94 -95

HISTORY
SACRED AND
PROFANE

Bampton Lectures for 1962

HISTORY
SACRED AND
PROFANE

ALAN RICHARDSON

D.D. (Oxon.), Hon. D.D. (Glasgow)
*Professor of Christian Theology
in the University of Nottingham*

The Westminster Press

PHILADELPHIA

10/1965
Rel.

© SCM PRESS LTD 1964

Library of Congress Catalog Card Number: 64-12393

TYPESET IN GREAT BRITAIN
AND PRINTED IN THE UNITED STATES OF AMERICA

DILECTISSIMAE CONIVGI
QVAE PLVRIMIS OCCVPATO NEGOTIIS
CONSTANTI CARITATE
HAEC OTIA PRAEBET DOMESTICA
QVAE STVDIA FOVENT

CONTENTS

Preface   9

Extract from the Last Will and Testament
of the Rev. John Bampton   15

1 THE CRISIS OF THE EIGHTEENTH CENTURY   17
   The 'Newtonian Philosophy'   18
   Locke and the Reasonableness of Christianity   20
   The Two Histories   23
   Humanist History   29
   Ecclesiastical History   33
   Antiquaries and Erudites   35
   The Twilight Period   41
   The Rationalist Attack upon Christian Faith   45
   The Nature of the Crisis   49

2 THE TWO WORLD SYSTEMS   54
   The 'New History' of St Augustine   55
   The Mediaeval Historical View   64
   The Mediaeval Synthesis   68
   The Achievement of the Middle Ages   75
   The Age of Transition   79

3 THE QUEST FOR HISTORICAL VERIFICATION   83
   The Anti-historical Element in Rationalism   84
   'Philosophe' History   90
   Hume and his 'Impartial' History   99
   Nineteenth-century Historiography   103
   Positivist History   109
   The Nineteenth-century Quest for Verification   118

4 DISENGAGEMENT FROM HISTORY   125
   Tillich and 'the Centre of History'   127
   Brunner, Barth and the 'Heilsgeschichte'   131
   Bultmann and the Kerygma Theology   139
   Existentialist Hermeneutics   147

5 INVOLVEMENT IN HISTORY 154
The 'Involvement' of the Historian 156
Moral Judgments in History 159
Dilthey, Croce and Collingwood 162
Edmund Burke and the 'Anglican' School 166
The Involvement of Ranke and Burckhardt 172
Meinecke and the Reappraisal of German History 181

6 HISTORY AND THE MIRACULOUS 184
Can Philosophy Answer Historical Questions? 185
What are Historical Facts? 190
The Nature of the Evidence for Christ's Resurrec-
tion 195
Christ's Resurrection as Historical Explanation 197
Personal Factors in the Judgment of Evidence 200
Is Christ's Resurrection an Historical Event? 206
The Unavoidable Decision of Faith 210

7 FAITH AND HISTORY 213
The Unique and the General 213
The Meaning of an Historical Faith 217
Disclosure Situations in History 223
'Factors' in History 227
The Revival of Old Testament Theology 229
New Testament Theology 234

8 THE WITNESS OF HISTORY 242
Myth and the Interpretation of History 243
Historical Relativism and 'the Climate of Opinion' 250
Historical Theology 254
Historical Theology and the Ecumenical Outlook 258
Christian Dogmatics as Historical Theology 261
The New Age of Universal History 265

Appended Notes
I The Deistic Controversy 273
II Classical History, Ancient and Modern 277
III The Philosophy of History 287

Bibliography 295
Index of Names 317
Index of Subjects 325

PREFACE

THE ground surveyed in these Lectures lies within the broad field of the History of Ideas. The methodical cultivation of this field is not yet well developed in Britain, although there has recently been considerable discussion of the danger of undue specialization in the universities. Acknowledgment should therefore all the more gladly be made of the progress which has been achieved in America, less hidebound and less pursebound than Britain. And here one should pay tribute from afar to the pioneering work of the History of Ideas Club founded in 1923 at the Johns Hopkins University, Baltimore, and in particular to the late Arthur O. Lovejoy, the 'father' of the Club and its chief inspirer. Professor Lovejoy died in the closing days of 1962 in his ninetieth year.[1] What is involved in the study of the History of Ideas is outlined in the first Lecture in his fine book, *The Great Chain of Being: a Study of the History of an Idea*,[2] itself the most distinguished exemplar of the study that has so far appeared.

The study of the History of Ideas, sometimes called Intellectual History, helps us to understand how people have come to think as they do by examining the thought-processes and unspoken assumptions of their age, listening carefully to the emotional and ideological reverberations, and thus feeling our way into their 'climate of opinion'. The ideas of an age must be illuminated by its characteristic ways of expressing itself, its literary and artistic predilections, its scientific opinions, its religious convictions and conventions, its social ideals and institutions, its historical myths, and so on, because ideas can be understood in their full historical or existential significance only in the rich context of living experience. This is clearly a very wide study indeed, but also a very concrete one, since it analyses only in order to understand the organic unity of thought. It crosses and recrosses the conventional

---

[1] An obituary notice appeared in the London *Times* on Jan. 1, 1963.
[2] Cambridge, Mass., 1942. See also 'The Historiography of Ideas' in his *Essays in the History of Ideas*, New York, 1955, together with the Foreword by Don Cameron Allen and the author's own preface.

boundary-lines between the academic disciplines, between the sciences and the humanities, between literature and ethics, between theology and history. Those who have identified scholarship with the investigation of the minutiae of a single discipline will pronounce it vague and unfocused. If this is a valid objection, it may well be brought against the attempt made in these Lectures to trace the course of man's age-long quest for self-understanding through his historical experience as over against his experience of nature, the continuing antithesis between the Hebrew and the Greek elements in the European tradition. The objection can be met only by a practical demonstration that such a study is worth while; the reader must be left to judge the issue for himself.

Until recent times the study of the history of ideas was regarded as falling within the province of the philosophers, although its content is much wider than the history of philosophy as such. Lovejoy was himself Professor of Philosophy at the Johns Hopkins University from 1910 until his retirement in 1938. Since the 'revolution in philosophy', which is said to have occurred during that period,[1] philosophers (in Britain at least) seem to have adopted a more restricted conception of their professional functions and have tended to confine themselves to the systematic (rather than the historical) study of ideas by paying scrupulous attention to the subtleties of the verbal forms in which they are expressed. It would thus seem to be coming about that the study of the History of Ideas is the latest of the disciplines to have emancipated itself from the tutelage of philosophy and to have achieved independence. Its academic footing in the universities is, however, another matter. History Departments do not usually consider it to be their affair; Schools of English have made considerable contributions to it (one thinks of the writings of the late Dr E. M. W. Tillyard and of Professor Basil Willey); the History of Science, itself something of a newcomer amongst the recognized academic disciplines, is clearly an important aspect of it; classical scholars and theologians, though they are often so busy digging their own plots that they do not look over the garden wall, have much to contribute. Nothing less is required than the active participation of every university department in the 'traffic in knowledge' which the study of the History of Ideas

[1] Cf. *The Revolution in Philosophy*, a collection of essays by Gilbert Ryle and others, London, 1956.

presupposes.[1] The goal is clear, even if the path through the academic undergrowth is not. One way of describing the goal would be to say that the ideal university would be one in which every member of the staff in every department read with intelligence and interest the *Journal of the History of Ideas*,[2] so long connected with Dr Lovejoy's name.

These lectures are concerned with the question whether man's understanding of himself as a being in history possesses a significance beyond anything that may be discerned through his being in nature. When we consider this question historically we find ourselves going back to two of the main sources of the European tradition: the Hebraic, with its strong historical sense and its constant expectation of significant disclosure-situations amidst historical events, and the Greek, with its tendency to regard the historical process as itself one of the rhythms of nature, and with its consequent hint—it is no more than that—of the possibility of a science of history. 'History' is a Greek word,[3] but after the confluence of classical and biblical thought, from the patristic period onwards, it assumed importance in the intellectual tradition of Christendom. Out of the quite disparate currents of Greek and Hebrew thought, there developed the wonderfully articulated scientific and religious world-view of the high Middle Ages, which survived until its own transformation into the new science of Galileo brought about its dissolution during the Age of Reason. The paradox of the alliance of biblical and classical thought has been strikingly expressed by Professor Lovejoy: 'The God of Aristotle had almost nothing in common with the God of the

---

[1] The curricula of undergraduate studies in some of the universities most recently founded or projected in Britain suggests a welcome breaking down of the old departmental barriers, though their concentration on 'modern' studies is an impoverishment. It is, however, doubtful whether the History of Ideas can profitably be handled at the undergraduate level, since it presupposes a basic education and a trained mind, such as the traditional type of honours school gives to the abler student.

[2] A Quarterly devoted to Cultural and Intellectual History; City University, New York 31, N.Y.

[3] It means 'an enquiry', the kind of intellectual exercise which the Greeks practised and the Hebrews did not. The verb *historein* occurs only once in the New Testament (Gal. 1.18)—significantly it relates to St Paul's having gone to Jerusalem to 'get to know' Cephas, presumably with a view to acquainting himself with the historical facts of the Christian story from the best available source. Cf. F. J. Foakes Jackson, *A History of Church History*, Cambridge, 1939, 1.

Sermon on the Mount—though by one of the strangest and most
momentous paradoxes of Western history, the philosophical
theology of Christendom identified them, and defined the chief
end of man as the imitation of both.'[1] The disintegration of the
mediaeval synthesis brought about the religious, moral and
political crisis of western Europe in the eighteenth century; it is
still our crisis, but today the whole world is being rapidly caught
up into it. It has made necessary a complete reassessment of the
classical and biblical inheritance of the West—and indeed (owing
to the expansion of Europe) of the world—in the light of new
scientific knowledge and, more important still, of new ways of
scientific thinking. To the revolution in scientific thinking
achieved in the seventeenth century there has been added the
revolution in historical thinking, which took place during the
nineteenth century; it completely transformed men's ways of
looking at the past by introducing a new quality of historical-
mindedness. We shall find it convenient to begin our enquiry with
the crisis of the eighteenth century, the twilight age—though it
thought of itself as 'enlightened'—between the scientific revolution, now come of age, and the historical revolution, hardly as yet
begun. From this starting-point we shall move backwards in time
to observe how the crisis had come about, then forwards towards
our own times, noting how in the nineteenth century (despite the
new historical-mindedness) classical notions of the possibility of
'scientific' history tended to predominate, whereas in the twentieth
century there has developed an increasing recognition of the
possibility of human self-understanding through involvement in
the challenges of history.

In the process of assessing the balance between the Greek and
the Hebraic emphases, between nature and history as sources of
our most important knowledge about ourselves and our destiny,
theological discussion (whatever other ends it serves) acts as a
useful barometer of the climate of opinion. It is a characteristic
of our age that most academic works seem to be written by specialists for specialists, and much theological writing today seems to
be of this kind. There is need for a new effort at mutual understanding in an age like our own, in which there seems to be a
growing recognition on many sides that it may be, after all,
through the understanding of history that the disclosure of mean-

[1] *The Great Chain of Being,* 5.

ing in human existence is possible. At least, some misconceptions might be removed—for instance, the frequent identification of 'theological statements' with 'metaphysical' ones. The affirmations of the Christian creeds are historical, not metaphysical, in character, and Christian theology itself is a matter of the interpretation of history. In any case, confronted as we are by the powerful and menacing secular myths of our time, the Christian and the humanist (classical or scientific) need to study afresh, and preferably together, the implications of *historical* thinking as such, as we move inevitably into an unprecedented phase of human existence, the new age of universal history which is rapidly being brought into being by the scientific and technological achievements of Christian-European civilization.

These Lectures, like all studies that pursue the history of an idea, are necessarily wide-ranging. Today we recognize that ideas and institutions can be understood only in the light of their history; but no one mind can master all that can be known about the various periods in which a single idea has grown up. Moreover, though ideas may be separated analytically from their context, they always belong to an organic complex of thought and experience apart from which they cannot be understood. The historian of ideas who desires a synoptic view will therefore be more than usually dependent upon the labours of scholars who are specialists in fields in which he may be only a layman, though a very interested layman. Let nothing said in this preface be taken to imply disrespect for specialists; the whole enterprise of the study of the History of Ideas depends upon the researches of specialists. Without the aid of students in many different fields a synoptic enquiry, such as that attempted in these Lectures, would be worthless. The Lecturer accordingly desires to express his gratitude to a great number of scholars, too many to enumerate, of whose help he has availed himself. Acknowledgment of indebtedness is implied in many of the footnotes, which have also been designed to assist the reader to pursue further his own enquiries into particular matters. The Bibliography likewise will, it is hoped, extend to others some of the benefits by which the Lecturer has himself profited. In these published Lectures the opportunity has been taken to expand considerably the content of the Lectures as preached, in accordance with Canon John Bampton's instructions, in the Church of St Mary-the-Virgin in Oxford on each of the

Sunday mornings of February and May 1962; the whole content of the Lectures as delivered is contained in this book in the order and under the title-headings of their original delivery.

It remains for the Lecturer, revisiting *Alma Mater*, to express his gratitude to all those who made profitable and enjoyable his renewed participation in 'the advantages afforded in this place'. He much appreciates the honour of the invitation from the Electors to the Bampton Lectureship; and he is glad to take this opportunity of expressing his thanks and those of his wife for the kind and hospitable welcome extended by many, in particular by the Vice-Chancellor and Mrs Norrington at Trinity College and by the Pro-Vice-Chancellor and Mrs Wheare at Exeter College. Lastly, as in the Bidding Prayer before each Lecture he invited his hearers to do, he praises God for the munificence of Founders and Benefactors, such as were Walter de Stapleton, founder of Exeter College, and John Bampton, of Trinity College, Prebendary of Salisbury and founder of these Lectures.

ALAN RICHARDSON

Nottingham
Easter Monday 1963

EXTRACT

FROM THE LAST WILL AND TESTAMENT
OF THE LATE
REV. JOHN BAMPTON
Canon of Salisbury

'. . . . I give and bequeath my Lands and Estates to the Chancellor, Masters, and Scholars of the University of Oxford for ever, to have and to hold all and singular the said Lands or Estates upon trust, and to the intents and purposes hereinafter mentioned; that is to say, I will and appoint that the Vice-Chancellor of the University of Oxford for the time being shall take and receive all the rents, issues, and profits thereof, and (after all taxes, reparations, and necessary deductions made) that he pay all the remainder to the endowment of eight Divinity Lecture Sermons, to be established for ever in the said University, and to be performed in the following:

'I direct and appoint, that, upon the first Tuesday in Easter Term, a Lecturer be yearly chosen by the Heads of Colleges only, and by no others, in the room adjoining to the Printing-House, between the hours of ten in the morning and two in the afternoon, to preach eight Divinity Lecture Sermons, the year following, at St Mary's in Oxford, between the commencement of the last month in Lent Term, and the end of the third week in Act Term.

'Also I direct and appoint, that the eight Divinity Lecture Sermons shall be preached upon either of the following Subjects—to conform and establish the Christian Faith, and to confute all heretics and schismatics—upon the divine authority of the holy Scriptures—upon the authority of the writings of the primitive Fathers, as to the faith and practice of the primitive Church—upon the Divinity of our Lord and Saviour Jesus Christ—upon the Divinity of the Holy Ghost—upon the Articles of the Christian Faith, as comprehended in the Apostles' and Nicene Creeds.

'Also I direct, that thirty copies of the eight Divinity Lecture Sermons shall be always printed, within two months after they are preached; and one copy shall be given to the Chancellor of the

University, and one copy to the Head of every College, and one copy to the Mayor of the city of Oxford, and one copy to be put into the Bodleian Library; and the expense of printing them shall be paid out of the revenue of the Land or Estates given for establishing the Divinity Lecture Sermons; and the Preacher shall not be paid nor be entitled to the revenue, before they are printed.

'Also I direct and appoint, that no person shall be qualified to preach the Divinity Lecture Sermons, unless he hath taken the degree of Master of Arts at least, in one of the two Universities of Oxford or Cambridge; and that the same person shall never preach the Divinity Lecture Sermons twice.'

I

THE CRISIS OF THE
EIGHTEENTH CENTURY

IN 1751, the year in which John Bampton died, David Hume
finished writing his *Dialogues concerning Natural Religion*. On the
advice of his friend Adam Smith, he locked the manuscript away
in his drawer, and the *Dialogues* were not published until three
years after his death, which occurred in 1776. They faithfully
reflect the divided mind of the eighteenth century, torn between
the affirmations of the Dogmatists and the doubts of the Sceptics.
Hume's own view, as distinct from the opinions which he puts
into the mouths of the disputants, is probably to be found in a
footnote in the last section (Part XII): 'Such disputes are com-
monly, at bottom, verbal, and admit not of any precise determination.' Thus, the Age of Reason[1] closes with the admission of its
acutest mind that reason cannot answer the question which it had
raised. Hume was the focus rather than the begetter of the doubts
of his age; as the American historian, Carl Becker, has remarked,
the notions encountered in the *Dialogues* were so widespread
during the second half of the eighteenth century that a most
convincing theory of their influence would certainly have been
put forward, had it not been known that Hume had locked away
the manuscript in his drawer.[2]

The truth is that the old traditional Christian world-view was
in a state of disintegration, and sceptical notions had been gaining
currency since the beginning of the Age of Reason, especially in
France. Behind the imposing façade of Versailles, literary men of

---

[1] Usually reckoned as extending from about 1650 to about 1780.

[2] *The Heavenly City of the Eighteenth-century Philosophers*, New Haven: Yale
Univ. Press, 1932, 71–75.

a sceptical turn of mind[1] were able to take advantage of the prestige and influence acquired by French language and culture for the dissemination of deistic and atheistic ideas. That Catholic monarch, Louis XIV, would have been distressed to learn that one of the achievements of his long and glorious reign was to establish a milieu for the ideas of his admirer Voltaire, who was a young man of twenty-one when Louis died. But the State was intent upon extirpating Huguenots rather than sceptics, since the former, unlike the latter, were potentially a political danger, with the backing of foreign military and economic power. Thus, there developed a movement of thought which aimed at establishing nothing less than a new, post-Christian world-view, based upon what was held to be 'the Newtonian philosophy' and undertaking to explain to the avid *bourgeoisie* what the new science was all about[2] and what conclusions should be drawn from it in the spheres of politics, morality and religion. The *philosophes* of eighteenth-century France re-enacted the role of the Sophists in the Athens of Socrates' day, with equally unsettling results as far as traditional religious ideas were concerned. It was they, and not the men of science themselves, who first put about the notion that there is a conflict between science and religion.[3] The year 1751 also saw the publication of the first volume of the massive *French Encyclopaedia*, which in the hands of Diderot and d'Alembert was to become the organ of all the radical and revolutionary opinion of the age.

The 'Newtonian Philosophy'

In England, where the revolution of 1688 had inhibited intolerant autocracy, and where the Protestant Religion had abated the oppressions of 'priestcraft', the new thought of the Age of Reason took a more moderate course. The English contribution to the achievement of that age was not smaller than the French, though it was less radical and less vociferous. Indeed, two Englishmen dominated the European intellectual scene all through the eighteenth century, and both were devoutly Christian. Never before or since the days of the fame and influence of Sir

[1] See on the *philosophe* movement Lecture III *infra*, 90-99.
[2] Voltaire himself was one of the great number who essayed the task; cf. his *Éléments de la philosophie de Newton*, 1738.
[3] See Herbert Butterfield, *The Origins of Modern Science, 1300-1800*, London, 1950, 149 f.

Isaac Newton and John Locke has English thought attained such a position of intellectual eminence on the European continent.[1] Newton (1642–1727), whose *Principia Mathematica* (1687) marked the consummation of the scientific revolution of the seventeenth century in a single work of genius, wrote to Richard Bentley in 1692 that in composing the *Principia* he had 'had an eye upon such principles as might work with considering men, for the belief of a Deity'. Newton, as Sir G. N. Clark has reminded us,[2] may not have been assiduous in his attendance at Trinity College Chapel and his biblical studies may have been intellectual rather than devotional, but he urged the first lecturer on the newly established Boyle Foundation to apply the Newtonian scientific conclusions to the 'confutation of atheism'.[3] That first Boyle Lecturer was Richard Bentley (1662–1742), held by many to be the greatest classical scholar England has ever produced.[4] Nothing could more strikingly demonstrate the oneness of that original Christian culture, from which the modern scientific movement was born, than that the greatest English scientific genius should have bidden the greatest English classical scholar to use his scientific work in the defence of the Christian faith. Nor could anything better illustrate the truth that, whatever the crisis of the eighteenth century might be, it was not occasioned by any conflict between natural science and religious belief as such. In England, indeed, the great scientific revolution had been consummated quietly and without fuss; there had been no persecutions of the new experimenters, who had enjoyed high patronage both in Church and State. And on the continent of Europe itself, the great leaders of the new scientific movements, Copernicus, Kepler, Galileo, Descartes, Pascal, a remarkable international array, had all without exception been men of deep and sincere Christian conviction; if they had encountered opposition, it was not because they had repudiated the biblical faith, but because they had fallen foul of

---

[1] See Gerd Buchdahl, *The Image of Newton and Locke in the Age of Reason*, London and New York, 1961.

[2] *Science and Social Welfare in the Age of Newton*, Oxford, 1937, 82f.

[3] The devoutly Christian Robert Boyle (1627–91), the 'father of modern chemistry' and one of the founders of the Royal Society, had left in his will a sum of £50 per annum for a series of eight lectures, delivered in London, against unbelievers. For Boyle see Roger Pilkington, *Robert Boyle*, London, 1959.

[4] Bentley's Boyle Lectures (1692) were entitled *Matter and Motion Cannot Think; or, a Confutation of Atheism from the Faculties of the Soul.*

the dogmas of the semi-canonized Aristotle. The scientific revolution of the sixteenth and seventeenth centuries is, historically, the supreme achievement of the human intellect, and its hidden causes will long remain a subject of research and discussion amongst historians of thought. Though it garnered the harvest of ancient Greek and mediaeval Arabic thought, it was a uniquely European achievement; as a distinguished historian of science has written, 'the transformations of philosophy, theory and method involved in it are not only unparalleled in the course of science at any other time or in any other civilization, they are unpredictable from the structure of science as it was in Greece, China or mediaeval Europe'.[1] Modern science is, in truth, the achievement of Christian civilization. If the rise of modern science was one of the factors which brought about the disintegration of the mediaeval Christian world-view in the eighteenth century, its very triumph in this regard testifies to the validity and vitality of those elements in the Christian humane tradition which made its emergence possible.

Locke and the Reasonableness of Christianity

John Locke modestly declared his ambition in relation to 'the incomparable Mr Newton' to be merely an under-labourer, clearing the ground and removing some of the rubbish. His life's work achieved much more than this,[2] and in the century after his death his name was constantly coupled with that of Newton as an equal. For Locke the clearing of the ground did not entail the demolition of the whole edifice of revealed truth, as it did for the deists and the *philosophes*. The culmination of his long epistemological enquiry is the conclusion that God's existence is 'the most obvious truth that reason discovers', and that the evidence for it is 'equal to mathematical certainty'.[3] We have indeed no innate

---

[1] A. R. Hall, 'The History of Science' in *Approaches to History: a Symposium*, ed. H. P. R. Finberg, London, 1962, 193.

[2] Locke's *Essay concerning Human Understanding* (1690) is probably the most important single English contribution to philosophy. His *Treatise on Civil Government* (also 1690) enunciated the principles underlying the English Revolution and provided the basic pattern on which the Constitution of the United States was framed after the American Revolution. Locke's insistence (against Hobbes) that natural law is independent of the State secured for the individual the right to think and live according to his conscience; the duty of the State was to safeguard this liberty.

[3] *Essay concerning Human Understanding*, IV, x, 1.

idea of God in our mind; but God did not make men as two-legged creatures, leaving it to Aristotle to make them rational.[1] He gave them reason, which is 'natural revelation', whereby they can, if they will but apply themselves, discover the truth about him. Furthermore, God gave men a revelation which, though it goes beyond what reason could prove, can be known to be true because our reason itself assures us that it comes from God, who cannot lie.[2] Revelation must always be tested by reason, which can never contradict it, for otherwise we might become victims of the delusions of the 'enthusiasts'. The biblical miracles were (as orthodox Christians since Aquinas had always affirmed) the rational guarantees of the truth of the scriptural revelation; and thus we have reason and Scripture, 'unerring rules', to prove to us whether a particular doctrine is true or false.[3] All this is but a philosophical presentation of the prosaic orthodoxy of the later seventeenth century; it is the intellectual basis of the much-admired Tillotsonian sermon, with its substitution of morality for grace and sentiment for adoration. Locke's general position was to remain the orthodoxy of loyal churchmen throughout the eighteenth century; and indeed, as Mark Pattison noted, the title of his shorter apologetic work, *The Reasonableness of Christianity* (1695),[4] epitomized the substance of English theology for a hundred years. Unhappily for the Church, the 'reasonableness' of orthodoxy made it impossible to offer any adequate reply to the deists in the great controversy which engrossed the first half of the eighteenth century:[5] if reason could establish the truth about God, could not revelation be dispensed with altogether? Neither the deists nor their orthodox opponents understood the biblical conception of a revelation through historical events; but whereas the misunderstanding is the essence of deism, it is also the root of the failure of the Church's orthodox apologists—whether weighty, like Butler, or blustering, like Warburton—to meet the challenge of the deists. The ground was cut from underneath both the deists and their opponents by the emergence of a real

[1] Ibid., IV, xvii, 4.
[2] Ibid., IV, xix, 4.
[3] Ibid., IV, xix, 14–16.
[4] Recently re-issued with an editorial introduction by Professor I. T. Ramsey in A. and C. Black's Library of Modern Religious Thought, London, 198.
[5] See Appended Note I, 'The Deistic Controversy', *infra*, 273.

sense of development in history towards the end of the eighteenth century, by which time the controversy was cold and dead.[1]

The Church's apologists during the first half of the eighteenth century failed not because they did not understand Newtonian science but because they did not understand the nature of the biblical revelation. Today in an age of specialization we stand amazed at the versatility of the scholars and divines who were able to follow the complexities of Newton's mathematics. They had grasped the implications of the scientific revolution; what they did not realize was that they were approaching the threshold of a revolution in human thinking even more subtle and far-reaching for man's view of his own nature and destiny than anything that was implied in the Newtonian philosophy.[2] The theologians had firmly grasped the truth that it was not from Newton's physics but from Descartes's metaphysics that the notion of a mechanistically determined universe was derived.[3] Thus, the eminent divine Samuel Clarke (1675–1729) brilliantly defended the Newtonian system against the Cartesian views still being taught at the turn of the century in the universities; in his Boyle Lectures (1704–5) he defended the existence of God against the Hobbesian free-thinkers and the idea of revelation against the deists. Nevertheless he illustrates the theological confusion of the age by his trafficking with Arianism and Unitarianism; he provoked one of the most violent controversies of the day by maintaining in his *Scripture Doctrine of the Trinity* (1712) that the early Church did not profess that dogma. William Whiston (1667–1752), Newton's successor in the Lucasian professorship of mathematics at Cambridge, actually

[1] Cf. Edmund Burke: 'Who now reads Bolingbroke? Who ever read him through? Ask the booksellers of London what is become of all these lights of the world' (*Reflections on the Revolution in France*).

[2] For the meaning of this phrase in the eighteenth century see the essay entitled 'Newton's Changing Reputation' by Henry Guerlac in *Carl Becker's Heavenly City Revisited*, edited by Raymond O. Rockwood, Cornell Univ. Press, Ithaca, N.Y., 1958, 6–25. An excellent summary will be found here of recent work by historians of science upon this aspect of the development of thought in the eighteenth century.

[3] Guerlac (op. cit., 15) shows that the crude materialism of some of the later writers of the century was not derived from Newton but from classical sources: 'We may with some justice speak of a Neo-Epicurean revival among the thinkers of the second half of the eighteenth century. This is an important matter if we wish to be clear about the religious implications of scientific progress in the eighteenth century. It is not from scientists (certainly not from Newton), but from philosophers, that the atheistic materialism of d'Holbach and Diderot can be legitimately and logically derived.'

became an Arian, and seriously suggested that the power to work miracles was withdrawn from the Church in AD 381, when the Council of Constantinople finally committed itself to the heresy of Athanasius. Happily Whiston provided a more worthy memorial of himself by his translation of Josephus. For all their ability and learning, mathematical and scholarly, the divines of the Age of Reason lacked the one thing which the questions then being asked required for their answer, namely, an historical approach to the Bible and to the formulation of Christian doctrine.

The Two Histories

Until the dawn of the Age of Reason the dual conception of history, which had gradually been evolving since the early Middle Ages, was the universally accepted way in which Christendom regarded the past. It is implicit in the good eighteenth-century phrase, 'history sacred and profane'.[1] The total of human historical knowledge could be divided into two quite distinct types, differing on account of the utterly disparate sources from which they came. Sacred history was, of course, the history of the world as it was divinely and therefore inerrantly disclosed in the Bible; this history was complete not only for all past time since the creation of the world, but also for all future time until its consummation in the Last Judgment, since it was believed that the apocalyptic sections of the Bible, notably the Books of Daniel and of the Revelation of St John, contained a prediction of the future course of things. Indeed, it was because Newton (who in respect of history belongs to the mediaeval rather than the modern world) believed in the 'revelation' that was contained in Daniel and in the Apocalypse of St John that he devoted so much of his later life to the task of finding by means of his astronomical studies the key to the secrets of future history which those books contained. Until the final disintegration of the mediaeval world-view in the eighteenth century, world-chronology had to be fitted into the sacred history of the Bible, as it had been since the time of Orosius in the early fifth century.[2] In the sixteenth and seventeenth

[1] An example of its eighteenth-century use will be found in the quotation from Hume *infra*, 187.

[2] St Augustine had commissioned his scholarly researcher, Orosius, to write a more orderly complement to his own discursive *De Civitate Dei*, which is discussed in Lecture II *infra*. Orosius' *Historiarum adversos Paganos Libri*, based on the work of earlier Christian writers like Eusebius of Caesarea and

centuries the work of scholars like Joseph Justus Scaliger (1540–1609), a French Protestant who succeeded Justus Lipsius (Joest Lips) (1547–1606) as professor at Leyden in 1593, had laid the foundation of modern chronology and had reduced to order the hitherto chaotic jumble of ancient history.[1] Much new knowledge was being gained, and the work of co-ordinating it with the age-long Orosian-biblical scheme was still proceeding vigorously in the seventeenth century. Fine scholars like James Ussher (1581–1656), Archbishop of Armagh, and the immensely learned Cambridge Hebraist, John Lightfoot (1602–75), had brought the mediaeval chronological scheme to its high point of perfection —a wonderfully scientific piece of reasoning, if the postulates of mediaeval thinking are granted—a century or so before the whole edifice of the mediaeval world-view finally collapsed.[2] Of course, the whole mediaeval 'universal history' was Europe-centred, and it would be anachronistic to expect it to be anything else; it is quite unhistorical to condemn (as Voltaire and many later writers have done) Bishop Bossuet for ignoring the rest of the world. J. B. Bossuet (1627–1704), the famous courtier, preacher and Bishop of Meaux, was born too soon for the new knowledge of China and the East, now beginning to flow in with the reports of the Jesuit missionaries, to have made much of an impact on his mind. His *Discours sur l'histoire universelle* (1681) is as mediaeval in its presuppositions as Newton's *Principia* in the same decade is modern: it is, in fact, the last *great* universal history in the traditional style.[3] But it is by no means the end of the old-style histories of the world. As late as 1735 there appeared Calmet's somewhat conventional *Historie universelle, sacrée et prophane*, in which, as in

---

of pagan historians like Livy and Suetonius, became the standard textbook on universal history for a thousand years; it was translated into English by King Alfred. Cf. R. L. P. Milburn, *Early Christian Interpretations of History*, Bampton Lectures of 1952, London, 1954, 92: 'Orosius' work, for all its defects, is the first attempt at a history of the world, and one which accords reasonably well with the demand of the ancient rhetoricians that narrative should be concise, clear and truthful.' See also Karl Löwith, *Meaning in History*, Chicago, 1949, 174–81.

[1] His (literally) epoch-making *De Emendatione Temporum* was published in 1583.

[2] It was from their work that the dates (e.g. Creation, 4004 BC) were taken and inserted in the margins of the Authorized (or King James) Version of the Bible printed after 1701.

[3] For a full account of it see R. Flint, *History of the Philosophy of History*, Edinburgh, 1893, 216–33.

Bossuet, *le doigt de Dieu* is the principal category of historical explanation; and in 1737 came the massive, composite English *Universal History from the Earliest Account of Time to the Present*.[1] The conception of a sacred history, derived from the infallible oracles of Holy Scripture, and supplying the frame into which all other histories had to be fitted, survived amongst loyal churchmen until after the close of the Age of Reason. It not only made it impossible to give a convincing answer to the rationalistic objections of the deists to the very idea of revelation; it made it impossible for scholars who remained loyal to the traditional belief to practise their craft on the documentary sources of the Christian faith. Since the Bible contained a history divinely disclosed, it was impious to examine its deliverances in a critical manner, since this would imply a doubt concerning the veracity of its divine Author. The Lightfoots and the Bentleys were thus inhibited from applying those acute critical methods to the Scriptures which they had so skilfully employed upon classical literature or the Talmud. Hence it was left to sceptics like Bayle, free-thinkers like Collins, or deists like Woolston or Reimarus[2] to essay the first English or German attempts at biblical criticism. The circumstances are understandable enough, but the consequences were none the less deplorable. Throughout the nineteenth century criticism tended to be viewed by sincerely believing Christians as the ally of rationalism and unbelief, while in the eyes of those who welcomed the new learning, loyalty to the traditional faith of the Church seemed merely a dull obscurantism. The controversy over *Essays and Reviews* (1860) was but the reverberation in the nineteenth century of a campaign which had been lost in the eighteenth. It required all the devotion and all the labours of scholars like Westcott, Lightfoot and Hort to demonstrate to a perplexed generation that faith and criticism might illuminate each other.

Profane[3] history, as contrasted with sacred history, was purely

---

[1] This work speaks in the preface of 'the only authentick and genuine History of Creation, that which has been left to us by Moses' (cited by J. H. Brumfitt, *Voltaire: Historian*, London, 1958, 85f.).

[2] For Reimarus see pp. 118 f. *infra*; Tindal's 'Deist's Bible' was published in a German translation in 1741.

[3] The adjective 'profane', customarily but incorrectly spelt 'prophane' in English usage down to about 1750, is derived from the Latin *profanus*, which literally meant 'before the temple', i.e. 'non-sacred', 'unconsecrated', 'secular'. The *Oxford Eng. Dict.* cites as examples: 1614, W. Raleigh, *Hist. World*, II (1634), 268, 'If there be any truth in prophaine antiquitie'; J. Bunyan,

a human enterprise; there was therefore an absolute qualitative difference between sacred and profane history. The latter was held in low esteem by all except a handful of antiquaries and their circle of devotees; to the philosophical mind in the Age of Reason all history was vitiated by the credulity of historians and their love of prodigies. Descartes, followed by Hobbes, had turned his back upon history as a source of knowledge; sceptics like Bayle regarded history as nothing more than a rubbish-heap of atomic facts; Bolingbroke sums up rationalist opinion about the middle of the eighteenth century when he condemns the search for historical facts as merely 'a specious and ingenious form of idleness'.[1] Not until the French *philosophes* and their Scottish fellow traveller David Hume discovered the propaganda-value of history-writing was history regarded as a serious occupation for 'men of discernment'. Such value as it possessed lay in its power to inculcate moral attitudes, especially amongst the young and those who were incapable of following the abstract reasonings of philosophers. The notion that there could be an existential encounter with the past, compelling men to make a decision concerning the present, or bringing them to a new self-understanding, was utterly foreign to the Age of Reason, as it is to rationalists in every age. Even the antiquaries of the period, who spent long hours in discovering, deciphering and editing the decaying records of the past, never understood their activities in such a light as this. They loved the past for its own sake, not for the sake of the present; and to this extent, despite the immense debt which is owed to them, they were something less than historians in the full contemporary sense. They were not interested in any moral lessons of history, still less in its entertainment-value; they despised those who esteemed history for its edificatory or diverting character, and they in their turn were despised by the 'men of reason' who stamped upon the age its characteristically rationalist outlook. For rationalist theologian and for earnest deist, for free-

---

Pilg. Prog., I (1678), 104, 'What you will; I will talk of things Sacred or things Prophane.' In such expressions as 'profane literature', 'profane history' no pejorative sense was implied. But, as today, the word could be used pejoratively, e.g. the Geneva Bible (1560) at Heb. 12.16, 'Let there be no fornicator, or prophane persone as Esau, which for a portion of meat sold his byrth right'; 1606, Chapman, *Monsieur D'Olive*, II, Plays (1873), I, 215, 'Said [of tobacco] 'twas a pagan plant, a prophane weede And a most sinful smoke.'

[1] For an expansion of the content of this sentence see Lecture III *infra*.

thinking sceptic and for sectarian enthusiast, history was not a source of genuine knowledge; it was at best a means of edifying pedagogy, at second best a mode of diversion, and at worst an indulgence of curiosity or idle speculation.

In such a climate of opinion the would-be orthodox Christian apologist had the cards stacked heavily against him; the distinctively biblical conception of revelation was essentially historical in character, and the orthodox apologist was hardly more aware of this than his deist opponent. Rationalism in theology had been developing in a straight and continuous line—despite a protest from such as Luther—from Aquinas *via* Lord Herbert of Cherbury to Matthew Tindal and Bishop Butler, and the logical conclusion of the development was not Butler's refusal to take the last step but Tindal's fully articulated rejection of an historical revelation altogether. In the changed climate of opinion the deists found it increasingly easy to show that the traditional conception of revelation as divinely communicated oracles written down in a book could not stand up to rational criticism, and in that age reason was the all-sufficient arbiter of truth. The idea of revelation could be dispensed with; all that rational men needed to do was to shun sectarian theology, mysticism and enthusiasm, and simply 'look through nature up to nature's God'.[1] The men of reason could no longer view the Bible with the uncritical eyes of the Middle Ages. They did not find in it what they thought they had a right to find. They would have expected the Intelligent Author of Nature, whom their reason assured them must exist,[2] to speak clearly, as Locke and Newton did; he could not be regarded as the author of the jumbled collection of tales and legends, prophecies and portents, which comprised the allegedly sacred history of the Bible. Poor Butler, with no better understanding of historical development than his opponents, was hard put to it to reply within the agreed terms of the debate. The Books of Moses spoke in riddles and obscurities; it was strange that the Author of the Book of Nature, which he had left open for the human reason to peruse, should be supposed to have addressed men of

[1] A. Pope, *Essay on Man* (1734), Ep. iv, 1, 332.

[2] There were few professed atheists in that age. Butler did not have to argue the existence of God. As he says, he was able to take 'as proved, and generally confessed to be proved', that there is 'an Intelligent Author of Nature' (*Analogy*, Works, ed. of 1874, I, 143, at the end of his section 'Of Natural Religion'; cf. also p. 6).

understanding through the enigmatical utterances of Moses and the prophets.[1] So inevitably the belief in a sacred history, immune from the critical judgment of reason, began to break down; the last phase of the disintegration of the mediaeval world-view was in process. The dichotomy of sacred and profane history was no longer tenable; sacred history was disappearing, so that there was only profane history left.

But profane history was not a source of assured knowledge; the partiality of historians and the unreliability of their evidence was a by-word amongst the men of reason. Therefore, when the biblical history thus was merged into the muddy stream of profane history, it lost its inviolable status and became what (in the opinion of the philosophers) all history is—a tissue of half-truths, unverifiable reports, legendary traditions and incredible tales of theophanies and miracles. It provided no foundation upon which philosophical truth or religious belief could be safely built. As Lessing declared in 1777 at the end of the Age of Reason, epitomizing in a sentence the judgment of that age, 'Incidental truths of history can never become the proof of necessary truths of reason.'[2] Or, as he put it very succinctly, 'If no historical truth can be demonstrated, then nothing can be demonstrated by means of historical truths.' There was no way across from history to rational belief. This was the 'ugly, broad ditch' which he could not leap, however hard he tried. If Christianity were an historical religion, so much the worse for Christianity. This was the challenge of the Age of Reason to the Church's faith in a divine revelation, and the Church's apologists in that age had no answer to it, save to reiterate the old belief in a sacred history. Nevertheless, in the new age of historical thinking which was dawning as the Age of Reason was passing away, new answers to the rationalistic challenge would be sought and found. Mark Pattison was doubtless right in holding that the ultimate utility of the deistic movement was that it 'forced upon theology the task of determining the true character of its own historic monuments',[3] but the task was long and arduous, and still today it awaits completion. The eighteenth

---

[1] Cf. J.-J. Rousseau in a letter to Mr. Beaumont (*Oeuvres*, 1823, VI, 115): 'Is it simple, is it natural, that God should go in search of Moses in order to speak to Jean-Jacques Rousseau?' Cf. Carl Becker, *Heavenly City*, 46–51; John Baillie, *Our Knowledge of God*, London, 1939, 185.

[2] Cf. Henry Chadwick, *Lessing's Theological Writings*, London, 1956, 31, 53.

[3] *Essays*, ed. H. Nettleship, Oxford, 1889, II, 226.

century amply illustrates the inutility of a literary criticism of the biblical records which is not infused by a sense of history.

Humanist History

To say that the eighteenth century lacked a sense of history, as we understand it today, does not mean either that there had not by that time been accumulated a very considerable amount of historical knowledge or that no people before or during that age were interested in history. Man in every age in which there is leisure for reflection is an historically minded animal;[1] what varies from age to age is the nature of his interest in history, or the perspective in which he looks at it. This interest or perspective does not arise from a purely academic or disengaged study of historical records, but from the living issues and present concerns of his own circumstances and conditions. Changed political, social and economic conditions always create a demand for a 'new history', that is, a new way of looking at the past in the light of the needs of the present. Thus, the felt need to express and evoke a sense of pride in belonging to *this* city or *this* nation is one of the most powerful stimulants both to the writing of history and to research into the past, though all too frequently the former activity may be undertaken with very little attention to the latter. To provide the myths—that is, interpretations of history—by which peoples express their pride in their own race or community has always been one of the most important functions of the historian as distinct from the antiquary. During the Middle Ages this function was often not prominent, because for long periods regional feeling was not intense; but during the age which is conventionally known as 'the Renaissance' a new stimulus was given to historical activity as a result of the rise of civic or national consciousness. And conveniently there lay to hand the newly recovered classical histories of Greece and Rome; with these as models the 'humanist' writers set about providing the new history which their times required.[2] To say this does not imply that no other motives than nationalist sentiment lie behind the rise of humanist activity in the field of history; historical writing reflects every motive and aspect of the age in which it is written. The historical myths of an age become impotent for its

[1] Cf. F. M. Powicke, *Modern Historians and the Study of History: Essays and Papers*, London, 1955, 227.

[2] See Appended Note II, 'Classical History, Ancient and Modern', *infra*, 277.

successor, because they no longer enshrine the sentiments and aspirations of a new generation; the common sense of the age gets to work on the old myths and clears them out of the way in order to make room for new ones. The legendary history of Geoffrey de Monmouth (*c.* 1100–54), with its stories of King Arthur and the Round Table, serves the age of chivalry very well; but in a new age common sense will reassert itself and a new history will be demanded. But the process by which common sense was made methodical, or scientific, was not completed before the nineteenth century, by which time it is called 'criticism'. The achievement of marrying the mythopoeic function of history to its scientific or fact-establishing function was not realized in any truly significant and widespread way before the nineteenth century, by which time a scientifically-minded age demanded a scientific history. Long after the accomplishment of the revolution in natural science, the old myths (interpretations) of history lived on. It was not the new physics and chemistry which killed the old historical myths; it was the new history. Humanist history had done much to break down the old Augustinian view of the control of history by Providence, and to create a secular or non-theological attitude towards profane history; but it did not succeed in producing a convincingly accurate reconstruction of the past. To the new scientists themselves humanist history seemed to lack the objectivity which they looked for in their own sphere, and it contrasted unfavourably with the revealed and certain truths of sacred history.[1] The need for objectivity in historical writing was recognized long before Ranke's day,[2] but the means of approximating

---

[1] Thus, Sir Robert Boyle contrasts the two histories: the Scriptures give us, he says, 'a history divinely inspired', and the 'secretaries' employed by their divine Author had no need to follow the universal practice of the profane historian, who gives himself the liberty of making speeches for orators and generals, 'and does not set down indeed what they said, but what he thought fit that such persons on such occasions should have said' (*Some Considerations touching the Style of the Holy Scriptures*, 1661; *Works*, ed. London, 1772, II, 260f.).

[2] E.g. Edmund Bolton, *Hypercritica* (Addresses II and III), 1618: 'All late authors that ever yet I could read among us, convey with them to narrations of things done fifteen or sixteen hundred years past the jealousies, passions and affections of their own time. Our Historian must therefore avoid this dangerous syren alluring us to follow our own prejudices, unless he mean only to serve a side and not to serve truth. . . . He is therefore simply to set forth, without prejudices, depravations or sinister items things as they are.' Cf. Ranke's famous 'wie es eigentlich gewesen'.

to it had not yet been acquired in the age of humanist history. Francis Bacon in his *Advancement of Learning* (Book II), as early as 1605, had outlined a remarkable programme of historical research, concerning which it has been well said that 'it is a striking testimony to the wide sweep of Bacon's genius that no century earlier than the nineteenth would have been able to appreciate the meaning of his advice, or could have attempted to act on it. Here, as in so much of his work, he surveys the promised land from afar; but it was left to distant generations to enter upon it.'[1] It is significant that Bacon's own *History of Henry VII* (1622) does not advance beyond the standards and ideals of the earlier humanist writers.[2] The historians of the age can do little more than retell the stories which they have found in their sources, for the critical method of historical verification was only now beginning to be hammered out, and there was a long way to go. John Milton's *History of England* (1670) is typical of its period.[3] He is well aware that many in his day had begun to doubt the veracity of his sources, yet, he says, he has decided to retain the 'ancientest' traditions, 'seeing that ofttimes relations hitherto accounted fabulous have been after found to contain in them many footsteps and reliques of something true'. Our English rhetoricians, he remarks, will know how to use them judiciously. So he tells how Brutus of Troy landed at Totnes, established his New Troy (London) and reigned over all Britain for twenty-four years. He goes down to the Norman Conquest, improving as his sources improve, but always protesting at the 'monkish' falsehoods in the sphere of ecclesiastical history. The humanist spirit had by no means distracted men's minds away from questions of the religious interpretation of history, and throughout the seventeenth century the question of the providential ordering of historical development remained near the centre of interest in history.[4] An earlier work, the entirely uncritical *Chronicles of the Kings of England*

[1] A. J. Grant, *English Historians*, London, 1906, xviif.

[2] G. N. Clark, *The Seventeenth Century*, Oxford, 1947, 278.

[3] Milton, of course, had a very much more profound conception of the place of Englishmen in the providential ordering of history than is conveyed in this conventional work. See William Haller's art., 'The Tragedy of God's Englishman' in *Reason and the Imagination: Studies in the History of Ideas, 1600–1800*, ed. J. A. Mazzeo, New York, 1962, 201–11.

[4] For the importance of Providence during this period see Herschel Baker, *The Wars of Truth*, Cambridge, Mass., 1952; for the general background see William Haller, *The Rise of Puritanism*, New York, 1938.

(1643) by Sir Richard Baker, represents the kind of history which Englishmen throughout this period enjoyed; it was the favourite readings of Sir Walter de Coverley. The revolution in the natural sciences had already achieved its mature expression with the publication of Newton's *Principia* in 1687, while the modern development of historical science was still in its infancy. Nevertheless a handful of specialists had made a start: Mabillon's treatise *De re diplomatica* was published in 1681.

We should never forget that it was one and the same movement of critical enquiry which first culminated in the seventeenth-century scientific achievement and later in the emergence of the fully developed historical critical method of the nineteenth century. The critical faculty, once awakened, could not rest satisfied with the successful exploration of the realm of nature; it was bound to go on from there to the critical investigation of the more intractable region of human nature, and, when the idea of development was fully understood, to seek to understand scientifically how, in fact, man and his institutions, have come to be what they are.[1] Since the nineteenth century it has been an axiom of Western thinking that men and their institutions cannot be understood apart from their history, or that to know what a thing is, it is necessary to give an account of its past. This is part, at least, and a very important part, of the meaning of the statement that we nowadays live in an historically-minded age. The historical revolution in human thinking, which was accomplished in the nineteenth century, is just as important as the scientific revolution of two centuries earlier. But they are not two separate revolutions;

---

[1] Cf. Sir F. M. Powicke, op. cit., 228: 'Just because man is historically minded, he is quick to see the bearing of scientific discovery upon his traditional conceptions of the past. Sometimes people talk as though the "higher criticism" of texts in recent times has had more influence upon the human mind than the higher criticism of nature. This seems to me to be nonsense. The higher criticism has been simply an application of an awakened critical faculty to a particular kind of material, and was encouraged by the achievement of this faculty to form its bold conclusions. If the biologists, the geologists, the astronomers, the physicists, the anthropologists, had not been at work, I venture to think that the higher critics would have been either non-existent or a tiny minority in a world of fundamentalists.' This statement is valid enough, but perhaps it should be added that there is a two-way traffic between the sciences and the humanities: Darwin's evolutionary hypothesis is inconceivable in any age before the nineteenth-century emergence of historical-mindedness (see *infra*, 97).

they are aspects of the one great transitional movement from the mediaeval to the modern way of looking at things.

Ecclesiastical History

It is usually a serious interest in the living issues of their own day which stimulates men to the study of history; and it is therefore not surprising to find that a new zeal for historical research arose out of the exigencies of ecclesiastical controversy at the time of the Reformation. The exposure of the so-called False Decretals in 1558 by the Lutheran 'Centuriators' of Magdeburg gave rise to the hope that by pursuing the methods of Matthias Flacius (1520–75) further breaches could be made in the papalist stronghold. As Lord Acton sadly remarked, 'forgery is a vice very common amongst zealous Christians', and indeed 'almost all societies begin with forged charters'.[1] The Middle Ages, as he said in his Inaugural Lecture, were 'content to be deceived, to live in a twilight of fiction, under clouds of false witness, inventing according to convenience, and glad to welcome the forger and the cheat. As time went on, the atmosphere of accredited mendacity thickened, until, in the Renaissance, the art of exposing falsehood dawned upon keen Italian minds.'[2] If keen Italian minds began the process, the very different cast of mind of the northern Protestants carried it forward until, by the end of the seventeenth century, a substantial amount of Christian literature was acknowledged by Catholic and Protestant alike to be unauthentic.[3] Thus, men of a markedly anti-humanist outlook, like Flacius himself, made a contribution to the development of critical historical study hardly less significant than that of the humanist scholars themselves. The Oratorians, notably Caesare Baronius (1538–1607), devoted much

[1] Acton Papers in the Cambridge University Library (Add. 4929, 185), quoted by Butterfield, H. *Man on his Past*, 76.

[2] J. E. E. D. Acton, *Lectures on Modern History*, London, 1907, 4f. (As early as 1440 the Italian humanist Lorenzo Valla (1406–57) had demonstrated the spuriousness of the so-called 'Donation of Constantine', the charter of the temporal power of the Papacy.)

[3] In Appendix II at the end of the *Lectures* (op. cit.) Acton quotes Duchesne: 'Ce n'est guère avant la seconde moitié du XVIIe siècle qu'il devint impossible de soutenir l'authenticité des fausses décrétales, des Constitutions apostoliques, des Récognitions Clémentines, du faux Ignace, du pseudo-Dionys, et de l'immense fatras d'oeuvres anonymes ou pseudonymes qui grossissait souvent du tiers ou de la moitié l'héritage littéraire des auteurs les plus considérables' (*Témoins anténicéens de la Trinité*, 1883, 36).

effort to the defence of the Church; Baronius's *Annales Ecclesiastici* in twelve folio volumes, a reply to the *Centuries of Magdeburg*, ensured that the serious study of history would henceforward be an indispensable feature of the controversialist's task. The remarkable Isaac Casaubon (1559–1614), the leading classical scholar of his age, a professor from Geneva who lived to write a defence of the Anglican position and who was buried in Westminster Abbey, was generally able to refute Baronius by reason of his superior scholarship; but he, like other scholars of his age, was never quite able to see the fathers of the ancient Church in an historical perspective, because their writings were invested with almost the same aura of sanctity as the canonical Scriptures themselves.[1]

The same judgment must be passed upon the work of the Anglican divines of the sixteenth and seventeenth centuries, whose contribution to the development of historical studies lay mainly in the field of patristics and early church history. Faced on the one side with the Puritan insistence that the whole polity and worship of the Church should be regulated solely by scriptural texts, and on the other by the demand of Rome for assent to doctrines unknown to the fathers, they appealed to 'antiquity', that is, to the faith and practice of the undivided Church of the early Christian centuries. Mark Pattison speaks of their work as nothing less than 'the opening of patristic antiquity', and he rightly describes it as 'a signal enlargement of the intellectual horizon of the English Church and the admission of a new stock of facts'.[2] His pessimistic assessment of the state of learning in the Church in his own day probably leads him to do less than justice to the work of the Anglican divines when he implies that it represented the late fruits of a dying tradition rather than presaged the future advances of historical scholarship.[3] 'Round the names of Pearson, Bull, Hammond, Stillingfleet, and the rest of the Caroline divines, gathers a faint lunar reflection of the noonday glory which surrounds the majestic edifice of the Catholic theology of the Middle Ages.'[4] Of course, Pattison is right in saying that the Anglican divines never conceived the idea of historical

[1] See Mark Pattison, *Isaac Casaubon*, 1875; ed. H. Nettleship, 1892.

[2] 'Learning in the Church of England' (1836) in *Essays*, II, 287.

[3] 'Like fruit in a wet autumn, learning in our Church promised well at first, but has hung on the tree ever since, still immature' (ibid.).

[4] Ibid., 286.

investigation as an end to be pursued for its own sake; they looked to primitive antiquity for just so much as served their purpose. Theirs was not the historical learning which 'resuscitates the whole spirit and form of a buried age'.[1] Before the nineteenth century, Pattison tells us in another essay, 'critical and historical conclusions had been employed by one side to pull down, by the other to maintain, the orthodox system, but there was no belief in criticism and history as scientific methods'.[2] This judgment is in general true, even though it overlooks certain rare spirits like Mabillon. But this should not obscure the indispensable service rendered by ecclesiastical historians, apologists though they were, to the development of scientific historical method as the nineteenth century came eventually to understand and practise it.[3]

Antiquaries and Erudites

When at the end of the seventeenth century Sir William Temple and his friend and former secretary Dean Swift, supported later by others such as Pope and Bolingbroke, lamented that there was no worthy History of England to put into the hands of 'foreigners and gentlemen of our own country',[4] they were voicing a widespread complaint. They stood in the humanist tradition, and they sighed for an English History which should be as patriotically stimulating, as morally edifying and as politically instructive as, say, Livy's magisterial History of Rome. Temple, Swift and Bolingbroke all toyed with the idea of attempting the task, but they got no farther than introductory sketches and essays. The

[1] Ibid., 286f.

[2] *Essays*, II, 228.

[3] Lord Acton well understood this point. At the beginning of his Inaugural Lecture (op. cit., 3) he says that ecclesiastical history 'opened the way in research and was the first to be treated by close reasoners and scholars of the higher rank' because of the 'graver issues' concerned in it. Since Acton's day, however, ecclesiastical history seems to have been increasingly disesteemed by academic historians in England and relegated to an intellectual ghetto which they rarely visit; the reason for this is doubtless in part because intellectual history has not yet achieved in England the status of an 'aspect' of history worthy of attention. In a symposium published in 1962, *Approaches to History* (ed. H. P. R. Finberg), cited above, there are chapters on Political History, Economic, Social and Local History, and so on, and chapters on the History of Science and of Art; but there is no chapter on Ecclesiastical History and (significantly) none on Intellectual History.

[4] For references see 'The Augustan Conception of History' by Herbert Davis in *Reason and the Imagination*, 213–29. See also Godfrey Davies, *Elizabethan and Jacobean Studies presented to F. P. Wilson*, Oxford, 1959, 231–4.

only men who could have written such a history from a basis of sound historical scholarship were not interested in the project; they were not historians in the humanist sense, and the humanists despised them. These were the men whom we would call antiquaries, but in their own day they were often called historians. They had amassed a very considerable amount of historical knowledge, and, what is perhaps even more important, they preserved a great number of original records for the use of all future historians, whose debt to them can hardly be overestimated. From about the middle of Queen Elizabeth's reign until about 1730, when the species seems to have died out, they concentrated on the task of recovering and preserving the relics of the past, and in the course of their work they acquired a mastery of the critical techniques of investigation which was not appreciated by their humanist and philosophical contemporaries, and which was lost altogether after 1730, for they had no real successors. Sir E. L. Woodward has said of them that 'if the critical methods laid down by these scholars had not been undervalued in England, if the material which they collected had been put to use, there would have been no need for Englishmen to learn over again from the Germans the scientific treatment of texts'.[1]

The antiquaries were not literary men; they wrote not for the edification of the public but for one another. They sought out and edited ancient texts, and they found patrons by whose aid their editions could be printed. Few scholars were fortunate enough to be able to use their position to promote their interest; Matthew Parker, who became Elizabeth's first Archbishop of Canterbury (1559), was a notable exception. The Church in the seventeenth century became a patron of scholarship, upholding the Laudian ideal of a learned clergy and championing humane studies against the attacks of the Puritans;[2] after the Restoration the Universities

[1] *British Historians*, London, 1943, 30.
[2] See 'The Humanistic Defence of Learning in the Mid-Seventeenth Century' by R. F. Jones in *Reason and the Imagination*. Cf. also F. Smith Fussner, *The Historical Revolution: English Historical Writing and Thought, 1580–1640*, London, 1962, 111: 'The Church after the Restoration set about the official encouragement and patronage of historical and antiquarian learning. Many, if not most, of the great books of late seventeenth-century mediaeval scholarship were written by churchmen. . . . William Nicolson and Edmund Gibson, both of whom rose to high positions in the Church of England, were passionate students of Anglo-Saxon antiquities who used their influence to promote such studies in the Church.'

and their presses greatly assisted the scholars who laboured upon the antiquities of England and published their work. But the most honourable names amongst the patrons of learning are those of a handful of private benefactors, to whom English historical scholarship owes so much: Sir Thomas Bodley (1545–1613), Sir Robert Cotton (1571–1631), Robert Harley (1661–1724), and a few others. The gentlemen of England who took pride in their own counties also deserve mention for their encouragement of local historians. Here we can do no more than mention them; nor indeed is this the place to describe the activities of the scholars whom they assisted.[1]

It is fascinating to ask what were the motives which compelled these men to the study of history. John Stow (1525–1605), the self-educated, middle-class scholar, who supported himself by tailoring and who found a patron in Archbishop Parker, virtually created a new *genre* of local history in his *Survey of London* (1598), after forty years of assiduous research, so superior was it in accuracy and plan to anything that had previously been attempted; it seems inadequate to suggest that pride in his native city was his sole inspiration. William Camden (1551–1623), a scholar of quite a different type, who was fortunate in the patronage of Lord Burghley, in his *Annales* of Elizabeth's reign lifted historiography far above the level of the mediaeval chronicle, and in his *Britannia* (1586) far transcended the ordinary standards of humanist history by reason of his original research into mediaeval antiquities. He was indeed a patriot who could write exalted panegyrics about his native land, but pride of country is hardly sufficient of itself to cause men to spend time and fortune on antiquarian research. His influence was considerable upon the company of antiquarian enthusiasts, and it has had lasting effect: Thomas Bodley was a pupil at Westminster School when Camden was second master there; but it was Camden himself who endowed the first University lectureship in history (now the Camden Chair of Ancient History at Oxford). What is the origin of that 'passion for the past' which drove a Norfolk gentleman like Sir Henry Spelman

[1] The task has been excellently and adequately performed in two outstanding books, F. Smith Fussner's work mentioned in the previous footnote, which takes the story down to the Civil War, and Professor David C. Douglas's delightful volume, *English Scholars*, London, 1939, which takes up the tale from the Restoration and carries it down to round about 1730, when the great period of antiquarian scholarship was over.

(1564–1641) to master Anglo-Saxon and to pioneer English philology and the study of the documents of English ecclesiastical history? What inner compulsion moved Sir William Dugdale (1605–86), the antiquarian of Warwickshire, to work on his *Monasticon Anglicanum*? How shall we account for the labours and achievements of Humfrey Wanley (1672–1726), Harley's librarian, when he was building up his famous collection of books and manuscripts; of Thomas Madox (1666–1727), who wrote the history of the Exchequer; of Thomas Hearne (1678–1735), the Oxford antiquary, who set new standards in his editions of the chronicles and sources of English history; of George Hickes (1642–1715), whose *Thesaurus* was not surpassed in the field of Anglo-Saxon studies until the nineteenth century? Should we simply say that their motive was curiosity, a desire to know for the sake of knowing? Curiosity was not highly prized as a virtue in the eighteenth century, which for the most part was willing to accept the advice of Ben Sira, 'Be not curious in unnecessary matters'; and all matters which were not directly edificatory, such as historical knowledge for its own sake, were deemed unnecessary. The Earl of Chesterfield's famous advice to his son, not to waste many hours on the five or six centuries after Charlemagne, is the typical verdict of the eighteenth century upon the value of mediaeval history. It was not 'edifying'; and certainly the antiquaries did not study mediaeval antiquities for the sake of edification. This was their offence in the eyes of humanists and philosophers. Many of them were shy and retiring, even to the point of unsociability; the most eminent of the later ones were Non-Jurors, who had virtually contracted out of civil society. To their contemporaries their studies seemed only a means of escape from the harsh present into the unresisting past, in Bolingbroke's borrowed phrase, 'a specious and ingenious form of idleness'. Throughout the whole period from Elizabeth's reign to the close of the Age of Reason the public image of the antiquarians was unattractive.[1]

---

[1] E. L. Woodward (op. cit., 24) quotes Sir Philip Sidney's caricature of the 'historian' as 'loden with old mouse-eaten records, authorising himselfe (for the most part) upon other histories, whose greatest authorities are built upon the notable foundation of Heare-say . . . better acquainted with a thousand yeeres a goe than with the present age . . . curious for antiquities, and inquisitive of novelties, a wonder to young folkes, and a tyrant in table talke' (*Apologie for Poetrie, c.* 1581).

On the Continent *les érudits*, as they are called, continued the researches of Scaliger and Lipsius into classical antiquity and they also opened up the scholarly study of the Middle Ages.[1] It may be true, perhaps, that interest in the latter had originally been awakened by the exigencies of ecclesiastical controversy, but, having once been kindled, it developed into a genuine desire to understand the past for its own sake. Amongst the 'erudites' the Benedictine monks of the Congregation of St-Maur, founded in 1621, were pre-eminent; during the seventeenth century the Maurists came to regard scholarship as a means of the service of God, in much the same way as other monks regarded manual labour. Amongst the Maurists the name of Jean Mabillon (1632–1707) is supreme; his *De re diplomatica*, says Marc Bloch, makes the year 1681 significant 'in the history of the human mind, for the criticism of the documents of archives was definitely established'. It is generally agreed that this work founded the science of diplomatic.[2] Ten years later Mabillon published his scheme of study for monks who regarded scholarship as a vocation, his *Traité des études monastiques*; it gave offence to the Cistercian Abbé Amand de Rancé, who in 1683 in his *Devoirs de la vie monastique* had permitted no other employment than prayer and manual work, prohibiting study. During the controversy that followed, the scholarly Bishop Pierre Daniel Huet[3] wrote to Mabillon congratulating him on having shown that ignorance was not a necessary qualification for a monk. In a chapter of the *Traité* entitled 'De l'étude de l'histoire sacrée et profane' Mabillon lays down thirteen principles of historical criticism, which remarkably anticipate the accepted methods of the nineteenth century.[4] Another Maurist, Bernard de Montfaucon (1655–1741), set a new standard in the presentation of patristic texts and is often said to

[1] For a survey of these developments see J. E. Sandys, *A History of Classical Scholarship*, Cambridge, 1908, Vol. II, 278–398.

[2] *The Historian's Craft*, Eng. trans. by P. Putnam, Manchester, 1954, 36.

[3] Huet had for ten years shared with Bossuet the responsibilities of tutor to the Dauphin (the son of Louis XIV); the celebrated Delphin Classics, of which sixty volumes were produced in twelve years, were edited by Huet, and, like Bossuet's *Discours*, were supposedly intended for the edification of the Dauphin. When the poor young man eventually escaped from his tutors, he restricted his reading to the announcements of births, marriages and deaths in the *Gazette de France*.

[4] This chapter is conveniently summarized in Norman Sykes, *Man as Churchman*, Cambridge, 1961, 12–15.

have created the science of Greek palaeography with the publication of his *Palaeographia Graeca* in 1708. The Bollandists, a succession of Jesuit scholars who continued the labours of John Bolland
(1596–1665), are usually held to have introduced a new era of
historical research by applying a severely critical judgment in the
production of their *Acta Sanctorum* out of the mass of half-
legendary materials before them. Amongst the many scholars of
the age who wrote no popular histories, but who published the
results of their researches for the benefit of other scholars, mention
must be made of Louis Sébastien le Nain de Tillemont (1637–98),
who attempted to get behind the outlines of the conventional
histories to the original sources, devoting himself wholly to
research after the austere and scholarly lay community of Port
Royal des Champs had been broken up during the Jansenist controversy. Perhaps the last and the greatest figure of the 'Age of
Erudition' is L. A. Muratori (1670–1750)—every theological
student has heard of the Muratorian Canon—the Italian antiquary
whose fifty-odd volumes of collected ancient and mediaeval annals
and antiquities constituted a treasure-house of riches for future
historians.

Many other names deserve mention, but enough has been said
to indicate that within the Age of Reason, yet concealed somewhat
from it, like a quiet backwater in a river, there existed an Age of
Erudition, the results of which were not utilized by historians
proper before the advent of Gibbon, and the spirit of which was
not renewed until the nineteenth century. It would be easy to
exaggerate the excellences of the erudites; in their approach to
history these men were not mediaevals, but equally they were not
moderns. 'Great as was their improvement', says Sir G. N. Clark,
their advances 'fell far short of what they were to become when
men of learning adopted in a later age what is sometimes called
par excellence the historical method'.[1] They accumulated a vast
store of historical data and they supplied future historians with
the materials of history; but, in the modern sense, they were not
themselves historians, for they had no myth, no interpretation, of
history to offer. They do not belong to the class of writers of
history in the sense that Clarendon and Burnet assuredly do; these
writers were indeed interpreting the events of their own times.
They are not in our stricter sense historians, because their great

[1] *The Seventeenth Century*, 287.

works do not re-create an age that is dead and gone, but make their own age live for us.[1] That is why Clarendon and Burnet may be read with enjoyment and profit by others than historians today. But the erudites did not and could not re-create the past: 'the method of Mabillon and his kind was not enough to bring the Middle Ages back to life'.[2]

The Twilight Period

The men of the eighteenth century thought of themselves as living in an enlightened age. There are constant references in the literature of the period to 'these enlightened days'.[3] Voltaire regarded the age that began in the reign of Louis XIV as one of the *'quatre âges heureux'* of mankind, the others being those of Pericles, of Augustus and of what we call the Renaissance. Today we are less sure that the eighteenth century was an age of light. It more probably seems to us a kind of twilight period, an age of half-seeing, between the fading brilliance of the mediaeval world-system and the dawn of our modern historically-minded age. This is especially true in respect of the quest for religious truth, which absorbed so much of the time and interest of the Age of Reason itself. It seems astonishing to us that, with all the accumulated knowledge and developed critical sense of the men of erudition, the eighteenth century did not solve the problem of biblical

---

[1] Edward Hyde, first Earl of Clarendon (1608–74), *History of the Rebellion and Civil Wars in England*; Gilbert Burnet (1643–1715), Bishop of Salisbury, *History of My own Time.*

[2] G. N. Clark, ibid., 284.

[3] The term 'the Enlightenment' seems to have entered our language as a translation of the German *Aufklärung* in the second half of the nineteenth century, when it was used pejoratively to designate the shallow intellectualism of the French *philosophes*, with their contempt for tradition, authority, etc.; cf. J. H. Stirling, *The Secret of Hegel* (1865), p. xxvii: 'Deism, Atheism, Pantheism, and all manner of *isms* due to Enlightenment, supported on such semi-information, on such weak personal vanity . . .'; E. Caird, *Philosophy of Kant* (1889), I, 69: 'The individualistic tendencies of the age of Enlightenment.' Professor Alfred Cobban (*In Search of Humanity: the Role of the Enlightenment in Modern History*, London, 1960), taking a favourable view of the achievements of the era (pp. 224f.), asks 'why . . . should we describe as the "Aufklärung" a movement which had . . . only a superficial and transient influence on the German mind?' and he laments the tendency of certain writers to ignore the English countribution (7f.). The significance of the use of 'enlightenment' in connection with the *philosophe* movement lies in the fact that what had formerly been considered a divine work of illumination is now regarded as an achievement of the unaided human reason.

origins and so begin to understand the character of the revelation in Christ as historical rather than literary. It seems almost incomprehensible to us that the scholars of the Age of Reason, who had progressed so far in developing the techniques of historical and textual criticism, should not also have gone on to develop the science of biblical criticism. But to think like this is to think unhistorically, to imagine that solutions which we see clearly could have been perceived equally clearly by men of former ages. Richard Bentley, the glory of English classical scholarship, evinces a critical acumen unsurpassed by scholars of later generations in the exposure of a classical forgery in his *Dissertation upon the Letters of Phalaris* :1699); had he lived a century or so later he might well have solved the Synoptic Problem or anticipated the methods of the Form-critics. He did not do these things, not because he had not mastered the techniques, but because he had not seen the problems. He lived in an age which by reason of its presuppositions could not have applied critical methods to sacred history. So far as the sense of history, as distinct from its methods, was concerned, the great scholars and the great scientists of the era were still mediaevals—Lightfoot and Ussher, Mabillon and Bentley, Boyle and Newton. Sometimes we come across the suggestion that Bentley was the Newton of the humanities, because he gathered into a great synthesis the results of all the labours of Scaliger and his successors. But there is no real parallel here. Bentley and his learned contemporaries might be more accurately likened to the later mediaeval scientists before Copernicus; they had made a great number of accurate observations, and they possessed a vast knowledge of detail, but they lacked the master-key, the new perspective which would enable the known facts to be integrated into a more coherent system. What Bentley and his age needed was not new facts, or a new method of discovering facts, but a new way of looking at the facts which they already possessed. New methods, a *novum organum*, are not (as rationalists from Bacon or Descartes to the present day suppose) nine-tenths of the matter. The new historical perspective, the historical dimension, the awareness of real development in the history of thought, did not arrive until somewhere about the end of the eighteenth century; and even then the rationalists of the nineteenth century never quite understood its significance. When the new perception came, it was not the work of any one mind, a

Copernicus of the new history;[1] it effected a significant change in the constitution of the Western mind itself, the acquisition of that new and almost indefinable quality which we call historical-mindedness.

One of the most interesting figures in the twilight period of the mid-eighteenth century is Conyers Middleton (1683–1750), a clergyman whose independence of mind lost him the preferment for which he longed and a Fellow of Trinity whose vendetta with the high-handed Master, Richard Bentley, cost him a considerable sum in a libel action.[2] He is significant rather for what he might have achieved than for what he actually accomplished, but in the deistic controversy he 'did something to infuse into it a new historical spirit'.[3] His approach was historical rather than philosophical or dogmatic, and the line of his argument tended towards the breaking down of the distinction between sacred and profane history, because he saw that a common historical criticism was applicable to both. Like his contemporaries, he was preoccupied with the question of miracles, but his approach (unlike Hume's) was historical. His chief work, *A Free Enquiry into the Miraculous Powers which are supposed to have existed in the Christian Church through several successive Ages*, was published in 1748, the

[1] For that matter the role of Copernicus in the scientific revolution is usually misunderstood by those who speak of a 'Copernican revolution'; see, e.g., Butterfield, *Origins of Modern Science*, chap. II, 'The Conservatism of Copernicus', 15–31. Perhaps a mild protest might be uttered here against the tendency to discover 'revolutions' in historiography at every point. We have noted already F. Smith Fussner's admirable volume, *The Historical Revolution:* that 'revolution, took place between 1580 and 1640. E. Cassirer plumps for Bayle as the one 'who carries out the "Copernican revolution" in the realm of historical science', though he is apparently the Galileo as well (*The Philosophy of the Enlightenment*, 1932, Eng. trans., Princeton, 1951, 207); it is all the more odd that in the chapter on History in Cassirer's *Essay on Man* (New Haven: Yale, 1944, 171–206) Bayle is not even mentioned. J. H. Brumfitt casts Voltaire for the role of Copernicus (see *infra*, 91 n.). G. Barraclough discovers that a Copernican revolution is going on today in the emergence of 'world-history' (in his essay in *Approaches to History*, ed. Finberg, op. cit., 101). Historical categories (e.g. 'revolutions in history') are necessarily imprecise in comparison with those of the exact sciences; perhaps it would be useful if some student of intellectual history would write a monograph on 'Copernicus' Role in Historiography'; it might help us to be less imprecise. In these Lectures we shall speak of an historiographical revolution only in connection with the emergence of the new historical perspective in the nineteenth century and the improvements in historical method which accompanied it.

[2] Happily, however, a judicious marriage had secured his fortunes.

[3] W. R. Sorley, *History of English Philosophy*, Cambridge, 1920, 153.

very year of Hume's Essay on Miracles; and Hume was generous
enough to admit that Middleton's work 'eclipsed' his own.
Middleton attempted to show that the same arguments which
were used to establish the historicity of the biblical miracles
would equally accredit the miracles of ecclesiastical history, and
that if the dogmas of the Bible were attested by the miracles, so
also the dogmas of the Roman Church were guaranteed by the
'evidences' of contemporary miracles. The argument, of course,
was designed to prove, not that the Roman claims were true, but
that the biblical dogmas were false. But it had the unintended
effect of converting the youthful Gibbon to the Roman obedience,
thus terminating his unprofitable undergraduate studies with the
dons of Magdalen College, sunk in 'prejudice and port' (1753);
the proselyte, however, soon lapsed, and a notorious section of
the *Decline and Fall* (chapter XV), still beloved of the rationalist
press, testifies to Gibbon's capitulation to the arguments of
Middleton. In attempting to apply to the records of sacred
history those critical techniques which had proved so successful
in the sphere of profane history, Middleton had taken a step in
the direction which must inevitably be followed;[1] had he not been
so ardent a deist, eager to expend his insights in the attack upon
the traditional orthodoxy, his contribution to the development of
the modern understanding of the Bible might have been considerable. But such a suggestion is anachronistic; only the truly
great thinkers can be other than what their age has made them, and
Middleton remained an 'enlightened' rationalist. His work did

---

[1] Cf. Leslie Stephen, *History of English Thought in the 18th Century*, 3rd ed.,
New York, 1949, 263f.: 'Middleton had, in fact, a more distinct view than
any of his contemporaries of the essential continuity of history. The dogma
of literal inspiration stood in his way, by giving the Bible a character entirely
disparate from that of all other historical records. The narrative itself, and the
events of which it spoke, were removed by a superstitious veil of sanctity
from the domain of historical criticism. To remove that veil and to apply
the same methods of enquiry to all periods and nations, and to show how the
supposed breaches of continuity disappeared under closer investigation, was
the aim of Middleton's writings. One of his posthumous tracts, called "Reflections on the Variations to be found in the Four Evangelists", expresses
very clearly the bearing of these principles upon the dogmas of literal inspiration. Considered as historical documents, he says, they are confirmed by their
trifling discrepancies. But this argument, familiar enough to apologists,
becomes, as he says, "wholly trifling and impotent on the theory which
represents the Evangelists as mere 'organs and pipes' for conveying the
utterances of the Divine Spirit to men".' (Cf. Middleton's *Works*, II, 341.)

nothing to relieve the perplexed minds of devout believers of the despondency which increasingly oppressed them.[1]

The Rationalist Attack upon Christian Faith

By the middle of the eighteenth century much had happened to cause distress and foreboding amongst faithful Churchmen. The religious unity of the English people had not been recovered after the Restoration, and Dissent was now a familiar feature of the religious landscape. There had been unedifying controversies even among Anglican divines about such central issues as the doctrine of the Trinity; the deists had denied both the fact and the need of a divine revelation. Though the works of Toland and Tindal might be burned by the common hangman, and though poor Woolston might languish in gaol for blasphemy, nevertheless open disrespect for Christianity was expressed with increasing impunity, until at last in the 1740s we descend to the scurrilities of Peter Annet and his kind. 'By about 1733,' says a recent writer, 'the cumulative effect of such deistic attacks on Christianity, abundantly aided by the confusions of the faithful, led to a real sense of despair among many of the latter.'[2] There is no certain foundation for the suggestion that Butler, while Bishop of Bristol, declined an offer of the see of Canterbury in 1747 on the grounds that it was 'too late for him to support a falling Church'; but he indeed took a gloomy view of the prospects of Christianity. In the 'Advertisement' prefixed to the first edition of his *Analogy* (1736) he writes: 'It is come, I know not how, to be taken for granted by many persons that Christianity is not so much as a subject of enquiry; but that it is, now at length, discovered to be fictitious. And accordingly they treat it as if in the present age this were an agreed point among all people of discernment; and nothing remained but to set it up as a principal subject of mirth and ridicule, as it were by way of reprisals, for its having so long interrupted the pleasures of the world.'[3] Nor could Churchmen of

[1] Of the many replies to Middleton's *Free Enquiry* the noblest was John Wesley's and the most ingenious was John Henry Newman's in 1843. See J. S. Lawton, *Miracles and Revelation*, London, 1959, 6of.; 73–75.

[2] R. N. Stromberg, *Religious Liberalism in Eighteenth-century England*, London, 1954, 49.

[3] Some words written in 1930 by C. D. Broad (*Five Types of Ethical Theory*, London, 1930, 54) in connection with this passage are worth recalling: 'This would certainly not be an accurate description of the attitude of "people of

Butler's intellectual cast of mind find comfort in the anti-rational mysticism of William Law,[1] while John Wesley's great work, just beginning, seemed to them merely (in Butler's words) 'a pretending to extraordinary gifts of the Holy Ghost', which (like all 'enthusiasm') was a 'most horrid thing'. The Church of Butler's generation was exposed for the first time to the inclemency of modern rationalism; not only were Christian morals openly derided, but the Church was represented as itself a source of bigotry and evil.[2] For long centuries, during which everyone had been baptized in infancy by order of the Government and disaffection had been punished by the magistrate, the Church had been shielded from that bitter hatred of God which the Bible uncompromisingly affirms to be buried deep in the human heart; but now, all at once, in the course of a few decades, the sheltering conventions were broken down. In any age, including our own, Christians shrink from the biblical realism which speaks of man's natural enmity towards God, and they are always surprised and hurt that men, otherwise 'decent' and 'progressive', should call good evil and rail against the Gospel of Christ with the implacable bitterness of an inverted religious zeal; when this new phenomenon of the modern period first appeared in open and powerful array, the Churchmen of the eighteenth century stood defenceless and dismayed before it. The clergy were ridiculed on the stage and in novels; nothing was too venerable to be impugned, too sacred to be mocked. 'Christianity is now railed at and ridiculed with very little reserve,' said the future Archbishop of Canterbury, Thomas Secker, 'and its teachers without any at all. Against us our adversaries appear to have set themselves to be as bitter as they can, not only beyond all truth, but beyond all probability, exag-

---

discernment" at the present time towards religion in general or Christianity in particular. We do indeed meet with such people; but they strike us as quaint and picturesque survivals of the eighteen-seventies who are rendered all the more amusing by their obviously sincere conviction that they are daringly advanced thinkers.'

[1] The outstanding devotional writing of the period is Law's *Serious Call to a Devout and Holy Life* (1728); for an excellent recent appraisal see C. J. Stranks, *Anglican Devotion, Studies in the Spiritual Life of the Church of England between the Reformation and the Oxford Movement*, London, 1961, 174–202.

[2] Cf. Bolingbroke, *Works* IV, 25; 'Christianity has been always a scene of dissension, of hatred, of persecution and of blood' (quoted by Stromberg, op. cit., 49).

gerating without mercy.'[1] It is not difficult for us to understand the motives which prompted John Bampton in such an age as this, when he made his will, to establish 'for ever' his annual courses of Divinity Lecture Sermons in Oxford 'to confirm and establish the Christian faith, and to confute all heretics and schismatics'.[2]

At this point it would perhaps be helpful to state what is meant by 'rationalism'. As the term is used in these Lectures, it denotes primarily belief in the power of the human intellect to elucidate with progressive or cumulative effectiveness the totality of things; it is faith in the total intelligibility—in principle, at least—of nature, including human nature. It is the affirmation that the only kind of knowledge is scientific knowledge (whether deductive or inductive) and the denial of the possibility of real knowledge derived from other sources, such as religious experience (mysticism), personal encounter or self-awareness (existentialism), or even practical living (tradition or inherited wisdom). Knowing is a technique to be mastered, which, when it is rightly applied, unlocks all secrets. Hence rationalism always insists on sweeping away the past, on the new start with a sounder technique. The 'new organ' of Bacon and the 'method' of Descartes are prime historical specimens of the rationalist appproach. It should be noted that our use of the word is quite different from its use in conventional textbooks of philosophy, in which Descartes, Spinoza and Leibnitz are 'rationalists', while Locke, Berkeley and Hume are 'empiricists'. As we use the word, Hume is an outstanding example of the rationalist mind. Rationalism, says Professor Oakeshott, is 'the assertion that, properly speaking, there is no knowledge which is not technical knowledge. . . . The sovereignty of "Reason", for the rationalist, means the sovereignty of technique.'[3] Nineteenth-century positivism and twentieth-century 'scientific humanism' are manifestations of the temper of mind

[1] Quoted by G. R. Cragg, *The Church and the Age of Reason, 1648–1789* (Pelican History of the Church), London, 1960, 127. Chapter 9, 'The Hanoverian Age in England', gives an excellent picture of the times.

[2] It is not surprising that, during the long struggle against nineteenth-century rationalistic agnosticism, many lecturers on the Bampton foundation should have directed their efforts towards its confutation in accordance with the Founder's wish. A century ago, for instance, the Bampton Lecturer for 1862, A. S. Farrar, chose as his theme *A Critical History of Freethought*.

[3] Michael Oakeshott, *Rationalism in Politics and other Essays*, London, 1962, 11. The title essay in this book is most suggestive in this connection.

which expressed itself so confidently in the eighteenth century's belief in Reason. The technique, once mastered, can in principle be better applied by machines (electronics) than by personal beings, for machines are incapable of those errors which arise from human prejudice and passion, to say nothing of the limitations of the individual human brain; even the complexities of the human sciences may one day be mastered by computers.[1] According to this philosophy, then, there is no such thing as religious knowledge, existential knowledge or traditional wisdom; there is only the knowledge which can be attained by a superhuman machine-brain which has mastered the technique of discovery and formulation. Hence the preoccupation of rationalism with certainty, its despising of poetic or imaginative awareness, and its reduction of all mystery to 'problems'. It is true that, since Marx and Freud, rationalism can never be quite as self-confident as it was in its pure eighteenth-century form; nevertheless the rationalist temper remains and still proclaims in our own days its assurance that what cannot be demonstrated by scientific method is at best mere opinion and at worst rank superstition. Such a philosophy, though not itself necessarily anti-religious (there have been theistic rationalists), becomes a useful weapon in the hands of those who are filled with that hatred of God which is for Christian people the strangest feature of human nature, despite the clear teaching of the Bible concerning it. Hence in modern usage the word 'rationalist' has become a synonym for 'anti-Christian' or 'anti-religious'. The weakness of the would-be apologists for Christian truth in the eighteenth century was, as we have said already, that they were themselves deeply infected by the presuppositions of a rationalistic age. Law and Wesley were, in their very different ways, more successful in their resistance to rationalism, because they were so largely emancipated from the

---

[1] 'The human sciences have failed to find as coherent a method as the natural sciences. . . . The simple reasoning of cause and effect which gave coherence to the physical sciences from the time of Hobbes onward is too crude to give an account of the interplay of human motives in a large society. It may be that the new concept which the human sciences require is a statistical one, and will turn out to involve nothing more radical than the application of large computing machines to social and economic problems. Or it may be that some more profound conception is required to marry the rational and the empirical approaches in the human sciences' (J. Bronowski and Bruce Mazlish, *The Western Intellectual Tradition from Leonardo to Hegel*, London, 1960, 494f.).

ideology of their age by their personal understanding of biblical truth. But their characteristic answers to the question raised by the crisis of the eighteenth century were practical rather than intellectual, and the eighteenth century found no apologist—not even Butler—who could meet the challenge of 'Reason' to the Christian faith in a divine revelation.

The Nature of the Crisis

The French historian Paul Hazard in a notable work[1] has spoken of the years between 1680 and 1715 as a time of acute crisis in the intellectual and moral development of Europe. But it was, he says, from 1715 onwards that there became apparent a continuing effervescence and diffusion of ideas so remarkable as to be without parallel in history.[2] That the crisis was a religious one can hardly be denied, but estimates of the importance of its religious aspect vary according to the particular standpoint of the historian, (that is to say) according to whether he holds that religious conviction is of decisive importance as a 'factor' in history or whether he regards it as merely epiphenomenal upon the broad stream of social and economic process. We shall hardly be surprised to find that amongst historians there are, in fact, widely differing interpretations of the nature and significance of the crisis of the eighteenth century. We will call attention to three mutually incompatible interpretations of the crisis.

In the last quarter of the nineteenth century the French historian Hippolyte Taine, the former radical extremist and exponent of scientific materialism, came to regard the 'enlightened' ideas of the *philosophes* as the source of all that was evil in the French Revolution and in the excesses of the Jacobins. France, having fasted under the Monarchy, became intoxicated by the bad brandy of Rousseau and endured a debauch of violence such as the world had never known before. For Taine the crisis of the eighteenth century came to a head in 1789.[3] This line of interpretation has

[1] *La crise de la conscience européenne, 1680–1715*, 3 tomes, Paris, 1935; Eng. trans., *The European Mind*, London, 1953.

[2] See Hazard, *La pensée européenne au XVIIIème siècle*, Paris, 1946; Eng. trans., *European Thought in the Eighteenth Century*, London, 1954.

[3] Hippolyte Taine, *Origines de la France contemporaine*; the first volume appeared in 1875 and the work was unfinished when he died in 1893. *L'ancien régime* appeared in 1876. See Adolphe Aulard, *Taine, historien de la Révolution française*, Paris, 1907; G. P. Gooch, *History and Historians in the Nineteenth Century*, London, 1913, 238–46.

more recently been brought up to date by J. L. Talmon, who has
traced the origins of our twentieth-century totalitarian 'democracies' to the stock of ideas of the eighteenth-century *philosophes*,
which 'branched out as a separate and identifiable trend in the
course of the French Revolution and has had an unbroken continuity ever since'.[1] Political messianism of the Marxist type is the
lineal descendant of the philosophy of the 'abstract man', the
purely egalitarian social ideal, which leaves the individual naked
before the State; and though in western Europe this political
salvationist faith had expended itself soon after 1870, it found a
more favourable climate in Russia and the East.[2] By marrying the
'general will' to 'popular sovereignty' Rousseau gave rise to
totalitarian democracy; and by his passion and by the fire of his
style he elevated the speculations of the eighteenth century into a
dynamic secular religion.[3] The crisis of the eighteenth century,
was, on this view, indeed a religious crisis.

On the other hand, Carl Becker in the early nineteen-thirties
was able to view the European scene with a proper academic detachment in the tranquil atmosphere of Cornell and perhaps also
in the isolationist perspective of his native Middle West. He could
adopt a more indulgent attitude towards the eighteenth-century
philosophers, admire their precocity and smile at their absurdities.
We need not, he seems to tell us,[4] take their pranks and posturings
too seriously; they were the adolescents of the modern world,
suffering its growing pains. Of course, they failed in their youthful
ambition to substitute faith in human reason for the mediaeval
faith in God. We, the disillusioned grown-ups of the twentieth
century, can see that both these faiths are absurd. Enlightened
reason is no cleverer than religious dogmatism when it comes to
building a Heavenly City out of human bricks and mortar. The
eighteenth-century philosophers ruthlessly demolished St Augustine's Heavenly City in the immature belief that it could be rebuilt
with more up-to-date materials; they were mistaken, but at least
they cleared away a lot of mediaeval ruins during the demolition
work, including, of course, childish notions about a revelation in
history. We are left with the impression that, in Becker's view,

[1] *The Origins of Totalitarian Democracy*, London, 1953, 249.
[2] Op. cit., 250–3.
[3] Op. cit., 43.
[4] In *The Heavenly City*, published in 1932.

these innocents at any rate were not responsible for the crimes of Hitler and Stalin.

A third and more favourable view is taken by Professor Alfred Cobban. He holds that the Enlightenment effected an ethical revolution[1] and that for the last century and a half the Western democracies have been living on its achievements.[2] The influence of Locke and Montesquieu ensured that the thought of the age did not turn into an apologia for absolutism.[3] The Enlightenment introduced an era of scientific and social progress, of political toleration and popular enfranchisement; it witnessed the decline of hereditary privilege and the abandonment of torture as an instrument of policy; even religion was purged of 'its grosser elements'.[4] But the area of its influence was regrettably limited to the eastern and western seaboards of the Atlantic;[5] it only superficially influenced the vast territories of the Habsburg, Hohenzollern and Romanov despotisms. Perhaps we notice here the inutility of umbrella-terms like 'the Enlightenment'; clearly Cobban is talking of the Enlightenment in terms of Newton, Locke and Montesquieu, whereas Talmon is speaking about a very different movement of thought, the French physiocrats, d'Holbach, Helvétius, Diderot, Voltaire, Condillac, Rousseau. So it is that Cobban can make a thoroughly optimistic assessment of the achievements of the Age of Reason; taking a view diametrically opposed to Talmon's, he tells us that, as a result of the achievements of the Enlightenment, 'the great totalitarian dictatorships (of the twentieth century) . . . now seem less the portentous anticipation of the future than the last monstrous survivals of an earlier age'.[6] A similarly optimistic estimate of the Enlightenment appears to be implicit in the recent Trevelyan Lectures of Mr E. H. Carr. In typically rationalist vein he seems to date modern history (perhaps even history itself in the full sense) from somewhere about 1760. 'Modern history begins when more and more people emerge into social and political consciousness, become

[1] *In Search of Humanity: the Role of the Enlightenment in Modern History*, 17.
[2] Op. cit., 241.
[3] Op. cit., 104.
[4] Op. cit., 104.
[5] It might be added that even there its success was not complete. See Jean Sarrailh, *L'Espagne éclairée*, Paris, 1954; H. R. Trevor-Roper, 'The Spanish Enlightenment' in his *Historical Essays*, London, 1957, 260–72.
[6] Op. cit., 224.

aware of their respective groups as historical entities having a past and a future, and enter fully into history. It is only within the last 200 years at most, even in a few advanced countries, that social, political and historical consciousness have begun to spread to anything like a majority of the population.'[1] On this view there is a good deal of history going on in the world today, far more than ever before. The participation in 'history' on the part of millions in Asia and Africa means the extension of 'reason' and its application on a world scale; and this is progress. Making appropriate allowances for the wear-and-tear of a couple of centuries, Mr Carr's interpretation is not substantially different from that of the eighteenth-century philosophers themselves. We *could* be moving towards the fifth 'happy age' of mankind.

Confronted by such widely differing interpretations of the crisis of the eighteenth century, we shall not here attempt to assess them. It is more to our purpose to call attention to the mythopoeic function of the historian, including the rationalist historian, who is usually less aware of it. The myths concerning the Enlightenment period are still living and active in the interpretations of our own times. Myths are interpretations of history, or of historical epochs, which arise in the historian's mind because he is existentially involved in the issues of his own day. This realization accounts for the widespread disillusionment of many, who discover with a shock that all historical interpretation involves subjectivity; they often become historical relativists and abandon the task of interpretation altogether; they may assert that interpretation is not the function of the historian at all and then confine their activities to a technical realm of 'objective' research which consists of particular enquiries about limited questions arising out of historical records under their noses. Then they will have adopted the attitude of the antiquaries and erudites of old, and dissociated themselves from the quest for a history that will be of value and interest to men like Sir William Temple, concerned with the tasks and duties of a living generation. For most of us (whatever a few academic historians may say) the fascination of history lies in its myths, in the interpretation of the past in the light of our engagement with the present. The past is our past, and it lives in our present. As Paul Hazard said, we are the lineal descendants of the

1 *What is History?* London, 1961, 144. Mr Carr detects a 'revolution in our conception of history' at this point; see note on p. 43 n. *supra*.

eighteenth century, and its crisis is our crisis.[1] To interpret the crisis of the eighteenth century is to make suggestions concerning the understanding of the twentieth century. The question which the eighteenth century most insistently put to itself was the question concerning religion; it had been raised acutely by the change which was coming over Western man's view of history. It would seem probable that our understanding of the significance of the crisis which the new historical attitude brought about cannot be complete if we leave out of our discussion—as do Becker, Cobban and Carr—the question of religion as a living, urgent issue. Today it is a hopeful aspect of the contemporary investigation of intellectual history', or the history of ideas, that it is more widely understood, especially by younger writers, that we are neglecting a clue of vital importance if religious ideas are dismissed as merely epiphenomenal.

[1] *European Thought,* Eng. trans., preface.

2

THE TWO WORLD SYSTEMS

FIFTY years ago it was usual to assert with Moellendorff that 'all our historical writing rests on foundations laid by the Greeks as does all our natural science'.[1] Today it would be widely agreed that new foundations have had to be dug not only for science but also for history. The latter part of the fifth century BC, when Socrates talked in the Athenian market-place and Thucydides was busy on his history of the Peloponnesian War, has been called the Greek Age of Enlightenment. But, as Mr M. I. Finley has recently reminded us,[2] it differed in at least one very important respect from the European Enlightenment of the eighteenth century: whereas the latter was at once followed by the birth of the new quality of 'historical-mindedness' and the emergence of modern historiography, 'Herodotus and Thucydides led nowhere'. Of the attempts to continue Thucydides' history only the *Hellenica* of Xenophon (*c.* 430–355 BC) survives, and it represents a sad decline from the master's standard. After that there is a gap of two centuries until we come to Polybius (*c.* 198–117 BC), of whom it has been said that he is 'the only surviving Greek or Roman historian with standards comparable to Thucydides'.[3] Mr Finley says categorically, 'Of all the lines of enquiry which the Greeks initiated, history was the most abortive.'[4]

---

[1] U. von Wilamovitz-Moellendorff, *Greek Historical Writing and Apollo*, Eng. trans. by Gilbert Murray, Oxford, 1908, 5.

[2] *The Greek Historians*, New York, 1959, 17.

[3] G. T. Griffith, art. 'Historiography', *Chambers's Encyclopaedia*, 1950, VII 118a.

[4] Op. cit., 20. For a fuller account of classical historiography see Appended Note II, *infra*, 278.

The 'New History' of St Augustine

If we ask why classical historiography 'led nowhere', we might profitably turn to St Augustine (AD 354–430), the sternest critic of its assumptions. He was not himself an historian in any modern sense; but he had been a professor of rhetoric, and in the ancient world rhetoric was concerned with the use that might be made of history and of historical illustrations in the development of the arts of persuasion. After his conversion (*c.* AD 386) Augustine found himself driven to a deeper consideration of historical questions by apologetic necessity. Two years after the sack of Rome by Alaric the Goth (AD 410) he began to write his *City of God*; he continued to work on it for fourteen years, so that it 'developed from a controversial pamphlet into a vast synthesis which embraces the history of the whole human race and its destinies in time and eternity'.[1] Replying to the accusation that the Eternal City had fallen because the worship of the Roman gods had been abandoned in favour of an oriental superstition, St Augustine found himself involved in a critique of classical ideology as a whole. Thus he came to compose the work which Mr Dawson declares to be the only writing of the Christian Fathers which the modern secular historian ever reads,[2] and the one which was generally regarded in the nineteenth century as establishing Augustine's right to be called the founder of the philosophy of history. But such a description is misconceived; and since in the twentieth century it would assuredly destroy his reputation as a thinker, it is worth while to consider its unsuitability. The philosophy of history is a nineteenth-century invention; it was elaborated in the philosophies of Hegel, Marx and the various positivist thinkers, after such prophets of the new age as Lessing, Condorcet and Herder had given literary expression to the newly-born notion of progress.[3] The Greeks did not entertain any idea of progress, and their cyclical view of history would have been incompatible with it. Even less was it possible for St Augustine, though he repudiated the cyclical view, to believe in progress in history such as could be measured by secular standards.[4] Belief in

[1] Christopher Dawson in *A Monument to St Augustine*, London, 1945, 43.
[2] Ibid.
[3] On the philosophy of history see Appended Note III, *infra*, 287.
[4] This is his fault in the eyes of modern classical-rationalist historians, who fail to understand the significance of Augustine's achievement in de-

progress is a very subjective matter: after all, it was even more difficult for those living in the days when the Roman Empire was violently disintegrating through barbarian invasion to believe in progress than it is for British historians in the twentieth century, when the British Empire is going into more or less voluntary liquidation. On the other hand, belief in progress might come more easily to the Goths and Visigoths in Augustine's day, or to Asians and Africans in ours; we are all tempted to identify our own ups and downs with the process of history as such.[1] In point of fact St Augustine's view of history is not based upon any inductions from allegedly observable trends in history or yet upon a philosophical analysis of the logic of history itself; it is profoundly unhistorical to try to make him a philosopher of history in any recognizably modern sense, and it is equally unhistorical to blame him, as Voltaire blamed the Middle Ages, for not thinking modern thoughts. It would be better to describe Augustine's view as a theology of history,[2] since it is based neither upon scientific history nor upon philosophy, but upon the biblical revelation, that is, upon 'sacred history'. His critique of the classical view of history, derived from Hebraic insights, was immensely significant for the future of European thought.

When we compare Greek and Hebrew ways of thinking about the past, we find an apparent paradox. The Greeks, who accepted the universal ancient and oriental view of history as a cycle of endless repetition, are nevertheless credited by modern rationalist thinkers with having invented the science of history. The Hebrews waged a relentless struggle against the mythological personification

---

stroying the cyclical view and thus making the modern conception of history possible. See J. B. Bury, *The Idea of Progress*, London, 1920, 22. Cf. G. P. Gooch, *History and Historians in the Nineteenth Century*, on his very first page: 'The atmosphere of the Middle Ages was saturated with theology. The influence of Augustine weighed with an almost physical pressure on the mind of Europe for a thousand years, diverting attention from secular history and problems'; the anachronistic attitude of eighteenth-century rationalism pervades the whole book; the Middle Ages are condemned for not being modern.

[1] Cf. Mr A. J. P. Taylor's remark, quoted by E. H. Carr (*What is History!* 106f.), that all this talk about the decline of civilization 'means only that university professors used to have domestic servants and now do their own washing-up'. To which Dr Carr adds that 'of course, for former domestic servants, washing-up by professors may be a symbol of progress'.

[2] So H. A. Hodges, *The Philosophy of W. Dilthey*, London, 1952, xv.

of the forces of nature and completely demythologized the nature-religion of the other ancient peoples; in so doing they developed a strong sense of history, but they are not credited by modern classical-rationalist scholars with having produced history at all. Collingwood, for instance, dismisses the Old Testament in a single page as 'mere theocratic history and myth'.[1] The explanation of this apparent paradox is that modern classical-rationalists accepted the nineteenth-century positivist view of history as a search for regularities amongst particular historical instances and they thought of historical enquiry as a quest for scientific explanation in terms of general laws. This might conceivably represent the idea at the back of Thucydides' mind, but, if so, he was virtually unique amongst Greek historians in attempting to carry it out, and in any case he did not consider the past to be a subject worthy of investigation; he confined his research entirely to the events of his own times. What the classical-rationalists liked about him was that he shunned supernatural explanations, at least with the top of his mind, although at a deeper level he believed as firmly as any other ancient historian in inexorable Fate. By the same token the classical-rationalists despised the Hebrews, because they wrote history unashamedly in terms of their encounter with the will of God in history ('mere theocratic history and myth'). Now, while it is possible to exaggerate the difference between the ancient classical and the Hebrew views of history,[2] it seems to be broadly true that the Graeco-classical view did not regard history as a source of real knowledge,[3] preferring philosophy and even poetry instead, whereas the Hebrews consistently held that history was the *locus* of all our knowledge both of God and of man, and that in nature only a 'whisper' of the truth concerning our existence was to be heard (Job 26.14). Thus, Greek historiography degenerated into a continual re-historicizing of the myth of Greek superiority;[4] the Hebrew prophets saw their whole history as standing under the righteous judgment of God. The classical view never developed beyond the identification of man with nature;

[1] *The Idea of History*, Oxford, 1946, 17. Cf. Wilamovitz-Moellendorff, op. cit., 3–26.

[2] Cf. the warnings given in James Barr, *Biblical Words for Time*, London, 1962, esp. 137–43.

[3] Cf. Aristotle, *Poetics*, 9.2f. (*The Works of Aristotle*, ed. W. D. Ross, ix, *De Rhetorica and De Poetica*, Oxford, 1924, par. 1451b).

[4] Finley, op. cit., 20.

the historical process was only the human counterpart of the periodic rotation of the heavens or the seasons; the repetitive patterns will go on for ever, thus making a 'scientific' view of history possible. But the Hebrews, unique amongst ancient peoples, were aware of themselves as having had a beginning as a nation and as having an historical destiny which was being fulfilled in successive stages.

It thus came about that modern classical-rationalist historians, believing that history is a science which searches for regularities as do the natural sciences, hailed the Greeks as innovators in the sphere of historiography, but failed to observe the genuine histori-cal-mindedness of the Hebrews. By historical-mindedness is meant: having a lively sense of real change and development in history, an awareness that successive ages are genuinely different from one another. In our modern age this historical attitude de-veloped out of the new sense of progress in history, which emerged towards the end of the eighteenth century (or perhaps it was *vice versa*: the discussion is of the hen-and-egg variety). In ancient Israel historical-mindedness was the result of the pro-phetic awareness of the inevitable accomplishment of a divine purpose in history; this was not dependent upon or measurable by any secular standards of progress (such as the spread of demo-cracy, literacy, etc.), and indeed the general Hebraic attitude to-wards historical development was that 'things will get worse before they get better'. The belief in a divine purpose in their history made it impossible for the Hebrews to accept the unhis-torical, naturalistic attitude of other ancient peoples, for whom history was a repetitive process comparable to the rhythm of nature; the perpetuation of this naturalistic attitude amongst the Greeks explains why the so-called Greek 'Enlightenment' did not lead to the emergence of a genuine historical-mindedness and why 'Herodotus and Thucydides led nowhere'. Rationalism in all its forms is fundamentally unhistorical. It looks to history not as itself a source of knowledge, not as the *locus* of insights into our own existential condition, but as something secondary, a means of corroborating or illustrating generalizations about human nature which have been derived from other sources (e.g. in modern times, the social sciences and psychology). The basic difference between the Greek and the Hebrew view is that the Hebrews regarded history as the *locus* of man's knowledge of himself and of

God in a way in which the Greeks did not.[1] The triumph of the Hebraic-Christian view over the classical, achieved by the time of St Augustine, made possible the ultimate emergence, after many centuries, of modern scientific historiography. To put the matter in another way, it was only in Christian civilization, more than two thousand years afterwards, that a great and dedicated international company of scholars was able to take up in a systematic way the enquiry (*historia*) which Herodotus began into the reason why men fight and behave as they do.[2]

In the Greek view the historical process reflects the periodic rotation of the heavens and the seasons; the repetitive patterns will go on for ever.[3] Herodotus conceives of these patterns as regulated by an ineluctable *nemesis*, a law of compensation which continually restores the balance of things. Man cannot avert his doom, and the bitter sorrow of history is that he can know so much and control so little.[4] Thucydides, eschewing supernatural explanations and masterfully developing empirical methods, hopes that men will learn wisdom in future crises, which will repeat the pattern of his own times; all that has happened in the past will happen again.[5] Beneath his 'scientific' attitude lie the philosophical presuppositions of classical naturalism, that the changeless is the real, that reason is able to detect the abiding patterns amidst the vicissitudes of history, that the circle is the perfect form of movement and that all things therefore inevitably return to their point of origin. When the Christian Church first carried its Hebraic heritage into the Graeco-Roman world, it must at once have come into conflict with the cyclical view of history.[6] Even

---

[1] On this whole subject see Thorleif Boman, *Hebrew Thought Compared with Greek*, Eng. trans. by Jules L. Moreau, London, 1960, esp. 168–71. Much suggestive material will be found, but Boman's conclusions should not be accepted without reserve. James Barr (op. cit.) criticizes some of his arguments on philological grounds, but he himself is in some danger of obscuring the truth that for the Hebrews, unlike the Greeks, history is the source of the profoundest knowledge that men possess. For the sense in which classical culture may be said to be 'ahistorical', see Reinhold Niebuhr, *Faith and History: a Comparison of Christian and Modern views of History*, New York, 1949, 16–22.

[2] Hdt., i, 1.

[3] For a brief and convenient documentation in respect of the doctrine of eternal recurrence see Karl Löwith, *Meaning in History*, 248, n. 15.

[4] Hdt., ix, 16.

[5] Thuc., i, 22; ii, 64.

[6] Cf. Justin Martyr, *Dial. Trypho*, I.

the Greek-minded Origen had protested against the notion that in another Athens another Socrates would marry another Xanthippe and drink another cup of hemlock.[1] For St Augustine the notion is intolerable. We might think it stupid to believe that the same Plato has sat in the same Academy teaching the same pupils at regular intervals throughout infinite ages of the past, and that he will do so again through all the cycles of an infinite future: it is morally impossible to believe such nonsense about Christ. The qualitative difference between Plato and Christ is apparent as soon as we are asked to believe that in another Jerusalem another Pilate would crucify another Jesus on another cross—to all eternity: 'Christ being raised from the dead dieth no more; death hath no more dominion over him' (Rom. 6.9).[2] This is the text which changed the outlook of European man upon history. The Christian experience of the conquest of death through Christ's resurrection brought to an end the classical view of history. The European mind was freed by the proclamation of God's saving act in history from the fatalistic theory of cyclical recurrence which had condemned Greek historiography to sterility. It is important to realize that this momentous change of outlook was brought about not by an effort of philosophical reasoning but by the preaching of the gospel of the resurrection; St Augustine gives us not a philosophy of history but a theology of history. The missing truth which he had not found amongst the philosophers, that the Word was made flesh and dwelt among us,[3] became, after the long interval of the Middle Ages, the fertilizing agent which brought to fruition the promise which Greek history had contained but had not fulfilled.

Other insights which Augustine had derived not from philosophy but from revelation were also important in the formation of the new historical outlook. The ancient belief in Chance or Accident was also at last overthrown. The rationalism of Thucydides led only to the irrationalism of Polybius (to say nothing of the lesser men), who virtually abandoned the search for historical causation and acknowledged Fortune (*Tyche*, the unpredictable) as the hidden controller of human destiny. The inexplicable reversals of Fortune—such as the disappearance from history of

[1] *Contra Celsum*, iv, 68; cf. v. 20.
[2] *De Civ. Dei*, xii, 14.
[3] *Confessions*, vii, 9.

the Persian world-rulers and their replacement by the Macedo-
nians who had sprung from nowhere[1]—were simply the result of
Luck (*Tyche*), and no other explanation need be sought. Luck had
smiled upon Rome and made her home there, and Polybius finds
the goal of history in the world-supremacy of the established
power: might is right, and thus, as C. N. Cochrane says, 'the quest
for a principle of historical intelligibility came to an ignominious
end'.[2] The Roman *Fortuna* had been worshipped in Rome above
all the gods, and after AD 410 it was the charge that the abandonment of her cult at Christian instigation had led to the defeat of
Roman arms which compelled Augustine to search for a 'new
history'. He thus comes to develop his doctrine of Providence,
which he opposes to the notion of Chance. What the pagans call
Fortuna, Chance or Luck, is only what is hidden from us; it is not
hidden from God. There is no such thing as accident or uncaused
occurrence in the universe. All history is controlled by the
rational purpose of God (Providence). Augustine is undismayed
by the pseudo-problems concerning freewill and historical
inevitability, which have vexed philosophically-minded historians
from Cicero to the present day, because of his own profound
conviction, based on experience, that the human will is never
more truly free than when it is most completely surrendered to
and controlled by the will of God.[3]

Because Augustine can now view history as standing under the
righteous judgment of God, he is able to offer a realistic critique
of all political pretensions. Rome had prospered not because she
was established on justice, as Cicero liked to believe,[4] or yet
because she was the favourite of Fortune, as her myth-making
historians had taught her complacent citizens fondly to imagine.
Rome had prospered because a *civitas terrena* was appointed by the
beneficent providence of God, who disposes of the kingdoms of
the earth,[5] to be the milieu out of which the reborn citizens of the
civitas Dei might be recruited. In his wisdom God entrusts to the

[1] Polyb., xxix, 21; cf. xxxvii, 4, xxxviii, 18.
[2] *Christianity and Classical Culture: a Study of Thought and Action from Augustus to Augustine*, Oxford, 1940, 474.
[3] *De Civ. Dei*, v. 9. For a development of this theme by a modern theologian
see D. M. Baillie, *God Was in Christ*, London, 1948, 106–18.
[4] Ibid., xix, 21, where Augustine criticizes Scipio's argument in Cicero's
De re publica.
[5] Ibid., v, 1.

earthly State the task of ordering human affairs on a basis of law, so that in peace and freedom men may learn the discipline and receive the privileges of membership of the Heavenly City. But successive earthly empires have transgressed their divinely appointed function and claimed a loyalty which is due to the Heavenly City alone. Kingdoms like Alexander's or empires like that of Rome ('the great Western Babylon—how many lives has her vanity cost!'[1]) are morally no better than gangs of pirates, for they have obtained their riches by attacking and enslaving other nations.[2] The divinity of the State is rejected along with all the idolatrous pretensions of political religion: what a contrast with the historians of the classical tradition, such as Polybius or Livy, who fed the people with the myth of Roman *virtus*! The new history of St Augustine, in the true Hebraic prophetic tradition, provides the classical world for the first time with a transcendental critique of the myths of the secular historians. Henceforward the insights of the biblical knowledge of the divine righteousness are available for the princes and governments of Europe.

St Augustine discovers the value of the individual and the significance of history at the same time. The State is not the goal of history and it exists only for the well-being of its subjects. It was not God's intention in the creation that some men should rule others, but government has been rendered necessary as a result of human sinfulness; the State is necessary only in a fallen world.[3] The earthly ruler should govern justly and firmly, like the father of a family; his ideal should be that all should live as members of the household of heaven, 'where command is wholly unnecessary'.[4] Then might the earthly city and the Heavenly City enjoy a peaceful co-existence, and the citizens of the celestial society might render perfect obedience to the secular authority.[5] But Augustine does not look forward optimistically to the perfect realization of this ideal in any age of history; he understands too well the wickedness of the human heart. History is the recruiting-ground where men and women out of every race and class and language are enrolled, one by one, as members of the Heavenly City. Thus, the significance of history does not consist in move-

[1] Ibid., xix, 7.
[2] Ibid., iv, 4.
[3] Ibid., xix, 15.
[4] Ibid., xix, 16.
[5] Ibid., xix, 17.

ment towards an ideal future on this earth; history is significant already, because in every age it fulfils its purpose in the providence of God. Every age of history is equally near to God.[1] History is the place where the two 'cities' intermingle, so that the citizen of the earthly society may pass over into the City of God. There is progress in history, but it is the progress of that company which in each generation is entering into the Heavenly City. No secular standards can be used to measure it, and Augustine disapproves of millenarian speculation and of all attempts to predict the future, whether good or bad, by using the Scriptures as an almanac in code.[2] Thus, meaning in history is not bound up with those eighteenth-century notions which Carl Becker derided as attempts to rebuild Augustine's Heavenly City out of up-to-date secular materials; all such notions involve the belief that those who are fortunate enough to live in the later periods of history are more blessed than those wretched ones who lived before the Enlightened Age. J. B. Bury intended to pass adverse judgment when he remarked, truly enough, that 'for Augustine, as for any mediaeval believer, the course of history would be satisfactorily complete if the world came to an end in his own lifetime'.[3] Bury in 1920 could hardly have envisaged an atomic era in which people then alive would seriously have to take account of the possibility that the world would come to an end in their own lifetime; he could hardly have understood that this reflection would no more disturb the faith of Christians than Augustine's faith was shaken by God's judgment upon 'eternal' Rome. For those who share Augustine's faith, history still derives its meaning not from secular progress but from the fact that it is the sphere in which the love of God for every individual soul is ceaselessly exercised for man's salvation, until his new creation, the Heavenly City, is complete. St Augustine can teach us that secular despair can be overcome by Christian hope, which enables men of faith to go on working while it is day, as Augustine worked even when the Vandals were encircling his city of Hippo. He lived in an age of despair more terrible than ours, an age in which the world—his world—was literally coming to an end; there would have been no Christian civilization of

---

[1] A view still held by Ranke, the doyen of the 'scientific' historians of the nineteenth century; see *infra*, 177.

[2] Ibid., xviii, 52f.

[3] *The Idea of Progress*, 21.

Europe, if he and the Church of the fifth century had yielded to secular despair.

The Mediaeval Historical View

In times of crisis the need for a 'new history' becomes manifest. The classical interpretation of history had broken down by the turn of the fifth century. The Romans had produced several outstanding histories, but they were all histories of Rome, enshrining the myth of Roman superiority. In strong contrast Augustine's new history, as expanded in scholarly style by Orosius,[1] was able to view the rise and fall of Rome as an episode in world-history: the Western Babylon was going the way of the Eastern one, and of Nineveh and Tyre, of Egypt, Persia and Greece. The idea of universal history was born; for the first time the notion that the world, and not merely the Roman world, had a single history entered the European mind.[2] It is hardly necessary to pause to emphasize how important was this step for the development of historiography. This first conception of the unity of human history was, of course, derived from the Bible, which supplied the frame into which could be fitted the histories of classical writers like Livy, or of earlier Christian writers like Eusebius of Caesarea. The idea of a *civitas terrena*, whose rulers were raised up by God to administer justice and keep peace, and who were brought down by God if in their pride they transgressed his law, remained the guiding political concept of mediaeval Christendom, and underlay the relationship of Church and State. This theological interpretation of history invested the secular order with dignity and significance; even Bury admits that men could never again be 'content to return to such views as satisfied the ancients, for whom human history, apprehended as a whole, was a tale of little meaning'.[3] The new theological outlook was able to appreciate and learn from the classical historiographers; throughout the Middle Ages great respect was felt for the achievements of antiquity. Before

[1] See footnote on p. 23, *supra*.

[2] The expression is used here for convenience, although it would be hopelessly anachronistic if taken in the modern sense: Augustine was not a European, but he is nevertheless one of the greatest of the makers of 'Europe'. On the gradual rise of a 'European' consciousness (which did not happen until long after the African churches had been swept away by Islam) see the fascinating study by Professor Denys Hay, *Europe: the Emergence of an Idea*, Edinburgh, 1957.

[3] *The Idea of Progress*, 22f.

the lights went out in Europe at the onset of the Dark Ages, the Venerable Bede had shown how the spirit and methods of classical historiography might be applied within the framework of the biblical view of time.[1] How historiography might have developed, had not the Dark Ages supervened, no one can tell; a long and slow process of the rekindling of the lamps was necessary.

In his own day and long afterwards Bede was famous not as an historian but as a commentator on the Scriptures; throughout the Middle Ages the Bible was the most studied book, and indeed, according to the standards of the time, the study of it was amazingly copious, diligent and sustained.[2] But those standards were not our standards, and there was little sense of a real development in history. The Bible came to be regarded as more like the script of a mystery-play than the text of a history-book; its theme was the drama of super-history, the history of salvation, rather than the story of actual flesh-and-blood historical events, which had happened in particular places and at precise times. In any age devoid of historical sense no appreciation of a revelation mediated through successive situations in a real history could have developed; no desire to establish actual historical events had arisen to check the mediaeval predilection for history as edifying romance[3] or to correct its understanding of the Scriptures as gnomic representations of divine truth. History was something to be *received*, whether from the divinely inspired biblical writers or from the respected wisdom of the classical authors; it was not something to be enquired into by curious minds. Though the mediaevals constantly used episodes from the narratives of the Patriarchs or scenes from the Gospels as paradigms of the Christian life, these bore as little relation to real history as did a morality play. The history in which mediaeval man was primarily interested was cosmic history, the drama of salvation which began in heaven and would end there.[4] After the eighteenth century interest in the Bible as history would be focused upon the Gospels; but up to the

[1] *A History of the English Church and People* (AD 731), Penguin Edition, 1955, trans. with introduction by Leo Sherley-Price.

[2] Cf. Beryl Smalley, *The Study of the Bible in the Middle Ages*, Oxford, 1952, xi and *passim*.

[3] Cf. the strictures of Lord Acton, p. 33, *supra*.

[4] Cf. E. M. W. Tillyard, *The Elizabethan World Picture*, London, 1943, 16: 'However widely biblical history was presented in mediaeval drama and sermon, even though many Protestants may have had the Gospels by heart, the part of Christianity that was paramount was not the life of Christ but the

end of the seventeenth century the Gospels were of historical interest primarily because they identified the place where the parabola of the cosmic drama of sacred history, in its course from heaven and back again to heaven, touched the earth at the lowest point of its descent (*ad infernos*). The plan of salvation was as well known to Abraham as it was to St Paul; there was no 'progressive revelation' in the Bible; what was patent in the New Testament was latent in the Old,[1] and it could be teased out of even the more obscure or even morally objectionable passages of the Old Testament by the use of the allegorical method. Gideon and Barak, Samson and Jephthah, were not primitive tribal war-leaders but philosopher-statesmen endowed with discernment beyond Plato's; the wisdom of Colomon exceeded all the science of Aristotle, and therefore his cryptic writings, dark with excess of light, must be searched till they rendered supernatural confirmation of what Aristotle had said in plainer language. Artists painted biblical scenes against Italian or Dutch backgrounds, and it did not occur to anyone until the eighteenth century that, for example, Shakespeare's *Julius Caesar* should not be played in 'modern' dress. It is hard for us, who live after the nineteenth century, to comprehend the unhistorical mentality of earlier ages, which had no notion at all that ancient times were in any important way different from their own.

This non-historical attitude towards the Bible, and especially towards the Gospels, imparts to mediaeval theology something of a docetic air in our modern eyes. The biblical history seems to become an elaborate mystery-play staged for our edification. But to think like this is to lapse into an unhistorical attitude ourselves and with the eighteenth-century *philosophes* to complain that the Middle Ages are not modern. Mediaeval men had their own way of affirming the essential humanity of Jesus, even if it were not our modern way of seeing him as a real historical person in real historical situations. For them Jesus was set in the midst of history, albeit a kind of supra-temporal history. Though their affections were set not on things on the earth but on the things above, the humanity of Christ was to them a precious reality. In

---

orthodox scheme of the revolt of the bad angels, the creation, the temptation and fall of man, the incarnation, the atonement, and regeneration through Christ. And this is as true of the Middle Ages as of the age of Elizabeth.'

[1] Augustine, *Quaest. in Heptateuch*, ii, 73.

the high Middle Ages devotion to Christ's humanity had assumed a new form, which expressed a type of piety that is still familiar in certain quarters today. In his Bampton Lectures for 1940[1] the late Dr G. L. Prestige described how in the twelfth century a revolutionary change occurred in the devotional attitude of the Western Church, which introduced a new kind of subjective and individualistic piety, unknown to St Athanasius or St Augustine. Inspired in its origins by St Bernard of Clairvaux, it was characterized by an intense personal devotion to the sacred humanity of the Lord, especially in his passion. Prestige quotes St Bernard: 'When I name Jesus, I recall to myself a man gentle and lowly in heart, kind, temperate, pure, pitiful, marked by every grace and holiness; a man, too, who is almighty God, who heals me by his example and fortifies me by his aid. . . . So I take my examples from his manhood and my assistance from his power.'[2] This later mediaeval individualistic piety continued amongst Catholics and Protestants alike long after the Reformation; in the eighteenth century it contrasts strongly with the prevalent deistic and moralistic attitude.[3] Some of its effects were unfortunate, since it obscured the corporate aspect of primitive and patristic Christianity, especially in the sphere of sacramental theology.[4] But it remains with us still today, a type of piety filled with evangelistic zeal, as blissfully ignorant as were the mediaevals of the historical problems which the eighteenth century uncovered for thoughtful Christians in the Western world. Its adherents would agree with St Bernard: 'Argue or discuss, and it has no flavour for me unless Jesus is echoed there. Jesus is honey in the mouth, music in the ear, rejoicing in the heart'—this Jesus who showed his love by dying for us.[5] Such testimony is salutary, because amidst our preoccupations with problems of history and its interpretation it reminds us that faith in Christ does not in the last resort rest upon the results of an historical investigation but upon Christ's own self-authenticating witness in our heart.[6]

[1] *Fathers and Heretics*, London, 1940, 382–420.   [2] *In Cant.*, xv, 6.
[3] Prestige points out that the Independent minister, Isaac Watts, who wrote 'When I survey the wondrous cross' in 1707, is not far from the spirit and temper of St Bernard (op. cit., 387). Compare other well-known evangelical hymns, such as 'How sweet the name of Jesus sounds' by John Newton (1725–1807), with *Jesu, dulcis memoria*, which, though often attributed to St Bernard, was probably written by an eleventh-century abbess.
[4] Cf. E. L. Mascall, *Corpus Christi*, 1953, 37f., 42, 177.
[5] *In Cant.*, xv, 6.   [6] Cf. John 5.34; 8.18.

The Mediaeval Synthesis

Mediaeval man derived his view of the significance and shape of history from the Bible. Though the content of the classical histories was absorbed into the biblical outline of world-history, the interpretative myths of the Greek and Roman historians had dissolved like phantoms with the coming of the morning light from the East. The biblical critique of naturalistic history triumphed in the West. But the Bible contained no comparable principle for the criticism of Greek science, for the men of the Bible found the kind of truth which they sought not in nature but in history. They were not interested in philosophical or cosmological speculation, and it is exceedingly difficult to say what precise cosmological views the Hebrew people held at the various stages of their development. They simply took over the dominant notions of their contemporaries, whether Babylonian or Greek, and adopted them for the time being. It would be impossible to construct a consistent cosmology from the biblical materials.[1] It would be ridiculous to suggest that when the Hebrew declared that heaven is God's throne and the earth his footstool, he imagined God to be sitting in heaven with his feet on the earth.[2] The Bible has so thoroughly demythologized the conception of God that it can use spatial language without implying any cosmological ideas at all. If God was in heaven, that implied his transcendence; but a man could set himself in heaven, too: that implied his arrogance (Isa. 14.12–15). If God was the God of Sinai, that was because of the disclosure-situation which had determined Israel's future history there. In short, the biblical conception of God's relation to the physical universe is more comprehensible in the light of the knowledge which we have today from modern astro-physics than it ever was in the days when Greek geographical conceptions of heaven and earth formed the traditional cosmological pictures in men's minds. The Hebraic awareness of God as transcendent and immanent, as everywhere

---

[1] Cf. Th. Boman, *Hebrew Thought Compared with Greek*, 182: 'The impossibility of writing a Hebrew cosmography dawns upon one when one attempts to determine God's dwelling place in the universe. He dwells everywhere (Ps. 139.7ff.) and nowhere (I Kings 8.27). The many different particulars of God's dwelling in the Old Testament are not to be interpreted geographically but either historically or theologically. . . .'

[2] Cf. Boman, op. cit., 182f.

and nowhere, fitted ill into the Greek cosmic geography of the concentric crystal spheres, which must logically assign an appropriate place in the universe to every gradation of being, including the highest. But the mediaevals had inherited Greek science, and, since they found neither a rival cosmology nor a critique of the assumptions of the Aristotelian-Ptolemaic system in the Bible, they took it over without disquietude. One of the most curious misapprehensions of our times, common to famous scientists and to men in the street, is that the mediaeval cosmology, which was shattered by the rise of modern science, derived its origin from the Bible. The extent of this misunderstanding serves to show how inseparably the mediaeval synthesis had riveted together biblical history and Greek science. It is still 'natural' to us, who have inherited Greek as well as Hebrew ways of thinking, to read the Bible with Greek eyes.[1]

Throughout the Middle Ages immense respect was accorded to the Greek scientific intellect, and some centuries had to elapse after the Dark Ages had been left behind before mediaeval science could begin to advance beyond the positions reached by the ancients. The physical universe was that of Aristotelian science, brought up to date by Ptolemy of Alexandria (AD 90–168), whose treatise *Almagest*—the Arabic name by which it was known in the Middle Ages—gathered up practically all the astronomical knowledge of the ancient world. The earth was the centre of the universe, and the rotation of the crystal spheres (to which the heavenly bodies were attached) around it seemed to account for the observed regularities of the skies.[2] The integrating metaphysical idea was that of 'the Great Chain of Being', or the hierarchical order of all things, which goes back beyond Plato to the Pythagoreans, and which later, by way of Alexandrian Judaism and Neo-Platonism, passed into the thought of the Christian Middle

---

[1] The problem is complicated by the fact that the Hebrews borrowed the cosmological ideas current in the dominant culture of an age. Thus, the New Testament uses the conventional notions of popular Hellenistic science. St Luke's account of the Ascension of Christ, while full of Old Testament motifs, is virtually unique in the New Testament in its use of Hellenistic cosmic geography to symbolize the truth of Christ's exaltation, which elsewhere in the New Testament is represented in quite different ways. The Lucan story, however, exercised considerable influence in the Middle Ages, because it seemed to endow Greek cosmology with canonical authority.

[2] For a readable account of ancient and mediaeval cosmology see Stephen Toulmin and June Goodfield, *The Fabric of the Heavens*, London, 1961.

Ages, combining in a wonderful synthesis science and religion, philosophy and mysticism.[1] A geographical place was found for every member of the hierarchy of being somewhere in the physical universe, from God and the Nine Choirs of Angels at the top of the ladder right down to the lowest crawling things or inert lumps of matter at the bottom of it: century upon century of this kind of thinking has made it almost impossibly difficult for modern men to rid themselves of spatial notions about God or Heaven as 'up there' or 'out there' and to get back to Hebraic thinking in terms which are far more suitable to the scientific cosmology of the twentieth century. The Hebrews were unique in dispensing with the idea of the Chain of Being; this was because their understanding of the absolute qualitative distinction between the Creator and the created made any notion of a gradation of being between God and the world quite unthinkable.

The acknowledged authority on the orders of being throughout the Middle Ages was the Pseudo-Dionysius,[2] who taught that there were three sets of three angelic beings, who constituted the downward links in the chain from God to man. These were (in descending order) Seraphs, Cherubim and Thrones; then Dominions, Virtues and Powers; and lastly Principalities, Archangels and Angels.[3] To each of these angelic orders there are assigned one of the nine spheres of the Ptolemaic astronomical system. The Seraphs, nearest to God, watched over the outermost sphere, the

[1] See Arthur O. Lovejoy, *The Great Chain of Being*, which is probably the most important contribution to the study of the history of ideas so far achieved, and which may indeed be said to have originated that study. Lovejoy traces the course of this ancient conception and its immense influence on men's thinking right down to the eighteenth and nineteenth centuries.

[2] Probably a Syrian monk, whose name is unknown to us, who (*c.* AD 500) wrote *The Celestial Hierarchy* and *The Ecclesiastical Hierarchy*, works which were for about a thousand years ascribed to that Dionysius who was converted by St Paul's preaching at Athens (Acts 17.34); hence his other title, 'the Areopagite'. Having by their false ascription obtained near-apostolic authority (officially recognized by the Lateran Council of 649), they were translated into Latin by John Scotus Erigena (*c.* 810–77) and were commented upon by many of the great theologians (including Albertus Magnus, Aquinas and Bonaventura). The Reformers questioned their authenticity as also did Catholic scholars of the period, such as Thomas Cajetan (1469–1534) and Petavius (1583–1652), though Cardinal Bellarmine still defended them.

[3] A handy mnemonic will be found in the first verse of the modern hymn, 'Ye watchers and ye holy ones', by Athelstan Riley (*English Hymnal*, 519; *BBC Hymn Book*, 288): exchange 'Princedoms' with 'Virtues' and we have the more usual order; considerable variations are found in the mediaeval lists.

primum mobile, which governed the movement of all the other spheres. Then came the sphere of the fixed stars, presided over by the Cherubim; then Saturn, the sphere of the Thrones; then successively the spheres of Jupiter (Dominions), Mars (Virtues), the Sun (Powers), Venus (Principalities), Mercury (Archangels), and finally the Moon, whose motions were supervised by the Angels, who also constituted the direct link between the lunar and the earthly regions. The sphere of the Moon constituted the real dividing line between the heavens and the earth; everything below it was compounded of the terrestrial elements, and was therefore mutable, imperfect and subject to change and decay; everything above it was immutable, perfect and eternal: as Tillyard remarks, 'the adjective *sublunary* contains a lot of meaning'.[1] Aristotle's assertion that the matter of the heavens was different in kind from terrestrial matter was one of his most serious blunders, and it held up the progress of scientific knowledge for a long time; the discovery by Kepler (1571–1630) of a comet beyond the regions of the moon provided empirical evidence of the falsehood of the Aristotelian doctrine of the immutability and perfection of the planetary spheres, but it brought him into disfavour with the Aristotelian theologians who had forgotten that the Scriptures had said that the heavens would grow old and pass away like an outworn garment (Ps. 102.26; Heb. 1.11f.). By the seventeenth century Aristotle's teachings, with the help they had received from the almost canonical Pseudo-Dionysius, had long been regarded as the official view of the Church itself.

In the sublunary sphere things were composed in varying proportions of those four 'elements', Earth, Water, Air and Fire, which go back at least as far as the four 'roots' of Empedocles (*c.* 493–433 BC). The heaviest and lowest of them, the cold and dry, is Earth, which is the centre of the universe; outside or beyond this is Water, the cold and moist element; beyond this comes the Air, the hot and moist element, from which the demons and elemental spirits take their 'aerial' bodies; and lastly there is Fire, the hot and dry, the highest and purest of the four elements. According to this simple physics, stones fall downwards because they naturally tend homewards, that is, to their proper place at the centre of the universe (or at the bottom of the ladder of being); fire, on the other hand, moves upwards towards its proper sphere

[1] Op. cit., 35.

next to the regions of the moon (the Empyrean, a Greek word which means 'fiery'). Boiling water was a mixture of two elements, water and fire, and so on. Such was the primitive condition of scientific knowledge up to about the time of the foundation of the Royal Society (1662); it was scarcely more advanced than in the days of the Ionian cosmologists before Socrates. Not only in regard to physics and chemistry was this simple philosophy of the elements considered adequate; it could also account for the phenomena of human physiology and psychology as well, to say nothing of the phenomena of the realm of 'spirits' and occult influences. Man is made up of the four elements in varying proportions, which determine his individual temper or disposition: for instance, his 'humour' will be melancholy, if the earth-element predominates, passionate if the fire element holds sway; his whole character depends upon their proper balance.[1] But man, like every other sublunary creature, is the victim of the strife of the elements, which are constantly at war with one another.[2] Earthquakes and tempests are evidence of this elemental strife in the realm of nature. It is the task of government to restrain the strife which is always liable to break out in the body politic; hence the importance of observing the hierarchy of the social order, the recognition of 'degree', which itself reflects the heavenly hierarchy,[3] and

---

[1] Cf. Shakespeare's *Julius Caesar*, V, v, 73–75:
> 'His life was gentle, and the elements
> So mix'd in him that Nature might stand up
> And say to all the world, "This was a man".'

Tillyard's *Elizabethan World Picture* cites other examples; indeed, his fine book reminds us how the mediaeval world-view, which it brilliantly sketches, still provided the cosmological background of poets and thinkers throughout the sixteenth and seventeenth centuries.

[2] Cf. Christopher Marlowe (1564–93), *Conquests of Tamburlaine*, Part I, lines 869ff.:
> 'Nature that fram'd us of four elements,
> Warring within our breasts for regiment,
> Doth teach our souls to have aspiring minds. . . .'

The idea of the strife of the elements is very ancient indeed; cf. Ovid, *Metamorphoses*, xv, 237–58, or Plato's strife of the rational and the spirited soul.

[3] Cf. Shakespeare's *Troilus and Cressida*, I, iii, 85–110:
> 'The heavens themselves, the planets and this centre
> Observe degree, priority and place,
> Insisture, course, proportion, season, form,
> Office, and custom, in all line of order. . . .
> . . . .
> Take but degree away, untune that string
> And, hark! what discord follows. . . .'

which in its turn is taught to mankind by the lower orders of nature herself.[1] When the strife of the elements is hushed and man's ear is attuned to hear it, then he can catch the sound of 'the music of the spheres', the heavenly harmony of the distant planets.[2] The individual man's place in the social hierarchy was fixed by God himself, who had 'ordained and constituted the services of angels and men in a wonderful order'.[3] Nevertheless there was one respect in which he was equal with every other man, whether king or duke or baron; he was equal before God and could 'aspire' to heaven with all the saints. The Augustinian conception of the recruitment of *all* ranks of men remained, and this in itself in a feudal society counted for something in respect of a man's dignity and value. Moreover, man alone of all terrestrial creatures was free, if he chose to avail himself of supernatural aid to exercise his freedom, from all those fatal influences of the astral powers which govern the course of mortal affairs.[4] This was another ancient and pagan idea, of which astrology was born, which had no place at all in Hebraic ways of thought; and the Church had to struggle continually against the deterministic implications of this debilitating pseudo-science.

In fact, as Professor Butterfield remarks of the mediaeval cosmology, 'in this whole picture of the universe there is more of Aristotle than of Christianity'.[5] It is based not upon biblical and Hebraic foundations, but upon the foundations laid by Greek science. It is compounded of the cosmology of the Ionian philosophers, the *Timaeus* of Plato, the physics of Aristotle, the *Almagest* of Ptolemy, the mysticism of Plotinus and the Gnostic

---

[1] Cf. Shakespeare's *King Henry V*, I, ii, 187ff.

[2] Cf. Shakespeare's *Merchant of Venice*, V, i, 60–65, where this ancient idea is expressed in some of the loveliest lines in English literature. The idea of the creation of the world as an act of music is found in Dryden's *St Cecilia's Day*, with its perfect representation of the mediaeval view:

'From harmony, from heavenly harmony,
This universal frame began . . .
Then hot and cold and moist and dry
In order to their stations leap
And music's power obey. . . .'

It is instructive to reflect that this Ode was written in 1687, the year of the publication of Newton's *Principia*.

[3] *Book of Common Prayer*, Collect of St Michael and All Angels.

[4] For an excellent account of the mediaeval view of the influence of the stars upon human life, see J. L. Lowes, *Geoffrey Chaucer*, London, 1934, 6–38.

[5] *Origins of Modern Science*, 21.

speculations of the Pseudo-Dionysius. Into this wonderfully integrated pagan frame is inserted the central picture of the biblical sacred history of man's creation and redemption, but the gorgeous details of the frame detract from the impression which the picture should make upon the beholder. Mediaeval man was hardly conscious of the discrepancy between the picture and the frame. Occasionally he found it necessary to reject a doctrine of the Greeks because it was flatly contradicted by the plain teaching of Scripture, as when, for instance, Aquinas reluctantly rejects the Aristotelian doctrine of the eternity of matter. On other occasions, however, the mediaeval mind was gladdened when it could find that a Greek notion could be corroborated by a biblical quotation; for example, when the ancient notion of the music of the spheres, accepted by Plato, derided by Aristotle, could be established by revelation in Job 38.7: 'When the morning stars sang together, and all the sons of God shouted for joy.' There was deep satisfaction to be gained from the contemplation of the wonderful hierarchy of being, in which everything in heaven and earth had its proper place. No 'problem of evil' could arise; according to the scheme, every conceivable gradation must exist between the highest and the lowest objects in the created order, the perfection of which consisted in providing for every degree of being (perfection) and non-being (evil, the absolutely unreal). Even an Iago or an adder *must* exist somewhere, since the ladder of being must contain every possible degree of perfection (and therefore of imperfection); everything that existed was necessary to the perfection of the whole—a point of view still held by eighteenth-century churchmen.[1] It is small wonder that theology was regarded as 'the queen of the sciences', since every link in the Great Chain of Being, in its own appropriate mode, reflected the glory of God, while the chain itself led upwards link by link to him. Hence according to 'the analogy of being' (*analogia entis*) every order of creation (the honey-bees, for instance)[2] expressed some truth about the divine realm, and in a real, though analogical, sense, it showed us truth about God himself. It was therefore possible to reason from nature to God (as, for instance, in the Cosmologi-

[1] Cf. Basil Willey, *The Eighteenth Century Background*, London, 1940, Chap. III, 'Cosmic Toryism', 43–56.
[2] See note 1 on p. 73 *supra*.

cal Argument[1] or in 'natural theology' generally). So impressive had this system of 'natural' knowledge become that in the later Middle Ages it was possible for a reputable theologian like Raymond of Sebonde[2] to maintain that the whole content of revealed truth could be discovered by the unaided human reason from the study of the realm of nature. But the more usual view was that of Aquinas, namely, that revelation (Scripture) was necessary, since it gave to man that knowledge of saving truth (the Incarnation, the Atonement, etc.) which he could not have discovered for himself, and which even Aristotle, the wisest of the ancients ('the Philosopher') did not know.

The Achievement of the Middle Ages

Rationalist historians of historiography usually explain the unhistorical attitude of mediaeval thought by saying that preoccupation with theology diverted attention from secular history,[3] and the statement is repeated from one book to another until it comes to be regarded as an established 'fact'. But unless careful distinctions are drawn, the true position will be obscured. Much depends upon what is meant by 'theology' in this context; if the word is understood to mean the whole system of classical-Hellenistic cosmological speculation, which culminated in the 'natural theology' of the later Middle Ages, then the statement is broadly true. But it must be borne in mind that this world-system had its roots in Greek thought, not in the Bible; it was Christian only in so far as it had been modified to accommodate the idea of creation by a personal God, whose attributes could in some measure be discerned analogically in his handiwork. The Bible nowhere argues from the world to God and does not suggest that nature provides us with analogies of truths concerning a divine realm. The heavens may declare the glory of God (Ps. 21.1) to those who have been obedient to his word in their own history, but 'nature' (for which there is no Hebrew equivalent) was not the source of a knowledge of God which was independent of or

[1] See E. G. Jay, *The Existence of God: a Commentary on St Thomas Aquinas's Five Ways of Demonstrating the Existence of God*, London, 1946.

[2] He died about 1435. His book, *Theologia Naturalis*, written originally in Spanish, was published posthumously in 1484 and was highly esteemed in the following century; but it was placed on the Index in 1595. See C. C. J. Webb, *Studies in the History of Natural Theology*, Oxford, 1915, 292–312.

[3] Cf. footnote 4, p. 55, *supra*.

supplementary to his word in history. This truth had been redis-covered by Protestant theologians at the Reformation, who had rejected 'the Aristotelian theology' upon biblical grounds before its scientific untenability had been demonstrated by the mathema-ticians and experimenters whose conclusions found expression in Galileo's *Dialogue* (1632).[1]

It is entirely incorrect to suggest that theology in the Middle Ages diverted attention from this world to a world beyond; on the contrary, mediaeval men were fascinated by the world of nature and found the study of it rewarding because all created things, from the honey-bees to the planets, could 'by a rule in nature teach the act of order to a peopled kingdom'. It was precisely upon the foundation of natural theology that there arose in the later Middle Ages the belief upon which Galilean science was founded, namely, that the contingent world of things, when investigated by observation and experiment, would disclose those regularities which it is the business of natural science to describe in terms of scientific laws.[2] The great step forward was achieved by the rejection of the pagan-classical view that the contingent was to be identified with the irrational; because the world of matter was created by the word or rational wisdom of God, it could not be understood by an aristocratic *theoria* of the Greek type, but only by a humble submission to empirical evidence, a following through of 'the wisdom of God in the works of creation'.[3] Chance, Accident (*Tyche*), 'the unpredictable', was at last banished from nature as, centuries earlier, it had been banished from history in the thought of St Augustine. And this was an achieve-

[1] See the trans. by Stillman Drake of Galileo's *Dialogue concerning the Two Chief World Systems—Ptolemaic and Copernican*, Univ. of California Press, Los Angeles, 1953. See also G. de Santillana, *The Crime of Galileo*, London, 1958; the latter writer contributed an introduction to Galileo's *Dialogue on the Great World Systems* (the Salusbury Translation), Chicago, 1953; and *The Private Life of Galileo* compiled principally from his correspondence and that of his eldest daughter, Sister Maria Celeste, London (Macmillan & Co.), 1870.

[2] Cf. the series of articles by M. B. Foster in *Mind* (1934), XLIII (N.S.), 446ff.; XLIV, 439ff.; and XLV, 1ff.; also E. L. Mascall's *Christian Theology and Natural Science*, Bampton Lectures for 1956, London, 1956, 94–98; and A. N. Whitehead, *Science and the Modern World* (Pelican ed., 1938), Chap. I.

[3] The phrase is the title of a treatise by John Ray (1627–1705), but all the new scientists of the seventeenth century, including Kepler, Galileo, Des-cartes, Pascal, Boyle and Newton, would have agreed that this was what they were doing. For Ray see C. E. Raven, *John Ray, Naturalist*, Cambridge, 1942.

ment of the high Christian civilization of the later Middle Ages. The convention which makes Copernicus the first of the moderns robs the mediaeval era of its supreme achievement and breaks the continuity of historical development. The great transition from the classical-mediaeval world-system to the new world-system of Galileo, the most momentous step ever taken in the history of thought, was a consequence of the development of mediaeval science itself; the refutation of the Aristotelian system was all along implicit in the work of those mediaeval investigators who themselves were consciously seeking to amend rather than to replace it.[1] The rationalist myth of history exactly reverses the truth when it makes 'the Renaissance' the age in which modern thinking was inaugurated by means of the recovery of the supposed empirical spirit of Greek science.[2] The ridding of European thought of the misconceptions of Greek 'science' is the theme of Galileo's *Dialogue*, and his contemptuous attitude towards Aristotle was the offence which incurred the displeasure of the conservative Aristotelian churchmen of the Inquisition. 'The Renaissance' may still perhaps be a useful conception in the history of art or of literature, but it has no utility in the history of science.[3] One of the more curious paradoxes of the history of thought is that, during the period in which the new scientists of Europe were eagerly throwing away Greek scientific notions with both hands, humanist scholars were no less eagerly rediscovering the long-forgotten accomplishments of the classical historians.[4] This was indeed a necessary step on the road to our modern conception of history, but there was a long way to go. The

---

[1] Cf. Marshall Claggett, *The Science of Mechanics in the Middle Ages*, Madison: Univ. of Wisconsin Press, 1959.

[2] On the rationalist myth see pp. 106–9, *infra*.

[3] The notion of 'the Renaissance' is little more than a hundred years old. It was given currency by the French historian Jules Michelet (1798–1874), a romantic revolutionary nationalist who as an anti-clerical hated the Middle Ages and as an anti-conservative hated the English. He called the seventh volume of his *Histoire de France* (Paris, 1855) 'Renaissance'; he defined the word as meaning the discovery of the world and of man, the genesis of the modern mentality as understood by nineteenth-century rationalism, i.e., as meaning 'post-Christian'. Today it is Burckhardt's conception of the Renaissance as primarily an Italian affair, involving the spheres of art and religion, which is usually intended by those historians who still use the term. See Herbert Butterfield, *Man on his Past*, 132–6.

[4] See pp. 277–80 *infra*.

emergence of a genuine sense of historical development still lay centuries ahead.[1]

When it is said that the mediaeval world-view was fundamentally unhistorical, more is meant than that the writing of history was not one of the characteristic interests or occupations of the thoughtful men of the age. Nor is it meant merely that such chronicling and history-writing as there was in the Middle Ages was uncritical of sources, credulous and primitive in literary form. What is meant is that the mediaeval mind did not regard history as a source of significant knowledge. Nature, not history, was the mirror of the divine realm. Rationalistic theology, in the Middle Ages, as in the eighteenth century, taught men to look through nature up to nature's God. St Augustine's strong sense of the revelation of God's will in the events of world-history, relived in the history of his own critical times, gave place during the succeeding centuries to the conception of a divine revelation written down in a book about history: the revelation was located objectively, so to speak, in the events narrated in the Scriptures, but it was apprehended subjectively by mediaeval men not in the events, which were no longer present, but in the written record of those events, a present possession divinely guaranteed. The task of the theologian did not consist in an engagement with history, but in a systematizing of the propositional truths of the Scriptures and in the rational drawing out of their conclusions. The Reformation, which is to be regarded as an incident in mediaeval church history rather than as the beginning of a radically new period of theology, did not in any way change this situation: Calvin would have agreed with Aquinas in his conception of the nature and task of theology as the systematizing of the revealed truths of Holy Scripture.[2] This is a profoundly unhistorical conception of the nature of divine revelation, since the effective medium of revela-

[1] Cf. G. N. Clark, *The Seventeenth Century*, 273: 'It is scarcely an exaggeration to say that the sixteenth-century writers had no idea of change, no idea that one age was different from another. Just as Shakespeare's Romans wore the dress of his own day, so the Renaissance historians did not know that men and events are made what they are by the character of the age to which they belong.' Also Herbert Butterfield, op. cit., 17: 'One is tempted to feel that this [historical-mindedness] is almost a new dimension added to our thinking—there is such a remarkable lack of it in the Renaissance and even in much of the eighteenth century.'

[2] An excellent account of the traditional conception of revelation will be found in A. L. Lilley, *Religion and Revelation*, London, 1932.

tion is no longer history but a literary communication. This un-historical attitude persisted until the religious upheaval ushered in by the Age of Reason, which marks the period of the real 'waning of the Middle Ages'.

The Age of Transition

History never stands still, and therefore every age is in a sense an age of transition. But the expression may be especially applied to the Age of Reason, because it witnessed the beginnings of a change in the very way in which men think; thinking *scientifically* has created a new world and is today leading mankind into a new age of universal history.[1] The disintegration of the mediaeval world-system in its Greek or scientific aspect would lead inevitably to profound changes of religious outlook and, after a long interval, to a new understanding of history as a source of significant knowledge about man and the world. It is not surprising that the awakened critical faculties should have achieved their earliest and most spectacular successes in the sphere of the natural sciences, for the world of nature is more open to inspection than are the deep recesses of human nature. But, though the process was slow and arduous, once the natural scientists had shown how by observation and experiment ancient dogmas about nature could be refuted or verified scientifically, the critical intelligence would inevitably go on to a scientific critique of man as an historical being, that is, as having a future which is conceivable only in the light of the interpretation of his past. Despite earlier beginnings, it was not until the nineteenth century that the quest for historical verification was undertaken with the same zealous and sustained effort as had already been exhibited in the exploration of the physical world. It is only in our own times that the significance of history for the understanding of man's existential predicament and destiny is gradually beginning to be recognized.

[1] See Lecture VIII, *infra*; cf. Herbert Butterfield, *Man on his Past*, 118: 'For my own part, I should like to cry from the house-tops that the publication of Newton's *Principia* in 1687 is a turning-point in history for peoples to whom the Renaissance and Reformation can hardly mean anything at all— peoples amongst whom the battle of Waterloo would hardly be calculated to produce an echo. And, before the Scientific Revolution, the great event in our history—the big new thing which made more difference to our world even than the fall of Rome—was surely the victory of Christianity in the civilization that surrounded the Mediterranean Sea.'

During the seventeenth century, though the ancient cosmological system was destroyed, the old historical attitudes survived. Ussher was bringing the mediaeval chronology to its final peak of perfection; Bossuet was producing the masterpiece of old-style universal history, and Newton himself was wrestling with the secrets locked away in Daniel and the Apocalypse. The poetry and literature of the age are saturated with the imagery of the classical world-view: the Chain or Ladder of Being, the War of the Elements, the Universal Harmony and Music of the Spheres, the Cosmic Dance, the Hierarchical Order of Angels and Spirits, Degree in the Body Politic, the Planetary Influences, and so on. It is instructive to reflect that *Paradise Lost* with all its traditional imagery was written by a man who, thirty years or so before its publication, had discussed natural philosophy with Galileo face to face. Tillyard quotes from Sir John Davies' *Orchestra* (1596):[1]

> 'Only the earth doth stand for ever still,
> Her rocks remove not nor her mountains meet;
> (Although some wits enricht with learning's skill
> Say heaven stands firm and that the earth doth fleet
> And swiftly turneth underneath their feet):
> Yet, though the earth is ever stedfast seen,
> On her broad breast hath dancing ever been.'

These lines were written, not by an old man nostalgic for the past, but by a student of the Inns of Court aged twenty-seven, who must have been familiar with all the 'advanced' ideas of his time. Tillyard comments: 'If Davies knew (as here he shows he does know) the Copernican astronomy, he must have known that this science had by then broken the fiction of the eternal and immutable heavens. But he trusts in his age and in the beliefs he has inherited, and like most of his contemporaries refuses to allow a mere inconsistency to interfere with the things he really has at heart.' Perhaps the men of that age knew better than we do that the truths symbolized by means of the imagery of the mediaeval world-picture are not of the kind which can be falsified by being scientifically disproved, and that they are more adequate to suggest the reality of man's status in the universe than the abstractions of the new mathematical cosmology can ever be.

In our own times it is not easy, though it is not impossible, to

---

[1] *The Elizabethan World Picture*, 99.

think in the picture-language of the mediaeval world-view after we have given up the literal sense which was generally intended in the Middle Ages. The difficulty is not an intellectual one but rather is occasioned by the failure of the historical imagination in a banausic age. A contemporary writer, Dr Heinz Zahrnt, in a fine book has thus characterized the intellectual movement of our time, in which the following phenomena appear side by side:[1] 'abstract art, atonal music, the reduction to a minimum of scenario, plot and action in a prominent trend of the modern theatre, the lack of descriptiveness in many scientific expressions which can be expressed only in formulae and can be comprehended only by purely mathematical thinking, existentialism in philosophy, and finally the demythologizing of the New Testament in theology. In all these almost contemporary phenomena we can detect a great "undertow of abstraction", a movement "from corporeality to a cipher".[2] This has without question led to the concentration of all expressions of life on the *punctum mathematicum* of human existence and thus to a stressing and intensification of its relations. In this way, so to speak, the quintessence of human existence has been distilled. At the same time, however, this abstraction has produced a loss of reality by depriving us of corporeal figures, concrete history and vivid reality; indeed, the very meaning of "abstract" is "that which has been taken away".' In an attempt to keep up with this current tendency towards abstraction, certain theologians have in our times sought to purge the language of religion of all its traditional imagery; they prefer to speak of God, not as Father, but as 'the ground of being', and of Christ, not as Son, but as 'the eschatological event', and so on. 'Ultimate reality' is characterized by abstractions such as 'mathematics' or 'love'. To the objection that the language of religion is the language of poetry it is replied that modern man has 'come of age', that he has outgrown religion and has no need of its picture-language; he is no longer a child, dependent upon authority, but is conscious of holding his fate in his own hands.[3]

---

[1] H. Zahrnt, *The Historical Jesus*, London and New York, 1963, 91; Eng. trans. by J. S. Bowden of *Es begann mit Jesus von Nazareth*, Stuttgart, 1960.

[2] The quotations are from Heinrich Vogel, *Jesus Christus und der religionslose Mensch*, Berlin, 1955, 11f.

[3] The expression 'religionless' means something quite different in English ears from what was intended by the German original, given currency by Dietrich Bonhoeffer (cf. his *Letters and Papers from Prison*, London, 1953,

The corrective for this tendency towards regarding the abstract as the real lies in the development of a genuine awareness of the significance of the historical. The spectacular successes obtained by abstract methods in the natural sciences and in mathematics not unnaturally encouraged men to follow the example of Descartes and Hobbes in turning their backs upon history as a source of significant knowledge in order to pursue the search for truth as the ultimate abstraction ('the ground of being', etc.), the final formula of reality. Obviously picture-thinking is irrelevant to such a purpose; the concrete imagery of poetry and the insights of the historical imagination are identified in the rationalist mind with the imaginary. Three centuries or thereabouts were to elapse before the mistake of Descartes could be clearly identified; throughout the nineteenth century historians tended to be mesmerized by the prestige of scientific abstraction, and for the most part they failed to understand the character of their enquiry as a concrete and existential exercise of the historical imagination. Of course, our twentieth-century understanding of history does not reinstate the mediaeval images of reality, based as they were upon the outmoded classical cosmology, and they can never again be accepted as literally true; but it enables us to see something of the reality which the mediaeval mind was trying to grasp, and it impels us to meet the challenge of history, theirs and ours, in the thought-forms of our own times.

---

published in America as *Prisoner for God*, New York, 1954). By 'religious' Bonhoeffer meant 'metaphysical', 'subjective', 'individualistic', 'pietistic'; 'religion' for him means what in English might be called 'religiosity'. In this sense 'religionless Christianity' would mean no more than 'Christianity', or, better, 'Christian faith'. Umbrella-words like 'religion' require careful definition; it is worth remarking that 'religion' is hardly a biblical word at all (cf. Alan Richardson, ed., *A Theological Word Book of the Bible*, London, 1950, 188). For an introduction to Bonhoeffer's thought see John D. Godsey, *The Theology of Dietrich Bonhoeffer*, London, 1960; esp. in this connection, pp. 248–59. See also Marten E. Marty (ed.), *The Place of Bonhoeffer*, London, 1963.

3

THE QUEST FOR
HISTORICAL VERIFICATION

BEFORE the great development of modern scientific historical method had begun to take place in the nineteenth century,
the idea that statements found in the records of the past could
be verified or falsified by rational processes had not been seriously
entertained by the majority of thoughtful men. The significance
of the researches of a Mabillon was not perceived; the labours
of the antiquaries were dismissed as the harmless eccentricity of
minds ill equipped for the pursuit of 'natural philosophy', which
was generally regarded as the only source of verifiable knowledge.
Montaigne, writing about 1572, voices the opinion of the age:
'I sometimes wonder whether it can be right for a prudent theologian, philosopher or other such person of precise and delicate
conscience to write history. How can they pledge their word on
a popular belief? How can they answer for the thoughts of unknown persons, and advance their own conjectures as valid
coin?'[1] The value of history resides in the moral lessons which
can be drawn from it: 'Let a tutor remember the purpose of his
duties, and impress upon his pupil the qualities of Hannibal and
Scipio rather than the date of the fall of Carthage, and not so much
where Marcellus died as why it was inconsistent with his duty
that he should die there. Let him be taught not so much the facts
of history as how to judge them.'[2] Historians, including his beloved Plutarch, make only a selection of the facts—a point
fastened upon later by Descartes—and do not give us the means

[1] Michel de Montaigne, *Essays*, trans. by J. M. Cohen, Penguin ed.,
London, 1958, 47.
[2] Ibid., 62.

of criticizing their judgments: 'it is a pity that men of understanding are so fond of brevity; no doubt their reputations profit by it, but the loss is ours. Plutarch would rather have us applaud his judgment than his knowledge.'[1] The general viewpoint of the sixteenth to the eighteenth centuries is that historical facts are too fragmentary and uncertain to provide us with genuine knowledge of the past, but that we may draw political wisdom and moral instruction from the behaviour and fate of those whose example has been preserved for us by the writers of histories. The fault of the antiquaries and erudites was that they were not moralists; they did not qualify as historians because they were not interested in any lessons of history. Dr Johnson was well aware of the vast accumulation of detailed knowledge of the past which had been gained during the age of the antiquaries and erudites, but he remains the mouthpiece of the sturdy 'common sense' of the eighteenth century: 'We must consider how very little history there is; I mean real authentic history. That certain kings reigned and certain battles were fought we can depend upon as true; but all the colouring, all the philosophy of history is conjecture.'[2]

The Anti-historical Element in Rationalism

It is not surprising that at the height of the intellectual ferment created by the scientific revolution in the seventeenth century, men should look for progress in knowledge towards the mathematical and physical sciences, with their definite and assured conclusions, and away from history, which seemed to be quite beyond the possibility of verification. The 'father of modern philosophy', René Descartes, had turned his back upon history, remarking that even the most faithful histories cannot possibly record everything that happened and therefore cannot represent the truth.[3] History cannot claim to be an exact science and must inevitably falsify the perspective of the past. 'On this theme,' writes M. Levy-Bruhl, 'Descartes' successors have written plentiful variations. They rarely missed an opportunity of showing historians and scholars that they had an extremely low opinion of the matters with which they were concerned. Malebranche, in particular, did not spare

---

[1] Ibid.
[2] Boswell, *Life of Johnson* (ed. Hill, 1887), II, 365f.; quoted by D. C. Douglas, *English Scholars*, 359.
[3] *Discourse on Method* (1637), Everyman ed., 1912, 6f.

his epigrams, jeers and even sarcasms at their expense. His example was followed by a number of Cartesians.'[1] The mention of Malebranche prompts an interesting comparison. Two members of the same religious community, the French Oratory, exact contemporaries, illustrate the opposing attitudes of the philosophers and the historians of the day. Nicolas Malebranche (1638–1715), the celebrated Occasionalist philosopher, followed the Cartesian practice and ridiculed historical research. Richard Simon (1638–1712), like his contemporaries, Spinoza and Bayle,[2] applied a dawning sense of historical development to the study of the Old Testament. Simon was a devout but free-thinking Catholic, to whom it seems to have occurred that, since the Bible was 'the religion of Protestants', it might be expedient to show by a critical examination that Scripture was very far from self-authenticating and that it needed the authorization of the Church. In his *Histoire critique du Vieux Testament* (1678) he anticipated the German nineteenth-century critics by pointing to the different literary styles and duplicate narratives of the Pentateuch and concluding that it was not written by Moses, but was compiled in the time of Ezra. But Simon was a hundred years or more in advance of his age, which was the age of Malebranche and Bossuet. Bossuet had the treatise suppressed in France (but it was published in full in Rotterdam in 1685), and he wrote his own refutation of Protestantism, in which he eschewed the inconsistencies of Moses and dwelt on those of the reformed theologians.[3] Fourteen years after its publication he observed that it contained all that there was to say on the Protestant question.[4] Simon was expelled from the Oratory in 1682 and spent his remaining years in retirement in Dieppe; Malebranche, though his treatise on Grace (1680) aroused opposition, was honoured in France as the philosopher who had shown that the Cartesian philosophy and the Galilean cosmology were consummated and crowned in Christian theology.

In England, Thomas Hobbes (1588–1679) is the outstanding

[1] L. Levy-Bruhl, 'The Cartesian Spirit and History' in *Philosophy and History, Essays presented to Ernst Cassirer,* ed. R. Klibansky and H. J. Paton, Oxford, 1936, 191.

[2] Each of the three has been mentioned as the putative father of biblical criticism, though their aims could hardly have been more various.

[3] *Histoire des variations des églises protestantes* (1688).

[4] E. K. Sanders, *Jacques Bénigne Bossuet,* London, 1921, 249.

example of the humanist scholar who abandoned history for the new scientific philosophy. A year after the publication of his elegant translation of Thucydides (1628), at the age of forty, he lighted by chance upon a copy of Euclid's *Elements* in the Cavendishes' house and thereafter developed his view that geometrical truth is the standard of philosophical reasoning and the type of all knowledge. Matter and Motion replace the humane studies as the objects of his attention. History depends not on reason but on memory; poetry depends upon imagination, and neither memory nor imagination is a source of knowledge for the rationalist Hobbes. Only deductive reasoning leads to certainty and therefore is alone worthy of the philosopher.[1] On the other hand, John Locke, the empiricist, does not despise the researches of the antiquarians; 'history', he says, 'is of great use. . . . I think nothing more valuable than the records of antiquity: I wish we had more of them.'[2] But he himself was engaged upon far more important matters, and it certainly never occurred to Locke that the human understanding could be investigated from an historical or genetic point of view.[3] Others, however, in the Age of Reason did not share the gentle Locke's fair and open-minded attitude towards history and its learned practitioners, even in the great age of English historians into which Hobbes long survived and Bolingbroke was born—the age of Hickes and Wanley, Brady and Wharton, Tyrrell and Hearne. The attitude of Henry St John, first Viscount Bolingbroke (1678–1751), the able negotiator of the Treaty of Utrecht (1713), contrasted strongly with that of his former cabinet colleague, Robert Harley, first Earl of Oxford and Mortimer (1661–1724), the illustrious patron of English mediaeval

---

[1] There is an excellent discussion of Hobbes' change of attitude in D. G. James, *The Life of Reason*, London, 1949, 1–62.

[2] *Essay concerning Human Understanding*, IV, xvi, 11. Locke was a friend of the historian, James Tyrrell, who was present at the meeting at Exeter House in 1671 at which Locke proposed the enquiry which led to the publication of the *Essay* in 1690.

[3] Cf. D. G. James (op. cit., 70): 'So far as he was a scientist, Locke was an experimental one, not, like Hobbes, a rationalist and deductive one; and his theory of mathematical knowledge as knowledge strictly "of our own ideas" quite denied him the intoxication Hobbes felt at the sight of a page of Euclid. Now deductive and mathematical science, scorning experiment, drove history out of Hobbes's scheme of things. But Locke can give a high place to historical knowledge; if mathematics provide certainty, it is certainty only about things of our own making; and history can provide probability so great as to be, for all time or purposes, certainty.'

scholarship, to whom (with his librarian, Humfrey Wanley) so much is owed in the preservation of the records of the past. Bolingbroke is hardly a philosopher worthy of the name, but his writings expressed many of the sentiments of the 'men of sensibility' of his day and were much admired by them—for instance, by Lord Chesterfield. In his *Letters on the Study and Use of History*, written between 1735 and 1742 during his retirement, Bolingbroke pours forth the scorn of the Age of Reason upon the historians and their labours. He avows 'a thorough contempt for the whole business of these learned lives, for all the researches into antiquity, for all the systems of chronology and history that we owe to the immense labours of a Scaliger, a Bochart, a Petavius, an Ussher, and even a Marsham. The same materials are common to them all, but these materials are few, and there is a moral impossibility that they should ever have more. They have combined these into every form that can be given to them: they have supposed, they have guessed, they have joined disjointed passages of different authors, and broken traditions of uncertain originals. . . . All these systems are so many enchanted castles; they seem to be something, they are nothing but appearances.'[1] History must not be made an excuse for the indulgence of a canine appetite, which devours without distinction everything that falls in its way. The accumulation of facts for their own sake is a culpable waste of time and intellect. History is useful only in so far as it concretely illustrates and imaginatively commends the abstract principles of moral philosophy; it is not an end in itself. 'An application to any study, that tends neither directly nor indirectly to make us better men and better citizens, is at best but a specious and ingenious form of idleness, to use an expression of Tillotson: and the knowledge we acquire by it is a creditable kind of ignorance, nothing more.'[2] In short, history ought to be 'philosophy teaching by examples'.[3] This, of course, was precisely the kind of history which the working historians of the age did not and would not

[1] *Letter* I.
[2] *Letter* II.
[3] 'I have read somewhere or other—in Dionysius of Halicarnassus, I think—that History is Philosophy teaching by examples' (*Letter* II). This Dionysius was a Greek rhetorician who came to Rome about 30 BC and wrote a pretentious history and some critical essays. His name became attached to the theory that it does not matter whether a history is true, provided that it is edifying and entertaining.

supply. For their part they despised history written for edification by men of letters and regarded it as largely fictional. But their day was passing, and by the second half of the eighteenth century the *philosophe* historians were ready with their new history, written to inculcate the ideals of the Enlightenment.

Pierre Bayle (1647–1706) had helped to prepare the way for the philosophers of the Enlightenment, but his attitude towards history was not yet theirs. His own name for it was 'historical Pyrrhonism'.[1] This does not mean that he doubted the possibility of genuine knowledge about the past: on the contrary, he differed from the Cartesians, holding that particular facts could be established, and he had a voracious though undiscriminating appetite for them. When they were established, they were useful for the work of demolishing every pretension to philosophical or theological knowledge. He might better be described as an historical atomist, because he denied the possibility of finding any causal connection between the facts of history or of drawing any philosophical or moral conclusions from them.[2] A Frenchman, the son of a Protestant pastor, educated by the Jesuits, Bayle grew to hate 'dogmatism'—the conviction that we are right and everyone else is culpably wrong—and he devoted his life in his exile in the Netherlands to the propagation of agnosticism in the cause of toleration. His *Dictionnaire historique et critique* (1695–7) achieved immense influence; it was translated into several languages and was the model for the French *Encyclopédie*; it was enlarged after his death, and by 1820 it had been expanded into sixteen volumes.[3] Like several of the *philosophes*, he took a sombre view of history, whose records reflected little credit upon the truthfulness and beneficence of the human species. Though neither very original nor very profound as a thinker, he did more than any other man of the seventeenth century to prepare the way for the eradication of the mediaeval division of history into 'sacred' and 'profane'.

[1] Pyrrho (*c.* 360–270 BC) was a Greek philosopher about whom little is known with certainty, but who had acquired the reputation of being the originator of absolute scepticism.

[2] It is strange that Cassirer should suggest that Bayle 'accomplished scarcely less for history than Galileo did for natural science' and—somewhat inconsistently—that 'it is he who carries out the "Copernican revolution" in the realm of historical science' (*Philosophy of the Enlightenment*, Eng. trans., 207).

[3] A useful introduction to it will be found in E. A. Beller and M. du P. Lee, jr., *Selections from Bayle's Dictionary*, Princeton Univ. Press, 1952.

Immoralities did not become moral when they were committed by King David or by any other character of sacred history; and the scriptural record itself was full of the same kind of ambiguities and inconsistencies as were found in other histories. The facts of history, when they were sought out, did nothing to assist either reason or faith to deliver the intellect from thorough-going scepticism.

There were many historians and many who wrote about history at the end of the seventeenth and the beginning of the eighteenth centuries. The age was searching for a 'new history' which should meet the challenge of the changing intellectual scene, but no significant fresh approach was achieved. La Mothe le Vayer anticipated the historical scepticism of Bayle, but maintained that only divinely revealed truths were credible at all;[1] yet this conviction did not restrict the flow of his works, which run to fourteen octavo volumes in the Dresden edition of 1756-9. The title of the anonymous *La Science de l'Histoire* (1665) raises expectations which are not fulfilled. The Abbé de Saint-Réal in his *De l'usage de l'Histoire* (1671) teaches that historical facts are worthless except to demonstrate the degradation of human nature. Father Tomassin of the French Oratory in his *Méthode d'étudier et d'enseigner chrétiennement et solidement les historiens profanes* (1695) swims against the current of thought in the Age of Reason and tries to demonstrate that even the pagan historians corroborate the truths of revealed religion and morality.[2] For any significantly new developments we have to wait for Montesquieu (1689-1755). In his earlier work (*Lettres Persanes*, 1721) he had taught the eighteenth century how the new geography could be made a means of criticizing French institutions and political absolutism under the form of a description of oriental society. In his great work *De l'esprit des lois* (1748) he stands in many ways nearer to the nineteenth century than he does to his own. He generalized the historical and comparative treatment of law and government in a way which significantly contributed to the development not only of legal and political thought but also to that of the social and economic sciences. Positive law ought to be the national or local expression of the human reason and therefore of moral principles. The book was at

---

[1] Cf. the title of his *Discours du peu de certitude en l'Histoire* (1668).

[2] For these and other writers of the period see R. Flint, *History of the Philosophy of History*, 202-16.

first published anonymously and was soon placed on the Index, but its influence was immediate and powerful. Professor Cobban says that it was the influence of Montesquieu combined with that of Locke which ensured that the thought of the Enlightenment did not turn into an apologia for absolutism; in trying to be a social scientist he did not cease to be a moralist.[1] Though not primarily an historian, Montesquieu possessed a sense of development in history which was rare in his century; the *philosophe* historians might have learnt from him the relativity of all historical standards and that it is profoundly unhistorical to carry back into remote centuries the ideas and moral norms of the historian's own day.[2]

'Philosophe' History

In the second half of the eighteenth century the demand for a 'new history' was met by the group of literary men who were associated with Diderot (1713–84) and d'Alembert (1717–83) and their massive *Encyclopédie*, which undertook to satisfy the educational demands of the advancing *bourgeoisie* by expounding the totality of human knowledge from the rationalist standpoint. They are known as the *philosophes*, though they were hardly philosophers in the strict sense: 'philosophy' for them meant the ideals of the Age of Reason, of which they were the self-appointed spokesmen and ardent propagandists. They were not scientists; they did not engage in research, but they were adroit in perceiving the points at which the new science could be utilized in the attack upon traditional and authoritarian ideas about religion and society. It was they and not the scientists themselves who invented the idea of a conflict between 'science' and 'religion', which has been sedulously fostered by rationalists for two centuries.[3] In this campaign the perennial Fontenelle (1657–1757) was able to direct operations from his strategic position as secretary to the Académie des Sciences for more than forty years. The *philosophes* wrote a great deal of literary history, but they were not historians in the sense in which the word has been understood since the nineteenth century; in accordance with the tradition of rationalism they

[1] A. Cobban, *In Search of Humanity*, 104.
[2] For the importance of Montesquieu in the development of historiography see the recent study by W. Stark, *Montesquieu: Pioneer of the Sociology of Knowledge*, London, 1960, esp. 35–39, 181–210.
[3] Cf. H. Butterfield, *The Origins of Modern Science*, esp. 149f.

despised historical research as an end in itself. Their original discovery was that history, like science, could be used for the inculcation of 'philosophy', not merely negatively, as Bayle had used it, to destroy traditional beliefs, but positively, to set forth the new rationalistic world-view as the self-authenticating judgment of 'all reasonable men'. The nearest representative of the *philosophe* point of view in England is David Hume, especially in regard to his view of history.

Voltaire (1694–1778) represents most of the diverse and sometimes contradictory tendencies of *philosophe* history. His own inconsistencies have given rise to widely divergent interpretations of his view of history.[1] He was already well known as a literary man, a poet and dramatist, when his *L'histoire de Charles XII* appeared in 1731. By the standards of his day his technique of historical investigation was excellent, but the work hardly breaks fresh ground in the development of historical writing. Ten years later he began the *Essai sur les moeurs*, the first complete edition of which appeared in 1756. Though not in the strict sense an historical work, it gives mature expression to the concept of history *en philosophe*. Voltaire deliberately begins where Bossuet leaves off, that is, in AD 800; and he begins with a chapter on China. Those who speak of Voltaire's 'Copernican revolution' in history seem simply to mean that he displaced the Christian European from his comfortable seat at the centre of the universe[2] rather than that he made any significant contribution to the growth of historical-mindedness. The Age of Reason loved the myth of the noble savage, born free and as yet untrammelled by the institutions of society.[3] Voltaire idealized the Chinese, the Mohammedans and

---

[1] The best guide is J. H. Brumfitt, *Voltaire: Historian*, 1958, though it may be felt that his own careful assessments hardly bear out his conclusion that Voltaire brought about a 'Copernican revolution in history' (165). The true assessment of Voltaire as an historian is well expressed a little later, when Brumfitt says that 'French Enlightenment historiography, as typified by its greatest and most universal figure, stands midway between that of the sixteenth century and that of modern times. The distance between Bossuet and Voltaire is great, but so too is the distance between Voltaire and Michelet or Taine' (168).

[2] Cf. Brumfitt, op. cit., 165.

[3] Cf. Dryden:

> 'I am as free as Nature first made man,
> Ere the base laws of servitude began,
> When wild in woods the noble savage ran.'
>
> (*The Conquest of Granada*, I, 1, i.)

the Indians, whom he represents as being nearer to that 'religion of nature' which all men had originally practised and which had been sadly obscured in Christendom by the superstitious prejudices (such as the dogmas of original sin and man's need of redemption) which had been invented for their own ends by a cunning and avaricious priestly caste. Such things as despotism in China or sutteeism in India were due to the thwarting of the noble ideals of the Mandarins and Brahmins by the superstition of a stupid populace. The picture of Confucius which Voltaire hung at Ferney symbolized not so much his love for China as his hatred of the Church. But, whatever the motives, and in spite of all the limitations of the new geographical knowledge, the widening of the horizons in the eighteenth century was a necessary and important step in the direction of the modern historical world-view. To this it must be added that the *philosophe* writers, especially Voltaire, took another significant step towards the historical outlook of the nineteenth century; they gave prominence to hitherto neglected aspects of history such as the development of the arts and of science, as well as to the importance of social institutions. Economic factors in history had not as yet come within their view; even Gibbon at the end of the Age of Reason nowhere considers the economic aspects of the decline and fall of the Roman Empire. But the widening of the scope of historical enquiry must be regarded as one of the achievements—perhaps the principal achievement—of *philosophe* history. Another achievement, though perhaps a negative one, was that by demonstrating the usefulness of history as a weapon in the ideological struggle of rival world-views, they called attention to the importance of the study of history and to the importance of getting the facts straight; thus they helped to make Europe history-conscious and prepared the way for the nineteenth-century quest for the unvarnished facts and for the sharpening of the tools of historical verification.

But the Enlightenment historians themselves, though they did not consciously distort facts, were not researchers and had no veneration for facts as sacred in their own right. Their viewpoint was that of Bolingbroke rather than that of Ranke. With the death of L. A. Muratori in 1750, the last of the great 'erudites' had passed from the scene, and there were few to value facts for their own sake. Cobban quotes Voltaire's advice to the historian: 'If you have nothing to tell us other than that one Barbarian succeeded another Barbarian on the banks of Oxus or Iaxartes, of what use are you to the public?' and again: 'Woe to details. They are a vermin that destroys great works.'[1] The value of facts lay in their philosophical and moral implications. Both the antiquarians before them and the disciples of Ranke after them are distinguished from the *philosophes* by their exclusion of moral interests from historical research; even materialists like Diderot and d'Alembert, as well as deists like Voltaire, believe firmly in the moral value of history. *Philosophe* history was to be above all things edifying, and the erudites were to be censured for failing to discriminate between what was edifying and what was not. That alone counted as historical which was useful in the campaign against *l'infâme*, the unenlightened. History thus becomes a broadsword in the passionate onslaught against tyranny, intolerance, torture, priestcraft and superstition, which amply atones for much that is crude and shallow in *philosophe* thinking and gives it an honourable place in the European story.

The Enlightenment writers are often given the credit for having invented the modern idea of progress. If such they indeed deserve, their invention rested upon their faith in reason rather than upon any inference from their empirical study of the direction of history. History was for them the story of a decline and fall from a pristine age of noble simplicity; man was born free, but is everywhere in chains.[2] The past was a mass of corruption from which it was better to avert the eyes.[3] Voltaire had declared that the history of the great events of the world was little else than a story of crime before Gibbon declared that history was 'little more than the register of the crimes, follies and misfortunes of mankind'.[4] 'Is this history which I have just finished,' Voltaire

---

[1] A. Cobban, *In Search of Humanity*, 109. The citations are respectively from Voltaire's *Dictionnaire philosophique*, art. 'Histoire', and his Lettre à J. B. Dubos, 3 Octobre 1738, *Oeuvres*, 1877–85, XXXV, 30.

[2] J.-J. Rousseau, *Du contrat social*, chap. 1.

[3] This was the attitude which caused nineteenth-century writers to complain that the eighteenth-century mind was fundamentally 'unhistorical'; J. S. Mill in his *Essay on Coleridge* (1840) says that it undervalued the past because it did not understand it, and he quotes d'Alembert's wish that 'all record whatever of past events could be blotted out' (*Mill on Bentham and Coleridge*, ed. by F. R. Leavis, 1950, 128f.). Becker cites Chastellux's declaration that there is 'far greater need of forgetting than of remembering', but notes that he nevertheless wrote a two-volume general history (*De la félicité publique*) 'retracing the unhappiness of humanity' (*Heavenly City*, 94).

[4] *Decline and Fall*, chap. 3.

exclaims, 'the history of serpents and tigers? No, it is the history of mankind; tigers and serpents would never treat their fellows so.'[1] The study of history could not provide the *philosophes* with any grounds for a doctrine of progress, apart entirely from the Cartesian notion, still potent in their mind,[2] that history affords no sure ground for philosophical conclusions. History was useful chiefly in affording terrible warnings about man's refusal to live according to nature (that is, reason). Reason was the ground of hope for 'the amelioration of society', and all future generations would pay tribute to the *philosophes* who had recovered the true principles of sanity and reason for the benefit of posterity. Meanwhile historical writing was not an end in itself and had no value in itself; 'history', said Voltaire in a famous phrase, 'is only a pack of tricks which we play on the dead'—and how he enjoyed the trick which he could play upon all the dead tyrants, oppressors, priests and charlatans, whose crimes and conceits he exhumed for the edification of posterity! Posterity was much in the minds of the *philosophes*, for whom the function of history was not so much to explain the past as to shape the future.[3] Karl Löwith cites Monsignor Knox: 'Those who had lost the sense of religious certainty enrolled themselves under the banner of optimism; the world's future occupied their thoughts instead of a future world, and, by a kind of inverted Confucianism, they fell to worshipping their grandchildren.'[4] Happily for Voltaire, he did not live to see the convulsions in which his fourth 'Happy Age of Mankind' ended; but the fate of Condorcet, the last of the *philosophes*, does not suggest that the aristocratic propagandists of Enlightenment would have been altogether satisfied with the judgment of posterity on the achievement of the Age of Reason.[5]

[1] Cited by Paul Hazard, *European Thought in the Eighteenth Century*, 407.

[2] Cf. Brumfitt, op. cit., 99.

[3] Cf. Becker's entertaining chapter on 'The Uses of Posterity' in his *Heavenly City* (119–68). Becker quotes Diderot: 'Posterity is for the philosopher what the other world is for the religious' (150).

[4] Löwith, *Meaning in History*, 230; the quotation is from R. A. Knox, *God and the Atom*, New York, 1945, 59.

[5] The Marquis de Condorcet (1743–94) was the leader of the 'ideologists', the materialist philosophers who offered a sensationalist explanation of the origin and nature of knowledge. In his writings the belief in progress has become fully explicit. He wrote his *Esquisse d'un tableau historique des progrès de l'esprit humain* (1793) while in hiding from the revolutionary extremists. He left his hiding-place in order not to implicate those who sheltered him and drank poison in prison. In this work he exults over the triumphs of the

When it is said that the thought of the Enlightenment is anti-historical, more is meant than that it was infected by the Cartesian doubt about the possibility of historical knowledge. The *philosophes* believed that some historical truths could be known with a relative degree of probability, and they wrote many volumes of 'probable' history. The fundamentally anti-historical element in their thinking is their assumption that historical truths are at best only second-class knowledge. The most that history could do was to corroborate the truths which reason had discovered about human nature; it was not itself an independent source of knowledge. The *philosophes* despised the erudites and themselves undertook no historical research, because they knew already from philosophy what the truth about human nature was. Lessing has formulated for all time the rationalist depreciation of history: 'Incidental truths of history can never become the proof of necessary truths of reason.'[1] This rationalist attitude towards history has constituted a very influential ingredient of the Western intellectual tradition down to our own times; it has, of course, changed its form, but not its basic assumption, that historical facts, even when verifiable, are not significant until they can be generalized under the form of scientific laws. In the eighteenth century those laws, the laws of human nature, were discovered by reason; they were (like the laws of nature itself) immutable and valid for all ages and places. Just as the laws of the Newtonian physics were valid for ancient Greeks or modern Chinese as well as for enlightened Europeans, so too the laws of human nature were the same for all men everywhere and in every stage of development. Montesquieu knew better, but he was in advance of his age; Vico in his remote Mediterranean backwater exercised no influence at all upon his own century.[2] Vico is the Melchizedek of the Age of

---

human spirit and looks forward to a coming ideal order to be established on the basis of that reason which can ascertain the laws of society as it has already ascertained those of nature. It is a pathetic and noble affirmation of belief in enlightened human nature: 'though he slay me, yet will I trust him'. Condorcet died, says Talmon, 'a victim of the triumph of his ideas' (*Origins of Totalitarian Democracy*, 18).

[1] Henry Chadwick, *Lessing's Theological Writings*, 53; cf. also 31.

[2] Cf. G. N. Clark remarks that, though Vico's book (*Principii di scienza nuova*, 1725) gathered up the learning of the seventeenth century, it was 'not written until the eighteenth, not read until the nineteenth, and not understood until the twentieth' (*The Seventeenth Century*, 286f.). Paul Hazard has said that the course of modern thought would have been very different if Vico had

Reason, without ancestors and also without progeny. He rejects the Cartesian view that that alone is knowledge which possesses the certainty and clarity of mathematics; history possesses its own certainty, but it is of a different order altogether from the deliverances of the scientific intellect. His book deals with many things; today we should describe it as a history of civilization. Vico is already historically-minded, that is, he views history as an evolution from the primitive to the advanced; his remarkable philological studies provide empirical evidence for his view. The sacred and the secular form one history; Vico does not have to unify history by denying the sacred. In all this he stands entirely outside the mind of the eighteenth century, removed as he was in far-away Naples from the north-western seaboard of Europe, where the new thought of the Enlightenment was finding its chief expression. He has read his Descartes, Hobbes and Bayle, but only to reject them. 'If ever there were two incompatible modes of speech,' says Paul Hazard, 'they were Vico's and Voltaire's.'[1]

Voltaire is so impressed by the success of Newtonian science in explaining the processes of nature by means of a single system of regular and immutable laws that he comes to conceive of human nature and history as being in principle similarly explicable. Brumfitt describes his view as an attempted application of the spirit of eighteenth-century science to history. 'As this concept of an ordered physical universe excludes the miraculous, the freak of nature, so does its transposition into the field of human history exclude similar aberrations. The laws of human conduct are as immutable as the laws of gravity. Man always was and always will be what he is. . . . Voltaire's universe is a static one without evolution or development. Just as his view of natural history is falsified by his opposition to the idea of evolution, so his view of human history is falsified by the search for unchanging principles of reason and behaviour.'[2] Every age and every incident was therefore to be judged by the 'enlightened' reason of the eighteenth century; nothing could have happened in history which

achieved a European audience in his own age (*European Thought in the Eighteenth Century*, 35). See *The New Science of Giambattista Vico*, Eng. trans. from the 1744 ed. by T. G. Bergin and M. H. Fisch, Cornell Univ. Press, Ithaca, N.Y., 1948; also *Time and Idea: the Theory of History in Giambattista Vico* by A. R. Caponigri, London, 1953.

[1] *European Thought in the Eighteenth Century*, 406.
[2] J. H. Brumfitt, op. cit., 103.

philosophe thought could not understand. If mediaeval men set out on Crusades, then it was a certification of their lunacy; if they admired Gothic Cathedrals, it was a proof of their barbarity. If Bossuet claimed to see the finger of God in history, it was evidence of his deceitfulness. Rational men could not sincerely do such things; they were contrary to human nature. The historical relativism of Montesquieu had not penetrated the mind of the Enlightenment. History was static, not developing; man's hope of progress lay in understanding and living according to those unchanging laws of human nature, the violation of which in the past accounted for the melancholy story of mankind which it was the historian's misfortune to have to recite. Voltaire's rejection of the theory of evolution is comparable to Aristotle's consideration of the hypothesis of a heliocentric universe, only to reject it.[1] It did not accord with his basic assumption. He could not rationally entertain the idea of the evolution of biological species, because he was not historically-minded. Darwin and Lyell could not have framed their hypothesis in the eighteenth century, because it required a revolution in historical thinking before it could have been taken seriously, that is, before anyone would have gone out and looked for the evidence which would verify it. The historical revolution of the nineteenth century is, after all, only an aspect, but an essential aspect, of that great movement of the human spirit which has created the scientifically-minded and historically-minded climate of opinion of today. There is only one 'culture'.

The reason why Voltaire's conception of historical causation is 'neither consistent nor profound'[2] is doubtless that causation in history does not correspond to the kind of causation which was described by Newtonian science. Voltaire vacillates between two types of causal explanation in history, both of which are outmoded today. The first is the 'Great Men' theory—the view to which Carlyle later gave classical expression when he declared

---

[1] The great naturalist Buffon (1707–88) had already had a kind of precognition of the Darwinian view concerning the mutability of species, but he lacked sufficient data to confirm it. Voltaire ridiculed the notion; he rejected Buffon's explanation of the presence of sea-shells in the Alps by means of the theory that the whole earth was once under water, although he had no better suggestion to make than that the shells must have dropped from the hats of passing pilgrims. See J. H. Brumfitt, op. cit., 87f., who remarks that 'the sight of the anti-Catholic Voltaire firmly rejecting the concept of evolution is not without its dramatic irony'.

[2] So J. B. Black, *The Art of History*, London, 1926, 7.

that 'the history of the world is but the biography of great men'.[1] Thus, in his *Siècle de Louis XIV* (1751), a work which may be described as modern in the sense that it transforms history from being a record of kings and their battles into the assessment of a civilization, he allows Louis to dominate the story and ascribes to him a large share of the credit for the achievements of the fourth 'Happy Age of Mankind'. (It is curious how the cosmopolitan Voltaire can identify the history of France with that of 'mankind'.) The other type of view which fascinates Voltaire and many of his contemporaries is the so-called 'Horse-shoe Nail' theory[2] of historical explanation—if indeed it may be called explanation, for in a sense it is the negation of rational explanation. It reintroduces into modern thought the whole conception of fate or blind chance which St Augustine had once exorcized from history. But we need not take it too seriously, since a modicum of linguistic analysis of the word 'accident' will quickly reveal that we are dealing here only with a pseudo-problem. The *philosophe* historians in their fatalistic moods enjoyed repeating anecdotes which showed that history was all a matter of fortune;[3] as actors in history, Voltaire remarked, we are like blind men playing cards; we are never allowed to see the face of the cards. Cartesian

---

[1] *Heroes and Hero Worship*, i, 'The Hero as Divinity'. Cf. his often-quoted remark that 'history is the essence of innumerable biographies' in his essay 'On History' (*Critical and Miscellaneous Essays*, I). The view was popular in the nineteenth century; Acton (*Lectures*, 329) quotes Charles Kingsley, an old-style Regius Professor of History at Cambridge: 'Instead of saying that the history of mankind is the history of the masses, it would be much more true to say that the history of mankind is the history of its great men.' See E. H. Carr, *What is History?* Lecture II, 'Society and the individual' (25–49); Carr calls this view 'the Bad King John and Good Queen Bess theory'.

[2] Cf. the nursery rhyme of how the kingdom was lost 'all for the want of a horse-shoe nail'. It is also often called the 'Cleopatra's Nose' theory; cf. the saying of Pascal: 'Had Cleopatra's nose been shorter, the whole aspect of the world would have been changed' (*Pensées*, ii, 162). All that needs to be said about this view may be read in E. H. Carr, op. cit., Lecture IV, 'Causation in History' (81–102).

[3] A single example from the many which Voltaire offers must suffice. In the *Siècle* (chap. XXII) he relates a tale of Bolingbroke's of how the Duchess of Marlborough upset a glass of water over Mrs Masham's dress, which so annoyed Queen Anne that the Duchess fell from favour and consequently the Whigs fell from power and were replaced by the Tories, who reversed Whig policy and concluded peace with France: thus, a glass of water was the 'cause' of the Treaty of Utrecht. (See J. B. Black, op. cit., 40f.) And Voltaire constantly criticizes Montesquieu's attempts at historical explanation by reference to geography and climate!

rationalism, from which Montesquieu had largely set himself free,[1] does not help to solve the problems of historical causation; and obsession with causation in natural science predisposed the eighteenth-century mind to rest content with purposeless and irrational mechanical explanations instead of truly historical ones. Even Gibbon constantly falls back upon accident as a means of explanation; he finds it especially congenial because it serves his aim of writing anti-Christian propaganda in the guise of history; it is a good counterstroke to the Bossuet-type of 'Finger of God' explanation.[2] And, though Hume the philosopher has had much to say about causes, Hume the historian has little to add to the stock ideas of the French *philosophes* in the matter of historical explanation.

Hume and his 'Impartial' History

It was 'philosophy', that is, the ideals of the Enlightenment, that the *philosophe* historians had undertaken to inject into history, and it was David Hume who was the successful innovator in Britain. He himself believed that he was undertaking something never before attempted, the writing of impartial English history. In his very brief sketch, 'My Own Life', he acknowledges the disappointment which he felt when his efforts were met on every side with 'one cry of reproach, disapprobation and even detestation' on the publication of the first volume of his *History of England* (1756), the volume on the Stuarts.[3] However, he consoles himself with the fact that the Primates of England (Dr Herring) and of Ireland (Dr Stone)—'which seems two odd exceptions'—sent him

---

[1] Cf. W. Stark, op. cit., 1–24.

[2] Again, a single example must suffice. We may admire the rhetorical skill with which he contrives to suggest that the chance outcome of a battle at Poitiers in 732 is responsible for the continued existence of the Christian religion in Europe: 'A victorious line of march had been prolonged above a thousand miles from the Rock of Gibraltar to the banks of the Loire; the repetition of an equal space would have carried the Saracens to the confines of Poland and the Highlands of Scotland; the Rhine is not more impassable than the Nile or Euphrates, and the Arabian fleet might have sailed without a naval combat into the mouth of the Thames. Perhaps the interpretation of the Koran would now be taught in the schools of Oxford, and her pulpits might demonstrate to a circumcised people the sanctity and truth of the revelation of Mahomet' (*Decline and Fall*, chap. 52).

[3] The fascinating and complicated story of the enthusiasm of his Edinburgh publisher and of the 'conspiracy of the booksellers' in London is told in E. C. Mossner, *The Life of David Hume*, London, 1954, 301–18.

messages 'not to be discouraged'. Hume's impartiality had allowed him to 'shed a generous tear for the fate of Charles I', but it caused men of the stamp of Warburton to denounce him as 'an atheistical Jacobite'. But, as often happens, denunciation and polemics proved good for sales; and by the time that the sixth and final volume was published, completing the history from Roman times, Hume was wealthy and renowned, having at last obtained the longed-for fame which his 'still-born' philosophical writing had not brought him. He had skilfully satisfied the needs of an expanding middle class in an age which was rapidly acquiring an appetite for history, and his work retained its popularity for more than a hundred years.

'The first quality of an historian,' Hume said in a letter, 'is to be impartial'; and, while he was at work upon his first volume, he remarked, 'I may be liable to the reproach of ignorance, but I am certain to escape that of partiality.'[1] On the latter point, as we have seen, he discovered himself to have been mistaken. We should note carefully that 'impartiality' does not mean for Hume what it has meant since the time of Ranke. Today impartiality means a disinterested search for the facts of the case and a determination to let them speak for themselves. But Hume undertook no research; he wrote his history (we are told) on a sofa with his feet up. He took what he wanted from earlier writers, and, when an original document came his way, he picked from it one or two 'curious passages'. Impartiality did not consist in letting the facts speak for themselves, but in giving them a 'philosophical' interpretation, that is, the interpretation which 'all reasonable men' would give them—men who were swayed neither by tradition nor by enthusiasm, and who therefore accepted the philosophical standpoint which Hume had already expounded in his *Treatise* and his *Enquiry*, before he began to write history at all.[2] To those

[1] J. B. Black, op. cit., 91.
[2] Carl Becker's assessment of Hume's history is unsurpassed: 'At first reading it seems no more than a dull and colourless chronicle of events, and one wonders why it should have been so eagerly read. . . . On more attentive reading the reason for its popularity is clear. Hume managed, with unobtrusive skill, to weave into the texture of the narrative a condemnation of the very things the eighteenth century wanted condemned—tyranny, superstition, intolerance. The story is a narrative of events, but it is after all well told, and above all told *en philosophe*: that is to say, not in order to trace the evolution of events but . . . in order to apply to them the ready-made judgments of the Age of Reason. It would be a dull reader indeed who would

who approved of Hume's philosophy Hume's history appeared impartial. Voltaire makes the matter quite plain. Writing in 1764, when Hume's final volume appeared, he declared:[1] 'Nothing can be added to the fame of this *History*, perhaps the best written in any language. . . . Mr Hume in his *History* is neither parliamentarian, nor royalist, nor Anglican nor Presbyterian—he is simply judicial. . . . The fury of parties has for a long time deprived England of a good historian as well as of a good government. . . . In the new historian we find a mind superior to his materials; he speaks of weakness, blunders, cruelties as a physician speaks of epidemic diseases.' One of the perennial illusions of the rationalist mind is that, because one is not an Anglican or a Presbyterian, not a Christian or a Marxist, and so on, one is therefore 'impartial'.[2] We cannot see our own ideological spectacles, and because our eyes are protected by them, we do not notice that as we throw our sand against the wind, the wind blows it back again.

Hume's thinking upon the subject of history does not advance beyond the general level of the *philosophes*. Though in the text-books of philosophy Hume is classified as an empiricist, we find in his *Enquiry* the veritable *locus classicus* of the rationalist view of history. Neither Hume nor Voltaire used history as a means of finding out empirically the truth about human nature, though they paid lip-service to the idea; they knew it already from philosophy. The doctrine of a static or undeveloping human nature had its antecedents in the Cartesian doctrine that truth is to be sought in the abstract principles of reason and not in the partial and inconsequential records of history. Hume states the rationalist dogma in its purest eighteenth-century form: 'Mankind,' he tells us, 'are so much the same, in all times and places, that history informs us

---

not carry away from such a book that most useful of lessons for the eighteenth century, namely, that *except* for the ambition of princes and politicians, the worldly interests and intrigues of priests, the emotional excesses of fanatics, and the fears of a superstitious and degraded populace—except for these recognized and remediable evils, the history of England might have been what the history of any people ought to be' (*Heavenly City*, 109f.).

[1] In *La Gazette Littéraire*, 2 mai; Mossner, op. cit., 318.
[2] For instance, after dismissing the various High Church or Dissenting biographers of Laud, H. R. Trevor-Roper adds: 'Only Gardiner, who treated him not as a churchman, but as a protagonist in English history, was able to look upon Laud in that secular spirit from which alone an impartial view can come' (*Archbishop Laud*, London, 1940, 6).

of nothing new or strange in this particular. Its chief use is only to discover (i.e. in twentieth-century English, to lay open to view, to uncover) the constant and universal principles of human nature.'[1] By presenting us with examples of how effect follows cause in human nature, as in the mechanical processes of physical nature, the study of history enables us to become acquainted with 'the regular springs of human action and behaviour'. 'It is universally acknowledged that there is a great uniformity among the actions of men, in all nations and ages, and that human nature remains still the same, in its principles and operations. The same motives always produce the same actions: the same events follow from the same causes. . . . Would you know the sentiments, inclinations, and course of life of the Greeks and Romans? Study well the temper and actions of the French and English.'[2] Hume follows up these remarks with a sentence which suggests that history is a data-gathering empirical science: the difficulty, of course, is that this is exactly what his presupposition about the fixity of human nature prevents him from doing. 'These records of wars, intrigues, factions and revolutions are so many collections of experiments, by which the politician or moral philosopher fixes the principles of his science, in the same manner as the physician or natural philosopher becomes acquainted with the nature of plants, minerals and other external objects, by the experiments which he forms concerning them.' The pages of history, that is to say, constitute the historian's laboratory in which he studies the laws of human behaviour, which he then formulates. But the very next sentence indicates that the truth about human nature and behaviour has already been decided upon before the research began: 'Nor are the earth, water and other elements examined by Aristotle and Hippocrates more like to those which at present lie under our observation than the men described by Polybius and Tacitus are to those who now govern the world.' Thus, in one paragraph of the *Enquiry* we see the two basic theses of the rationalist doctrine of history: first, the doctrine of static human nature ('the constant and universal principles of human nature'), and second, the view that the method of history is fundamentally the method of the natural sciences: history is already in

[1] *Enquiry concerning Human Understanding*, Sect. VIII, Part I, § 65 (ed. L. A. Selby-Bigge, Oxford, 1894, 83).
[2] Ibid.

principle a branch of social science, although it remained for the nineteenth century to develop what is implied in this conception.[1]

Nineteenth-century Historiography

During the nineteenth century the former of these rationalist theses, the doctrine of static human nature, came gradually to be abandoned, or at least modified even by those historians who still subconsciously accepted it. Montesquieu's preliminary intimation of historical relativity and Vico's suggestion of the organic growth of nations now at last attained explicit recognition in the European mind. The perspective of history became three-dimensional; the past was no longer viewed in the flat from the vantage-point of 'constant and universal principles', valid for all nations and epochs, as it had been viewed by Voltaire, Hume and even Gibbon.[2] Western man became historically-minded in the nineteenth century, as in the seventeenth century he had become scientifically-minded. As the natural sciences had then liberated themselves from the control of philosophy, so now history also was freed from servitude to philosophy, and by the end of the nineteenth century had become an enquiry in its own right.[3] Thus the historical revolution of the nineteenth century completed the great transformation of the human understanding which was involved in the transition from the mediaeval to the modern world-view. As there developed a genuine sense of the uniqueness and particularity of every separate age of the past, the nineteenth century came more and more to regard the eighteenth century's

---

[1] For Hume's view of miracles, see Lecture VI, *infra*, 187–90.

[2] Gibbon, of course, was an historian in a sense in which Voltaire and Hume were not. He dissented strongly from the *philosophe* denigration of historical research; his first literary venture, the *Essai sur l'étude de la littérature* (1761), was a defence of the erudites; and his supreme literary achievement constitutes a marriage of history *en philosophe* with historical research. Cf. G. M. Young, *Gibbon*, London, 1932 (pp. 32f. in ed. of 1939). But Gibbon's aim is not yet the nineteenth-century ideal of the disinterested search for facts; his is still propaganda-history. His view of the Middle Ages is that of Voltaire, not that of the Romantics or their successors.

[3] Cf. Carl Becker, *Heavenly City*, 18: 'In the early nineteenth century, history could still be regarded as the Transcendent Idea realizing itself in the actual. In our time, history is nothing but history, the notation of what has occurred, just as it happened. . . . No respectable historian any longer harbours ulterior motives; and one who should surreptitiously introduce the gloss of a transcendent interpretation into the human story would deserve to be called a philosopher and straightway lose his reputation as a scholar.'

static viewpoint as profoundly unhistorical.[1] An unparalleled
effort of vigorous and sustained historical activity now began. Not
only the intelligentsia but the whole educated middle class became
aware, in a new and intense way, of history as a process of real
change and development; for the first time the European mind
began to view all things historically—every idea, every institution,
every social custom, every economic condition. In England a
remarkable series of talented men of action and men of letters,
mostly outside the universities, directed their energies to satisfying
and at the same time to stimulating the voracious public appetite
for history as the re-creation of the living past in all its rich
variety. In Germany the passion for historical knowledge took a
more scientific turn. The new historians enlisted under the watch-
word of Leopold von Ranke, who became Professor of History at
Berlin in 1825: 'wie es eigentlich gewesen'—'as it really happened'[2]—not propaganda, not philosophy, but facts for their own
sake. The diligence of the nineteenth-century German historians
in finding and recording the facts of every period of the past and
of almost every region of the world cannot be overpraised. Sometimes the Rankean way of regarding history as the disinterested
pursuit of facts for their own sake is called 'historicism',[3] but we
intend to avoid this ill-defined term and we shall speak of history
in the Rankean mode simply as 'scientific history', in a colourless

[1] Cf. the quotation from J. S. Mill, *supra*, 93 n.

[2] These famous words appeared in the preface to the youthful Ranke's
Geschichte der romanischen und germanischen Völker, 1494–1535 (1824). The
significance of Ranke as an historian is discussed in Lecture V, *infra*.

[3] 'Historicism', the English equivalent of the German *Historismus*, has
been used in at least the following senses: (1) the Rankean view of history as
the distinterested search for facts, or presuppositionless research; (2) the
view that theological or philosophical truths can be established by 'objective'
historical research (as in the 'life-of-Jesus' movement; see the next section of
this chapter); (3) the philosophy of history; (4) the positivist view that the
aim of historical research is the establishment of general laws about human
behaviour or social development; (5) the view that historical prediction is
the principal objective of the social sciences; (6) the view that to give an
adequate account of the nature of an idea or an institution is to describe
historically how it came to be what it is; (7) historical relativism; (8) simply
the study of history as such. E. H. Carr (*What is History?* 86 n.) would add
the view that historicism is the collection of all the opinions about history
which Professor Popper dislikes; cf. Karl Popper, *The Poverty of Historicism*,
London, 1957. Carr says that 'Professor Popper's widely read writings on the
subject have emptied the term of precise meaning'. At any rate we agree with
Carr in avoiding the word altogether because of its lack of agreed and precise
meaning.

and non-pejorative sense. History had indeed become scientific in the sense that the method and the tools—critical, philological archaeological, and so on—which were now used were improved even beyond the standards of Mabillon and the acutest of the erudites.

Nevertheless, nineteenth-century historiography in its main line of development[1] did not entirely succeed in freeing itself from the incubus of eighteenth-century rationalism. Three considerations deserve attention in this respect. First, although it was now generally agreed that accurate knowledge of every past epoch is an end earnestly, even passionately, to be desired and pursued, many historians made little effort to see the past from the point of view of the men and women of the past, and not from that of the nineteenth century. A consciousness of the superiority of the nineteenth century in moral as well as in scientific judgment made it impossible for them to see, for example, the Middle Ages through mediaeval eyes. A long tradition of rationalism in history stretches across the nineteenth century and into the twentieth— Hallam, James Mill, Grote, Macaulay, Buckle, and many more, right down to J. B. Bury and Dr G. P. Gooch in almost our own times. Hallam's *Middle Ages* (1818) and his subsequent works are based upon honest, painstaking and disinterested research upon original authorities, and they set a high standard of accuracy; but he is lacking in that quality of historical imagination which can bring the past to life. Not all who took advantage of the intense interest awakened by the Romantic movement in the Middle Ages had any real insight into the mediaeval mind: Sir Walter Scott's characters in his historical novels are nineteenth-century men and women in period dress.[2] Macaulay, who has been called 'the most popular writer of history the world has ever seen', and (much more absurdly) 'the English Ranke', is the outstanding example of the rationalist historian. He is the great exponent of the myth of progress, and every past age is condemned as falling short of

[1] Another line, implicit in the thought of Burke and Coleridge and developed by those whom they influenced, is discussed in Lecture V *infra*.

[2] Nor indeed was Scott careful about historical accuracy. Lord Acton reminds us that it was the shock of the discovery that Scott in *Quentin Durward* had tampered with Commynes in his presentation of Lewis XI that made the youthful Ranke resolve to be an accurate historian (*Lectures on Modern History*, 19). On the rationalism of Scott see Duncan Forbes, *The Liberal Anglican Idea of History*, Cambridge, 1952, 190f.; and note especially the Dedicatory Epistle for *Ivanhoe*.

the materialistic prosperity (for the *bourgeoisie*) of the nineteenth century. Macaulay is intensely aware of real change and development in history, as every reader of the opening chapters of his *History of England* (1848) will know; but his total inability to understand that men of past ages must be judged by the standards of their own time leads a distinguished historian of today to conclude that his mental attitude towards the past is 'in the deepest sense unhistoric'.[1] The nineteenth century loved Macaulay because he was (in Geyl's words) 'so exclusively and intolerantly English'; he will always be read because his *Essays* are masterpieces of style, epigram, wit, argument, vituperation and onesidedness, and his *History* is enthralling and dramatic; but as an historian, apart from his awareness of real development, he is still the polemical and propagandist *philosophe*. He is not, of course, typical of nineteenth-century historiography; he illustrates the rationalistic element within it, as did Buckle in another way, by exaggerating it. The century remained to the end confident that its own criteria of judgment were the fixed and unquestionable standards of the rational mind as such. Lord Acton at the end of the century remained convinced of the universal validity of nineteenth-century moral standards, which he thought that the historian should apply in his work,[2] and he believed that the accumulated results of historical research were leading towards 'ultimate history', the final settlement of all the disputed points which still await liquidation.[3]

The second point which we should consider is that the underlying 'myth' of nineteenth-century historiography was the

[1] Pieter Geyl, *Debates with Historians*, Groningen, 1955, 27. Geyl's chapter on Macaulay (19–34) amply illustrates and justifies this conclusion. Macaulay condemns the early Christians for not finding in the Bible what the sons of the Enlightenment and the Utilitarians found there; he praises James Mill's *History of British India* because it judges the Indians strictly from the British and rationalistic point of view; he treats the authors of the Toleration Act as bigots because they did not go the whole length of Catholic Emancipation, and so on. He has no sense that he and his age stand on the achievements of the past: 'Just so (says Geyl) have we heard a baby, mounted on the shoulders of its father, cry out: "How much taller am I than Papa!" '

[2] See *infra*, 160, 250–2.

[3] Cf. *The Cambridge Modern History: its Origin, Authorship and Production*, Cambridge, 1907, 10–12. Contrast Sir George Clark's introduction to *The New Cambridge Modern History*, I, Cambridge, 1957, xxiv–xxv. Some limitations of the latter work in the sphere of intellectual history, doubtless the result of the lingering rationalist attitude, are pointed out in an art. by Basil Hall in *The Journal of Theological Studies*, N.S. Vol. XI, April, 1960, 110–17.

rationalist myth. By 'myth' is meant the overall interpretation or perspective by which historical development as a whole is unified in the collective mind of an epoch. It is largely ideological in the sense that no one thinker has given birth to it, and most historians in any age (especially those most completely dominated by it) are almost entirely unaware of it; it is for them just the way in which they (and 'all reasonable men') look at things. Myth differs from serious attempts at the constructive or critical interpretation of history in being largely unconscious, though, of course, it is consciously articulated by many writers, including historians. 'It is the historians', writes Professor Geyl, 'who are the guardians of mankind's collective memory. It must be admitted that they often use (or abuse) their guardianship to help in creating the legends which substitute themselves for the reality, and many are the great writers of history whose immediate influence on their contemporaries and on the world's affairs has been due, more than anything else, to the legendary or mythical features in their presentment of their subject. But criticism never slumbers, the argument without end that is history can never rest, and indeed, to track down legend and to show up myth is the function that the professional historian today will look upon as his special contribution to society; a contribution making for sanity, for clarity of vision, for a heightened sense of individuality, for balance and for moderation of judgment.'[1] Today we are all so self-conscious about our ideology and embarrassed at the suggestion of it that many academic historians retreat to a stratum of 'technical history'[2] from which all questions of interpretation are supposedly banished, or to a remote and vanished period which arouses no ideological passion in the breast and where the scientific historian may practise his virtuosity in peace for the delectation of a handful of fellow specialists.[3] There is no real escape from the

[1] Op. cit., 237. Geyl is discussing Sir Isaiah Berlin's exposure of the fallacy and danger of the myth of determinism or *Historical Inevitability* (in his book of that title, published in 1954).

[2] For the explanation of this notion see H. Butterfield, *Man on his Past*, 94, 98, 137–41, 229.

[3] From this point of view, as Professor W. H. Walsh points out, 'the history of the nineteenth century, which stirs our passions because it is so near to us and because the men of that time were at once so like and so unlike ourselves, will be less suitable for serious study than the history of the fourteenth, which we can regard with comparative equanimity. All periods are equally near to God, as Ranke told us, but some, those we should norm-

problems of ideology and interpretation by means of scientific history, since the latter, properly defined, means nothing more than the methodology of establishing the reliability or otherwise of the materials upon which a judgment concerning 'what happened' ('facts') may be made. Ranke himself, the great protagonist of scientific history, is the founder of the Prussian myth, and Karl Marx, who provided the proletariat with a revolutionary variant of the nineteenth-century myth, had much to say about scientific history. The pseudo-escape route is to accept the conventional myth or ideology of the day, because then, if one's history is attacked, its critics will stamp themselves as eccentrics and outsiders, whose animadversions may be ignored. In our decade, however, there is a clash of ideologies; there is no one generally accepted myth of history, and so escape from the noise of battle is less easy.

But the situation was different in the nineteenth century, which was largely dominated by the rationalist myth inherited from the Enlightenment. According to this myth the Greeks had laid the foundations of science and of history and had kindled the torch of intellectual freedom. Then, alas, there supervened upon the conversion of Constantine in the fourth century AD the long night of ecclesiastical dogmatism, and the onward march of mankind was halted during the mediaeval age of 'barbarism and religion'. But happily the men of science at the Renaissance, with the rekindled lights of Hellas shining in their eyes, threw off the shackles of theology. The whole myth is focused in the legendary picture of Galileo at the Inquisition, which historical criticism has even yet scarcely begun to erode in the popular mind. Perfection, whether inevitable or conditional, is the goal of the upward march of mankind; science is the means by which it is achieved. Myths of this kind are little affected by sober historical criticism; they expire only when a new and dynamic myth arises to take their place, after they have grown old and anaemic. Today the rationalist myth, given classical expression in Bury's *Idea of Progress* (1928), underlies many popular histories of science and many accounts of

---

ally care about relatively little, enjoy Ranke's successors' particular favour': art. 'The Limits of Scientific History' in *Historical Studies*, III (Fourth Irish Conference of Historians), London and Cork, 1961, 48.

the nature and function of the social sciences.[1] Its vitality amongst the intelligentsia of England in the nineteen-sixties is illustrated in the announced curricula and ideals of the most recently founded universities, which give the impression that little which was said or done before about 1750 is worthy of the serious attention of modern undergraduates.[2]

Positivist History

The third characteristic which imparts to nineteenth-century historiography its rationalistic flavour results from the immense prestige of the natural sciences, including applied science, during the era. This inevitably gave rise to the view that 'history is a science, no less and no more'.[3] Now, everyone today presumably agrees that history should be scientific, in the sense defined above —the sense in which historical enquiry in the hands of a Ranke (or, for that matter, of a Mabillon) was scientific. But Bury's school of thought intended much more than this. For them the natural sciences were the model of what all science should be, including historical science. Such views are often called 'positivist', a word which owes its admittance into intellectual history to Auguste Comte. In these Lectures 'positivism' denotes the theory that the only truth which can be known to be true is that which can be verified by scientific method of the type which is practised in the natural sciences. Positivist history is historiography based

[1] The egregious example is Barbara Wootton's *Testament for Social Science: an Essay in the Application of Scientific Method to Social Problems*, London, 1950.

[2] The nature of historical myths is dealt with further in Lectures V and VIII *infra*. For a brief assessment of the rationalist myth against the evidence concerning the way in which the modern scientific outlook did, in fact, arise see Alan Richardson, *The Bible in the Age of Science*, London, 1961, 15–125.

[3] These famous words were uttered by J. B. Bury in his Inaugural Lecture at Cambridge in 1902 on 'The Science of History' (reprinted in his *Selected Essays*, London, 1927). The discovery of truth was the historian's proper task and it was to be carried out by the same methods of organized research as had proved so successful in natural science; the 'complete assemblage of the smallest facts of human history' would 'tell in the end'. (Bury was one of the editors of the *Cambridge Modern History*.) Historians should abandon their literary ambitions, sink their personal feelings and devote themselves to the search for scientific-historical truth. G. M. Trevelyan replied to Bury on behalf of humanist history in *Clio, a Muse* (London, 1931), which also contains Trevelyan's own Inaugural Lecture on '*The Present Position of History*', when he succeeded to Bury's Regius chair in 1927. A valuable discussion of the issues at stake will be found in W. H. Walsh, 'The Limits of Scientific History' (op. cit.).

on the theory that historians scientifically ascertain facts, which then somehow arrange themselves into a pattern of general laws or are capable of being so arranged by sociologists (another word invented by Comte); the object of history is the formulation or verification of generalizations concerning human behaviour by means of the study of human development down the ages. This is the nineteenth-century version of Hume's view that the chief use of history is 'only to discover the constant and universal principles of human nature'. It is anti-historical in the sense that it involves measuring the past by the standards of the present; nature, including human nature, is regular, and history, like natural science, aims at discovering regularities. Nothing could have happened in the past which does not happen today, nor could men have thought or felt or acted in former ages in ways different from the ways of today. Positivism, like Marxism, was philosophy, though it masqueraded as science; it was based upon the now out-moded notions of the nineteenth century concerning the nature and procedures of science, and consequently has lost much of its original appeal;[1] but it still lives on as an ingrained habit of thought among uncritical minds. One of the genuinely ideological assumptions of Western society today is that truth as such is that which has been established by scientific method of the type which has been so successful in natural science: everything else, such as religious truth, artistic standards, ethical norms, is a matter of 'opinion' and will remain so until 'science' (especially psychology and the social sciences) is in a position to settle questions about religion and human destiny definitively. The temper of our times is in this sense positivistic. It is important in such a climate of opinion to note that enthusiasm for scientific methods in modern historical study in no way commits us to a positivistic view of the nature of history. To admire Ranke it is not necessary to venerate Comte.[2]

---

[1] Cf. E. H. Carr, *What is History?* 50–68. Nowadays positivists usually prefer to be called 'scientific humanists', a term which helps to disguise the the parentage of their thinking in nineteenth-century philosophy.

[2] Positivists from many countries still gather on September 5 in the cemetery where Comte is buried in Paris. As the self-announced Messiah of the Religion of Humanity which he founded, with its grotesque parody of Catholic worship, Comte gave expression to faith in man's divinity, thus providing an object of adoration for many in the age of progress. But these paranoiac posturings of his later years caused misgivings amongst those who, like J. S. Mill, had once hailed him as a great thinker. It was Mill who had

Auguste Comte (1798–1857) said little of lasting significance, yet his reputation amongst advanced thinkers in his own day was immense; he was not a scientist—Herbert Spencer said that he knew nothing about physical science—yet he was accepted as the genius who had at last made philosophy scientific. The secret of his success was doubtless that he articulated the ideological aspirations of his age: now at last science had placed in man's hand an instrument by which he could control both his environment and his own unruly behaviour, so that the promise of the wonderful new age of progress might be brought to fruition. Comte believed that he had discovered the laws of human historical and social development, and that henceforward the accumulation of facts in the light of these laws must lead to universal happiness. Sociology could now reform the world according to scientifically verified laws. 'Now that history has been for the first time systematically considered as a whole, and has been found, like other phenomena, subject to invariable laws,' Comte declares, 'the preparatory labours of modern science are ended';[1] and in his *Cours de philosophie positive* he describes these 'invariable laws' and interprets all history by means of them. It is unnecessary for our purpose to detail the historical and sociological laws which Comte thought he had discovered; it is relevant only to point out that, in that age of scientific synthetic philosophy, the laws 'scientifically' established in the various systems differed just as widely as the old, pre-scientific philosophical theories had done. Herbert Spencer's *System of Synthetic Philosophy* (in several volumes,

---

rescued Comte from penury by enlisting financial support from George Grote, the radical wealthy banker, and from others; and it was Mill's patronage which secured for him a following in England such as he had not obtained in France. The best short introduction to Comte will be found in the chapter entitled 'Comte's Secular Religion' in John Bowle, *Politics and Opinion in the Nineteenth Century: an Historical Introduction*, London, 1954, 117–33, where a full bibliography will be found. J. S. Mill's *Auguste Comte and Positivism* (1865) and Edward Caird's *The Social Philosophy of Comte* (1885) are standard works; Basil Willey's *Nineteenth Century Studies*, London, 1948, is helpful. Comte's diffuse six-volumed *Cours de philosophie positive* (1830–42) was translated and abridged by Harriet Martineau in *The Positive Philosophy of Auguste Comte* (2 Vols., 1853). Comte's reputation was at its zenith in the middle of the century, when, for instance, a writer like G. H. Lewes in his *Biographical History of Philosophy* (3 vols., 1845–6) could conclude that the philosophical activity which he had traced from Thales was now at an end, philosophy having been replaced by positivism.

[1] Quoted by John Bowle, op. cit., 123.

1862–93), though based upon all known scientific knowledge, turned out to be vastly different in its elucidation of the laws of human progress from the allegedly no less 'scientific' philosophy of Karl Marx. That the nineteenth century did not notice these strange contradictions of 'science' was doubtless due in some measure to the fact that it confined Marx to a proletarian ghetto: ideologies and their rationalizations are not taken seriously until they have been backed by military and economic power, such as was placed behind the ideas of Marx after the Russian revolution of 1917. A hundred years after Comte a dedicated propagandist of latter-day positivism could say that 'we must admit that as yet there are few laws in social science which can claim the universality of, say, the law of gravity'[1]—one wishes that she had named one such law—while one of the most eminent sociologists of our times has said that 'it must be admitted that sociologists have not so far succeeded in establishing any general laws of social development'.[2] But this does not in the least imply that the human or social sciences are less worth pursuing than the natural sciences or that the knowledge to which they lead is less valuable than knowledge gained through natural science; most of us would doubtless agree that the very success of the latter makes the pursuit of the human sciences all the more urgent.

By the middle of the nineteenth century the achievements and prestige of the natural scientists had induced amongst students of the humanities a marked sense of inferiority. History, too, must become scientific and uncover the laws of human progress in the way that the sciences had elucidated the laws of nature; but, alas, history and history's laws still lay hid in night: no historical Newton had yet appeared to make all light. Thus, Mark Pattison laments: 'The driveller and the philosopher seem equally helpless when they tread that shifting quicksand called History. The difference between them disappears or dwindles to that of literary qualification. We read a Grote or a Michelet with the same intellectual gratification which we derive from a superior novel . . . (we) look around for the aid of some scientific method to which appeal may be made, and which shall coerce the dissidents, and silence controversy, as effectually as it is silenced by the onward

---

[1] Barbara Wootton, op. cit., 180.
[2] Professor Morris Ginsberg, art. 'Sociology', *Chambers's Encyclopaedia*, Vol. XII, 1950, 674 (b).

progress of discovery and physical science.'[1] It was because H. T. Buckle promised to be the Newton of historical science and declared that he was about to produce a new kind of scientific history, which would elucidate the laws of progress, that he aroused such intense and widespread interest in his day. Buckle was one of the more remarkable and colourful personalities of the Victorian age; his prodigious reading, his astonishing memory and his graphic and rounded style enabled him to express (as he boasted) 'the spirit of the age' in a way which immediately made him a best-seller. Only two introductory volumes of his projected *History of Civilization in England* (1857 and 1861) had appeared when their author died of fever in Damascus a year after the publication of the second volume at just over forty years of age.[2] Buckle asserted (as indeed Fontenelle had done as long ago as 1688) that the progress of civilization depends upon the accumulation of knowledge; the historian's proper business, therefore, is to trace the growth of knowledge and hence the progress of civilization. Scientific history takes no account of individuals as such; the behaviour of groups and classes provides the materials of science, and the aim of history is to demonstrate inductively the laws governing historical change, just as natural science discovers the laws which govern the processes of nature. Social history must be based not upon a selection of individual incidents, which are precariously reconstructed, but upon a wide statistical induction over sufficiently long periods.

Mark Pattison sympathizes with Buckle's aim, but laments his failure to achieve it. He is ready to believe, though it is not easy to establish *a priori*, 'the abstract doctrine that social changes have the same character of uniformity that physical changes have'.[3] We may indeed believe in the uniformity of history, just as scientists believe in the uniformity of nature, though neither belief can be shown to be more than an article of faith. But Buckle, says Pattison, has not produced the evidence, nor validated his 'laws of progress', nor yet written a new kind of history. His unequalled sketch of the progress of society in France (in his first volume) is just like any other history. He does not, in fact, write about

[1] *Westminster Review*, 1857; reprinted in *Essays*, II, 414f.
[2] An excellent account will be found in Giles St Aubyn, *A Victorian Eminence: the Life and Works of Henry Thomas Buckle,* London, 1958.
[3] *Essays*, II, 419f.

'general averages', but about individuals—especially about 'the force exerted on national life by the single will of a Louis XIV'. By his own definition of history, Buckle's *History* is excluded from any claim to that title. It bears as much relation to history (as Buckle defines it) as the Rothschild story bears to the science of political economy. There is still a wide gulf between history and social science, and Buckle has not bridged it. Even his one great scientific induction, the law of progress, is based only on observations taken in favourable European localities; the great stationary societies of China or Hindustan are not mentioned, nor is, for example, the decline of Italy since the fifteenth century. The one boasted law of the new historical science is an illusion: there is no such thing as an irresistible advance of knowledge at all. A wider induction would have shown that all man's achievements are local and precarious. Today, a hundred years after Buckle's death, there is little reason to modify Mark Pattison's reluctant conclusions. History is still a 'quicksand' in the sense that it never provides an unyielding foothold; Grote and Michelet have been superseded, as has every historian of the nineteenth century, and it is generally conceded that the writing of a 'final' history of any period whatever (such as Lord Acton still thought attainable) is in principle impossible. Whatever the value of historical study may be, it is not nowadays usual to locate it in its power to elucidate sociological laws; and the view that the progress of the human race consists in the accumulation of scientific knowledge has turned out to be an illusion: the progress of scientific knowledge is just as likely to destroy civilization, because it does not appear to be paralleled by any 'law' of moral and political progress. Positivist history is not a gospel for the space-age.

Nevertheless, varieties of historical positivism still today find some distinguished advocates. It is, for instance, sometimes suggested that history is more like an applied science than a positive science; it is concerned with particular events rather than with general laws, in much the same way as an engineer is concerned with particular bridges or tunnels; but behind both the historian and the engineer stands the scientist who elucidates the underlying generalizations. Thus, Professor Karl Popper holds that there are no historical laws as such; history certainly uses universal laws as elucidated in the generalizing sciences of sociology and so on, but these provide no selective and unifying perspective for history.

This is the reason why interpretations of history are not scientific in character.[1] Because there are no laws of history, there can be no 'universal history' and no meaning in history. 'History' in the sense in which most people speak of it ('the history of mankind') does not exist; there are only particular histories, such as political history. The latter is history as taught in our schools, and it would be just as sensible to treat the history of embezzlement as history *par excellence,* because 'the history of power politics is nothing but the history of international crime and mass murder.'[2] The history of art or of civilization would have told a different story about mankind. The attempt to discover man's inevitable destiny from so-called laws of history (historical determinism) is what Popper calls 'historicism'; it is doomed to failure because history has no laws and no meaning. Historicism is dangerous because it leads to fanaticism; it is false whether it assumes a Christian form[3] or the 'scientific' form of Marxist Messianism.[4] History has no meaning and no inevitability, but we can nevertheless give it a meaning: 'we can make it our fight for the open society. . . . It is up to us to decide what shall be our purpose in life, to determine our ends.'[5] And indeed Popper's crowded and brilliant pages constitute an impassioned plea for political freedom, a moving tract for the times, first published (significantly) in 1945. 'Facts have no meaning; they can gain it only through our decisions': Hitler's Reich is destroyed; what happens next is 'up to us'. History, in Professor Popper's philosophy (though he might not call it that), is like nature, a flowing stream of purposeless process. It is like the St Lawrence River (though he might repudiate the simile), which follows its immemorial course with utter indifference to any purposes

[1] Cf. Karl Popper, *The Open Society and its Enemies*, 1952, II, 248–56; also the reply to Morton G. White, 'Historical Explanation' in *Mind*, Vol. LII, 1943, 212ff. in Popper, ibid., 343f. Cf. also C. G. Hempel, 'The Function of General Laws in History' in *Readings in Philosophical Analysis*, ed. H. Feigl and W. Sellars, New York, 1949, 459–71.

[2] Ibid., II, 257.

[3] For example, in John Macmurray's *The Clue to History*, London, 1938; see Popper, ibid., II, 230f., 260f.; Popper approves of Barth's denial of the revelation of God in (secular) history (259).

[4] Popper, ibid., II, 77–211; 239–43; and see Popper, *The Poverty of Historicism, passim.*

[5] *The Open Society*, II, 265.

or meanings; it acquires significance only when engineers harness Niagara or convert the river into a mercantile waterway for the Middle West. Historians do not find meaning in history; they bring meanings to it; they are really engaged in the task of social engineering, and their interpretations of history will be ancillary to the purposes of sociologists, planners and politicians.

Now, this understanding of the function of history, as we shall see in Lecture V, is a true aspect of the historian's task, but it is not the whole of it and not the heart of it. The chief weakness of positivist views about history is that they do not describe what, in fact, historians actually do, and they do not touch the heart of the historian's real interest. We have already noted that the history which Buckle wrote bore little relation to his exposition of the principles of scientific history. We might have illustrated the same dichotomy by reference to Taine, whose conception of history and the moral sciences as a kind of human 'botany', achieving the same kind of certainty as the natural sciences, happily did not inhibit him from writing the same sort of history as the 'literary' historians.[1] Or again, the learned German historian Karl Lamprecht (whose twelve-volume *Deutsche Geschichte* appeared between 1891 and 1904) claimed to have established conclusively the laws of social psychology which all civilizations *must* follow, and thus to have made history an exact science; his theory was widely accepted by sociologists, but repudiated by almost all historians, thus raising a heated controversy about the method and aim of historiography.[2] Since that time it has become clear that the great majority of working historians do not think of themselves as social scientists in any sense, but regard their discipline as one which exists in its own right.[3] Historians do not, of course, despise

[1] See Ernst Cassirer, *An Essay on Man*, 192–6.
[2] See F. Seifert, *Der Streit um Lamprechts Geschichtsphilosophie* (1925); Cassirer, op. cit., 199–202.
[3] That their view is nowadays generally conceded is attested by the existence of departments of History within the Faculties of Arts in the English Universities, not in the Faculties of Social Science; but this is, of course, a comparatively recent development. 'It is perhaps difficult for anybody less than fifty years old to appreciate how long it took for history to win the place it occupies today in the established organization of scholarship. . . . Not until 1923 could that great pioneer of the Manchester school, T. F. Tout, write: "The battle for the recognition of the subject is as good as won" ' (H. P. R. Finberg in his editorial introduction to *Approaches to History, a Symposium*, vii). It should also be recalled that our present-day historical methods were developed (so far as England is concerned) by men like Stubbs

generalization as such, and the relation between history and the social sciences will always be one of close interaction. The discussion of this relation proceeds vigorously today and is of great interest and importance.[1] History is nowadays *sui generis*, but it is related to every branch of human enquiry. Historians do not go to work with the intention either of discovering or applying social laws, nor yet to illustrate general truths which were already well known in advance of their study.[2] There is something essential to historical study, as it is practised today, which is absent from positivistic theories of history that put the emphasis upon general laws. This 'something' was hardly noticed in the nineteenth century, except perhaps by a few forward-looking thinkers like Dilthey; it has been the characteristic contribution of the twentieth century to elucidate it. Anyone wishing to understand the great difference between nineteenth-century historiographical thinking and that of the twentieth century might profitably read Ernst Cassirer's chapter on 'History' in his *Essay on Man*.[3] In the quest for truth, Cassirer tells us, the historian is bound by the same strict rules as the scientist, but his decisive act is one of the imagination, because the reality of history is not a uniform

---

and Mandel Creighton in remote country parsonages such as Navestock and Embleton, not in the Universities.

[1] It is far too extensive and complicated to enter upon here. A short but suggestive essay is Professor Cobban's 'History and Sociology' in *Historical Studies*, III, London and Cork, 1961, 1–8. See also *The Social Sciences in Historical Study*, Social Science Research Council Bulletin 64 (1954); Michael Oakeshott, *Experience and its Modes*, Cambridge, 1933, 158–61; Patrick Gardiner, *The Nature of Historical Explanation*, London, 1952, 28–33, and the criticism of Gardiner in William Dray, *Laws and Explanation in History*, London, 1957, 118–31; W. H. Walsh, *An Introduction to the Philosophy of History*, London, 1951, 48–59; E. H. Carr, *What is History?* 50–80; C. A. Beard and Sydney Hook, 'Problems of Terminology in Historical Writing' in *Theory and Practice in Historical Study: a Report of the Committee on Historiography*, Social Science Research Council Bulletin 54 (1946).

[2] Historical study unquestionably has a deep and lasting effect upon social and political activity, but it does not provide ready-made models for action. A study of *coups d'état*, for instance, might be more likely to inhibit action than to supply practical rules for revolutionaries. In his book *The Conspirators: a Study of the Coup d'État* (London, 1962), Major D. J. Goodspeed examines six *coups* of this century, but concludes that, though there is a general element in them all, 'in every case their outcome is unpredictable' (236). Such a conclusion, however, will not cause historians to suppose that they are not worth studying as a type of human behaviour, or revolutionaries to refrain from having a go.

[3] Op. cit., 171–206.

sequence of events, but the inner life of man. The deep implications of this judgment will be drawn out more carefully in Lecture V.

The Nineteenth-century Quest for Verification

By the middle of the eighteenth century the literary criticism of the Bible had been attempted in earnest. In 1750 J. D. Michaelis, Professor of Oriental Languages at Göttingen, published his *Introduction to the New Testament*, a work of rationalist criticism. In 1753 the Catholic French physician Jean Astruc published anonymously in Brussels his analysis of Genesis into a Yahwe source and an Elohim source.[1] About the same time as Hume was composing his *Dialogues* (that is, from 1744 onwards) Hermann Samuel Reimarus (1694–1768) was engaged upon a work which he entitled 'Apology for the Rational Worshippers of God'. He is the critic with whom Albert Schweitzer begins his account of the nineteenth-century quest of the historical Jesus.[2] An earnest deist, with a passion for rationalization, Reimarus was shocked by the immoralities of the Old Testament; being completely devoid of any historical sense of an evolution from more primitive to higher moral conceptions, like other rationalists of his day, he dismissed the idea of revelation in the Bible as childish. Like Hume, he prudently locked away his manuscript in a drawer; but after his death it came into the hands of the philosopher G. E. Lessing, who published portions of it (the Wolfenbüttel Fragments) between 1774 and 1778 under the title *Fragmente eines Ungenannten*. The last portion appeared the year before Hume's posthumous *Dialogues* saw the light; it dealt with 'The Aims of Jesus and his Disciples'. Reimarus held that the New Testament must be treated like any other human writing, and he described the intentions of Jesus and his followers in eschatological terms. During the controversy which arose in Germany Lessing suffered

---

[1] The title of his work is *Conjectures sur les Mémoires originaux dont il paroît que Moyse s'est servir pour composer le Livre de la Genèse*; a German translation appeared in 1783. See A. Lods, *Jean Astruc et la critique biblique au XVIIIᵉ siècle* (1924).

[2] *Von Reimarus zu Wrede*, 1906; Eng. trans., *The Quest of the Historical Jesus*, London, 1910. See also *Fragments from Reimarus* (1879), Eng. trans. by C. Voysey of D. F. Strauss, *H. S. Reimarus und seine Schutzschrift für die vernünftigen Verehrer Gottes* (1860); Paul Hazard, *European Thought in the eighteenth century*, Eng. trans., 426–8; A. C. Lundsteen, *H. S. Reimarus und die Anfänge der Leben-Jesu-Forschung*, Copenhagen, 1939.

much vilification with complacency. The attitudes of Reimarus and his sponsor Lessing exerted a powerful influence over New Testament research, which was being intensively pursued in the new age of historical activity now dawning. Without the new historical sense, literary criticism in the hands of a Reimarus was largely sterile; it might distinguish various sources, but it could say nothing about their historical relationships. It had to await fructification by the new historical criticism. It was in Göttingen, where from about 1760 onwards a remarkable revival of historical study was taking place, that the combination of literary and historical criticism was genuinely achieved. At Göttingen, where J. C. Gatterer was appointed to the chair of History in 1759, a succession of historians of a new type, including J. G. Schlözer and J. S. Semler, opened up the wider study of history, especially modern history, by applying the critical methods of research which they had learned from philologists and from biblical scholars. They foreshadowed Ranke and the nineteenth-century developments in their determination to ground history upon a critical evaluation of sources in contrast to the 'wind-bag' blustering of the *philosophe* literary historians.[1] In 1787 J. G. Eichhorn (who had studied at Göttingen and became a professor there in 1788) in his studies in Genesis invented the phrase 'the higher criticism' and established his claim to be the real founder of Old Testament criticism in the modern sense.[2] By 1806 W. M. L. De Wette, at the age of twenty-five, had laid the foundations of Pentateuchal criticism in his remarkable work, published at Halle, entitled *Contributions to the Introduction to the Old Testament*. Thereafter the study of the Old Testament began to assume its modern shape.

Lessing himself, who died in 1781, was a deist with a difference. With one foot planted firmly in the Age of Reason, his other foot touches the threshold of the historical-mindedness of the nineteenth century. The publication of his *Education of the Human Race* (1780) marks the end of an era. Revelation he regards as a *progressive* enlightenment. The Old Testament is only a preliminary stage, suitable for the instruction of the human race in its childhood.

---

[1] For an account of the Göttingen historians see H. Butterfield, *Man on his Past*, 26–58.

[2] See J. Estlin Carpenter, *The Bible in the Nineteenth Century*, London, 1903, 112.

The New Testament marks a higher stage in the process; and, though Lessing (unlike Voltaire) has a warm respect for traditional Christianity, he does not regard it as the final step in man's religious development; it will be superseded by the coming of a truly rational awareness of the divine purpose for mankind. The fruition of man's religious and moral perfection would assuredly be achieved by future generations. In all this Lessing anticipates nineteenth-century ideas about inevitable progress. But he is still an eighteenth-century deist: religious truth is a matter of reason and certainty, not of faith and history. Incidental truths of history can never become the proof of necessary truths of reason; in other words, the notion of a final revelation in history is self-contradictory. From the eighteenth century Lessing transmits to the nineteenth the dogma that the rational understanding of nature precludes both special revelations in history and miraculous divine interventions in it. Such things are contrary to reason as such; nineteenth-century positivism never questions the proposition. The biblical narrative must be judged by the standards of the modern scientific understanding of the world as governed by fixed and unalterable laws of nature. The Bible itself, even the New Testament, must be judged by the literary and moral canons which we would apply to any other ancient writing. The title of Lessing's posthumous essay, published in 1784, is significant: 'A New Hypothesis concerning the Evangelists considered simply as Human Historians'. Lessing's great prestige as a philosopher gave impetus to the new kind of research which was now being undertaken, namely, the study of the New Testament along the lines of the critical and historical methods developed by the Göttingen historians in different fields of investigation.[1]

The rationalistic assumptions of the eighteenth century, being carried over into the nineteenth, affected the historical interpretation of the New Testament in various ways. The grotesque rationalizations of H. E. G. Paulus (1761-1851) were aimed at removing the obstacles created by the presence of the miraculous element in the Gospels. The mythical interpretation of D. F.

[1] For Lessing see H. Chadwick, *Lessing's Theological Writings*, Eng. trans., where selected passages are translated; Karl Barth, *From Rousseau to Ritschl* (Eng. trans. of *Die Protestantische Theologie im 19 Jahrhundert,* 1952), London, 1959, 118-49; John Baillie, *The Belief in Progress,* London, 1950, 118f., 130-2, 165ff.; Paul Hazard, *European Thought in the Eighteenth Century,* 430-3.

Strauss, whose *Life of Jesus* startled the Christian world in 1835,[1] was designed to show that behind the legends of the Gospels (all of them second-century creations) and the dogmas of the Councils lay man's archetypal hope of the 'resurrection' of 'humanity', as expressed in the beautiful myths about Jesus. But Strauss's theory, like Bultmann's in the twentieth century, offered no explanation of how the myth-creating community came into existence in the first place; it merely (in Mark Pattison's phrase) 'dispersed history into the air'. The celebrated Tübingen School in the eighteen-forties made the first consistent attempt to explain the origins of Christian doctrine by the principles of historical criticism. Its weakness, like that of so much German biblical criticism, was that it took over an *a priori* scheme from the then fashionable philosophy (Hegel's) and forced the evidence into it: the dialectic of the Petrine and Pauline elements within the Church resulted in the synthesis of second-century Catholicism. The initial assumptions of the school precluded a strictly historical investigation, which was made subservient to a philosophy; amongst these assumptions was the conviction of F. Ch. Baur, the brilliant and learned founder of the school, that the question of the resurrection of Christ lies outside the sphere of historical enquiry—an assumption which has dominated German theology right down to Bornkamm at the present day, and which has precluded a serious consideration of the historical evidence in its own right.[2] Others, especially those influenced by Schleiermacher, fearing (*pace* Lessing) that the incidental truths of history were too problematical to guarantee religious certitude, looked to Christian religious experience to provide the foundation for a Christian theology. In the result, theological enquiry tended to become the interrogation of the religious consciousness with a view to discovering in it the assurance of truth. The traditional confidence in a divinely guaranteed sacred history had now been undermined by criticism; and hence the historical stream of religious experience, rather than the 'incidental facts of history', was taken as the starting-point of theological reconstruction.[3] The Ritschlian School, whose influence was paramount during

---

[1] Eng. trans. by George Eliot and Miss Barber, 1846.
[2] See Lecture V *infra*, where this matter is discussed.
[3] See the chapter 'From Schleiermacher to Barth' in Alan Richardson, *The Bible in the Age of Science*, 77–99.

the second half of the nineteenth century, determined to ground the truth of Christianity upon the one certain historical basis which could be empirically investigated, namely, the impression made by Christ upon the soul confronted by him, and the loyalty, confidence and peace which flow from this encounter. Albrecht Ritschl himself, the leader of the school, after his break in 1857 with his former Tübingen ways of thinking, tended to be conservative in matters of New Testament criticism; but many of his followers found it possible to adopt extreme views about the historicity of much of the contents of the Gospels, especially the miraculous elements. Like W. Herrmann, Ritschl's most distinguished disciple, they generally held that even a negative criticism cannot destroy the powerful influence which the perfection of Christ's personality, as presented in the Gospels, makes upon the sincere believer. The miracles are of minor importance to those who have found in Christ their spiritual freedom and the forgiveness of sins.[1] The resurrection and the living power of Christ are an inference from his historical personality and do not rest upon the ability of historians to reconstruct what happened on Easter Sunday. Thus we arrive at the famous distinction drawn by the most learned and prominent of the Ritschlians at the end of the century, Adolf von Harnack (1851–1930), the distinction between the Easter message and the Easter faith.[2] The message concerning the Empty Tomb is a legendary accretion in the Gospels; the Easter faith is the conviction that the Crucified attained an inward victory over death and entered into life eternal. Belief in the resurrection in its traditional sense is replaced by the assurance of the absolute value of the individual and therefore of immortality. Indeed, throughout the Ritschlian period there was a constant tendency to make the cross rather than the resurrection the culminating point of the Gospel story.[3]

[1] W. Herrmann, *Communion of the Christian with God* (Eng. trans., 1930), 180.

[2] Harnack's widely read lectures, *Das Wesen des Christentums* (1900), translated into English under the title *What is Christianity?* have recently been reprinted (New York and London, 1958).

[3] For the development of criticism in the nineteenth century see R. J. Knowling, art. 'Criticism' in *Hastings's Dictionary of Christ and the Gospels*, I (1906), 383–94; J. Estlin Carpenter, op. cit.; and for the general background see F. Lichtenberger, *History of German Theology in the Nineteenth Century*, Edinburgh, 1899; O. Pfleiderer, *Development of Theology in Germany since Kant*, New York, 1890; and K. Barth, *From Rousseau to Ritschl*.

Concentration upon the historical personality of Jesus gave to the Ritschlian period one of its most characteristic features, namely, the so-called 'life of Jesus movement'. The assumption underlying the remarkable series of 'lives' of Christ which appeared in the later nineteenth century was that the wonderful personality of Jesus would provide a solidly historical foundation such as would guarantee the truth of his teaching concerning the Kingdom of God and of the deliverances of the Christian religious consciousness which derived from encounter with him. Theology might be freed from the embarrassment, so keenly felt in the positivist atmosphere of the age, of dogmatic Christological formulations and of the miraculous accretions in the ancient records; but, of course, those healing works which science might recognize as falling within the scope of the ascertainable psychological laws of nature would serve to enhance the wonder of Jesus' personality. The firm ground of historical truth upon which the Christian faith was established was Jesus himself; the impression which he made upon his contemporaries is reproduced in the experience of his disciples in every age, creating in them loyalty, conviction and peace. The personality of the historical Jesus could be scientifically investigated; it was a fact of history, and it is a fact of experience today. It is the truly miraculous element in Christianity; no other miracles are needed. The first-century legendary embellishments of the Gospel story may be stripped away; and then we may see Jesus as he really was. Under the influence of such ideas the many 'lives' of Jesus, written by theologians or by literary men (like the Frenchman, Ernest Renan), enjoyed an enormous vogue; they represented almost every kind of approach, from the mildly conservative to the radically humanistic.[1]

The variety of reconstructions thus offered led inevitably to the recognition of the subjective character of such histories: the different interpreters looked down into the well of history and saw at the bottom of it, not the historical Jesus, but the reflection of their own face. The rediscovered Jesus of history turned out to be the embodiment of a nineteenth-century ideal figure, who died for the causes dear to the age of progress. The collapse of the

[1] Amongst them may be mentioned those by Th. Keim, B. Weiss, W. Beyschlag, H. J. Holtzmann, A. Edersheim. There were English counterparts, including Sir John Seeley's *Ecce Homo* (1865) and F. W. Farrer's *Life of Christ* (1874). In England and America the vogue continued for some time after it had ceased in Germany.

whole Liberal 'Jesus of history' movement was at hand when
Johannes Weiss published a small work entitled *Die Predigt Jesu
vom Reich Gottes* in 1892, which was followed in 1901 by Albert
Schweitzer's *Messianitäts - und Leidensgeheimnis*. In these works it
was suggested that the apocalyptic element was, in fact, not a first-
century 'husk' but the very kernel of Jesus' teaching. According
to Schweitzer the historical Jesus, whom the nineteenth century
had sought with such persistency, was 'one unknown', 'a stranger
and enigma to our time'. Both Weiss and Schweitzer remained
liberals of the Ritschlian type; they made no attempt (as did, for
instance, George Tyrrell in *Christianity at the Crossroads*, 1909) to
establish a post-Liberal theology based upon the rediscovery of
the apocalyptic element in the Gospels. The power of Schweitzer's
historical Jesus to command men's obedience across the centuries
remained an 'ineffable mystery'. The religious hero of the Liberal
'lives' could not have driven a famous New Testament scholar to
study medicine and to practise it in the primaeval forests of
equatorial Africa; but then, neither could the courageous but
deluded Jewish apocalyptic fanatic, who threw himself upon the
wheel of history in order that he might return from death upon
the clouds of heaven in the glory of the angels. Schweitzer tells
us so himself. 'It is not Jesus as historically known who is significant for our time and can help it. . . . The abiding and eternal
in Jesus is absolutely independent of historical knowledge, and
can be understood only by contact with his spirit which is still at
work in the world.'[1] The sustained quest of the nineteenth century
for the historical verification of the truth of the Gospel was pronounced irrelevant by the historian of that quest. A leading
German New Testament scholar, Professor Günther Bornkamm,
has recently written that today no one is in a position to write a
life of Jesus, and that the enquiry which for almost two hundred
years of prodigious effort has aimed at recovering the historical
Jesus, freed from all embellishment by doctrine and dogma, has
ended in failure. 'Albert Schweitzer in his classical work, *The
Quest of the Historical Jesus*, has erected its memorial, and at the
same time has delivered its funeral oration.'[2]

[1] *The Quest*, Eng. trans., 399.
[2] G. Bornkamm, *Jesus of Nazareth*, Eng. trans., 1960, 13.

4

DISENGAGEMENT
FROM HISTORY

THROUGHOUT the nineteenth century the shadow of
eighteenth-century rationalism made it difficult for the Protestant theologians of Europe to discern the truly historical
character of the biblical revelation. Søren Kierkegaard (1813–55)
anticipated in a remarkable way the reaction of twentieth-century
Continental theologians against the characteristic nineteenth-
century solutions of the problems which the rise of positivistic
historiography had created for theology. He is haunted by Lessing's dictum that 'incidental truths of history can never become
the proof of necessary truths of reason'; he quotes it on the title-
page of the *Philosophical Fragments* (1844), a work which deals
urgently with the question of faith and history.[1] Faith, he insists,
is not founded upon historical research, which can neither verify
nor refute it. Faith is the acceptance of an 'absolute paradox' or
'basic absurdity', namely, that the Eternal Truth has entered
history, that God has been born an infant and grown to manhood
as other men do. The contemporaries of Jesus were in no better
position to understand this paradox than are those who live
eighteen centuries afterwards, for it can be known only subjectively, not historically; those who accept the paradox of faith are
as 'contemporary' with Jesus as were the apostles themselves.
The labour of scholars who seek to reconstruct the historical life
of Jesus is irrelevant to the understanding of the paradox, since
even the most brilliant reconstruction would yield only approxi-
mate results and would therefore provide an insecure basis for
man's eternal happiness. The God-Man is not a 'truth of reason'

[1] Eng. trans. by David F. Swenson, Oxford and New York, 1936.

but an object of faith. Kierkegaard's answer to Lessing is therefore that 'the object of faith is the reality of the God-Man in the
sense of his existence: but existence involves particularity, and
the particular cannot be thought, but only the universal: the
object of faith is thus God's reality in existence as a particular
individual, the fact that God has existed as an individual human
being'.[1] The absolute paradox can therefore be known only by
being believed on the attestation of the apostles; it is impossible
to attain objective knowledge by historical research into the life
of Jesus. Subjectivity is truth. An individual can do no more than
testify that he has believed the paradox, and this is enough. Therefore Kierkegaard's answer to the scepticism of Strauss is simply
this: 'If the contemporary generation had left nothing behind
them but these words, "We have believed that in such and such a
year God appeared among us in the humble figure of a servant,
that he lived and taught in our community, and finally died", it
would be more than enough. The contemporary generation
would have done all that was necessary; for this little advertisement, this *nota bene* on a page of universal history, would be
sufficient to afford an occasion for a successor, and the most volu-
minous account can in all eternity do nothing more.'[2] The fact
that we have no objective certainty about the Jesus of history is
irrelevant to our faith in him. As Bultmann was to say nearly a
hundred years later, 'To understand Jesus all that is necessary is
to proclaim that he has come.'[3]

Kierkegaard's influence upon his own century was slight. How
far he has directly influenced the theologians of the twentieth
century is an open question, but at least he was prophetic in this
sense: like the white mice which were formerly carried aboard
submarines, he exhibited symptoms of distress long before normal
human beings had become aware of the noxious elements in the
atmosphere. After 1919, the year of the publication of Barth's
Römerbrief,[4] which is generally said to have brought the 'century
of Schleiermacher' to an end, European theologians, led by Barth,
became aware of these noxious elements and an immense posthu-

---

[1] *Concluding Unscientific Postscript to the Philosophical Fragments* (1846); Eng.
trans. by David F. Swenson, Princeton Univ. Press, 1941.

[2] *Philosophical Fragments,* 87. See further, Hermann Diem, *Kierkegaard's
Dialectic of Existence,* Edinburgh, 1959, 81–100.

[3] See below, 140.

[4] Eng. trans. by E. C. Hoskyns, *The Epistle to the Romans,* Oxford, 1932.

mous interest in Kierkegaard was awakened. Though the new 'neo-orthodox' theologians departed widely from many of Kierkegaard's characteristic positions, they took the same general direction; they attempted to disengage Christian faith from the relativities of history. Though they differed considerably from one another in standpoint, they shared a certain common feature: they carried over, as happens in almost all strong reactions, an important element in the outlook from which they were reacting. More precisely, they carried over the old assumptions of the positivistic attitude towards history, without subjecting it to radical criticism, and thus adopting a submissive attitude towards it. Instead of asking what the fact of divine revelation through historical events implies for our conception of history, they have exhibited a tendency to assume the 'scientific' validity of positivist notions of history, and then, finding that there is no standing-ground for revelation within such a conception of history, to look around for a sphere of super-history or of existential encounter in which the salvation events may have taken place. The attitude of such dominant theologians of the first half of the twentieth century as Tillich, Brunner, Barth and Bultmann represents in one form or another a disengagement of theology from history.[1]

Tillich and 'the Centre of History'

Paul Tillich was born in 1886, as also was Barth; Brunner was born three years later; Bultmann was born in 1884. During their

[1] Reinhold Niebuhr, who is indeed one of the dominant theologians of the period, should not be included among those who seek a disengagement from history. Though he holds that 'the centre, source and fulfilment of history lie beyond history', he insists that 'the Christian faith is centred upon one who was born in a manger and died upon the cross' (cf. the preface to *Beyond Tragedy: Essays on the Christian Interpretation of History*, New York, 1937). Myth is for him an important category of understanding, but he does not suggest that the events of the biblical history are myths. On the contrary, he maintains that the biblical history is the clue to all history. The whole character of the Christian religion is involved in the affirmation that the Word became flesh. This affirmation 'declares that an event in history can be of such a character as to reveal the character of history itself; that without such a revelation the character of history cannot be known. It is not possible to arrive at an understanding of the meaning of life and history without such a revelation' (ibid., 13f.). Again, 'the Christian faith begins with, and is founded upon, the affirmation that the life, death and resurrection of Christ represent an event in history, in and through which a disclosure of the whole meaning of history occurs' (*Faith and History: a Comparison of Christian and Modern Views of History*, 26).

formative years the influence of Ritschlianism, or Liberal Protestantism of the Harnack type, was paramount. On the one hand,
there was confidence in the ability of historical research to uncover
for us the wonderful personality of Jesus and the impression
which he made upon his contemporaries as the source of the
abiding religious experience which Christians still enjoy.[1] On the
other hand, under the influence of the *religionsgeschichtliche Schule*
(the 'History of Religion School') of W. Bousset, R. Reitzenstein,
W. Heitmüller and others, there developed a disposition to regard
the particular events in the Gospel history—a virgin birth,
miraculous healings and other portents, the resurrection of a dead
teacher and his marvellous ascension into heaven—as instances of
the general tendency of all religion to proliferate legendary and
miraculous occurrences for the edification of the faithful; they
are data not for the constructive theologian but for the comparative study of religion. Behind this disposition the assumptions
of positivism are not difficult to discern: particular historical
instances, even if they could be held to be credible in themselves,
are of no significance until they are seen in the light of general
laws, just as particular occurrences in the natural order are meaningless until they are subsumed under the laws of physics and
chemistry. The biblical history was to be explained according to
the laws of the development of religion in general, as enunciated
by the science of 'comparative religion', and whatever would not
conform to these general laws must be explained away. Positivist
philosophy has no room for the action of God as a category of
historical explanation. When, after the First World War, the
methods of form-criticism (long ago developed by H. Gunkel and
other leaders of the *religionsgeschichtliche Schule* in the study of the
Old Testament[2]) were applied to the study of the Gospels, it was
the positivist assumptions in the minds of the leading form-
critics which led to scepticism concerning the possibility of any

[1] Donald Baillie quotes Principal A. M. Fairbairn (1838–1912), *Christ in
Modern Theology*, 1893, 3f.: 'We feel Him more in our theology because we
know Him better in history. His historical reality and significance have
broken upon us with something of the surprise of a discovery. It is certainly
not too much to say: He is today more studied and better known as He was
and as He lived than at any period between now and the first age of the
Church.' See D. M. Baillie, *God Was in Christ*, 33; chapter II contains an
excellent discussion of this whole subject.

[2] See A. R. Johnson in *The Old Testament and Modern Study*, ed. H. H.
Rowley, Oxford, 1951, 162–81.

real knowledge of the historical Jesus; there is nothing in form-criticism as a literary method which determines the historical truth or falsehood of the narratives under discussion. The discovery that our historical records of Jesus are themselves the products of the faith of the early Church does not of itself imply that they are useless as sources of historical knowledge about Jesus, as Tillich, following the early form-critics, still assumes.[1] The *ultimate* conclusions, as distinct from mediate ones, drawn from the employment of any strictly scientific literary or historical method do not follow from the use of the method itself but from the assumptions which are brought initially to the study. The original form-critics brought with them the positivist assumptions of the *religionsgeschichtliche Schule* of which they were the leaders or in which they spent their formative years. These assumptions appeared to Continental theologians in the period between the two World Wars not as the dogmas of positivist philosophy but as the postulates of scientific historiography as such. As T. E. Hulme remarked, 'there are certain doctrines which for a certain period seem not doctrines, but inevitable categories of the human mind. . . . People do not see them, but other things *through* them.'[2]

Long before the appearance of the New Testament form-critics, Tillich had concluded that the historical facts of the life of Jesus were far too dubious to be used as a foundation for Christian theology; and he was therefore driven into opposition to Liberal dogmatics, which had sought to replace the crucified Christ by the historical Jesus.[3] It was, in fact, Albert Schweitzer who had convinced him that the historical truth about Jesus could never be reconstructed, and the conviction has remained with him.[4] The Christological question is entirely independent of the problems of historical enquiry into the facts behind the biblical picture of Christ. 'The exposition of these facts,' he says, 'can lend only probability—and with respect to the historical Jesus, a very faint probability.'[5] He develops his conception of Christ as 'the centre of history', which, he says, must be made visible, not by historical research, but by being shown to be the

[1] *Systematic Theology II*, New York and London, 1957, 101–17.
[2] *Speculations*, ed. Herbert Read, 2nd ed., London, 1936, 50f.
[3] *The Interpretation of History*, New York, 1936, 110.
[4] *Systematic Theology*, II, 102–6.
[5] *The Interpretation of History*, 265.

power that gives meaning to our existence and overcomes 'the threat of meaninglessness'. He tells us that 'to look at this centre, to interpret it, to relate it through negations and affirmations to the whole of history, to make its claims comprehensible and to argue for the superiority of its claim in theory and practice—that is Christology today'.[1] Such statements read like a despairing attempt to replace the vanished Jesus of history by a Christ-Principle which, though the 'centre' of history, is nevertheless beyond history, a *gnosis* from an ontological realm which cannot be assailed by the acids of historical criticism. At any rate, Tillich is quite clear that, whatever the basis of the Christian faith may be, it has very little to do with history in the ordinary sense of the word. He says explicitly, 'the foundation of Christian belief is not the historical Jesus, but the biblical picture of Christ. The criterion of human thought and action is not the constantly changing and artificial product of historical research, but the picture of Christ as it is rooted in ecclesiastical belief and human experience.'[2]

It is no part of our purpose to follow Tillich into the realm of ontological shadows into which he ascends out of the world of history. Most modern folk, hearing that the Gospel history deals only in very faint probabilities, are unlikely to find reassurance in speculation. Professor John McIntyre has pointed out that a logically permissible contrary of Tillich's words about 'a very faint probability' would be the statement that 'the exposition of the facts about the historical Jesus can lead only to a high degree of

[1] Ibid.

[2] Ibid., 34. We are reminded here of the remarkable book of Tillich's old teacher, Martin Kähler, *Der sogenannte historische Jesus und der geschichtliche biblische Christus*, Leipzig, 1892, 2nd ed., 1896. On its original appearance it was greeted with disfavour because its attack on the Liberal 'lives of Jesus' was thought to be destructively sceptical. It anticipated many of the positions of the form-critics and of the subsequent kerygma theology; in recent years it has attracted more attention than at its first appearance; the first edition was re-issued in 1953. Kähler maintained that faith does not rest upon the tortured and uncertain conclusions of the subjective 'lives' and that limits must be set to the 'papal pretensions' of the historians (73–5). The real Christ is not a supposed Jesus *behind* the Gospels, but the Christ whom the apostles preached, the Christ of the whole of the New Testament, the Christ of faith (63–66); the *biblical* Christ is the only historically credible Christ (96). But, unlike Tillich and Bultmann, Kähler held that the Gospel picture of Jesus represents the true and imperishable impression which the Man Jesus left upon history (78f., 87–79). For a discussion of Kähler's position see Paul Althaus, *The So-Called Kerygma and the Historical Jesus*, Eng. trans. by David Cairns, Edinburgh, 1959, 19–37.

improbability'.[1] If it is highly improbable that Jesus ever lived, then it is highly improbable that the Incarnation ever happened. 'It is curious that a movement which rebelled against the Liberal anti-historical tendencies should fall into precisely the same errors. . . . The neo-Orthodox have produced a view of history which leaves little room for the Word to enter, and none for him to leave traces of his having been there.'[2] Christ is related to history at large, but not to that portion of history where the Church proclaims that he actually appeared. The author of a fine expository and critical study of Tillich's thought has recently concluded that 'Tillich has simply not been radical enough in criticizing Liberal theology. He has not seen that historians who doubt the value of the records have failed to establish their point. Here, Paul Tillich remains a child of his generation, a victim of the historicism of the last century.'[3]

Brunner, Barth and the 'Heilsgeschichte'

Emil Brunner and Karl Barth share Tillich's Cartesian scepticism concerning the possibility of historical knowledge, but unlike him they have inherited the Ritschlian distrust of metaphysics. The miraculous revelation of the Word of God assures them (as speculation could not) of a realm of super-history where the saving events of the Gospel have taken place. These saving events have occurred on a different plane of history from that which secular historical method can investigate, and consequently the activities of Jesus during his earthly life have at best only a marginal bearing upon the faith of Christians. Though Brunner and

[1] 'Christ and History' in *The Reformed Theological Review*, Melbourne, Victoria, Australia, Vol. VIII, No. 3 (August 1949), 15.

[2] Ibid., 16.

[3] George H. Tavard, *Paul Tillich and the Christian Message*, London, 1962, 112. By 'historicism' here Tavard means what we have called positivistic historiography. He adds that Tillich has failed to show the meaning of history because 'his interpretation of the Christ as the appearance of essence in the conditions of existence, of the New Being in the garb of the old, has given his historical analysis a philosophical slant which is both disappointing and misleading'. In his *Systematic Theology* Tillich has laid stress on the transhistorical New Being, insisting on the ontological more than on the historical dimension of Jesus as the Christ (ibid.). Cf. Tillich, *Systematic Theology* II, 114: 'Participation, not historical argument, guarantees the reality of the event on which Christianity is based. It guarantees a personal life in which the New Being has conquered the old being. But it does not guarantee his name to be Jesus of Nazareth.'

Barth differ on certain theological questions, which seem very important to them,[1] their basic affinity is founded upon their shared attitude towards the historical basis of the biblical revelation.

Like Tillich, Brunner was oppressed by the thought that history deals only in probabilities. 'Dependence on history as a science leads to a state of hopeless uncertainty. Therefore, when a thoughtful person refuses to build his relation to the eternal on anything so unsafe as historical science, he is acting rightly; for such building is indeed a glaring example of building one's house upon the sand.'[2] Faith in Christ, Brunner admits, depends upon the historicity of certain facts—for example, the crucifixion— 'although with regard to these facts there is only a relative certainty, that is (from the historical point of view) a mere probability'.[3] The most that can be said is that historians have never produced the disproof of these facts; the Christian believer has inner grounds for the conviction that they will never be able to do so. It is a misunderstanding to regard the object of Christian faith as a fact of history.[4] The preference of nineteenth-century theologians for the Synoptic Gospels is a sign of their bondage to the historical point of view. Faith is not concerned with the Jesus of history, as historical science sees him; the only adequate basis of the Christian faith is the witness of Scripture as a whole, which includes witness to the resurrection. The latter would not seem to be a fact of history, since 'the historian lacks knowledge of the resurrection'.[5] Thus, Brunner places himself decisively in the long line of European theologians stretching from Ferdinand Christian Baur, the founder of the Tübingen School, to Günther Bornkamm today, who regard it as axiomatic that the resurrection of Christ lies outside the sphere of historical scholarship. Brunner assumes without questioning that 'the historian' works only within the positivist rules concerning the limits of the historically permissible, and the historian is contrasted with 'the believer'.

---

[1] See footnote on p. 127 of Alan Richardson, *Christian Apologetics*, London, 1947, or, for more detail, Peter Fraenkel, *Natural Theology*, London 1946.

[2] *The Mediator*, Eng. trans. by O. Wyon (London, 1934) of E. Brunner, *Der Mittler*, 1927, 156.

[3] Ibid., 168.

[4] Ibid., 156.

[5] Ibid., 159.

'It is of the very essence of revelation and of faith that we should become Christians not through the historical picture of Jesus but through the picture traced by the Gospels in the light of the resurrection faith.'[1] The manner of verifying historical facts (such as the crucifixion) differs for faith and for historical science; facts which for the latter have only probability carry for the believer absolute certainty.[2] Because the validity of Christian faith does not rest upon historical science, there can be no conflict between criticism and faith. The believer as such, indeed, has no historical interest: 'the Christian faith has just as little to do with the influence of Jesus on the history of the world as it has to do with his historical personality. It is not interested in "the Founder of Christianity", nor his influence upon history.'[3] In the ordinary sense of the word 'history' the Christian faith is not concerned with history at all.[4] History in its secular sense merely represents humanity as a whole in its need of redemption.

But there is apparently another sense of the word 'history' which is peculiar to Christian faith and cannot be understood apart from it. There is only one example of history in this special Christian sense, namely, the Incarnation of God in Jesus Christ. This is a unique event, not merely in the way that some philosophers have said that all historical events are unique (as contrasted with occurrences in the natural order). It is unique because the Incarnation of God happened only once. Moreover, it is a fact in the world of facts, although it is of an order which cannot be investigated by historians. This means that the believer cannot make or unmake facts at will, because the unique fact of Jesus Christ is given once for all in the scriptural revelation. 'Our relation to Jesus is not a particular instance of our general attitude to history; it does not form part of a reverent attitude to history as such. Owing to this element of uniqueness, indeed, this particular instance is completely isolated. And the Christian faith *is* this special relation to this unique event, as to something absolutely unique, and thus to it alone.'[5] In this way Brunner is driven to offer an alternative definition of Christian faith in place of the robust declaration of the New Testament and of the historic

[1] Ibid.
[2] Ibid., 165.
[3] Ibid., 81.
[4] Ibid., 153.
[5] Ibid., 154.

Creeds that God raised Jesus Christ from the dead in the very
midst of ordinary, everyday, secular history. The Ritschlian
ignoring and undervaluing of the Old Testament is conspicuous
in Brunner's isolating of the 'absolutely unique event' of the
Incarnation not only from profane history but also from the
acts of God to which the kerygma of the Old Testament bears
witness. And so he escapes from his entanglement in positivist notions about general laws of history by flight into a realm of
Heilsgeschichte, or supra-history, where the critics cease from
troubling and the faithful are at rest. But he also evades the biblical affirmations about the living God who acts in the history of
this world.[1] Against all such attempted solutions of the problem
of criticism and faith, we must insist that there is only one history,
and that if it is incredible that the acts of God were worked in it,
then the revelation in Christ cannot be salvaged by recourse to a
Heilsgeschichte that runs parallel to secular history, never really
intersecting it, and inaccessible save through some extra-historical
perception known as faith.

Karl Barth in his reaction against the Liberal view that faith in
Christ was founded upon the historical Jesus has in many respects
gone further than any other twentieth-century theologian towards
the total disengagement of faith from history. He does not believe
in the 'wonderful personality' of Jesus at all. In a widely quoted
passage in the first half-volume of his *Dogmatik* (1932) he wrote of
'the Rabbi of Nazareth, historically so difficult to get information
about, and when it is got, one whose activity is so easily a little
commonplace alongside more than one other founder of a religion
and even alongside many later representatives of his own "religion"'.[2] He was gratified by the scepticism of the form-critics
concerning the possibility of any genuine knowledge of the
historical Jesus, since this had destroyed the 'Jesus-cult' which the
Liberals had fostered. The personality of Jesus is wholly irrele-

[1] It should be noted that there is another and quite unexceptionable sense
of the expression *Heilsgeschichte*, namely, to refer to the acts of God for our
salvation in the midst of the history of our world. It is in this acceptable sense
that it is used, for example, by Oscar Cullmann in his *Christology of the New
Testament* (Eng. trans., 1959), *passim*. See also chap. VI, 'The *Heilsgeschichte*
Theology', in Alan Richardson, *The Bible in the Age of Science*, 122–41. The
undefined use of this ambiguous expression has created much confusion.

[2] Eng. trans., *The Doctrine of the Word of God*, *Church Dogmatics* Vol. I,
Part I, Edinburgh, 1936, 188.

vant to the Christian faith, and it is a matter for satisfaction that criticism is no longer committed to 'chasing the ghost of an historical Jesus in the vacuum behind the New Testament'.[1] The so-called historical Jesus is only the figment of the imagination of this or that historian; the real Jesus, as he actually was, remains unknown because of the lack of authentic information. As the person of Jesus was quite unremarkable, so also is his recorded teaching; it can be paralleled in the sayings of other religious and ethical leaders, and in any case it achieved little. In the earthly life of Jesus there is no revelation of God; on the contrary, there is in it a veiling of God, a hiding of the divine form. The revelation of God is hidden in history, not made manifest by it. We can therefore afford to be indifferent to the conclusions of the historical critics; their researches are irrelevant to the faith of the believer.

But all this does not, of course, mean that Christ is a non-historical being; on the contrary, that the Word became flesh, that God entered history, is the very centre of the Christian faith. What it means is that 'the miracle of Christmas' is not accessible to historical investigation and can be neither proved nor disproved by it. The revelation of God takes place not in the public history of this world, but in a supra-history beyond it; that which is veiled in the historical life of Jesus is made manifest in the events of the Resurrection and of the Great Forty Days, as indeed it had been indicated in the preceding sacred history, the Virgin Birth of Christ, his Miracles and Transfiguration. The *Deus absconditus* has come forth out of his utter hiddenness and has become the *Deus revelatus*; at the Incarnation he veiled himself in the history of the world and at Easter he unveiled himself in the miracle of the Resurrection. The Virgin Birth indicates and the Empty Tomb demonstrates that God has disclosed himself to the eyes of faith.[2] All the affirmations of the Christian faith concerning Jesus, for example, his sinlessness, do not rest upon empirical observation but upon faith in the Word of God; beside them such affirmations as historians may find themselves able to make concerning him are of no particular interest to the believer, since they do not concern the real, historical Christ. 'The real historical Christ is none other than the biblical Christ attested by the New Testament, that

[1] *The Doctrine of the Word of God, Church Dogmatics*, Eng. trans., Vol. I, Part II, Edinburgh, 1956, 65.
[2] Op. cit., Vol. I, Part II, 181–3.

is, the incarnate Word, the risen and exalted one, God manifested in his redeeming action as the object of his disciples' faith.'[1] As the years have passed, this emphasis upon the real historicity of the salvation-events has become even stronger in the later volumes of the *Dogmatik*. For instance, in the volume on 'The Doctrine of Reconciliation' which Barth completed in 1953 we read: 'The atonement is history. . . . To speak of it we must tell it as history. To try to grasp it as supra-historical or non-historical truth is not to grasp it at all. It is indeed truth, but truth actualized in a history and revealed in this history as such—revealed therefore as history. But the atonement is the very special history of God with man, the very special history of man with God. As such it has a peculiar character. . . . The atonement takes precedence of all other history. . . . To say atonement is to say Jesus Christ. To speak of it is to speak of his history. . . . What takes place in this history—the accusation and conviction of man as a lost sinner, his restoration, the founding and maintaining and sending of the community of God in the world, the new obedience of man—is all decided and ordained by him as the one who primarily acts and speaks in it. . . .'[2] What is clear from such passages as this is that, although this history is said not to be 'supra-historical', it cannot conceivably be the history which historians are engaged upon in the ordinary course of their work.

In truth it is very difficult to understand what Barth means by history or to relate his 'very special history' to the history which historians actually investigate day by day. The difficulty is that of attaching any meaning at all to the idea of historical happenings which are *in principle* beyond the reach of the historian, or of conceiving some kind of Platonic realm of historical essences to which the historian *qua* historian has no access. Is not Barth really talking about interpretations of certain historical events, which historians can investigate, but about which they differ according as to whether they are believers or unbelievers? But in that case the investigation of the historical events by historians, whether Christian or non-Christian, would assume truly critical importance, and this would invalidate everything Barth has said about the irrelevance of historical criticism. Is any other view than this intelligible at all? There is, indeed, another *possible* view, namely,

[1] Ibid., 64.
[2] *Church Dogmatics*, Vol. IV, Part I, Eng. trans., Edinburgh, 1956, 157f.

Bultmann's existentialist view; and the passage which we have just quoted from Barth was doubtless written with Bultmann's teaching in mind and in deliberate repudiation of it.[1] In an Excursus in an earlier volume of the *Dogmatik*[2] Barth had criticized Bultmann's existentialist view of history, and Bultmann replied in his essay on 'The Problem of Hermeneutics'[3] written in 1950. In the latter Bultmann asks that Barth should give an account of the 'abstract categories' which he uses in setting up his view of history. 'He concedes to me', Bultmann writes, 'that the resurrection of Jesus is not an historical fact which can be established by means at the disposal of historical science. But from this he thinks it does not follow that it did not happen. History of this kind may well have happened. We may well accept as history that which good taste prevents us from calling " 'historical' fact", and which the modern historian will call "saga" or "legend" on the ground that it is beyond the reach of his methods, to say nothing of his unavowed assumptions.[4] My question is, what does Barth understand by "have happened" and "history"? What kind of events are those about which it can be said that they "have really taken place as history in time far more certainly than everything which the historian can establish as such"?[5] It is perfectly clear that Barth is interpreting the pronouncements of Scripture by means of an imported body of abstract categories. What is the origin and meaning of this apparatus of abstract thought?'[6] The question remains whether Bultmann himself fares any more satisfactorily with a theology for which 'the resurrection of Jesus is not an historical fact', and whether he is able to answer convincingly

---

[1] As is suggested by Heinrich Ott in *Kerygma and Myth*, II, ed. H.-W. Bartsch, Eng. trans. by R. H. Fuller, London, 1962, 325. Note also Barth's own acknowledgment in his Foreword to *The Doctrine of Reconciliation* that Bultmann's 'subject' is 'always present', even where he has consciously ignored him (p. ix).

[2] Vol. III, Part II, 1948, 534–7; Eng. trans., 1960, 443–7.

[3] To be found in *Essays Philosophical and Theological*, Eng. trans. by J. C. G. Greig (of Bultmann's *Glaube und Verstehen*, II, 1952), London, 1955, 234–61.

[4] This quotation is from Barth's *Church Dogmatics*, Vol. III, Part II, Eng. trans. 446.

[5] The quotation is from ibid., 535f. In Vol. IV, Part I, Eng. trans., 334–7, Barth speaks of the events of salvation history as 'pre-historical'—like the creation-story they are from the viewpoint of modern scholarship 'saga' or 'legend'. He says that 'the death of Jesus Christ can certainly be thought of as history in the modern sense, but not the resurrection' (336).

[6] *Essays Philosophical and Theological*, 260.

the criticisms which Barth and others have made of his own existentialist position.[1]

It is doubtful whether historians generally, including Christian historians, would find the notion of a 'real history' behind their own history any more attractive than the old Bossuet-type of explanation by means of 'the finger of God'. Mr E. H. Carr, however, rejecting the view that religion may be treated like the joker in the pack of cards, to be reserved for really important tricks that cannot be taken in any other way, commends Barth for having 'pronounced a total separation between divine and secular history, and handed over the latter to the secular arm'.[2] But it is likely that most Christian historians would have serious misgivings about earning Mr Carr's commendation in this way. Doubtless Barth is expressing in his own language, a language in which words do not bear their normal everyday meaning, many profound truths which Christians sincerely believe; but unless one takes the trouble to learn the Barthian language, these truths remain unilluminated. Barth's talk about a real history in which events happen which are nevertheless conceded not to be historical facts creates so many pseudo-problems—that is, problems of a purely linguistic order—that we never get through to the only question which really matters, the question whether God has or has not revealed himself in the history which *historians* talk about. 'Secular' historians will fold their arms and conclude that Christians have abandoned the claim that God has acted in history. And this is not what Barth intends to say. What he means to say is that God's action in history is not capable of investigation by the methods of historical research which are used in the investigation of the action of, say, economic or social forces. And in this, of course, he is right. It was necessary for Barth to say this insistently thirty or forty years ago, when the idea that Christian truth could be established by historical evidence still lingered in certain Liberal quarters. Barth has made his point emphatically; and it would be hard to name any serious theologian who today believes that Christian truth can be verified by 'objective' historical research. But to say that Christian truth cannot be attained by

[1] Barth's criticism was continued in *Rudolf Bultmann, ein Versuch ihn zu verstehen* (Zürich, 1952), of which an Eng. trans. will be found in *Kerygma and Myth*, II, 83–132.

[2] *What is History?*, 69.

historical enquiry apart from the insight of faith is a very different thing from saying that the historical facts which criticism can investigate are irrelevant to Christian belief. To say the latter is to agree with Schweitzer that 'it is not Jesus as historically known who is significant for our time and can help it. . . . The abiding and eternal in Jesus is absolutely independent of historical knowledge.' The course of theological discussion in European Protestantism itself during the last two decades seems to point to a growing dissatisfaction with Schweitzer's conclusion.

Bultmann and the Kerygma Theology

Rudolf Bultmann has written much on the theme of history, but there are certain obscurities and even contradictions in his works and it is scarcely possible to be sure what his real meaning is. Even his most ardent apologists admit that he has made statements that are inconsistent with what they take to be his 'real intention'.[1] His earlier work, in what was then the new form-criticism, was done while he was under the influence of the *religionsgeschichtliche* school, which tended to regard early Christianity as merely one of the cults of a dying-and-rising god which flourished in the Hellenistic world; its symbolic truth was connected only accidentally with the historical Jesus of Nazareth. Indeed, Bultmann edited the posthumous second edition of the leading exposition of this view, Wilhelm Bousset's *Kyrios Christos* (1913), which appeared in the same year as the first edition of his own *Geschichte der synoptischen Tradition*, namely, 1921.[2] In the English-speaking world it is widely held that Bultmann's subsequent adoption of an existentialist theology represents a genuinely evangelical attempt to escape from the negative and sceptical consequences of his fundamentally positivistic Gospel-criticism, even though it is achieved at the expense of divorcing the kerygma of the Church from any possible sources of it in the life and teaching of Jesus. Bultmann and his apologists, however, deny this.[3] The decisive event in Bultmann's transition from the *religionsgeschichtliche* to the existentialist point of view was the

---

[1] E.g. Schubert M. Ogden, *Existence and Faith*, New York, 1960, 20f.

[2] Third ed., Göttingen, 1947; Eng. trans. by John Marsh, Oxford, 1963.

[3] R. Bultmann, *Glauben und Verstehen*, I, 1933, 101; James M. Robinson, *A New Quest of the Historical Jesus*, London, 1959, 74f.; S. M. Ogden, op. cit., 11f.

publication of Barth's *Epistle to the Romans* in 1919.[1] In the famous debate between Barth and Harnack in *Die Christliche Welt* (1923)[2] Bultmann already stood on Barth's side. Both rejoiced that the quest of the historical Jesus had ended in failure, because the attempt to achieve security by means of scientific historical investigation was a form of unfaith and therefore an illegitimate theological procedure. Faith was not a favourable assessment of historical probabilities but a response to the proclamation of the Word of God in the living present. Bultmann rejected the *religionsgeschichtliche* view that the historical reality of Jesus himself was irrelevant because Jesus was significant only as the symbol of a religious attitude; on the contrary, he maintained, the 'happenedness' of 'the Christ-event' is essential to the Christian faith.

But Bultmann also maintained that the factual *details* of the life of Jesus are a matter of historical probability only, and are irrelevant to faith in the Christ *event*: 'To understand Jesus all that is necessary is to proclaim that he has come.'[3] The Gospels do not mediate an historical encounter with the historical Jesus. In order to understand this attitude we should note that the expression 'the historical Jesus' is ambiguous and may mean either Jesus as he really was (the Jesus whom the nineteenth-century 'quest' sought to recover) or the Jesus who can be pieced together by means of scientific historical criticism. When, more than a generation ago, Bultmann in a notorious passage wrote that about the historical person of Jesus we can know 'virtually nothing',[4] he probably intended the former of these meanings, since in his other writings he has told us something about the Jesus who can be known by means of historical research as he has practised it. He intends to say that Christianity is not a 'personality cult' of Jesus and that all the psychologizing 'lives' of him are worthless alike from the standpoints of scientific history and of Christian faith.[5] But equally the scientific account of the historical Jesus is

---

[1] Cf. Bultmann's review of this work in *Die Christliche Welt*, XXXVI, 1922.

[2] Reprinted in K. Barth, *Gesammelte Vorträge*, III, 1957, *Theologische Fragen und Antworten*, 'Ein Briefwechsel mit Adolf von Harnack', 7–31.

[3] *Kerygma and Myth*, I, ed. by H. W. Bartsch, Eng. trans. by R. H. Fuller, London, 1953, 117.

[4] *Jesus*, Berlin, 1926, 12 (Eng. trans., *Jesus and the Word*, London, 1935, 8).

[5] Cf. James M. Robinson, op. cit., 19n., who cites what Bultmann wrote in 1927: 'The Christ according to the flesh does not concern us; how things looked in Jesus' heart I do not know and do not wish to know' (*Glaube und Verstehen*, I, 1933, 101).

not kerygma and is not the object of Christian faith. It is at this point that the process of disengagement from history becomes marked. Our scientific knowledge of Jesus is a matter of probability and is irrelevant to the proclamation of faith in Christ. With one half of his mind Bultmann remains firmly in the old positivistic tradition of Ritschlian liberalism; this is the part which he uses when he is engaged upon his scientific historical criticism. The kerygma must not be used as a source of knowledge concerning the historical Jesus.[1] As recently as 1957 Bultmann could write that dogmatic presuppositions must not be allowed to answer such questions as whether Jesus was conscious of being the Messiah: 'any such Messianic consciousness would be an historical fact and could only be exhibited as such by historical research. Were the latter able to make it probable that Jesus knew himself to be the Messiah, this result would have only relative certainty, for historical research can never endow it with absolute validity. . . .'[2] The nineteenth-century conception of 'facts' as the objects of historical research and the rationalist insistence upon the relativity of all historical knowledge take precedence over any twentieth-century insights concerning the nature of historical facts as judgments of evidence which are not merely conditioned but actually made possible by the personal standpoint (or faith) of the particular historian. Moreover, though absolutely presuppositionless history is agreed to be impossible, 'dogmatic' (i.e. Nicene or Chalcedonian) presuppositions are on principle excluded, while the old Liberal presuppositions are accepted as 'scientific'. It is a 'dogma' of Liberal criticism that any kerygmatic or Christological statements that appear in the Gospels—such as that Jesus thought of himself as the Messiah—must be deemed to be unhistorical, since they must be a reading back of the kerygma of the post-Easter Church into the life and times of Jesus. Any other standpoint appears 'unscientific' in the eyes of Bultmann's entourage. Thus, it is difficult to gain a hearing for an alternative hypothesis, such as that the theology of the New Testament as a whole is based primarily upon Jesus' own interpretation of his mission and person in the light of his understanding of the Old

[1] Cf. *Glaube und Verstehen*, I, 208.
[2] 'Ist voraussetzungslose Exegese möglich?' in *Theologische Zeitschrift*, XIII, 1957, 409–17; Eng. trans. in Schubert M. Ogden, *Existence and Faith*, 289–96.

Testament.[1] Such a suggestion appears hopelessly old-fashioned, even pre-critical, to those brought up in the neo-Ritschlian atmosphere breathed today by many Continental New Testament scholars.[2] It would be as easy as it is futile to indulge in mutual charges of being old-fashioned: on the one side 'Ritschlian', 'Liberal' and so on, and on the other side 'dogmatic', 'pre-critical' and the like. In our view the only true historical method is to frame various hypotheses (which are not to be adopted or dismissed as 'dogmatic' presuppositions) and then to test them by critical methods with a view to discovering which of them most satisfactorily explains the New Testament evidence. This is the way in which historians do, in fact, arrive at their interpretations of evidence or historical explanations; the notion that they first discover 'facts' and then exhibit their causal connections (Taine's maxim) is no longer acceptable amongst historians themselves.[3]

In his essay 'Is Exegesis without Presuppositions Possible?'[4] Bultmann tells us that the exegete should eliminate his own individuality or personal standpoint as he seeks to understand the text, but that he cannot dismiss the historical method, since the latter is presupposed by the fact that exegesis is a part of the science of history. 'The historical method includes the presupposition that history is a unity in the sense of a closed continuum of effects in which individual events are connected by the succession of cause and effect. . . . This closedness means that the continuum of historical happenings cannot be rent by the interference of supernatural, transcendent powers and that therefore there is no "miracle" in this sense of the word. Such a miracle would be an event whose cause did not lie within history. While, for example, the Old Testament narrative speaks of an interference by God in history, historical science cannot demonstrate such an act of God . . .; it can only leave every man free to determine whether he wants to see an act of God in an historical event that it itself understands in terms of that event's immanent historical

---

[1] This hypothesis forms the principle of interpretation which is put forward in Alan Richardson, *Introduction to the Theology of the New Testament*, London, 1958.

[2] Cf. the review by W. G. Kümmel of the volume referred to in the previous note in *Theologische Literaturzeitung*, 1960, Nr. 12, 922–6.

[3] Cf. Patrick Gardner, *The Nature of Historical Explanation*, London, 1952, 70–80; and see *infra*, 190ff.

[4] Schubert M. Ogden, op. cit., 289–96.

causes.'[1] Thus Bultmann in 1957 makes it very clear that he still adheres to the positivist conception of the nature of history which dominated the *religionsgeschichtliche Schule* of his youth and with which he has worked as a New Testament critic throughout his life. The historian, he tells us, cannot dispense with these presuppositions, because they are those of the historical method as such. It is at this point that the basic fallacy of Bultmann's whole position is located. His fundamental presuppositions concerning history are not the presuppositions of historical method as such but of the positivist conception of history. Recent discussion within the sphere of the critical philosophy of history, even though inconclusive as philosophical discussion usually is, has at least shown that other views of the nature of history and historical method are possible, and that the nineteenth-century positivist view is no longer the dominant conception amongst those philosophers and historians who have given attention to the problem. History is indeed a 'closed continuum' of causes and effects; but the action of God as a factor in historical causation is not to be ruled out on philosophical grounds in advance of the historical enquiry into the biblical evidence for it.

From his fundamental positivistic presuppositions all the characteristic features of Bultmann's theology follow. The demythologizing programme is necessary because the kerygma of the Bible affirms the acts of God in history; but since 'science' knows nothing of the acts of God, the biblical affirmations must be understood as mythological ways of expressing existential truths.[2] The testimony of the prophets and the apostles to the action of God in Israel's history (which, in Bultmann's view, has no special or unique interest for Christians)[3] is set aside as irrelevant to the task of historical explanation; and Bultmann on the basis of his acknowledged presuppositions reconstructs what he supposes to have been the way in which the obscure Galilean preacher, who summoned men to existential decision, was eventually transformed in second-century Catholicism into the Gnostic saviour God-man, who came down from heaven, imparted esoteric saving

[1] Ibid., 291f.

[2] Bultmann's lecture *Offenbarung and Heilsgeschehen*, which began the discussion about demythologizing in 1941, may be found as the opening essay, 'The New Testament and Mythology', in *Kerygma and Myth*, I, op. cit.

[3] See his essay on 'The Significance of the Old Testament for the Christian Faith' in *Glauben und Verstehen*, I.

gnosis, and finally ascended into heaven again. The theology of the New Testament is thus a curious amalgam of Jewish apocalyptic fanaticism and Hellenistic speculation concerning the Heavenly Man.[1] It is totally incredible to the modern man, who 'ought not to be burdened with the mythological element in Christianity. . . . The preaching of Christ must not remain a myth for him.'[2]

When the process of demythologizing is completed, we are left with 'Jesus the Word', not to be identified with the Jesus of history. The latter is not kerygma; the Gospels are not historical accounts of the life and work of Jesus, but forms under which it was natural to present the kerygma in the Hellenistic age. That is why they are inferior as historical sources. The Jesus whom they preach is not an historical figure but a present message, a kerygma which challenges us to existential decision. The salvation-event which meets us in the preaching is a present event, not an event of past history. This present event is the real substance of what Bultmann calls 'the Easter faith', rather curiously (as used to be said of Harnack) in view of the fact that nothing in particular happened on the Third Day. 'Christ meets us in the preaching as one crucified and risen. He meets us in the word of preaching and nowhere else. The faith of Easter is just this—faith in the word of preaching.'[3] The preaching brings to us a true understanding of our existence (in the full existentialist sense of that term, which is so hard to convey by means of the rather colourless English word), and this effects that change in our very being by which we pass from 'unauthentic' to 'authentic' existence.[4] Bultmann makes it very clear that Christ's resurrection is not a real event in history (not even a probable one!), such as he allows the crucifixion to have been: 'The resurrection is not itself an event of past history. All that criticism can establish is the fact that the disciples came

[1] Cf. Bultmann's *Theology of the New Testament*, Eng. trans. by Kendrick Grobel, 2 vols., 1952, 1955, New York and London.

[2] *Kerygma and Myth*, I, Eng. trans., 122.

[3] *Kerygma and Myth*, I, Eng. trans., 41.

[4] The use made by Bultmann of the existentialist philosophy of Martin Heidegger may be studied in Ian Henderson, *Myth in the New Testament*, London, 1952; John Macquarrie, *An Existentialist Theology: a Comparison of Heidegger and Bultmann*, London, 1955; L. Malevez, *The Christian Message and Myth: the Theology of Rudolf Bultmann*, London, 1958; H. P. Owen, *Revelation and Existence: a Study in the Theology of Rudolf Bultmann*, Cardiff, 1957. Cf. also Heinrich Ott, *Geschichte und Heilsgeschichte in der Theologie Rudolf Bultmanns*, Tübingen, 1955.

to believe in the resurrection. . . . The historical problem is scarcely relevant to Christian belief in the resurrection.'[1] The disengagement from history is complete: despite Bultmann's stress on the 'happenedness' of 'the salvation event', the kerygma (as he conceives it) is grounded neither upon the historical life of Jesus nor upon his historical resurrection.

Obviously the matter could not be left here. There must be some real historical connection between the kerygma of the apostolic Church and the life and teaching of Jesus. It is not surprising that Bultmann's own disciples, now amongst the most distinguished theological teachers in Germany, should during the last decade or so have devoted serious attention to the question. Out of their discussion has emerged what has come to be called 'the new quest of the historical Jesus'.[2] It is stressed that this new quest differs significantly from the old one; those who pursue it have not renounced the lesson which they had learnt from Bultmann, namely, that the Gospels are not reliable sources of biographical information about Jesus, but are primarily interpretations of the significance of Christ as the primitive Church had come to believe in him. There is some disagreement amongst Bultmann's apologists concerning the attitude of the master towards this development amongst his disciples. According to Ogden, the so-called 'new' quest was all along implicit in Bultmann's teaching; he had held from the start that Jesus' call to decision implied a Christology and that, whether or not Jesus thought of himself as Messiah, the Church rightly interpreted his intention by giving him that designation.[3] Robinson, on the other hand, speaks of Bultmann's 'shift in position' and says that he 'seems to have moved with the "post-Bultmannian" move of his pupils with regard to the historical Jesus and the kerygma'.[4] We may leave the ambiguities of the master's statements to the discretion of his interpreters; it is more relevant here to notice that the question was brought into the open by the publication of an

[1] *Kerygma and Myth*, I, Eng. trans., 42.

[2] A lucid and informative account of this development will be found in the monograph by James M. Robinson referred to above, *A New Quest of the Historical Jesus*.

[3] Schubert M. Ogden, op. cit., 11f.; cf. Bultmann, *Glauben und Verstehen*, I, 265f.

[4] Op. cit., 19–21.

address delivered by Ernst Käsemann in 1953,[1] whether in fact it
initiated a 'new' quest of the historical Jesus or not. Criticism is
able, Käsemann suggests, to distinguish between those elements
in the Gospel tradition which derived either from Judaism or
from the early Church and those which were original with Jesus;
it then appears that, though Jesus himself spoke in terms of his
divine mission rather than of his person, the Church correctly
interpreted what was implicit in his teaching when it proclaimed
him as Messiah and Son of God. Thus, historical investigation
can legitimately point to a real connexion between the historical
Jesus and the kerygma of the Church.

Ernst Fuchs and Günther Bornkamm are likewise distinguished
pupils of Bultmann's who have taken up a position analogous to
Käsemann's. Fuchs[2] sees in the *actions* of Jesus—for example,
eating with publicans and sinners—an implicit claim that God
was now in the last times drawing near to sinful humanity in
mercy and judgment; the parables and sayings of Jesus are to be
understood as commentary upon his deeds. The implicit eschatological understanding of Jesus' person and mission, which his
disciples had absorbed from him, became explicit in the kerygma
of the Church. Bornkamm stresses more particularly the *words* of
Jesus, but his deeds also can be historically and critically assessed:
'the Messianic character of his (Jesus') being is contained *in* his
words and deeds and *in* the unmediatedness of his historic
appearance'.[3] The implication of Jesus' life and words, that is to
say, is Messianic, even though it must be critically concluded that
the Messianic elements in the Gospel tradition reflect the post-
Easter kerygma. Thus, Bornkamm on the basis of rigorous critical
scholarship agrees that, though the Gospels do not furnish
psychological and biographical data for a life of Jesus in the old
sense, they supply sufficient historical evidence to justify the
conclusion that the Church's kerygma is firmly rooted in the
words and deeds of Jesus himself. Some such verdict as this seems

---

[1] 'Das Problem des historischen Jesus', *Zeitschrift für Theologie und Kirche*,
LI, 1954, 125–53.

[2] 'Die Frage nach dem historischen Jesus', *Zeitschrift für Theologie und
Kirche*, LIII, 1956, 210–29; Fuchs's writings on this theme since 1932 are
collected in his volume *Zur Frage nach dem historischen Jesus, Gesammelte
Aufsätze* II, Tübingen, 1960. (An English translation of selections from this
collection is in preparation.)

[3] *Jesus of Nazareth*, Eng. trans., 178.

to be the outcome of the intense discussion which has been taking place during the last few years.[1] Thus, W. G. Kümmel in his study of the eschatological teaching of Jesus concludes that in his own person, as well as in his words and deeds, there is a real eschatological presence, challenging men with God's 'now' which discloses the future as God's future.[2] In general, it seems true to say that there has been during the last decade a renewal of interest in the question of the historical element in the Gospels and a new appreciation of its theological importance. It is true that this new concern is entirely different from the subjective and unscientific interest of the older quest in the 'personality' and 'psychology' of Jesus and that there is radical discontinuity as well as continuity between the new quest and the old. The new attitude has made possible a rapprochement between exegetes and systematic theologians, who have for some time been experiencing a 'problem of communication' between the two sides.[3] Systematic theologians of Barthian affinities have turned their attention once more to the theological significance of the actual history of Jesus and his disciples as it may be known through scientific research.[4] Those who believe that the Christian faith stands or falls by its witness to what happened in history will find encouragement in these developments.

Existentialist Hermeneutics

For the 'post-Bultmannian' writers, faith cannot be made

[1] See Helmut Ristow and Karl Matthiae (eds.), *Der historische Jesus und der kerygmatische Christus*, Berlin, 1960, which contains essays by forty-eight New Testament scholars. An English translation by A. G. Hebert of Helmut Gollwitzer's essay, 'Der Glaube an Jesus Christus und der sogenannte historische Jesus', appeared in *Theology*, Vol. LXV, No. 501 (March 1962). See also H. W. Bartsch, *Das Historische Problem des Lebens Jesu* (Theologische Existenz Heute, Neue Folge, 78), Munich, 1960; Joachim Jeremias, 'The Present Position in the controversy concerning the Problem of the Historical Jesus' in *The Expository Times*, LXIX, No. 11 (August 1958); T. W. Manson, 'The Life of Jesus: Some tendencies in Present-day Research' in *The Background of the New Testament and its Eschatology* (ed. W. D. Davies and D. Daube), Cambridge, 1956, 211–21.

[2] *Promise and Fulfilment*, Eng. trans., London, 1957, 151–5.

[3] Cf. Hermann Diem, *Dogmatics*, Eng. trans. by Harold Knight, Edinburgh, 1959, 38–40.

[4] E. G. Hermann Diem, ibid. For further documentation see James M. Robinson, op. cit., 22–25, who speaks of the 'increasingly positive evaluation of history on the part of Karl Barth' and refers specifically to the basic Christological sections of his volumes on Reconciliation (*Church Dogmatics*, Vol. IV, Parts I and II).

dependent on the relativities of historical judgments. There is no
security in history (such as was the object of the old quest) which
enables us to avoid the decision about Christ. Lessing's *dictum* may
be brought up to date: 'Incidental truths of history can never
become the proof of kerygmatic truth.' Genuine faith, Bornkamm
tells us, is certainly not dependent on the course of New Testament research.[1] There is another kind of knowing upon which
faith depends, namely, existential knowledge. Just as by his words
Jesus confronted men with the immediacy of his own historical
presence, so that the response of faith was inexorably demanded
of them, so today, according to Bornkamm, the Jesus of the
Gospels confronts men here and now with his unmediated
presence and demands their commitment to his authority. In the
Gospels, then as now, Jesus' authority is always immediately and
authentically present. 'This encounter compels everyone to step
out of his customary background. This bringing to light of men
as they really are takes place in all the stories about Jesus.'[2] 'In
reading Bornkamm's *Jesus of Nazareth*', says a recent writer, 'we
feel that critical research has become unobtrusive, and has been
shifted from being an end in itself, producing faith, to being a
means towards letting the Gospels confront us with the person of
Jesus as the One who brings God near.'[3]

By urging that there is another kind of knowledge of Jesus in
addition to that provided by objective historical research the
Bultmann school does not mean that some historical knowledge
can be established by historical investigation while other historical
facts can be known by some non-historical perception, such as
faith. Such a view would be more like Barth's notion of a *Heilsgeschichte* inaccessible to secular historians. One of the strongest
emphases of the whole Bultmann group is its insistence that the
truth of the kerygma cannot be verified by historical research; all
that the new quest seeks to establish is that the historical Jesus

---

[1] *Jesus of Nazareth*, 15; cf. Fuchs's criticism in his article 'Glaube und
Geschichte' in *Zeitschrift für Theologie und Kirche*, LIV, 1957, 117–20. Bornkamm himself, of course, does not deprecate criticism as such; on the contrary, he practises it and says, 'It is precisely historical criticism which, rightly
understood, has opened up our way anew to this history, by disposing of
attempts along biographical, psychological lines. We can now see more
clearly' (ibid., 24).

[2] *Jesus of Nazareth*, 61.

[3] Hugh Anderson. 'Existential Hermeneutics' in *Interpretation, a Journal
of Bible and Theology*, Richmond, Virginia, XVI, 2 (April 1962), 155.

intended encounter with himself to be an eschatological encounter with God.[1] Confrontation with the historical Jesus was already confrontation in some sense with the kerygmatic Christ. Today the kerygmatic Christ confronts us in the word of preaching, that is, in the kerygma of the New Testament. According to Bultmann there is no need to postulate a special 'Christian' or 'theological' hermeneutic method. General hermeneutics as understood in the light of the existentialist phenomenology of man, or understanding of the human situation, is all that is required to make the issue clear. The understanding of the text before us (whether biblical or non-biblical) requires an openness on the part of the reader whereby he allows himself to be challenged and to have his existence called in question. Through such existential challenge the kerygma of the New Testament brings us to a new understanding of our existence, destroying all the false securities in which we had sought refuge and offering us a new 'openness to the future' which marks our entry upon 'authentic existence'. The exegete's task is to 'interpret the phenomena of past history in the light of man's understanding of his existence and so to make us aware of it as furnishing a basis for our present understanding. His duty is, by making the past live again, to bring home to us the truth: *Tua res agitur.* It concerns you yourself.'[2] Again and again in his various writings Bultmann returns to this theme, and his insights are penetrating and suggestive.[3] He is expressing in his own way—or, more accurately, in the language and thought forms of Heidegger's existentialist analysis—what has been said in many different ways by historians of various types during the twentieth century. It is not necessary to adopt or even to understand Heidegger's philosophy in order to appreciate the existential (*existentielle*) dimension of historiography; and most historians nowadays acknowledge this dimension without concerning themselves at all with any articulated existentialist (*existentiale*) Philosophy.[4] (In

---

[1] James M. Robinson, op. cit., 76f.

[2] Bultmann, *Das Urchristentum*, 1949, 8; Eng. trans., *Primitive Christianity in its Contemporary Setting*, 1956 (Fontana Library edition, 1960, 12).

[3] Attention may specially be drawn to his essay on 'The Problem of Hermeneutics' in *Essays Philosophical and Theological*, and to *History and Eschatology*, Gifford Lectures, Edinburgh, 1957 (*passim*; see esp. p. 133).

[4] There is wisdom in Karl Barth's aphorism, 'If we do not commit ourselves unreservedly and finally to any specific philosophy, we will not need totally or finally to fear any philosophy' (*Church Dogmatics*, Vol. I, Part II, 735).

these lectures 'existential' must not be taken to imply 'existential-ist' in the philosophical sense.) Dr James M. Robinson rightly speaks of a dimension which has entered into historical thinking in the twentieth century which was absent in the nineteenth—though, as we shall see, it was not entirely absent in England amongst those who had been influenced by Burke and Coleridge.[1]

The involvement of the historian in the subject-matter which he interprets has become a question of vital interest amongst critical philosophers of history today. It underlies Bultmann's conception of *Geschichtlichkeit*, which implies existential involve-ment in the past situation which the historian seeks to interpret and also the involvement of the interpreter himself in his own genuinely historical life-situation. There is a two-way traffic be-tween the past situation and the present existence of the historian; the one illuminates the other. As we shall see, many philosophers and historians today are ready to acknowledge this truth. It is obvious that its recognition carries significant implications for the interpretation of Scripture. Here the work of the existentialist New Testament scholars has much to teach us; indeed, it may be said that the writings of Ernst Fuchs on this subject are as impor-tant as anything which has emerged from the Bultmann school.[2] The particular problem which arises is that of the relation of the

[1] See *infra*, 166–72. Dr Robinson says: 'We have come to recognize that the objective factual level upon which the nineteenth century operated is only one dimension of history, and that a whole new dimension in the facts, a deeper and more central plane of meaning, had been largely by-passed. The nineteenth century saw the reality of the "historical facts" as consisting largely in names, places, dates, occurrences, sequences, causes, effects—things which fall far short of being the actuality of history, if one understands by history the distinctively human, creative, unique, purposeful, which distinguishes man from nature. The dimension in which man actually exists, his "world", the stance or outlook from which he acts, his understanding of his existence behind what he does, the way he meets his basic problems and the answer his life implies to the human dilemma, the significance he had as the environment of those who knew him, the continuing history his life produces, the possibility of existence which his life presents to me as an alternative—such matters as these have become central in an attempt to understand history. It is this deeper level of the reality of "Jesus of Nazareth as he actually was" which was not reached by "the reconstruction of his biography by means of objective historical method" ' (op. cit., 28f.).

[2] See especially Fuchs's *Hermeneutik*, 2 Auflage mit Erganzungsheft, Bad Cannstatt, 1958; and his collected papers, *Zum hermeneutischen Problem in der Theologie: Die existentiale Interpretation, Gesammelte Aufsätze* I, Tübingen, 1959; also 'Glaube und Geschichte' in *Zeitschrift für Theologie und Kirche*, LIV, 1957, 117–56, and 'Jesus und der Glaube', ibid., LV, 1958, 170–85.

historical Jesus to the kerygmatic Christ, and it is agreed that we cannot have the one without the other, that, in fact, there are not two Persons but one Person. As we listen to the discussion we are constantly reminded of the Christological controversies of the fourth and fifth centuries: the question of the relation of the humanity to the divinity of Christ is being debated in a twentieth-century transposition. Perhaps this is not well appreciated by the existentialist theologians themselves, with their horror of all 'dogmatics', though it is doubtless true that the ancient discussions were just as 'existential' for the participants in their day as are the modern ones for us. At any rate it would seem that the four famous adverbs of the Chalcedonian Formula might in the view of the existentialist theologians be applied to the union of the Jesus of history with the Christ of the kerygma; 'unconfusedly, unchangeably, indivisibly and inseparably'.

And yet, despite this satisfactory conclusion, a misgiving remains. Even though there is no final sundering of the one Christ, there is a bifurcation of the mind of the Christian historian. On the one hand, he knows Christ through the kerygma, that is, not historically but existentially. 'Jesus can be encountered in the kerygma. In this sense faith is not dependent on historiography, which as a matter of fact has been all but non-existent with regard to Jesus during most of the centuries of the Christian faith.'[1] On the other hand, theology today 'is committed to a kerygma which locates its saving event in an historical person to whom we have a second avenue of access provided by the rise of scientific historiography since the Enlightenment'.[2] The latter consideration indeed provides the theological *raison d'être* for the new quest. We have on our hands, therefore, a 'problem of the two avenues of encounter with Jesus'.[3] The problem is solved by allowing the second avenue—scientific historiography—to dictate the shape of the knowledge of Jesus which we have by the grace of the first avenue, the kerygmatic, although faith is said not to be dependent on historiography. The reason for this is that 'scientific historiography' means, along with certain twentieth-century existential insights, the nineteenth-century positivist conception of history which, as we have already noticed, is explicitly reaffirmed by

[1] James M. Robinson, op. cit., 85.
[2] Ibid.
[3] Ibid., 85f.

Bultmann: the view that history is a naturalistic continuum of causes and effects, in which 'miracles' do not happen and in which the activity of God cannot be a factor in causal explanation. On such a view as this the biblical interpretation of certain events as acts of God—the kerygmatic element of both the Old and the New Testaments—must be set aside or, in the language of the school, 'demythologized'. In the view of the existentialist theologians the New Testament kerygma is falsely 'objectivized': it says, for example, that on the third day God raised Jesus from the dead and makes several other statements which are incompatible with positivist scientific historiography. The kerygma is therefore demythologized, so that it then becomes not a witness to the acts of God but to 'the meaning of Jesus'. It testifies not to the act of God in raising Jesus from the dead but to 'the act of God in which transcendence is made a possibility of human existence. The kerygma is not the objectification of a new, "Christian" religious principle, but rather the objectification of an historical encounter with God.'[1] The New Testament certainly attests the truth that for those who believed in Jesus 'transcendence' became a 'possibility of human existence' (if we care to use such language), but it also affirms as an historical fact that this possibility arose, after contact with the earthly Jesus was no longer possible, because God had raised him from the dead. The refusal to speak of the resurrection of Christ as an historical event, and not simply as a realization of transcendence within human existence (whatever that may mean), is made out of deference to the canons of positivist 'scientific historiography'. It is this deference which, despite all the protestations of the 'new quest' theologians, gives to their presentation of the historical element in the Gospels its faintly docetic air; the facts of the Gospel-story, if not the Gospels themselves, seem to be accorded a status similar to that which the Reformers allowed to the Books of the Apocrypha: they may be used for example of life and instruction of manners, but not applied to establish any doctrine.

Despite its many valuable features the existentialist hermeneutic fails because its theory of 'the two avenues of encounter with Jesus' does not account for its own deepest insights. Dr Robinson has well said that 'the objectivity of modern historiography consists precisely in one's openness for the encounter, one's willing-

[1] James M. Robinson, op. cit., 84.

ness to place one's intentions and views of existence in question, i.e. to learn something basically new about existence and thus to have one's own existence modified or radically altered'.[1] It should have been added that this 'openness' must include also the willingness to allow one's pre-Christian positivistic presuppositions about history as a closed continuum likewise to be modified or radically altered. When the Gospel of Christ was first preached in the Hellenistic world, its acceptance involved the repudiation of all 'modern' pseudo-scientific astrological notions about the forces which rule human history. So today, when the kerygma of the Church of Jesus Christ is accepted, positivistic superstitions about a closed historical continuum, 'scientifically' based on nineteenth-century physics, dissolve into the air like the insubstantial phantoms which used to haunt the Colossians. There is no *scientific* presupposition of historical method which requires historians to rule out the possibility of divine action in history. It is an error to imagine that in order to be 'objective' or 'scientific' we have to accept certain presuppositions which all historians (including non-Christians) are supposed to share; it is positivistic philosophy, not historical method, which decrees that the resurrection of Christ cannot be regarded as an historical event. To accept the kerygma of the New Testament means to know that God acts in history and to be liberated from all theories which enslave the human mind by dispiriting fables of a continuum of causes and effects in which the arm of the Lord is powerless to intervene. The kerygma of the whole Bible is a proclamation that God is a God who intervenes in history and is Lord of history. The biblical language about God's mighty acts in history certainly needs interpreting; but it does not need demythologizing, because it is not a myth. It does not speak in mythological terms of an existential meaning disclosed in a certain historical situation, but of how God intervened in the stream of events and altered the course of history. Existentialist hermeneutics does not salvage the historical element in the biblical kerygma from the wreckage of the historic faith in the shallows of positivist philosophy.

[1] Op. cit., 76f.

5

INVOLVEMENT IN HISTORY

IN the previous Lecture we found that the attempts made by certain eminent theologians in recent years to disengage sacred history (whether in the form of *Heilsgeschichte* or of existential truth) from the relativities of 'profane' history (the history with which 'secular' historians concern themselves) are not entirely convincing. We must now go on to suggest that they are not really necessary. They arose out of the positivistic assumption that it is the task of historians (like other scientists) to establish 'facts', which may be objectively ascertained by following recognized scientific procedures, and that the causally interconnected account of historical facts, thus determined, constitutes (in principle, at least) a corpus of verifiable knowledge to which 'all reasonable men' must assent. There cannot be Christian (or Marxist or anything else) historical facts, any more than there can be Christian chemical or geological facts. This view loses its persuasiveness as soon as we begin to analyse what is meant by 'facts', but we will postpone this discussion to the next Lecture. It gains such plausibility as it possesses from the way in which one kind of historian (in our modern period) works.[1] This is the kind of historian who

[1] Some comments by a philosophical critic of this view, in a valuable analysis of 'facts', are illuminating: 'The squirrel theory of history is the theory which holds that it is the duty of the historian to gather up facts from county record libraries and then bury them again in university libraries. It is based on the argument that since history is a reputable discipline like the natural sciences, it is itself a science, and concerned with the discovery of facts. Historians who discover facts are doing their job: historians who do not discover new facts are not really historians at all, but merely popularizers, pedagogues or journalists. . . . I do not wish to decry the historian's scrupulous regard for facts: inaccurate history is not history at all: no historian can be any good without mastering large masses of detailed facts, and some historians may be right in concentrating their efforts on accumulating and establishing more facts. What I deplore is the heresy that this is the

is bred under the competitive university-structure of our Western world, with its emphasis upon 'research': he employs a non-controversial technique to establish non-controversial facts; he eschews 'interpretation'; he is the twentieth-century counterpart of the seventeenth-century erudite and antiquarian. He is doubtless a worthy labourer in the vineyard of knowledge, who supplies the materials of history, even if he does not concern himself with history in the fuller sense, the history which moulds the future by the very act of interpreting the past. If he were the only kind of historian, the positivist account of history as a science dealing with facts would be plausible, at least until we started asking what is meant by 'facts'. His activities would fit comfortably into the theory that historians discover facts which may then be subsumed under the general 'laws' of social science, even though they themselves are concerned only with facts and resolutely leave the formulation of laws or the discerning of patterns to others. How far, indeed, historians of this kind exist in reality is open to question; they exist on paper, but it is probable that beneath the academic surface there often lies concealed the deep concern for the present which redeems historical research from irrelevance and triviality. In the last resort, it would generally be conceded, nothing can be *historisch* without being in some way *geschichtlich;* no 'facts' can be 'mere facts', and every 'fact' that can be discovered is worth discovering because all history is somehow significant.[1] To say this does not imply that an historian must

---

sole business of historical research, that if I succeed in showing that a charter has been misdated by two years, I have done well, but if I rewrite the history of England over a century or more, however convincingly I re-create the motives and personalities of that time, however soundly I judge of the relative significance of the different tendencies and movements then, however coherently I work together the whole, I am not an original historian, and my work is only derivative, secondary and second-rate. Why should a historian confine himself so? Only if he believes that there is a special class of entities called facts, and that they alone are sacred and objective. . . ' (J. R. Lucas, art. 'On Not Worshipping Facts' in *The Philosophical Quarterly*, April, 1958).

[1] It is sometimes said that it is a defect of the English language that it has only one word to do duty for the two German words, *Historie*, the merely historical, and *Geschichte*, the significantly historical. But at least the English usage helps to remind us that there is only one history and to prevent us from thinking of an abstract history, in which facts have no existential significance, alongside a supra-historical sphere which lies outside the scope of historical scholarship.

commit himself to any theory about historical significance; many great historians (Burckhardt, for instance) would affirm the value of historical truth while repudiating any interest in the philosophy of history, which deals in theories about it. In just the same way, one can affirm the beauty of a work of art (Burckhardt will again serve as an example) without discussing aesthetics. History in the full sense is both science and art; the writing of history involves being as 'public' in the presentation of evidence as a scientific periodical and as 'personal' as an artist in the exercise of the interpretative imagination.

The 'Involvement' of the Historian

There is a story that when A. F. Pollard once prophesied that there would come a day when there would be many professors of History in the University of London, those who heard him laughed disdainfully. Today there are many kinds of history—constitutional, economic, social, and so on—all of them respected and well established in the curricula of our universities. The historical-mindedness of our age expresses itself in the conviction that we cannot understand our society and its institutions, even our lives and their problems, without understanding how they came to be what they are. The human situation itself, if it is understandable at all, must be understood historically. The historian (in all his varieties) is an indispensable agent of our self-understanding. This is why what we have called history 'in the full sense' is not a 'merely academic' subject in the pejorative sense of that phrase. It is the study of man himself, because it is human self-knowledge historically understood. The proper interest of the historian is not any supposed causal nexus of 'facts' conceived in terms of nineteenth-century physics; his ultimate concern is man, not as a possible subject of generalized laws (that is the concern of the social sciences), but man in his concrete individuality in this particular situation or that. This is precisely an *historical* interest, a humane interest, and the general recognition of this truth accounts for the fact that history is established in our universities amongst the humanities, not amongst the sciences. Man is the object of study of many of the sciences (for example, the biological, psychological and social sciences), and the historian will take account of all that they have to say; but his own study of man differs from theirs in being concretely particular and personal in character. This is true, perhaps especially true, even of those aspects of historical study which for convenience we call constitutional history, political history or social history.

In this 'full' sense of 'history' it is surely the historian's own involvement in humanity (though he himself may never have stopped to reflect upon it) which determines his quality as an historian; his own participation in the life of his nation, his locality, even his college (if he is an academic), is what stimulates his powers of sympathetic interpretative imagination. What we have called his historical interest, his humane interest, however it has been awakened, rests upon a conviction that *some* human beings at least, those who are truly *historical* persons, are worth getting to know in a personal way for their own sake; and again whole societies, whole epochs, are worth getting to know for their own sake, for the sake of their essential humanity. Of course, countless millions—the great majority—of those who have lived in past ages cannot be 'historical' in this sense, because the means of our ever knowing anything significant about them are perished beyond recovery; similarly, too, countless millions in past times lived 'non-historically' as undifferentiated units in primitive societies; what can be known about them is material for the archaeologist and anthropologist rather than for the historian. But, allowing for all this, there are still very many people, and the societies in which they lived, who can be known by means of the historian's craft; and the historian seeks to know them, in as fully personal a way as possible, because, being human, they are worth knowing, good and bad alike, or, to omit any moral reference, congenial or repugnant as they may be to us. The historian's interest can best be described in the familiar words of the classical humanist poet: *Homo sum: humani nil a me alienum puto.*[1] It is an interest in *real* men and women in *real* historical situations, persons who once were just as alive as we are today, and who through the historian's craft can be known, at least to some extent, as living people with understandable motives and ambitions, hopes and fears, virtues and failings. Historical study in this sense achieves the discovery of the essential humanity of individuals and societies that have passed away, not in the unhistorical eighteenth-century sense of a generalized science of behaviour (Hume's 'constant and universal principles of human nature'), but

[1] Terence, *Heauton Timorumenos*, I, i, 25.

in the sense that the human predicament of past generations, in circumstances very different from our own, nevertheless reveals itself to us as our predicament; the men and women of history speak to us in our own situation today. History involves the recognition of the humanity which is both ours and theirs, without which both the literature and the history of past ages would be irrelevant to our concerns. Here lies the essential difference between the humanistic and the rationalistic approach. In the sphere of natural science, truly enough, every new advance means that an old hypothesis becomes obsolete and must be discarded; henceforward it belongs to the museum of the history of science. But in the sphere of the humane studies, on the contrary, the achievements of the past never become obsolete: were it otherwise, the plays of Aeschylus would be as out of date as the physics of Aristotle; Jeremiah's prophecies would be as irrelevant to our condition as the psychology of Protagoras; and the Dialogues of Plato would be as 'dated' as the astronomy of Ptolemy. The rationalist mind fails to observe the distinction between the two types of knowing. The historical interrogation of the past is relevant and of vital concern to us today because that which makes us *men*, beings who are defined by our basic relation to God and to our fellows, remains just what it was in the days of the ancient dramatists, historians, prophets and philosophers. The humane tradition attests the perennial recognition of this truth.

To bring to life real people in their own historical life-situation is the fine achievement of the historian. To accomplish it he must have mastered many difficult scientific techniques; by accomplishing it he demonstrates that scientific method is not the whole of history. If useful generalizations or illustrations concerning human behaviour at large can be drawn from the historian's re-creation of the past, well and good; but such things are a by-product of his labours rather than the goal at which he aims. The true historian can re-create even a (to us) repugnant society or epoch, so that we may view it with compassion. To take an example, the Aztec civilization destroyed by Cortés was surely one of the most obsessively bloodthirsty and (to us) repellent civilizations that have ever existed; yet a reviewer of a recent historical study of it can write that the author 'has the rare quality of entering into the minds of those he is studying and seeing things from their point of view; the result in this case is that for perhaps the first time it is possible to understand the Aztecs and sympathize with them in their painful predicament'.[1] The reviewer adds that 'the book is one of the best ever written about the Aztecs: his portrait of their society is a triumph of scholarship, understanding and literary skill'. These, surely, are the three qualities necessary in the historian who successfully re-creates a former age; scholarship, the mastery of the materials and techniques of research; understanding, the sympathetic entering into and reliving of the experience of a vanished society; and literary skill, the capacity of communicating to others the experience thus re-created.

Moral Judgments in History

It is the ingredient here called 'understanding' with which we are now more particularly concerned. It involves a certain quality of personal relatedness between the investigator and his subject which is essential to all the humanities.[2] This does not at all imply a superior attitude of moral judgment on the part of the historian; the best word for this personal relatedness is 'compassion'. Professor Butterfield has well spoken of the historian's 'passion for the past' as 'a kind of flame which is simply a compassion for human beings', an intensity of understanding such as might lead us neither to condone nor to condemn, but to feel with even a Catherine de' Medici on the eve of the massacre of St Bartholomew.[3] The historian's task is not to pass moral judgments but to

[1] *Times Literary Supplement*, Nov. 10, 1961 (No. 3,115), 800; the work under review is Jacques Soustelle, *The Daily Life of the Aztecs*, Eng. trans. by P. O'Brian, London, 1961.

[2] In saying this it is not implied that this quality constitutes a difference in kind between history and the natural sciences, and there is no intention to deny the argument of Michael Polanyi (*Personal Knowledge*, London, 1958, *passim*) that 'scientific detachment' is a false ideal in the exact sciences and that 'personal participation' is an ingredient of *all* acts of understanding.

[3] H. Butterfield, *History and Human Relations*, London, 1951, 128. In an instructive essay in this volume, entitled 'Moral Judgments in History', he considers the case of Catherine de' Medici. Assisted by all the resources of historical enquiry and by all the humanity we possess, we are called as historians 'to resurrect the whole occasion and to see with Catherine, feel with her, hold our breath with her, and meet the future with all her apprehensions. If by imaginative sympathy we can put ourselves in her place in this way, not only envisaging the situation in all its detail but apprehending in all its vividness and intensity until we reach the point at which we could almost conceive ourselves making the drastic decision, or at least have a sense of just what it would take to carry us across the border to such a decision—then we are historians indeed' (124).

understand. Moral indignation always obscures judgment, whether we are studying past events, such as those of August 23, 1572, or contemporary ones, such as the Anglo-French assault upon Suez in November 1956: moral indignation is part of the stock-in-trade of politicians, not of historians. This does not at all mean that the historian should himself be devoid of moral convictions; it means that, after he has entered intimately into the lives and shared the perplexities of the men and women he has known in his studies, he will ask himself whether, if he had been in their place, he would have acted any more wisely. Croce in a moment of insight remarks that, as soon as we hear the murmur of Christ's admonition, 'Judge not, that ye be not judged', the verdict of condemnation will die on our lips; and today historians would seem to agree with Croce on this point rather than with Lord Acton: history for Croce is not a great high court of judgment, and in this sense at least *die Weltgeschichte* is not *das Weltgericht*.[1] Acton shared with the Enlightenment historians the conviction that there was an objective and universal moral standard, and, being a Victorian, he thought he knew what it was.[2] Today, in the changed atmosphere of the twentieth century, compassion rather than condemnation is more generally deemed to be the appropriate attitude of the historian. This is largely because, while it has not ceased to be scientific, history has become essentially one of the humanities again, and the words 'humane' and 'compassionate' are near synonyms.[3]

The true aim of the historian, and his reward, is the understanding of humanity in its concrete wholeness. His thinking, like

[1] B. Croce, *History as the Story of Liberty*, Eng. trans. by S. Sprigge, London, 1941, 207–9.

[2] Acton criticized Bishop Creighton for not having condemned the persecuting Popes (such as Sixtus IV) in his *History of the Papacy during the Reformation*, 5 vols., 1882–94. In a letter to Creighton he declares 'it is the common, even the vulgar, code that I appeal to'. He finds that, since 'power tends to corrupt, and absolute power corrupts absolutely', therefore 'great men are almost always bad men': 'I would hang them higher than Haman, for reasons of quite obvious justice, still more, still higher, for the sake of historical science' (*Historical Essays and Studies*, ed. Figgis and Laurence, London, 1907, 504f.). Cf. also Acton's *Lectures on Modern History*, 23–28.

[3] On the question of moral judgments in history see also Michael Oakeshott, *Experience and its Modes*, 158; E. H. Carr, *What is History?* 69–72; David Knowles, *The Historian and Character*, Cambridge, 1955. The view that the historian ought to pass moral judgments has recently been reaffirmed by Sir Isaiah Berlin, *Historical Inevitability*, 76f.

all rational activity, involves generalizations, but he does not undertake it with a view to demonstrating general truths which were in his mind before his study began. He does not investigate Aztec civilization in order to provide empirical evidence for a generalization, such as that *tantum religio potuit suadere malorum*;[1] nor does he study the Popes or the Medicis in order to demonstrate the general truth that 'power tends to corrupt'. He pursues his task regardless of the truth or falsity of the contention of those philosophers who assert that there are, in fact, no universal generalizations in history but only collective or enumerative judgments.[2] Nor is he disturbed by the criticism that historical judgments are rarely verifiable by methods comparable to those of the natural sciences, or that they are frequently incapable of being falsified.[3] History is *sui generis*, and historical judgments cannot be reduced to any form of scientific generalization, because historical characters are not laboratory specimens but men and women who in their historical individuality are the objects of human regard and compassion. The historian's own self is involved with theirs in a manner analogous to the involvement of his own life with that of the people he meets every day in his neighbourhood and in his place of work; and, as Croce said, the historian will not pass beyond the 'obscure intimacy' of his own feelings 'unless he can judge himself and mediate his own history, which is only his in so far as it is an integral part of the history of the world'.[4] The historian indeed makes judgments, but they are not moral judgments; their *sui generis* character does not permit history to be reduced to ethics any more than to science or to philosophy. The historian is involved in history in a way in which the natural scientist is not involved in nature: the latter cannot, even imaginatively, live the life of amoebas or molecules, in order to understand their behaviour, nor does he need to do so; but the

---

[1] Lucretius, *De Rerum Natura*, I, 101.

[2] E.g. Michael Oakeshott, *Experience and its Modes*, 161.

[3] Cf. Patrick Gardiner (*The Nature of Historical Explanation*, 95) quotes Stuart Hampshire: 'The historian is not primarily concerned to establish general statements falsifiable by experiment, but . . . his conclusions (if any) are judgments about particular persons and particular events . . .' 'It is the distinguishing characteristic of practical and historical judgments (as opposed to statements of fact and scientific statements) that the conditions of their falsification are not exactly prescribed' ('Subjective Conditionals' in *Analysis*, October, 1948).

[4] Op. cit., 213.

historian must in some sense get inside the mind of the persons
or the societies which he studies, if he is to attain historical understanding. The recognition of this truth is the reason why in recent
discussions of the historian's task we have heard so often such
words as 'intuition', 'insight', 'understanding', 'projection',
'imagination', 'sympathy', 'empathy', 'compassion' and 'involvement'.[1]

Dilthey, Croce and Collingwood

Nineteenth-century thought, as we noted in Lecture III,
tended to regard history as a science, or perhaps as an applied
science of human behaviour, and hence there arose the kind of
theories of the type which are known as positivist. During the
twentieth century, however, the movement of thought has on the
whole been away from such positions and towards regarding
history as an enquiry *sui generis*, following its own methods which
are not those of the natural sciences or even of the social sciences,
because of the element of personal identification or 'empathy'
which must be brought to the task of making historical judgments
or of interpreting the historical evidence. It is no accident that
this development was largely stimulated by philosophers who
were themselves considerable historians, as they came to reflect
upon the nature of their own historical work. Wilhelm Dilthey
(1833–1911), though most of his life was lived in the nineteenth
century, was one of the seminal thinkers whose thought has profoundly affected the attitudes of the twentieth century; its abstract
and Germanic character has unfortunately somewhat restricted
its direct influence in the English-speaking world.[2] Dilthey
pointed the way in showing that the human sciences (*Geisteswissen-*

---

[1] For an historian's statement of the importance of empathy in historiography see H. Butterfield, *History and Human Relations*, 145f.; for a consideration of the matter from the point of view of the critical philosophy of
history see W. Dray, *Laws and Explanation in History*, Oxford, 1957, 118–55,
where references to recent discussions will be found.

[2] The best introduction to Dilthey's thinking about history is *Meaning in
History: W. Dilthey's Thoughts on History and Society*, edited with introduction
by H. P. Rickman, London, 1961; a translation of the most relevant passages
is made (pp. 66–168) from Vol. VII of Dilthey's works (Teubner Verlag,
Stuttgart). Excellent introductions to Dilthey's thought as a whole will be
found in two books by Professor H. A. Hodges, *Wilhelm Dilthey, an Introduction*, London, 1944 (see esp. 11–35; 121–4), and *The Philosophy of Wilhelm
Dilthey*, London, 1952 (see esp. 332–41). The former contains selected passages in translation.

schaften), such as sociology, are not to be considered inferior to the natural sciences because they develop a method of their own which is different from the methods of natural science. Especially is this true of history. The historian, because he is himself an historical being, can project himself into the experience of others and thus enlarge his own present experience through the understanding of the past. Historical understanding means to relive (*nacherleben*) the past experience of others and so to make it one's own; there is nothing that corresponds to this in the non-human sciences, and the latter can tell us nothing about mankind except the physical facts.

Benedetto Croce (1866–1952) and R. G. Collingwood (1889–1943) are thinkers who in rather different ways viewed history from the standpoint of idealist philosophy. Their metaphysical interests are somewhat unfashionable today, and in any case they do not concern us here. Collingwood prefers to speak of 'thought' rather than with Dilthey of 'experience': the historian cannot experience what Julius Caesar experienced, since an individual's feelings are private to himself. But his thought is accessible to other rational beings, and the historian can think again Julius Caesar's thoughts and so relive his thought. But Collingwood is not entirely consistent in his use of words, and the substance of his theory is contained in these sentences: 'Historical knowledge is the knowledge of what mind has done in the past, and at the same time it is the redoing of this, the perpetuation of past acts in the present. . . . To the historian, the activities whose history he is studying are not spectacles to be watched but experiences to be lived through in his mind.'[1] There are no such things as past events; all history exists only in people's minds and therefore is a subject of rational explanation; and since all history is the history of thought, causation in history is simply the thought in the mind of the person by whose agency the event came about, and this thought is not something other than the event but 'the inside of the event itself'.[2] Whether this kind of language clarifies the issue we will leave an open question; what it does indicate is Collingwood's clear recognition that history is nothing apart from the historian's ability to re-create the past and make it present for us.

For Croce all history is contemporary history and the facts of

[1] *The Idea of History*, 218.
[2] Ibid., 214f.

history are present facts. Indeed, they are not in time at all, because they exist only in thought, and thought is not in time. From the point of view of our present interest, Croce, like Collingwood, is important not because of any metaphysical implications which he thought that he had discerned in his study of history, but because he was giving expression to a truth, much neglected during the nineteenth century, which in our own times has become increasingly recognized. Croce saw that historical writing is determined by contemporary needs and develops out of present situations, in which historical facts 'vibrate'. History is an act of consciousness arising out of a moral need which prepares and invokes action and is always related to action in the present: clearly Croce would not consider the publication in the learned journals of academic essays about mediaeval laundry-lists or rent-rolls to be 'history' in any sense at all. Both Croce and Collingwood helped to articulate the important truth that the experience of the present is the reality which lies behind the activity of the historian, since the latter is concerned not with a dead past but with thought and action in the present.[1]

It is today virtually a commonplace to speak of history as a two-way traffic between the present and the past. Almost all the world's great historians before the nineteenth century were men who had had practical experience of affairs; Livy is practically the only classical historian who approached his study 'academically', and he was intensely concerned about the politics and morals of the Rome of Augustus; all the characteristic historical works of the Renaissance humanists were written by men who were acquainted at first hand with the problems of statecraft.[2] Sir Charles Webster, equally at home in the lecture-room and in Whitehall, has told us that 'the past . . . ceases to have meaning unless it is relived in the light of the experience of each succeeding generation';[3] and even Gibbon, who would have found Croce's view of history as practical somewhat difficult to understand, discovered that 'the captain of the Hampshire grenadiers . . . has not been

---

[1] See B. Croce, *History as the Story of Liberty*, esp. 19, 78–118, 175; *Theory and History of Historiography*, Eng. trans. by D. Ainslie, London, 1921, 289–314; for a general introduction to Croce see H. Wildon Carr, *The Philosophy of Benedetto Croce*, London, 1917; C. J. S. Sprigge, *Benedetto Croce: Man and Thinker*, Cambridge, 1952.

[2] See *infra*, Appended Note on Classical History, 277–86.

[3] *The Art and Practice of Diplomacy*, London, 1961, 151.

useless to the historian of the Roman Empire'.[1] Croce himself was active in Italian affairs, though during Mussolini's ascendancy a period of retirement was forced upon him; while Collingwood, a lifelong don, a philosopher and an historian of Roman Britain, devoted his energies to the understanding of modern society with a view to the maintenance of free institutions within it.[2] Whether the historian has himself participated in practical affairs or not, it is essential to his calling that he should be seriously concerned to understand the moral, political and social issues of his own day; if he is not thus 'involved' in his own age, he will not be able to bring a past age to life. This is why there can never be a final and definitive version of history, 'ultimate history', such as Lord Acton in 1896 believed was being progressively attained;[3] the 'truths' of history cannot be stated once and for all, as the truths of the physical sciences may be—for example, the truth discovered by Boyle in 1662, that the pressure and volume of a gas are inversely proportional ('Boyle's Law'). Every generation must write history afresh in the light of its own experience. This is not because new 'facts' have been discovered (though fresh evidence may indeed have come to light), but because new judgments of the old evidence are required when it is looked at in a new perspective. There is no escape from the consequent problems of ideological distortion and of historical relativism, as we noticed in Lecture III,[4] by attempting to revive the nineteenth-century fiction of an objective 'scientific' history; after having partaken of the insights of the twentieth century, only the timid would seek a fundamentalist security in the dogmas of positivism. The question of myth, ideology and relativism must be resolutely faced in the light of a careful observation of the way in which historians actually go about the task of representing the past; and to these questions we shall return in Lecture VIII. Here it is relevant to note that, since new historical experience necessitates new interpretations of history, the demand for a new history is most urgent in times of rapid and far-reaching social and political change. The age of the French Revolution was just such a period, and the man who achieved a new understanding of history in that age was Edmund

---

[1] *Autobiography*, World's Classics ed., 166.
[2] Cf. his work, *The New Leviathan*, 1942.
[3] See *supra*, 106.
[4] See *supra*, 107f.

Burke (1729–97). If the lessons which had been learnt by Burke and his successors had not been forgotten during the heyday of positivism and materialistic prosperity in the later nineteenth century, it would not have been necessary for Dilthey, Croce and Collingwood to discover over again the truths which they had enunciated.

Edmund Burke and the 'Anglican' School

After the upheaval of a great revolution or a major war, a new order comes into being and with it a new perspective from which the past is viewed. The revolutionaries themselves, as Lord Acton noted,[1] want to break with the past and so they repudiate history; they are 'ready to destroy its records and to abolish its inoffensive professors'. But what happens is the reverse of their intention: history is reborn because fresh assessments must be made. In Acton's view, the French Revolution was a direct cause of the great new era of historical activity which began in the second quarter of the nineteenth century and developed into a movement more significant even than the revival of learning at the Renaissance.[2] He regards Burke as perhaps the first great historical thinker, though he was an historian *manqué*.[3] Professor Butterfield speaks of Burke as 'the presiding influence over the historical movement of the nineteenth century'.[4] Others, amongst them Croce and Fueter, have designated Burke as the father of Romantic history;[5] certainly Burke's attitude was diametrically opposed not only to that of the anti-historical Jacobin intellectuals but also to the Enlightenment view that history provides only a succession of stereotypes of 'the constant and universal principles of human nature'. The revolutionary temper of his age drove Burke to make a reappraisal of English institutions and their

---

[1] *Lectures on Modern History*, 14.

[2] Ibid. Cf. also the quotations from Acton's unpublished works in H. Butterfield, *Man on his Past*, 66f., 98.

[3] Burke's early work, *The Abridgement of English History*, was described by Acton as his most remarkable literary production. He refers to the story that Burke decided not to write a history when he heard that Hume had begun one and he comments, 'It must be regretted that the reverse did not occur' (Butterfield, ibid., 69). As regards the story, see Thomas W. Copeland, *Edmund Burke: Six Essays*, London, 1950, 128, footnote 21.

[4] Ibid., 18.

[5] Sir Ernest Barker calls Burke's view 'historical romanticism' in *Essays on Government*, Oxford, 1945, 226.

history. Social institutions were not for him fetters (as they were for Rousseau) which hampered the universal progress of mankind, but providential means by which particular societies (nations) within Christendom, especially in England, had been continually improving. Burke was a Whig who desired to preserve those values which had been established by the conservative English Revolution of 1688 and which were obviously jeopardized by the success of the radical French Revolution of 1789. To understand those values, as enshrined in such institutions as Parliament itself, was to understand their history, and this carried the study back into the time of their beginnings in the Middle Ages. In its turn, this meant seeing the Middle Ages with new eyes: what had been for Gibbon 'the rubbish of the Dark Ages' became for the new historians the cradle of European civilization. The rediscovery of the Middle Ages now became one of the most exciting enterprises of the Romantic Age. The word 'Gothic' ceased to be an epithet of abuse (not only in architecture),[1] and novelists, painters, church builders and railway architects were soon vying with historians in re-creating the 'enchantments of the Middle Age'. The verdicts of the Enlightenment had to be revised because the perspective of a new age had focused the light of practical history upon the pages which hitherto only the antiquarians had turned, and at last their labours were put to profitable use. Most important of all, a sense of history and of real development through the centuries had been born. Henceforward historians were to become increasingly aware that their task consisted not in baking the bricks of an edifice of 'ultimate history', and not even primarily in discovering new 'facts', but in the never-ending task of the reappraisal of past history in the light of new experience.[2]

How far Burke himself was directly or indirectly responsible for these developments it is impossible to say; there is plenty of work still to be done upon this question, which seems never to have been thoroughly investigated by historians of ideas. Indeed,

[1] On the use of the word 'Gothic' and the abuse of 'Gothic, barbarous and monkish' architecture, etc., in the Age of Reason see the fascinating essay 'The First Gothic Revival and the Return to Nature' in *Essays in the History of Ideas* by Arthur O. Lovejoy, 136–65.

[2] During the nineteenth century the constant reappraisal of the French Revolution itself was a compulsive preoccupation of historians. See Daniel Halévy's *Histoire d'une histoire*, Paris, 1939, a short survey of histories of the Revolution; and see P. Geyl's illuminating essay 'Michelet and his History of the French Revolution' in his *Debates with Historians*, 56–90.

much still awaits elucidation in the matter of Burke's own view of history.[1] The task is one of great difficulty, because Burke's thought has to be sifted out of a mass of various utterances given forth at various times by a statesman who was grappling with the realities of a crisis in which the old order of European society was giving place to a new age, amidst scenes of unparalleled violence with their aftermath of confusion. Burke recoils in aversion from the Roussseau-type of anti-historical exaltation of 'conscience' which, discounting 'the virtue which is practicable', confers infallibility upon the morality of the moment and pronounces absolution upon the excesses of revolutionary fanaticism.[2] History in Burke's view involves an encounter of every generation in its turn with the eternal moral order: 'moral values are disclosed through the movement of Providence in the temporal process. The moral significance of a situation is to be sought by an active response to the moment itself in its integrity'.[3]

Burke's historical thinking was carried forward into the nineteenth century by friends and admirers who had come under his influence. Amongst the latter was S. T. Coleridge[4] (1772–1834), an unsystematic writer whom J. S. Mill nevertheless called 'one of the two great seminal minds' of the nineteenth century (the other being Bentham, a strangely assorted pair). After his early enthusiasm for the revolution in France, from which he had recovered by 1798, he came to value continuity and tradition, much

[1] The most adequate treatment of the subject known to the present writer is a substantial article by John C. Weston, Jr., entitled 'Edmund Burke's View of History' in *The Review of Politics*, Univ. of Notre Dame Press, Indiana, Vol. 23, No. 2 (April 1961), 203–29. The author discusses such problems as that of the reconciliation of providence and freewill in Burke's thought. Burke's historical views are touched upon in Alfred Cobban's early study, *Edmund Burke and the Revolt against the Eighteenth Century*, London, 1929 (reissued with a new preface, 1960); Cobban discusses somewhat vaguely how the new historical perspective came into being about the end of the eighteenth century. There is suggestive material in an excellent study by Charles Parkin, *The Moral Basis of Burke's Political Thought*, Cambridge, 1956.

[2] See Charles Parkin, op. cit., 131–8.

[3] Ibid., 131.

[4] See esp. his *Confessions of an Inquiring Spirit*, recently edited by H. St J. Hart, London, 1956. It is difficult to lay a finger on any particular part of his diffuse writings as specially illustrative of his attitude to history. Most of what has been written about him deals with his poetry and his literary criticism. For an introduction to his philosophy see J. H. Muirhead, *Coleridge as Philosopher*, London, 1930; also E. K. Chambers, *S. T. Coleridge*, London, 1938.

in the vein of Burke, though his moderate Toryism did not inhibit his support for measures of social reform. His pervasive influence affected in particular a group of energetic churchmen, who after about 1820 developed a line of thinking about history which provided an alternative to the major current of eighteenth-century rationalistic thought carried into the nineteenth century by such writers as Hallam, James Mill, Grote, Macaulay and Buckle. Less than justice has been done to this group of historical thinkers by rationalist historians of nineteenth-century historiography, such as Dr G. P. Gooch. Happily the injustice has been somewhat redressed by the publication in 1952 of Mr Duncan Forbes's Prize Essay entitled *The Liberal Anglican Idea of History*. The group, whom Mr Forbes calls 'Liberal Anglicans', includes Thomas Arnold (1795–1842) of Rugby, who became Regius Professor of Modern History at Oxford; Connop Thirlwall (1797–1875), later Bishop of St Davids; J. C. Hare (1795–1855) of Trinity College, Cambridge, who with Thirlwall translated Niebuhr's *History of Rome*; H. H. Milman (1791–1868), the rather stolid historian who was Professor of Poetry at Oxford, and. became Dean of St Paul's; and A. P. Stanley (1815–81), the pupil and biographer of Dr Arnold, the redoubtable secretary of the Royal Commission (1850) which enquired into the state of Oxford University, who subsequently became Dean of Westminster. They shared Coleridge's enthusiasm for German thought, especially in its aspect of historical Romanticism.[1] They admired, though not uncritically, the new German historians, especially B. G. Niebuhr (1776–1831). They learned from Niebuhr not only the principles of historical criticism, such as Milman might apply to the Old Testament (though anonymously at first) and Thirlwall

---

[1] The word 'Romanticism' has a bewildering variety of meanings. A valuable clarification will be found in A. O. Lovejoy's address (1923) 'On the Discrimination of Romanticism', republished in his *Essays in the History of Ideas*, 228–53, in which volume other contributions relevant to this theme will also be found. He points out 'the palpable and important historical fact that the one "Romanticism" which . . . has an indisputable title to the name was conceived by those writers as a rediscovery and revival, for better or worse, of characteristically Christian modes of thought and feeling . . . such as had been for a century alien to the dominant tendencies in "polite" literature' (247f.). He adds that Schleiermacher's famous *Reden* (1799) was the first important formulation of Romanticism for religious philosophy (Eng. trans. by J. Oman, 1893: *On Religion: Speeches to its Cultured Despisers*; new ed., New York and London, 1958).

to the New;[1] what was perhaps even more important, they learned what it meant for a working critical historian to be 'involved' in history, both past and present, if a former age is to be brought to life. The lesson was a congenial one, for they were all 'practical' historians.[2] History was not antiquarianism, admirably defined by Arnold as knowledge of the past enjoyed by one who has no lively knowledge of the present.[3] 'The scientific observer', said Thirlwall, 'stands aloof from the object which he submits to his experiments. . . . The progress of society is something in which the student of history has a deep personal concern. He is himself part of that which he sees. He is carried along by the movement which he scans, and contributes in some measure to modify it by his presence.'[4]

---

[1] Milman's *History of the Jews* appeared in 1829, and its author did not long remain anonymous; Stanley later described it as the first indication that the Bible could be treated both critically and reverently at the same time, but his Broad Church outlook was not universally shared. Thirlwall, after his youthful indiscretion of translating a critical work of Schleiermacher's on St Luke's Gospel, did not venture into the field again. His chief work, *The History of Greece* (8 vols., 1835–44) was mostly written in the living of Kirby Underdale in Yorkshire. When Lord Melbourne appointed him Bishop of St Davids, he learned Welsh; thereafter he took part in all the great ecclesiastical issues of the age.

[2] For the detailed explication of this statement Mr Forbes's book, mentioned at the beginning of this paragraph, should be read in full. He summarizes the matter thus: 'For them history was nothing if not practical. It was by no means an end in itself, a study of the past for its own sake, an intellectual exercise or emotional experience barren of results in the outer world, and unrelated to the duties and aspirations of everyday life, to the larger problems, social, political, religious. The science of history was related to the social and political problems of the day; the philosophy of history to a way of life and thought. History, if it were not a guide, was nothing. It was, moreover, in its very nature a force in the world. . . . History, for the Liberal Anglicans, was practical because it was a relation of past and present to form a whole which included the historian. As Thirlwall pointed out, the historian is himself in history, his very thoughts about the past are themselves a part of history. The historian cannot sever himself from the historical context or stand aloof from the processes of history as the scientist stands apart from the processes of science. Unlike the scientist, the historian is part of his subject. . . . The historian has a responsibility to society. . . . Thus the practical history of the Liberal Anglicans is not a mere recourse to history for eristic purposes, for examples, cases, precedents. History for them is practical, not in the eighteenth-century sense of philosophy teaching by examples. . . . If the historian, therefore, wishes to understand the past, that is, to live actively in the past, he must live actively in the present' (87).

[3] Forbes, ibid., 169. For an example of the way in which this insight is now generally understood by historians see M. Bloch, *The Historian's Craft*, 43–47.

[4] Forbes, op. cit., 168. The mass of writings of the 'Liberal Anglicans' are

It is clear that those who stood in the tradition of Burke and Coleridge realized that it is the practicality of history which imparts to it the sense of reality, even of urgency; thus, Arnold, with his eye on Niebuhr, writes of 'that sense of reality about the Romans—that living in a manner amongst them, and having them and their life distinctly before our eyes—which appears to me so indispensable to one who would write their history'.[1] Niebuhr himself, with the aid of the critical scientific techniques which he had mastered, brought the Romans to life precisely because he was concerned about the needs of his own Germany. He was anxious to hold up Rome as a model of political radicalism. The strongest passion of his life (Forbes quotes Seeley as saying) was his hatred of the French Revolution. The Anglican historians, especially Milman, were not unaware of his tendency to idealize Roman history or of the motive for it; and they looked for inspiration beyond Niebuhr to Vico and to his view of the unity of history as a whole.[2] Being men of the nineteenth century, influenced by German thought, it is natural enough that they should have spoken hopefully about the construction of a philosophy of history, such as, in fact, they never achieved. Rationalist interpreters of nineteenth-century thought have tended to dismiss them summarily as mere philosophical, or, worse still, theological idea-spinners, as a species of latter-day Bossuets, who contributed little to the development of 'scientific' history;[3] in the age of the increasing dominance of positivist ideology, it was not noticed that positivist history was only another variety of philosophical interpretation, even though it called itself scientific. Yet today it is clear that many of the ideas which the 'Liberal Anglicans' put forward concerning the practicality of history are widely accepted by working historians, who do not concern themselves with the problems of philosophy, as a true description of the nature of their activity. Their influence upon the development of English theo-

---

so diffuse and often inaccessible nowadays that the student will be grateful to Mr Forbes for the generous selection from them which he gives (153–200). It is tempting to quote more, but enough has been cited here to indicate that much of value is to be found in what Mr Forbes has selected.

[1] Forbes, ibid., 168.
[2] Cf. Forbes, ibid., 17–20.
[3] Thus, Dr G. P. Gooch dismisses Arnold in a couple of pages; he is 'rather the theologian than the historian' (*History and Historians*, 320).

logy (and, indirectly, historiography) has apparently never been
adequately investigated and assessed. It was probably considerable. In an age when Evangelicals and Tractarians combined to
oppose the application of the new methods of historical criticism
to the understanding of the biblical revelation, their confident
acceptance of those methods prevented the English Church from
yielding to obscurantism. On the other hand, although Arnold
and his friends were (and still often are) branded as Liberals whose
spiritual home was in Germany, it would seem to have been the
'Liberal Anglicans' who, by providing a non-positivist attitude
towards history, rendered it unnecessary for English theologians
to embark upon that unfortunate strategy of disengagement from
history which has characterized Germanic theology from Ritschl
to the disciples of Barth and Bultmann. Because of their influence,
the methods of historical science, properly so called, were not in
England believed by theologians necessarily to presuppose the
assumptions of positivism. The great English scholars of the
nineteenth century, Lightfoot and Hort—critical scholars, said
Lord Acton, surpassed by neither Frenchman nor German[1]—
together with Westcott, the third of the great Cambridge trio,
were able to accomplish their biblical and historical work without
feeling constrained to make any concessions to positivist conceptions of what might or might not be allowed to be historically
possible. In an age of religious bewilderment, they demonstrated
that the wholehearted acceptance of modern critical methods was
entirely compatible with a serene and confident allegiance to the
unreduced faith of the Catholic Creeds. Westcott said of the facts
recited in the Apostles' Creed what few leading German theologians from Ritschl to Bultmann have ever quite found themselves
able to say: 'They belong to life. They are in themselves unchangeable. They stand before us for ever in their sublime
majesty, part of the history of the world.'[2]

The Involvement of Ranke and Burckhardt

The course of the development of historiography since the year
in which the great Leopold von Ranke succeeded to his chair at
Berlin (1825) graphically illustrates the truth perceived by the
'Liberal Anglicans' concerning the practical character of history.

[1] *Lectures on Modern History*, 17.
[2] *The Historic Faith*, 1883; 5th ed., 25f.

For more than half a century after that date Ranke presided over the vast and thorough historical enterprise of searching out the facts ('wie es eigentlich gewesen')[1] and presenting them in an objectively scientific form, the form of 'ultimate history', free from all bias and presupposition: the historian's task was simply to let the facts speak for themselves. On this view, detachment is the cardinal virtue of the historian. Facts were to be rescued from the conflict of opinion; this was the business of the new historians. Lord Acton characterized the Rankean view of history as something that was detached from the questions on which men differ—religion, politics, philosophy, literature. It is the laying out of a story on which all men and all parties can form what judgments they like when they have read it, but they will not be able to dispute the facts themselves. The science of history deals with what must be true for all interpreters: 'Ranke holds that concerning the facts about Martin Luther and the figure of the man as he appears in history, there is no reason why Protestant and Catholic, conservative and liberal, should ultimately differ.'[2] This is the view which has come to be known as Ranke's view, though Ranke himself, while insisting on the primary importance of 'what happened', held deeper views. It is certainly not an accurate description of Ranke's own activity as an historian. Ranke was, after all, an historian 'in the full sense', an historian in the 'Liberal Anglican' sense of the term; he was no mere 'technical historian', as so many of his lesser admirers have tried to be. He was in truth the interpreter or myth-maker of the Prussian State.

'We historians', said Carl Becker in his famous essay in 1910, 'are of that ancient and honourable company of wise men of the tribe . . . to whom in successive ages has been entrusted the keeping of the useful myths.'[3] This statement is just as applicable to Ranke as to any other true historian, as recent German discussions of historiography have abundantly illustrated. History 'in the full sense' is an interaction between the past and the present, and the historian always interprets the past in the light of his

---

[1] *Supra*, 104.

[2] Quoted by H. Butterfield, *Man on his Past*, 94. This kind of view, sometimes called 'scientific history', is also called 'technical history'. Cf. Butterfield, ibid., 137–41. In German it is usually known as *Historismus*.

[3] 'Detachment and the Writing of History', *Atlantic Monthly*, CVI, Oct. 1910; cf. *Everyman his own Historian: Essays on History and Politics*, New York, 1935, 247.

involvement in the great religious, moral and political issues of his own day. The positivist ideology of the nineteenth century obscured this truth in that era from all except the followers of the tradition of Burke; but it was just as true of the rationalist historians themselves as of any others; and the realization of this state of affairs constitutes the main difference between the thinking of the twentieth century about the nature of history and that of the nineteenth.[1] The largely unconscious ideals and aspirations of an age—properly called its ideology[2]—are not seen for what they are until that age has passed away; then everyone laughs at the prejudices of his grandfathers ('Victorianism') and demands a new history which shall embody the outlook of contemporary society. This is why history must always be re-written and why historians, whether they like the office or not, are the keepers of the useful myths. They have a responsibility to society, and if reputable historians do not discharge it, demagogues and propagandists will supply the public demand. Becker during the period between the two World Wars, we are told, often used to wonder why historians had done so little to prevent the catastrophe of 1914. Since Becker's death in 1945 much has been written on this theme, especially in Germany, and the activity of Ranke as a 'wise man of the tribe' has been much debated. The crisis of the twentieth century, of world upheaval and of social change, besides which the crisis of 1789 seems hardly more than a palace-revolution, has inevitably created a demand for a new history, and it is not surprising that many historians today envisage their task in terms

---

[1] Cf. E. H. Carr, *What is History?* 30f.: 'Grote, an enlightened radical banker writing in the 1840s, embodied the aspirations of the rising and politically progressive British middle class in an idealized picture of Athenian democracy, in which Pericles figured as a Benthamite reformer, and Athens acquired an empire in a fit of absence of mind. . . . Writing in the 1850s . . . Mommsen was imbued with the sense of need for a strong man . . . to save Germany from ruin . . . the lawyer-politician Cicero, that ineffective chatterbox and slippery procrastinator, has walked straight out of the debates of the Paulkirche in Frankfurt in 1848. Indeed, I should not think it an outrageous paradox if someone were to say that Grote's *History of Greece* has quite as much to tell us today about the thought of English political radicals in the 1840s as about Athenian democracy in the fifth century BC, or that anyone wishing to understand what 1848 did to the German liberals should take Mommsen's *History of Rome* as one of his textbooks. Nor does this diminish their stature as great historical works.'

[2] For the correct and useful sense of this much-abused word see Alan Richardson, *Christian Apologetics*, 72–78.

significantly different from those of the positivist historians of a vanished age.[1]

As might have been expected, it is in Germany that the re-appraisal of history is today being undertaken with the deepest sense of urgency. As far back as 1921 Becker had written that, when times are out of joint, historians 'will be disposed to cross-examine the past in order to find out why it did not usher in a better state of affairs . . . approving or disapproving in the light of present discontents. The past is a kind of screen upon which each generation projects its vision of the future; and so long as hope springs in the human breast, the "new History" will be a recurring phenomenon'.[2] The words might have been written in 1961 with the great German post-war debate about history in mind.[3] In the course of this discussion the paradox has become apparent that Ranke, who has been called the Newton of modern scientific history, is now discovered to have been the foremost myth-maker of the Bismarckian National State. After 1825 the old eighteenth-century myth of universal reason had faded, along with the cosmopolitan culture of the age of Frederick II, and a new national awareness, stimulated by the excursions of Napoleon, was awakened in Europe. Scientific history provided the

[1] Professor Geoffrey Barraclough has written feelingly of the dilemma of those historians who before 1939 had been brought up in the cult of 'historicism' (presumably Rankean history as characterized by Acton). He describes how, when they returned from war service after 1945, they found that the 'old grooves', though not entirely obliterated, no longer served the purposes of a contemporary and relevant post-war approach to history (*The Historian in a Changing World*, Oxford, 1955, 8f.; the whole book is highly illuminating for the understanding of the historian's task today).

[2] In a review in the *American Historical Review*, XXVI (July 1921), of H. G. Wells's *Outline of History* (1920), an uncompromisingly rationalist piece of propaganda history, aimed (not unsuccessfully) at the younger generation.

[3] The best account of post-war developments in German historical thinking will be found in *German History: Some New German Views*, edited by Hans Kohn, London, 1954, where a full bibliography down to that date is given. The Editor's essay, 'Rethinking Recent German History', is followed by reflections upon this theme by leading contemporary German historians. The reassessment of Bismarck, which forms the starting-point of the new historiography, is treated by Franz Schnabel in 'The Bismarck Problem'; Ludwig Dehio's 'Germany and the Epoch of World Wars' is especially instructive, and Walther Hofer's 'Toward a Revision of the German Concept of History' is particularly relevant to our theme. Not the least service performed by the volume is its inclusion of F. Meinecke's address, 'Ranke and Burckhardt' (1948).

myth by means of which national ambitions for the future could
be thrown on to the screen of the past. Ranke came to conceive
of the progress of mankind as bound up with the development of
sovereign national states, 'spiritual essences', 'God's thoughts',
each differentiated from the others by its own individual virtues
and achievements. A conservative by temper and conditioning,
Ranke at first had serious misgivings about Bismarck's violent
methods; but his apprehensions were gradually overcome as
Bismarck's success enabled Ranke's native Prussia to realize her
virtues and greatness, especially between 1866 and 1871. Meinecke
quotes Ranke as having said on his ninetieth birthday (1885), 'In
the events we have experienced, we may see principally a defeat
of the revolutionary forces which make impossible the regular,
continued development of world-history. If these forces had stood
their ground, there would have been no question of the continued
creation of historical forces, or even of an unpartisan examination
of them. World history in the objective sense would have been
impossible.'[1] And thus, while Ranke presided over historiography in Germany, the Bismarck myth was born; the historians
were making history in the twentieth century in the very act of
writing history in the nineteenth. Ranke's responsibility in the
matter is endlessly debated, and it is not necessary for us to join
in the controversy. How far had Bismarck, as Ranke supposed,
held in check the forces of 'revolutionary democracy', or how far
had he strengthened those elemental powers which Hitler subsequently invoked to establish National Socialism in 1933? The
course of events certainly proved Ranke to be right on one point
at least: the triumph of the revolutionary forces put an end to
objective historiography, which was one of the earliest casualties
in the Third Reich. Once more Acton's assertion that revolutionaries seek to abolish history was proved to be well founded: the
Nazis had even less use for objective history than had the Jacobins; yet once more the reverse of their intention was what, in
fact, came about: history was reborn because fresh assessments
must be made, and the radical reappraisal of German history has
been the liveliest aspect of academic historiography in Germany
since the collapse of the post-Bismarckian national state in 1945.

Subsequent developments or perversions of Ranke's myth of
National States cannot fairly be laid at his door. He was mistaken,

[1] Meinecke's art. in Hans Kohn, op. cit., 145.

as events were to prove, in thinking that Bismarckian policies could avert the triumph of demonic revolutionary forces and preserve such values of civilization as the love of objective truth. If he was naïve in his belief in the beneficence of conflict between National States or in the good intentions of the autocratic Prussian Government (which, incidentally, had afforded him protection), he was entirely sincere in his belief in a European community enriched by the diversity of national civilizations.[1] Moreover, subsequent perversions of his views about nationality (which were turned into nationalism) would have been utterly repugnant to his deep religious awareness (expressed in 1854 in his lectures before King Maximilian of Bavaria) that 'every epoch is immediate to God and that its value in no way rests upon what it produces, but upon the very fact of its existence . . . this is the way in which the historian must look at things'.[2] He never lost his early conviction, stated in a letter of 1820, that God is observable throughout history and that witness to him is to be found in 'the connecting line that runs through history'.[3] For Ranke moral standards were immutable, as for Acton; and if in the name of scientific history he excluded moral judgments from his works, he could not foresee that there would come after him, even from among his own pupils, those for whom 'moral' would mean 'German nationalist'. The so-called Prussian School of historians Droysen, von Sybel and Treitschke, says Geyl, placed their services unreservedly in the service of the Prussian Idea.[4] On the post-Rankean version of the Prussian myth, Bismarck and Luther became the twin impersonations of the new nationalist ideology, the political and spiritual cult-heroes respectively. More disturbing than Becker's question about why historians had done so

[1] Cf. P. Geyl's admirable essay 'Ranke in the Light of the Catastrophe' in *Debates with Historians*, 6.

[2] Ranke, *Weltgeschichte*, IX (1888), 5 f.

[3] P. Geyl, ibid., 7. On Ranke's religious view of history see Hans Liebeschütz, *Ranke*, Historical Association Pamphlets, 1954, 4f., 8f.; also Meinecke's art., op. cit.

[4] Ibid., 11. Heinrich von Treitschke (1834–96) succeeded to Ranke's chair at Berlin in 1874. By his glorifying of power politics and of war, by his fervent nationalism and anti-Semitism, he prepared the way for the triumph of Prussianism over the German spirit. Geyl quotes his exclamation at the victory of 1870: 'Who can be so blind as to deny that in the wonderful happenings of these days works the divine Intelligence that compels us Germans to become a nation?' (*Use and Abuse of History*, New Haven, Yale Univ. Press, 1955, 43).

little to avert 1914 is the question why after 1918 German historians (whose function, of course, is to destroy myths as well as to
create them) did so little openly and effectively to puncture the
Prussian myth. Even after 1918, writes Dr Hans Kohn, 'German
historians, instead of re-examining the foundations of the Bismarckian Reich and of the Ranke tradition, set their hearts on the
vindication of the past . . . and viewed the world situation as if
it had begun with the Allied "crime" of Versailles'.[1] And so there
came into being, open and unashamed, Alfred Rosenberg's *Myth
of the Twentieth Century*, and in 1934 its author was put in control
of all political and intellectual education in the Party, while
Baldur von Schirach was charged with the indoctrination of
German youth.

When Ranke retired from his chair at Berlin, Jakob Burckhardt (1818–97) was invited to succeed him, but he declined the
honour.[2] A member of one of the oldest and most respected
families in Basel, he became professor of History there from
1858 to 1893. He was known during his lifetime chiefly as an
historian of art, on which he constantly lectured; for him history
was essentially the story of civilization, and the preservation of
culture and of the arts of civilization was to him more important
than the depressing reality of power politics and national egotism.
Burckhardt thought Bismarck was a great man, and therefore
potentially evil; he found his personality 'obnoxious'. As a young
man he had sat in Ranke's seminar and had reverenced his teacher;
but he never thought that 'facts' as such were worth knowing for
their own sake. He was naturally conservative and took an even
more gloomy view than did Ranke of the smouldering forces of
revolutionary socialism; but, unlike Ranke, he did not believe
that Bismarck's policies would safeguard civilization from their
destructive violence. The Germany he loved was the Germany of
Weimar and Goethe; the Germany which stifled him was the
Prussia of Potsdam and Bismarck; the Germanic city in which he

[1] Hans Kohn, op. cit., 25.
[2] 'I would not have gone to Berlin at any price; to have left Basle would
have brought a malediction on me. Nor is my merit in the matter great; there
would be no helping a man of fifty-four who did not know where his modest
portion of (relatively) good luck lay. . . . It is a great triumph for Treitschke
—good luck to him!' (Letter dated 28 June 1872 to von Preen; *The Letters of
Jacob Burckhardt*, selected and translated by Alexander Dru, London, 1955,
152.)

could be himself was the Basel of Erasmus and Holbein. Burck-hardt was a humanist who added 'the history of art' to the 'aspects' of history which are nowadays included in academic curricula;[1] but in a deeper sense his humanist attitude to history has profoundly interested thoughtful people in the last decade or two, and he has undoubtedly been taken more seriously than he ever was in his lifetime.

Burckhardt was not appreciated in his own age because he resisted its ideological assumptions. In an age of optimism he was pessimistic. It was an illusion to imagine that the nineteenth century was superior morally, culturally or even intellectually to its predecessors.[2] He had discerned portents in history which boded ill for the future, where others had observed tokens of progress—for example, in the France of Louis XIV, 'the first *perfected* example of the modern State with supreme coercive power exercised on nearly all branches of culture' (contrast Voltaire and Buckle).[3] Money-making, 'the main force of present-day culture', postulates the omnicompetent State, which (as the crisis of 1870-1 showed him) would pursue war as an instrument of policy because it was, amongst other objectives, an effective way of disciplining the revolutionary-prone workers.[4] But this would lead eventually to the triumph of the revolutionary forces, since they would have to be taken into partnership as industry and commerce were geared ever more scientifically to war; a-moral men, despisers of culture, would become dictators, 'terribles simplificateurs', upstarts who would usurp the powers of the old, effete dynasties. Here, in a letter to a friend, dated 26 April 1872, is surely a most remarkable prediction of the events

[1] His guide to Italian works of art appeared in 1855, *Der Cicerone*; his *Civilization of the Renaissance in Italy* (1860) was translated into English by S. G. C. Middlemore (1878; reissued 1944); his *History of the Renaissance in Italy* appeared in 1867. His earliest work, *The Age of Constantine the Great*, was published in 1852. These were the only works published during his lifetime. His *Weltgeschichtliche Betrachtungen*, edited from his notes, was published posthumously in 1905 (Eng. trans. by 'M.D.H.', *Reflections on History*, London, 1943). There is an attractive biographical introduction in the *Letters*, ed. A. Dru, op. cit., 1–34. See also B. Croce, *History as the Story of Liberty*, 100–10; Karl Löwith, *Jakob Burckhardt der Mensch inmitten der Geschichte* (Lucerne, 1936); and Alfred von Martin, *Die Religion Jakob Burckhardts* (1942); also his *Nietzsche und Burckhardt* (1940).
[2] *Reflections*, 62.
[3] Ibid., 83.
[4] Ibid., 116f.; 136f.

which took place in Germany some sixty years later: 'Bismarck
has only taken into his own hands what would have happened
in due course without him. . . . He saw that the growing wave
of social-democracy would somehow or other bring about a state
of naked power . . . and said: *Ipse faciam*, and embarked on
three wars, 1864, 1866, 1870. But we are only at the beginning.
Don't you feel that everything we do now seems more or less
amateurish, capricious, and becomes increasingly ridiculous by
contrast with the high purposefulness of the military machine
worked out to the last details? It will be most interesting for you,
my dear Sir [his correspondent was von Preen, a German district
Prefect], to observe how the machinery of State and administra-
tion is transformed and militarized; for me—how schools and
education are put through the cure, etc. Of all classes, the workers
are going to have the strangest time; I have a suspicion that . . .
the military State will have to turn "industrialist". The accumulations of beings, the mounds of men in the yards and factories
cannot be left for all eternity in their need and thirst for riches;
a planned and controlled degree of poverty, with promotion and
uniforms, starting and ending daily to the roll of drums, that is
what ought to come logically.'[1] The future which was depicted
on the screen of history—the same history which Ranke was
determined to read objectively—was seen much more clearly by
Burckhardt than it had been seen by Ranke.

Burckhardt was a pessimist, but not ultimately so. In life he
was cheerful, serene and contented. Though he had lost his
ministerial vocation and his belief in dogmatic orthodoxy in his
student days, when Strauss was putting forward his 'mythical'
theory concerning the Gospels (Burckhardt's early letters are full
of echoes of the debate), he remained profoundly Christian in
temper, rejecting the alternatives of rationalism ('a kind of
religion, too')[2] and of Liberalism. His pessimism was essentially
that of the Christian faith: 'according to Christian doctrine, the
prince of this world is Satan. There is nothing more un-Christian
than to promise virtue a lasting reign, a material divine reward
here below. . . . It would be a horrible sight if, as a result of the
consistent reward of good and punishment of evil on this earth,
all men were to behave well with an ulterior motive. . . . The

[1] *Letters*, ed. A. Dru, 151f.
[2] *Reflections*, 54.

time might come when men would pray Heaven for a little impunity for evil-doers.'[1] Burckhardt's studies in history had taught him the need of immense compassion for all those nameless multitudes who have suffered while 'great men' have redirected the course of history and established those civilizations in which culture has become possible,[2] and one cannot read the concluding pages of his *Reflections*, his maturest thought, without sensing his passionate belief that they had not suffered in vain.

Meinecke and the Reappraisal of German History

The retrospective surveys often given to us by eminent historians, when towards the end of their working lives they look back over developments in historiography and historical points of view in their own times, are invariably fascinating and instructive. One such retrospect in recent years stands out above all the rest as moving testimony to the historian's involvement in history. Friedrich Meinecke, born in 1862, was brought up in the tradition of Ranke and became its historian;[3] he occupied Ranke's chair at Berlin from 1914 to 1928; for forty-two years he edited the *Historische Zeitschrift*, which commemorated his ninetieth birthday in its issue for October 1952, and which contained a complete bibliography of his works. He was not uncritical of the Ranke tradition of scientific history ('Historismus' in its normal German usage); already by 1927 he had asserted that historical reality cannot be apprehended by a method which leaves value (especially political and ethical value) out of account.[4] The connection between historiographical positivism and nationalism, including the assistance which the former has unintentionally given to the latter, has probably never been thoroughly investigated; and a beginning might be made by historians of ideas through a study

---

[1] Ibid., 214.

[2] 'Culture' is defined as 'the sum total of those mental developments which take place spontaneously and lay no claim to universal or compulsive authority' (*Reflections*, 55).

[3] *Die Entstehung des Historismus* was published in 1936.

[4] Art. 'Kausalitäten und Werte in der Geschichte' in *Historische Zeitschrift* (CXXXVII, 1927). J. A. von Rantzau says of this essay: 'He sees, unabashed, the distinctive marks of a true historical work to consist in the attitude toward the primal ideas of the good, true and beautiful, hopelessly antiquated as they must seem to many of his positivist and nationalist colleagues' (art. 'The Glorification of the State in German Historical Writing', 1950, in Hans Kohn, op. cit., 173).

of the development of Meinecke's historical thinking. In his *Die Deutsche Katastrophe* (1945) the octogenarian doyen of German historical studies courageously declared that modern German history had turned aside from the true German and Western spirit of Goethe and Europe and that Germany must now rediscover herself, not as a Great Power, but as a leader in the peaceful ways of civilized humanity. His last testament was his address to the German Academy of Sciences, 1948, one of the most moving confessions of our times.[1] We will not here attempt to summarize it; it should be read in its entirety. The historian must remain 'poised high over the world as free as he can be of partisan outlook', even amidst the downfall of his own ideals. He cannot, however, be a detached spectator, because 'in the historian's own mind, historical observation and the experience of living in his own time and sharing in its destiny form an indivisible inner unity. . . . The things we have lived through in the past fourteen years thrust before us quite novel aspects and problems in our historical past. There is much we must relearn.'[2] The address enumerates 'the factors comprising Burckhardt's greater excellence in his judgment of the present and the future'. Meinecke's conclusion is that, 'cautious as we may be, still we must say that Burckhardt saw more deeply and acutely into the essential historical character of his own time. As a result, he was able to see the future, too, more definitely and certainly than Ranke could.'[3]

The events of German history in the twentieth century have profoundly affected the contemporary understanding of the nature of the historian's task, more particularly as this concerns his responsibility to society. For one thing, it has to be recorded that the historical myths of the superiority of the Aryan race and of Hitler's Reich as the bulwark against Communism were not overthrown in the German mind by historians, but by events, by the outcome of campaigns such as those of Stalingrad and Normandy, and by the violent entry of foreign soldiers into Berlin. Furthermore, it was not merely historical myths that were destroyed: a theory about the nature of historiography itself, the orthodox academic view of scientific history to which all histo-

---

[1] Reprinted under the title 'Ranke and Burckhardt' in Hans Kohn, op. cit., 142–56.
[2] Ibid., 144.
[3] Ibid.

rians, except a few outsiders like Burckhardt, had subscribed for more than a hundred years, was utterly discredited. As the searching reappraisal of German history since 1945 has abundantly demonstrated, it is not merely a new history (or new historical myth) which is demanded, but a new historiography, one which takes account of humane values and does not open the door to demagogues by pretending that historians, being scientists, are not concerned with moral issues. After the Nazified history-books had been burnt, what was the new 'image' of Germany and her history that should be written into the new ones? How is the post-war generation of historians to discharge its responsibility to society? This question has been seriously and endlessly debated by historians in Germany since 'the catastrophe'. Behind all questions about a new 'image' or interpretation of history lies the more fundamental question of the nature of historical thinking itself. One quotation only must suffice to illustrate some of the lines of approach now being discussed; it is taken from a lecture given by a Swiss historian (born in 1920) who became *Dozent* at the Free University of Berlin: 'Though concealed in the conception of history is the notion that we have in our mind a picture of the historical past, the theory of historiography has long since recognized that we should not take "picture" here in the sense of faithful copy of the past. Naïve historical realism, according to which something like recognition of an historical object "in itself" (*an sich*) is possible, has long since been overcome. The picture which we form of the past must not be compared to a photograph but to a painting. And, just as we can see a landscape only from a given place, similarly all historical vision is determined by that place from which we view it. It means seeing in *perspective*. Broadly conceived, an historical problem, therefore, is always a question by the present to the past. Hence, in point of fact the questioner's interest and principle of selection, and in the final analysis his value system and his ideology, are decisive factors in the definition of the question. An understanding of history is never achieved by cognition without prior assumptions, but with understanding of the specific assumptions. Only when these assumptions enter into our calculations as conditions can we speak of historical objectivity.'[1]

[1] 'Towards a Revision of the German Concept of History', art. by Walther Hofer in Hans Kohn, op. cit., 188.

6

HISTORY
AND THE MIRACULOUS

IN the preceding Lecture we considered the change in men's thinking concerning the nature of history and of the historian's task which has come about during the course of the twentieth century. This change, as we saw, did not result from any abstract philosophizing, which on the whole has tended to run in the contrary direction. Even the idealistic speculations of Croce and Collingwood look today like rationalizing attempts to provide a philosophical justification for their insights into the nature of their own activity as historians, rendered necessary because those insights ran counter to the mainstream of positivist thinking in their days. The truth is that in an age of revolutionary change, and therefore of historical reappraisal, twentieth-century historians found themselves abandoning the nineteenth-century notion of 'scientific history' not for philosophical reasons but for historical ones. When it was discovered that neither Ranke himself nor anyone else had written presuppositionless history, and that behind the laboratory-jackets of the 'scientific historians' were disguised the 'wise men of the tribe' spinning their myths, it was sensibly concluded, not that Ranke and his fellow workers were not historians, but that the theory which represented history as an objectively factual science, like the physical sciences, must be wrong. Twentieth-century historians, have, in truth, learnt from the course of events themselves what the nineteenth-century historians, by and large, failed to learn from Burke. Contemporary historians for the most part have abandoned positivist conceptions of history for the same reasons that in an earlier revolutionary age Burke and his followers had abandoned the rationalist conception of history of Hume and the *philosophes*.

We saw in Lecture IV that the most eminent leaders of continental theological thought during the first half of our century had attempted to disengage the Christian revelation from that sphere of history with which 'secular' historians are concerned, and that they had endeavoured to find a home for it in a realm either of sacred history (*Heilsgeschichte*) or existential experience, to which historians, *qua* historians, had no access. We noted also that the reason why they felt obliged to adopt this desperate strategy of withdrawal was that they had come to accept the positivist theory of history as the indisputably scientific account of it. Now that the positivist view has itself disentegrated before the march of events and today no longer represents what most historians think about history, it is time to reopen the question and to ask whether there are any good *historical* reasons for supposing that a divine revelation, such as the Bible attests, cannot have been vouchsafed in the midst of ordinary, everyday 'secular' history, the history which working historians handle. Such an enquiry, of course, raises the whole question of the miraculous. How do we go about answering this question in the light of contemporary attitudes towards history? In order not to be too discursive, we will concentrate the enquiry upon the resurrection of Jesus Christ from the dead, since the whole Christian faith in God's revelation in history is focused upon this miracle. Our question is: whether the resurrection of Christ may reasonably be held to be an historical event.

Can Philosophy answer Historical Questions?

Now that history has become 'just history', an enquiry in its own right, seeking historical explanations which cannot be reduced to generalizations drawn from other enquiries, a number of the old philosophical objections are perceived to be—as Hume in a moment of honesty confessed—'at the bottom verbal, and admit not of any precise determination'.[1] Of course, historians generalize, since rational discourse of any kind is impossible without generalization; and of course they make use of the generalizations of every other science, from the law of gravity to the law of diminishing returns. But their own generalizations, necessary

---

[1] See p. 17 *supra*.

indeed in the task of historical explanation, *are* their own; precisely because they are historical, they have a character of their own, and they are not less useful because they do not partake of the exactness and verifiability of the generalizations of the natural sciences. Thus, to take a recent illustration, when an historical writer in giving us a profound and brilliant historical interpretation of the period from 1789 to 1848 in terms of a conception of the 'dual revolution' which he finds in this era, it is unlikely to disturb him when it is alleged that his general concept 'revolution' is unscientific because it embraces (in his usage) two quite different movements of events, namely the French Revolution and the Industrial Revolution, which have nothing in common except the word 'revolution'.[1] The historical general concept 'revolution' (cf. also 'the historical revolution') is used in the way in which historians use *their* general concepts, that is, analogically and not univocally, which is not the way in which scientists use *their* general concepts; the former are of use in the interpretation of historical evidence and the latter are not (except incidentally, as, e.g., the law of gravity). History, unlike science, does not progress by making wider and wider generalizations; it progresses by giving more coherently rational explanations of the available historical evidence, so that in the end we are bound to agree that 'it must have been like that'.[2] Historical method does not rule out the possibility of an event's having taken place because it does not fit into a system of generalizations; it decides that an event has *probably* taken place because the assumption that it has done so makes better sense of the evidence. There are no historical generalizations (or laws of history) which determine in advance of the historical enquiry whether an event may have happened or not; historical generalizations arise out of the evidence and are not *a priori* conditions of thinking which precede it. The general concept 'revolution' does not arise out of observed regularities in

[1] The reference is to E. J. Hobsbawm, *The Age of Revolution: Europe from 1789 to 1848*, London, 1962.

[2] This is the generally accepted criterion of whether an historical explanation is a good one or a bad. To take an example at random: Mr Harold Nicolson in a review of Professor Lacey Baldwin Smith's recent biography of Catherine Howard, *A Tudor Tragedy* (London, 1961), writes: 'Professor Smith has in fact so excellently caught the atmosphere of the Tudor age that the tragedy moves inexorably to its end, so that the reader does not exclaim "But this could not possibly be true!" but exclaims "Of course, it was all a logical consequence!" ' (*The Observer*, London, Sunday, June 18, 1961).

historical events, but out of analogies discernible by the historical imagination.

Eighteenth-century rationalism believed that what might or might not have taken place could in many vital respects be determined in advance of historical enquiry by a consideration of certain laws of nature, which are the same for all men in all ages and places. This was the reason why, as we noted, *philosophe* history before Gibbon dispensed with historical research and despised the erudites. Historical questions were to be settled dogmatically by reference to 'the constant and universal principles of human nature', not by scrupulous examination of the evidence followed by the attempt to give a coherent account of it. As a Victorian bishop remarked of another kind of dogmatism (during the *Essays and Reviews* controversy), 'where the conclusions are prescribed, the study is precluded'. David Hume attempted to settle the historical question about miracles by an appeal to supposedly universally valid generalizations called 'the laws of nature'; being a rationalist he did not, of course, distinguish between laws of nature and laws of history (or of human nature). In Section X, 'Of Miracles', in his *Enquiry concerning Human Understanding* he wrote: 'I flatter myself, that I have discovered an argument . . . which, if just, will, with the wise and learned, be an everlasting check to all kinds of superstitious delusion, and consequently, will be useful as long as the world endures. For so long, I presume, will the accounts of miracles and prodigies be found in all history, sacred and profane.'[1] 'A wise man', he tells us, 'proportions his belief to the evidence', a statement with which no one could disagree, since it enunciates a rule which is true not only for historians but for law-courts and for everyday life. But Hume himself does not really believe it, because he is going on to tell us that the evidence does not matter, that the question about miracles can be decided without bothering about evidence, since no conceivable historical evidence could establish a miracle. His 'decisive argument' is that evidence from the past can be rightly evaluated only upon the assumption that the same fundamental regularities obtained in the past as are observable today. Of course, Hume, lacking the historical attitude, assumed that what eighteenth-century natural philosophy believed to be the fundamental regularities would for ever remain unalterably

[1] Ed. L. A. Selby-Bigge, 110.

the same in every subsequent age; but we will let this pass, and
agree with his contention that the historian in determining what,
in fact, happened will take into account all the scientific evidence
available in his own day concerning the kind of world we live in.
If that evidence no longer requires him to think that historical
causation is explicable by means of the causal sequences described
by the physical sciences, that will be a factor in the process by
which he arrives at his judgments about facts. Hume, however,
considered that he had here a knock-down argument, valid for all
time, against miracles. He makes the argument easier for himself
by defining 'miracle' in a way in which no theologian from St
Augustine onwards would have done; a miracle, he tells us, is 'a
violation of the laws of nature'; it is what never happens in the
common course of nature.[1] Of course miracles do not happen, if
they are defined as that which does not happen. Laws of nature,
Hume explains, are established by 'a firm and unalterable experience', and he gives as an example of a law of nature the proposition that 'all men die'. The 'uniform experience' that all men die,
he says, amounts to proof against the possibility of resurrection
from the dead. (But surely all that it 'proves' is that Jesus must
have *died*, as indeed the historical evidence says that he did.) 'The
plain consequences is . . . that no testimony is sufficient to
establish a miracle, unless the testimony be of such a kind that its
falsehood would be more miraculous.' One should always reject
'the greater miracle'.[2]

The conclusion of Hume's argument is that nothing short of a
divine revelation could attest the occurrence of a miracle; *no*
human witness, *no* historical evidence, could do so. There are still
some philosophers who remain impressed by it.[3] But nowadays
it is not usual to hold that there are any fixed laws of nature in the

[1] Ibid., 114f.
[2] Ibid., 115f.
[3] For example, Professor A. G. N. Flew has recently attempted to bring
it up to date by urging that what is historically impossible is what is logically
incompatible with a true law of nature: 'Any proposition which might
express a law of nature will be open and general and of the form *any such
thing must be so and so*. The typical historical assertion is particular and in the
past tense. . . . Propositions of the first sort can in principle be tested at
any time and in any place. Propositions of the second sort cannot any longer
be tested directly at all. It is this which gives the former their vastly greater
logical strength, justifying their use against the latter' (*The Listener*, London,
Vol. LXV, No. 1679, June 1, 1961, 963f.).

sense of generalizations from 'uniform experience' which are somehow endowed with logical necessity, so that they are capable of proving a universal negative.[1] Still less are there any laws of history (such as the law of progress) which can be used to answer historical questions without the fatigue of having to look at the evidence. History is not a generalizing science which tells us that if such and such circumstances occur, then such and such results will follow; it does not attempt to formulate general propositions of the type 'any such thing must be so and so'. All that Hume is really telling us is that the more surprisingly a reported event runs counter to our experience, the stronger the testimony will have to be before we shall be willing to accept it. But this is an observation in the sphere of the psychology of belief, which applies to everybody, including historians. The historian's particular expertise is precisely that of assessing the value of the evidence of the past. He is *par excellence* the wise man who proportions his belief to the evidence.[2] The one thing he will not consent to do is to accept an interpretation of historical events before he has been allowed to study the evidence for himself. The integrity of history as an autonomous discipline demands, as Collingwood saw, that the historian should reject all ready-made answers;[3] and this is true whether the answers are offered by actual participants in the particular events or by philosophers discoursing upon the nature of events in general. The question whether a particular event

[1] Cf. J. F. Ashton, S.J.: 'Professor Flew states that "the expression 'Law of Nature' is so used by scientists that to speak of violating such a law must be contradictory and without sense". This is simply rubbish. A scientific law is not an affirmation of a logical necessity; it is an affirmation of an observed regularity in nature. It states what *does* happen, not what *must* happen. That is why all scientific laws are in principle open to refutation. They never acquire the logical necessity that Professor Flew would wish upon them. If they did, they would cease to be informative and become mere tautologies' (Letter in *The Listener*, Vol. LXV, No. 1681, June 15, 1961, 1049f.).

[2] Much has been written about the cross-examination of historical witnesses as a primary duty of the historian since F. H. Bradley raised the question about historical testimony in his remarkable pioneering essay on 'The Presuppositions of Critical History' (1874; reprinted in *Collected Essays*, Oxford, 1935, I, 1–70; see esp. 38–45). One of the best introductory discussions is that of Marc Bloch, *The Historian's Craft*, 79–137. From the theological side attention may be called to John Knox, *Criticism and Faith*, New York and London, 1953, and D. E. Nineham, 'Eye-Witness Testimony and the Gospel Tradition', art. in *The Journal of Theological Studies*, NS, Vol. IX, 2 (Oct. 1960).

[3] *The Idea of History*, 257.

happened is an historical question and cannot be settled by philosophical ratiocination; it can be settled only by the employment of the methods which historians use in the assessment of historical evidence. How one should define 'miracle' is a philosophical (or theological) question and one which is irrelevant to our present concern. Whether, in fact, Christ rose from the dead is an historical question and one which involves the assessment of historical evidence.

What are Historical Facts?

There are, however, as we have already noticed, some theologians who do not regard the resurrection of Christ as a matter for historical enquiry at all. For instance, Professor Günther Bornkamm tells us that 'the event of Christ's resurrection from the dead, his life and his eternal reign, are things removed from historical scholarship. History cannot ascertain and establish conclusively the facts about them as it can with other events of the past.'[1] Two assumptions about the nature of history seem to be implied in this statement. The first is that history *can* establish conclusively the facts concerning some past events; and indeed Bornkamm's *Jesus of Nazareth* is (in comparison with other writings of the Bultmann school) notable for its positive affirmations concerning the historical Jesus. But, secondly, his words imply that a distinction must be made between such facts, which may be conclusively established, and certain beliefs or interpretations which cannot thus be established; amongst the latter is the resurrection of Christ. It will be immediately apparent that we are here back once more in the old nineteenth-century positivist conception of 'scientific history'. Historians establish facts, and they can establish some facts conclusively; the interpretation of the facts is not their concern at all. That is the business of philosophers or theologians; historians deal only with facts, which it is their task to establish and then tie together by means of a string of causal connections: 'après la collection des faits, la recherche des causes'.[2] The trend of contemporary thinking about history seems to be against the distinction between facts and faith, or between history and interpretation. It appears to be widely held today that there are no such things as bare facts and that history is from first

[1] *Jesus of Nazareth*, Eng. trans., 180.
[2] 'Taine's Maxim'; see *supra*, 142.

to last interpretation. The reasons for thinking thus become apparent as soon as we begin to examine what is meant by 'facts'. There are several historical thinkers to whom we might turn for a critique of the theory that facts precede interpretation in historiography. Croce, somewhat obscurely, and Collingwood, more incisively, have criticized the view; but since they may be suspected of harbouring illicit idealistic purposes, we will turn to Carl Becker, who cannot be accused of nourishing any ulterior ambitions as a philosopher. He was pre-eminently the historian for whom history was 'just history' and nothing else.

From the time when Becker wrote his celebrated article on 'Detachment and the Writing of History' in the *Atlantic Monthly* (1910), his views remained consistent and unwavering until his death in 1945.[1] He sustained a devastating onslaught upon the generally received view that facts are one thing and interpretations another. During the nineteenth century it had been mistakenly believed that a fact is a purely objective thing, something that could be pressed with the thumb to test its solidity, something that does not change. If earlier historians had been discredited, that was because they had worked unscientifically and so got their facts wrong; the more scientific an historian was, the more he concentrated on the hard facts, leaving it to others to interpret them or make a synthesis. But this is a naïvely uncritical view of the nature of history. Doubtless in the sense of 'what happened' the facts are indeed immutable, but in this sense they are just what the historian can never directly know. It is not the reality which the historian takes apart, but only 'sources'. He never gets at the uninterpreted facts, 'what really happened', because the uninterpreted facts-in-themselves constitute a noumenal reality which lies beyond the forms of our perception. Just as for Kant the mind is

[1] Two books will be found especially helpful in the elucidation of Becker's thought, which has provided a focus for much historical discussion in America: Charlotte Watkins Smith, *Carl Becker: on History and the Climate of Opinion*, Cornell Univ. Press, Ithaca, N.Y., 1956, and Burleigh Taylor Wilkins, *Carl Becker: A Biographical Study in American Intellectual History*, M.I.T. Press and Harvard Univ. Press, Cambridge, Mass., 1961. See also Raymond O. Rockwood, ed., *Carl Becker's Heavenly City Revisited*; Cushing Strout, *The Pragmatic Revolt in American History: Carl Becker and Charles Beard*, New Haven, 1958. Of interest in this connection is Charles A. Beard, 'Written History as an Act of Faith', *American Historical Review* XXXIX (1934), 219–31. There is a very considerable literature, and a full bibliography may be found in Wilkins, op. cit., 231–42.

the law-giver of nature, so for the critical philosopher of history the historian is the law-giver of the human past. Just as we cannot experience the raw material of nature (*noumena*), but only nature as conditioned by the forms of our perception, so the historian cannot see the historical reality but only the images in his own mind. 'The facts of history', said Becker in 1910, 'do not exist for any historian until he creates them, and into every fact that he creates some part of his individual experience must enter.' The distinction between facts and interpretation is therefore untenable, because facts are only interpretations of evidence. Becker accordingly calls facts 'mental images', but it might be better to call them 'judgments of evidence', because the latter term is more precise (after all, poets and opium-smokers enjoy mental images) and also because the expression 'mental images' suggests an idealist view of history of the Croce-Collingwood type. Such a view was not at all Becker's conclusion; he eschewed philosophical construction and aimed only at elucidating the nature of the historian's activity; all that can be said is that Becker calls attention to those aspects of the historian's work which lend to idealist theories such plausibility as they possess. The historian's facts are mental in the sense that they are nowhere if not in someone's mind; as such they are present facts, and how they are related to the noumenal or immutable past facts is a question not for the historian but for the critical philosopher of history.[1] The assigning

[1] Whether Becker was philosophizing is a matter of verbal definitions; he was essentially an historian reflecting upon the nature of his own activities. But that a philosopher could arrive at the same kind of conclusions is demonstrated by F. H. Bradley's long-neglected 'Presuppositions of Critical History' of 1874. Bradley had urged that all history is a matter of inference, prejudication and presupposition (*Collected Essays*, 20); that awareness of its own presuppositions is its only protection from the caprices of fiction (21); that it 'rests in the last resort upon an inference from our experience, a judgment based upon our own present state of things, upon the world personal in us' (24); it is inextricably blended with the historian's own experience and beliefs (26f.); 'facts' are criticized testimonies from the past, tested and reconstructed by the historian in the light of his own principles and convictions (29–31); unlike the natural sciences, history can test past facts only by analogy with the present (31–36); it is therefore only probable (38); its interest is not in scientific generalization but in 'the oneness of humanity in all its stages and under all its varieties' (39); because it is always personal, it is rooted in the historian's own time and place, and therefore history will always have to be rewritten (45). But all this was far in advance of the historical thinking of Bradley's own day. If it had been discussed and assimilated, Becker's views of 1910 would not have seemed so unorthodox to his own generation.

of importance in historical explanation comes first, because without it facts (judgments of evidence) cannot come into view; the interpretative concept precedes the facts and determines them. There are no uninterpreted facts which form the raw material for the scientific historian; the assumption that there are such facts prevents historians from asking the right questions. It is not the historian who sticks to the facts; the facts stick to him: 'the really detached mind is a dead mind, lying among the facts of history like unmagnetized steel among iron filings, no synthesis ever resulting in one case or the other to the end of time.' What the historian can never detach himself from is the 'climate of opinion' of his own day; it is because of this that he notices certain 'facts' and ignores others; what he does with his evidence is determined by his belonging to a particular age and place; his interpretation of history and his view of what are and what are not 'facts' is conditioned by the dominant ideas of the age in which he lives. Becker thus raised in an urgent form the problem of historical relativism; it seemed as though the objectivity of scientific history was being replaced by a subjectivity from which in view of his own historical conditioning the historian could not escape. But we will defer the discussion of this important question until Lecture VIII.[1]

Since Becker's essay of 1910, which brought the matter into the foreground of discussion, his views seem to have obtained wide acceptance amongst historians who have reflected upon the nature of their own activity; how far this is due directly to Becker's influence, which at least in England does not appear to have been strong, or how far he was giving expression to a change which was inevitably coming about in the sphere of historical thinking, it is not our business to enquire. Today it would seem to be widely understood that historical facts are simply judgments of evidence; 'objective' facts are nothing more than judgments of evidence which have been agreed upon by a large number of historians; they do not seem as objective in one age as in another, not (as a rule) because the evidence alters or is significantly enlarged, but because of changes in 'the climate of opinion'. What one age thinks of no importance may be very

[1] For a fuller exposition of Becker's view of 'facts', adequately documented by reference to his writings, see Charlotte Watkins Smith, op. cit., 52–58.

highly rated in another.[1] We do not at once recognize the real character of history because of the way in which we all (inevitably) learned history at school. If a schoolboy learns and accepts the fact that in 1066 a battle at Hastings resulted in the establishment of Norman rule in England, he is only assenting (at second hand) to a judgment of evidence which has been agreed upon by a lot of historians. We all accept as 'facts' a great number of other people's judgments at second hand, and most of us have very little notion of how those judgments were arrived at in the first place; indeed, every historian has to accept masses of second-hand judgments, however critical he tries to be, because it is impossible for him to verify every single 'fact' of history for himself. Thus, for most of us history looks like an objective photograph of the past, and we forget that the determinative factors in it were originally the mental activity, judgments of importance and scale of values of a large number of people whose interpretation of the evidence was determined in part by their own personal beliefs and qualities and in part by the 'climate of opinion' of their particular age. When he hears the cliché that 'it's no use arguing about facts', the critical historian will smile, because he knows that the facts referred to are nothing other than the present stage of an on-going argument. Historical facts form the most profitable of all topics for argument.[2]

[1] Cf. F. H. Bradley: 'It is a commonplace that the past has recorded too much of that we could well spare and too little of that we would most gladly know. Will it not be so always? What we think the important phenomena of 1870 and 1871 may perhaps have eluded our accurate observation, and in 1971 may with other things be a matter of controversy, while as for the interest of the historian of 1971, and the facts which bear most in his mind on progress, of these perhaps we have simply no notion' (op. cit., 44f.).

[2] An illustration of how historians have come to hold a view not dissimilar from Becker's may be taken from Sir F. M. Powicke's address entitled 'After Fifty Years' to the Historical Association, New Year's Day, 1944: 'Can anybody *know* a historical fact? If he tries to establish or even to verify a fact, he finds himself faced by a long elaborate process, so long and so elaborate that, at every turn, he has to cut it short by reliance on the work of others. The establishment of a fact is an achievement in deduction, and all of us derive our "knowledge" of history, regarded as a whole, at second, third, fourth, up to nth hand. Moreover, the history which we read, though based on and facts, is, strictly speaking, not facts, but a series of accepted judgments, what we call historical generalizations are judgments about judgments. Yet, as a subject of systematic instruction, whose results in the pupil's mind are submitted to a hierarchy of tests by examination, it inevitably comes to be regarded as a body of objective truth, a sort of photograph of the past. The process of discovery and judgment is lost to view' (*Modern Historians and the Study of History*, 231).

The Nature of the Evidence for Christ's Resurrection

It is hard to see how it can be denied that history is not a direct knowledge of past events, but is rather a mental construction made by historians in order to comprehend the traces of the past which have come down to us in memory, tradition, written records, archaeological relics, and so on. If this is so, it would also seem difficult to deny that the mental activity of the historian who creates history by interpreting these traces of the past is conditioned by the presuppositions, beliefs, interests, moral values, prejudices and anxieties of his own life and times. The very stuff and essence of history are not objective facts and scientific laws but personal and therefore challengeable judgments of evidence. If this, or something like it, is the usual view today of what history is, we may pass on to our central concern in this Lecture and ask in the light of it: What sort of evidence might lead to the judgment that the resurrection of Christ was an event of history? And here, of course, we mean ordinary, secular history, the order of history which Becker was writing about, not some eschatological realm of sacred history in which the secular historian's tools cannot be used. Two conditions would have to be fulfilled before the judgment could be reached that the traces of the past point towards the resurrection of Christ as the most coherent explanation of the evidence. First, there would have to be credible attestation on the part of witnesses to happenings which could not be more rationally accounted for by some alternative hypothesis; and, secondly, the event attested would have to accord with the historian's own deepest understanding and experience of life. In practice these two conditions cannot be separated, because our view of the credibility of the witnesses will be determined by our whole attitude to life, its nature and meaning. Hume was stating an undeniable psychological truth when he said that no testimony however strong can make us believe that things have happened which our experience has convinced us could not happen, or, at least, do not happen. But conversely we shall be the more ready to believe witnesses who tell us about events which help us to understand matters of which we have had personal experience.

First, then, let us deal with the question of the attestation of Christ's resurrection by reliable witnesses. Carl Becker held that almost all historical evidence is the testimony of witnesses. Now, we do not possess any eyewitness accounts of Christ's resurrection; the Gospels imply that there were no human witnesses of the event itself. Nor, except in the case of St Paul and possibly the writer of the Apocalypse, do we have the personal statements of any of the witnesses who were believed by their contemporaries to have seen the Risen Lord. The resurrection narratives at the end of each of our four canonical Gospels are not now regarded by scholars as the factual accounts of eyewitnesses; and consequently the type of pre-critical arguments used in, say, Sherlock's *Tryal of the Witnesses of the Resurrection of Jesus*[1] are entirely valueless today. These resurrection narratives are now recognized as being the outcome of a long period of growth in the tradition. This does not mean that they do not contain important supporting evidence for Christ's resurrection,[2] and they are, of course, of first-class historical value as evidence of the way in which the sub-apostolic Church presented or recited its belief in Christ's resurrection as an historical event.

The primary evidence for the resurrection of Christ as an historical event is the emergence of the faith which carried the news about Jesus far beyond the boundaries of Judea and Galilee and within a few decades had brought into being communities of people, who shared a new and distinctive quality of fellowship and life, in almost every city in the Roman world and in the lands beyond its eastern limits. An historical explanation has to be found for the rise and power of this faith. Professor Bornkamm tells us in effect that no such historical explanation is possible; 'the last historical fact' available to scholars, he says, is 'the Easter faith of the disciples'.[3] But such an attitude involves the abandoning of historical method altogether, for the historian cannot admit that there are any 'last facts' in history, for they would be causeless events. They are what (if we may adapt Hume's phrase) never happens in the common course of history; they would be miracles in Hume's sense. History is a causal nexus in which there can be no breaks, no events which are in principle inexplicable. The historian, if he is to be true to his calling, is bound to go on to

[1] Cf. *infra*, 274.

[2] The most scholarly presentation of this evidence will be found in C. H. Dodd, 'Essay in the Form-Criticism of the Gospels' in *Studies in the Gospels*, ed. D. E. Nineham, Oxford, 1955, 9–35.

[3] Op. cit., 180.

consider the various possible explanations of the alleged happening or, if he can, to find a new and a better one. He might, of course, say that he found the evidence inconclusive or insufficient and suspend judgment; he might decide that he himself was incompetent to weigh the complex issues involved; he might even say that he had more important matters to attend to; but the one thing which he as an historian could not say would be that no explanation was in principle possible. After all, the matter under discussion is not some remote by-way of an obscure region of history; it stands in the main stream of world-history, and indeed it could be argued that no other event of ancient history has done so much to shape the subsequent course of the history of the world as has the rise of the Christian faith and the Church which came into being with it. Moreover, there is no shortage of historical materials concerning Christian origins; there is indeed an abundance of it, and it has been worked over again and again by scholars for centuries. A not inconsiderable amount of this historical material actually dates from the period in which the events, whatever their character, took place, which gave rise to the faith of the Christian Church. This latter material, which during the first three centuries or so of the Christian era was gathered together in the book we now call the New Testament, has been more rigorously, continuously and minutely scrutinized, with all the resources of modern critical methods, than any other historical documents that have ever been written. In the opinion of the overwhelming majority of the scholars who have undertaken this scrutiny, the books of the New Testament collectively represent the mind and teaching of those who at first hand witnessed to the events, whatever they were, which brought into existence the community of new faith and new life which later became generally known as the Church of Jesus Christ, a new form of religious and social organization, transcending every division of race, class and language, to which there was no parallel in the ancient world. Here is historical testimony in abundance, and it demands historical explanation. What was the cause (in the historical sense of 'cause') of 'the Easter faith of the disciples'?

Christ's Resurrection as Historical Explanation

There are only three lines of answer to this question, and they are all well known. The first is that which is unanimously advanced in the New Testament by the writers who recorded the testimony of the original witnesses, namely, that faith in Christ, like the Church itself, was called into being by the resurrection of Jesus from the dead and by nothing else. This answer has recently been concisely restated in the light of contemporary scholarship in a fine chapter of his book *The Nature of Faith*[1] by Brunner's successor at Zürich, Professor Gerhard Ebeling. The clause in the Creed, 'he rose again from the dead', Ebeling points out, is not based upon this or that passage in the New Testament, or upon a particular section or book within it, as are other clauses in the Creed—for example, 'born of the Virgin Mary'. It is central to every book of the New Testament. It might be added that even the most radical members of the form-critical school, as we have noticed, insist that every portion of the Four Gospels, including their accounts of the passion and death of Jesus, are written in the light of faith in his resurrection; and this is why they suppose it to be so difficult to obtain an undoctored or historical account of his earthly life. The pervading truth which can be learnt from every part of the Gospels, and not merely from their concluding sections, is that the central conviction of the communities in which and for which they were written was faith in Jesus as the Risen Lord; without this faith the Gospels would not have been written.[2] Faith in the resurrection is not one aspect of the New Testament teaching, but the essence of it. Faith in Christ was not faith in 'the teachings of Jesus', but precisely faith in the Risen Christ. The teaching of Jesus, as summarized in (for example) the Sermon on the Mount, was collected and formulated only gradually over a number of decades; and this happened because of the belief that the Risen Jesus was Lord. The Christian way was not a new ethic but a new life, which was empowered by the Spirit of the Risen Lord. The joyous experience of this new quality of life with which the New Testament is radiant, the sense of liberation from sin and from the fear of death, did not derive from the

---

[1] Eng. trans. by R. Gregor Smith, London, 1961.

[2] Thus, Bornkamm, who distinguishes between the certainty of the Easter *message* (i.e. the proclamation of the Risen Lord) and 'the ambiguity and historical problems of the Easter *narratives*', speaks of the certainty 'even in a completely historical sense' that 'there would be no gospel, not one account, no letter in the New Testament, no faith, no Church, no worship, no prayer in Christendom to this day without the message of the resurrection of Christ . . . ' (*Jesus of Nazareth*, 181).

teaching of Jesus but from his resurrection. And this resurrection is everywhere represented as an event of recent history, not as the unhistorical manifestation of a celestial being, a mysterious irruption of a Gnostic heavenly man, but as the exaltation of one already known and dear to those who had companied together 'all the time that the Lord Jesus went in and out among us, beginning from the baptism of John, unto the day that he was received up from us' (Acts 1.21f.), those who became the 'witnesses of his resurrection'. As Professor Ebeling says, 'the testimony to the resurrection of Jesus . . . is closely bound up in the source material with the testimony to specific historical events'.[1] These events were the actual circumstances of his arrival in Jerusalem, his arrest and trial before Pontius Pilate, his condemnation, crucifixion, death and burial—a grimly historical story which no one would have invented in order to commend the divinity of a cult-hero. Faith in Jesus Christ is indissolubly connected with real historical happenings, the last of which called it into being and defined its content. In creed, life and worship, the origin of the Christian 'way' is grounded in a series of historical events. The earliest *credo* or proclamation (kerygma) was that Jesus, whom his disciples had followed from Galilee to Jerusalem, was the Risen Lord. The life of the Church was from the beginning not a new ethical code but a new being, 'risen with Christ'. The earliest worship of the Christian communities took the form of a recitation of the events of the dreadful night on which the Master had been betrayed and arrested, when he broke the bread and blessed the cup: the celebration of the judicial murder of a dead leader would have provided no occasion of joy or source of power apart from the certainty that Jesus was risen from the dead. Considerations of this kind lead us to assent to the conclusion of Professor Ebeling: 'The resurrection of Jesus is not to be regarded as one object of faith alongside others, as though Easter only added the resurrection of Jesus as something to be believed along with everything else. Rather, faith in the Resurrected One simply expresses faith in Jesus. This is not something additional to the Person of Jesus, but Jesus himself.'[2]

Thus, the historical evidence for the event of Christ's resurrection arises from the community which came into being for the

[1] Op. cit., 62.
[2] Ibid.

express purpose of bearing witness to his resurrection, understood as having set the seal of the divine approval upon his life
and work. This is the evidence which requires historical explanation. Most of the documentary evidence concerning the faith and
life of this community of witness is contained in the New Testament; indeed, almost all the surviving first-century evidence is
brought together from many different sources in this convenient
form, but, of course, like all other historical testimony, it must
be understood against its environment. We often hear it said that
it is a weakness in Christian apologetic that according to the
evidence Christ after his death showed himself alive only to his
disciples and unfortunately did not appear to any unbiased outside
witness. It might, of course, be pointed out that, if this were so,
it was entirely consistent with his refusal during his earthly life to
perform mighty acts to impress the curious and the sceptical. But
the statement is not an entirely accurate description of what is
recorded as having taken place, and it obscures the vital point;
we must be careful to notice what the New Testament evidence
actually is. It does not say that Jesus appeared to believers; on the
contrary, he appeared to men whose hopes had been shattered and
who were in despair: 'we trusted he was to be the redeemer of
Israel but he was crucified three days ago' (cf. Luke 24.20f.). This
is a truly critical point in the interpretation of the evidence, which
has to be explained one way or the other. All the evidence is
unanimous with regard to it. It points to the judgment that the
Church did not create the belief in the resurrection of Christ; the
resurrection of Christ, historically speaking, created the Church
by calling faith into being.

Personal Factors in the Judgment of Evidence

This is indeed a satisfyingly historical account of the origin of
the Christian Church with its distinctive faith, life and worship.
It is satisfying because it accords with the testimony of those who
had been nearest to the first-hand participants in the events which
require interpretation, and also because it leaves us with no break
in the causal series, that is, in the coherent pattern of historical
explanation. It does not leave us with any 'last fact' which cannot
be further investigated by the historian and which has to be
referred to some non-historical realm of existential experience or
of super-history. On purely critical grounds alone, it provides a

rational historical explanation of all the available evidence. But, as we have seen, history is more than criticism and the historian's judgment is determined by a number of other factors, ranging from his own personal experience of life to 'the climate of opinion' of the age in which he lives. His judgments of evidence are therefore formed not by a disembodied critical intellect but by the man who he has come to be. If our question were simply one of interpreting the evidence on a strictly critical basis, ruling out all other considerations, the judgment would have to be that the Church came into existence (historically speaking) as the result of the resurrection of Christ. But now, as we should expect from our study of how historical judgments are actually made, it is precisely at this point that the interpretative concepts in the historian's mind come most powerfully into play. And here we may turn for help to a most illuminating reflection of Carl Becker's, the more so because he is not discussing Christ's resurrection, nor indeed is he speaking from the point of view of a Christian believer at all.[1]

Becker is speaking about the historian's inability to believe that certain kinds of events are possible, however much reliable testimony is brought to support them.[2] 'When the historian is confronted by testimony to the occurrence of a specific event, of a kind which he is profoundly convinced cannot possibly occur, he always says that the witnesses, whether two or two hundred, are self-deceived.' This, says Becker, is what we expect him to do; 'and yet,' he continues, 'if we inquire into it we perceive that he is really abandoning his normal procedure, denying the very presuppositions that he ordinarily relies upon to validate his activities'. He then goes on to tell us why the historian does this disconcertingly unprofessional thing. The reason is that it is not true that the historian has an open mind and no preconceived ideas. His preconceptions are determined by the climate of opinion around him. 'Living in this climate of opinion he has

[1] Becker had reacted against the churchgoing Methodism of his parents. His biographer records his exclamation in 1928: 'If Methodism is slowly dying in Iowa there is hope for the world.' He became a rationalist who laughed at the absurdities of rationalist claims, a sceptic in whose outlook there remained a hangover of Christian philosophy. See Burleigh Taylor Wilkins's biographical study, op. cit., 12–28, 150, 177.

[2] The passage occurs in an unpublished paper written by Becker in 1937 and quoted in Charlotte Watkins Smith, op. cit., 88–90, where an instructive discussion will be found.

acquired unconsciously certain settled convictions as to the
nature of man and the world, convictions which interpret human
experience in such a way that it is easier for him to believe that
any number of witnesses may be self-deceived than it is to believe
that the particular event testified to has ever happened or can
ever happen.'

This honest statement makes the issue plain. It is not a purely
technical critical judgment which determines on which side of
such a question as that of Christ's resurrection the historian will
come down. As we have had many occasions to notice in the fore-
going Lectures, the view that historical questions can be settled
by purely intellectual or scientific procedures has been steadily
losing ground during the present century, as the central importance of the historian's own personal faith and values in the
making of historical judgments have come to be increasingly
recognized. Becker, we are told, cheered the decline of 'scientific
history', because he thought that it prevented the right questions
from being asked.[1] We must finally abandon the view that the
historical as such is constituted by those facts upon which all
historians are agreed, the view to which Lord Acton and many
historians of his day had given their support.[2] 'The conflict of
opinion', from which Acton thought it necessary to rescue 'facts',
is the very stuff of history, for history in practice consists in a
kind of ongoing Socratic dialogue concerning what is the right
judgment of the evidence, that is, a dialogue concerning the
'facts'. The historical Luther is not, as Acton supposed, the series
of facts upon which all historians must agree; such facts constitute not history ('in the full sense') but chronicle: that he
entered the monastery at Erfurt in 1505, nailed his theses to the
door of the Schlosskirche at Wittenberg in 1517, that he died in
1546—these are the kind of 'facts' upon which Catholic and
Protestant and rationalist historians can all agree, but all of them
together, hundreds and thousands of them, as many as could be
found by a thousand researchers working for a thousand years,
would not add up to an historical account. The historical Luther
is a controversial figure still as he was in his life, as he has been
ever since he died: he is the Luther into whose knowledge of
justification one may enter, or the Luther whose morbid sub-

---

[1] Charlotte Watkins Smith, op. cit., 68.
[2] Cf. *supra*, 106, 175.

jectivity destroys the unity of the Catholic Church, or the Luther whose anti-reason is a menace to the progress of society, or the Luther who lives in the German pantheon along with Bismarck as the abiding spirit of a *Volk*. A truly historical account of Luther will not be 'detached'; it will make us aware personally of Luther's greatness and compel us to feel in our inward self the agony and the peace which Luther knew; it will dare to tell us which of these Luthers was 'the historical Luther'. Or perhaps it will make us see how it came about that he could 'in fact' have been all these Luthers in one man; and if it can do that, convincingly and without distortion, it will indeed be a great history. It will remain a great history, even when, a century later in a changed climate of opinion, a fresh reappraisal will have to be made, not because new facts will have been discovered (though they may have been, even if it seems improbable to us), but because what Luther means to one generation in its historical task will not be quite what he means to another, as it faces a different historical predicament, its own particular and unrepeatable crisis of belief and action.

The historian's final judgment of the evidence will, then, in the last resort, and after as rigorous a critical appraisal as he can make, be determined by the man he is. Nothing can abolish the personal element from the decision about what is and what is not a 'fact' when once we have moved outside that realm of technical history, which, being more or less verifiable by anyone who has acquired the necessary expertise, is relatively detached and non-controversial. It is only after this stage has been passed that the personal qualities of the historian himself come into full activity, where those gifts of understanding, empathy and compassion, of which we have spoken, are displayed. Now the judgments of the evidence in its entirety (or 'wider generalizations', if we regard the expression as useful) are made in the light of what Becker calls the historian's 'settled convictions as to the nature of man and the world', 'convictions which interpret human experience'. It is because of these convictions, as Becker says, that the historian decides whether this or that historical testimony is valid; the crucial 'facts', 'what happened' at the most critical points in the story, are determined in the light of them. The historian makes his judgment because he is the man he is, because he himself is an historical being, who in personal reaction towards and against the

historical situation of his own day, and in his personal commitment to those features of his own experience which he regards as
significant, concludes that it *must* have happened in this way and
not that, that such-and-such an event must or must not be a fact.
This is not, of course, a logical 'must'; it is a personal 'must', and
without this kind of 'must' history 'in the full sense' cannot be
written.

Becker himself exaggerated the importance of the 'climate of
opinion' in the determination of an historian's judgment, and he
underestimated the importance of the historian's personal decision in regard to the challenges of the rival faiths of his day.
This is doubtless because the circumstances of his academic
existence and the sceptical inclination of his own temperament
combined to make decision and commitment somewhat distasteful
to him, though in the end, as his biographers show, he did take
sides in some of the great political and moral issues of the years
between the wars. His own inclination to dissociate himself from
the historical decisions of his age makes it all the more intriguing
that he should have been one of the first to criticize trenchantly the
illusion of detachment in the writing of history. It was, in the
opinion of his biographer, Becker's youthful questioning of the
miraculous element in Christianity which first led to his interest
in historiography[1] and brought him eventually to make what is
probably the most significant American contribution to that
subject, though his projected book about it was never written.[2]
He spoke of the historian's belief in or rejection of miracles as in
either case an 'act of faith' which was determined by 'the historian's settled convictions as to the nature of the universe and the
kind of fact that can occur in it'.[3] Becker held that those convictions were in their turn settled for the historian by the 'climate
of opinion' of his age. For a mediaeval man miracles were the
order of the day and any testimony would do; for a modern man

[1] Burleigh Taylor Wilkins, op. cit., 197.
[2] Cf. Harry Elmer Barnes, *A History of Historical Writing*, Oklahoma,
1937, 266–8. Barnes declared that if Becker's paper on 'What are Historical
Facts?' (1926) were ever published, it would 'probably come to have the
same place in historical science that the theory of indeterminacy occupies in
contemporary physical science'. Becker refused to publish it, and it appeared
posthumously in *The Western Political Quarterly*, VIII, 327–40 (Sept. 1955).
See Wilkins, op. cit., 201.
[3] In his paper 'On Historical Evidence', MS. 1 (1937), quoted by Wilkins,
ibid.

they were ruled out by his preconceived ideas: 'if the historian hasn't a preconceived idea as to what must have happened, he at least has preconceived ideas as to what could not have happened'.[1]

'Acts of faith'—the phrase is C. A. Beard's[2] and it was adopted by Becker—are not, however, determined solely by the 'climate of opinion' of an age. If they were, all the life would be drained from historical writing, which thrives on the clash of judgment against judgment. Becker, 'the nearly absolute relativist', has made the mistake of identifying his own mental furniture or preconceived ideas with the universally valid judgment of his own age—valid, that is, until the 'climate of opinion' changes again and twentieth-century ideas (including Becker's relativist ideas) are replaced by other ideas. There are today as in every age several 'climates' in which we may choose by an act of decision to live, for men are not passive sufferers of their climate. There is, for instance, a climate of opinion within the Christian Church in which a quite different atmosphere from the pervading positivist ideology is breathed. The metaphor no longer serves, because this Christian climate is historical, stretching down time, rather than across space. Preconceived ideas acquired from the positivist ideology of a passing age are not something clamped on us, about which we can do nothing; it is a frequent Christian experience that they can be changed, gradually or suddenly, by a radical conversion which involves nothing less than a death of the old self and a being born again to a new and living hope. Historically it cannot be disputed that such a conversion, such a breaking down of settled convictions, was the result of the first proclamation of the event of Christ's resurrection from the dead, or that such a conversion has been brought about through all the Christian centuries and still takes place today. Deterministic notions about impersonal climates of opinion will not disturb Christians who know that they have themselves by the great mercy of God been begotten again to just such a new and living hope by the resurrection of Jesus Christ from the dead (I Peter 1.3). They will not be disconcerted to hear that it is not by any supposedly impartial examination of historical evidence that men are brought to believe that Jesus rose from the dead, because they have known this all along.

[1] Wilkins, ibid.
[2] Cf. his art. 'Written History as an Act of Faith' (1934), op. cit.

Is Christ's Resurrection an Historical Event?

We said above that there were only three possible lines of
answer to the question whether the resurrection of Christ was
an event of history. The first is the one which we have discussed,
namely, that the testimony of the earliest Christian community to
the occurrence of that event is to be accepted as the most rational
historical explanation of the evidence. But before the historian
can make this judgment he will first have to rid himself of preconceived ideas which compel him to believe that it *could* not have
happened; he will have to rid his mind of all eighteenth-century
conceptions of miracle of the kind articulated by Hume. More
positively he will have to know in his own life something of that
self-transcendence which enables men in every age to relive the
historic reality of the original Christian community to which the
New Testament bears witness. This is what in Christian terminology is called 'faith', and it is the Christian counterpart of what is
meant when it is said that historical interpretation involves an
act of faith. Christian theology has never suggested that the 'fact'
of Christ's resurrection could be known apart from faith.

Another line of historical explanation of the rise of the Christian Church is diametrically opposed to this interpretation. It is
probably as old as the first century (cf. Matthew 27.63f.), but it may
be dealt with briefly. It is the hypothesis that the Easter message
was deliberately fraudulent, the disciples having conspired to
deceive the world about the fate of their unfortunate rabbi. No
serious scholars today entertain this theory, presumably because
it is incredible that a faith which brought reconciliation with the
all-holy God and peace and charity amongst men could have
originated in a fraudulent conspiracy. As Hume remarked, we
must always reject the greater miracle.

The third line of explanation adopts the hypothesis that the
earliest Christian witnesses, though sincere, were nevertheless
mistaken in their interpretation of the factual basis of their kerygma. There are many varieties of this type of attempted explanation of the evidence; it would take too long even to attempt to
classify all of them. They do not share any preconceived idea as
to what must have happened, but they do share settled convictions
as to what could not have happened. They are all in their various
ways expressions of the rationalist attitude of the eighteenth

century, which developed into nineteenth-century positivism and gave rise to the notion of 'scientific history'. Some of them are strongly anti-Christian, like the Christ-Myth theories of Arthur Drews (1865–1935), who taught that Christianity was a variant of Gnosticism and that Jesus never lived.[1] Then there are the strictly 'scientific' historians, for whom it would be a dereliction of their scientific vocation to allow any personal convictions to creep into their research; the theories of the *religionsgeschichtliche Schule*,[2] which found parallels to the Gospel-story all over the world of Hellenistic religion, ended by making faith in Jesus and the resurrection merely a variant of the Hellenistic cult-pattern of the dying and rising god. This school neatly illustrates Becker's contention that the trouble with 'scientific history' is that it prevents people from asking the right questions; its members went out to look for evidence to corroborate a preconceived idea, and, of course, they found it; but, while it vastly enriched our knowledge of the mystery-religions, the theory itself did not convince those who did not begin from the same presuppositions. Then there were those who started with positivist preconceptions but with a broadly Christian intention, such as Harnack and those Ritschlians who distinguished between 'the essence of Christianity' and its first-century envelope of miracle and myth.[3] In more recent times there have been the followers of Brunner, Barth and Bultmann, who in quite different ways found it necessary to disengage the Christian kerygma from history because for them the latter meant 'scientific history'. The historical was defined as that nexus of cause and effect which was open to investigation by all truly detached investigators, who apart entirely from any 'faith' or presuppositions could agree on all the scientifically ascertainable facts. Since the resurrection of Christ could never be found amongst the latter, a place for it must somehow be found outside history. Hence Brunner's repeated contrasting of 'the historian' and 'the believer'.

Barth and Bultmann rejoiced, as we noted,[4] that the Liberal quest of the historical Jesus on the basis of 'scientific history' had ended in failure. They held that the attempt to achieve security by means of scientific proofs was a form of unfaith and therefore

[1] Cf. his *Die Entstehung des Christentums aus dem Gnosticismus* (1924) and *Die Bestreitung der Geschichtlichkeit Jesu* (1926). This still represents official Marxist doctrine.

[2] Cf. *supra*, 128. [3] Cf. *supra*, 122f. [4] Cf. *supra*, 140.

theologically illegitimate. Faith could never be the outcome
of a scientific balancing of historical probabilities. Their insight
was, of course, completely right. What, alas, they did not realize
is that historical judgments as such are not things which in
matters affecting our view of the meaning of life are determinable
apart from faith or basic presuppositions. Once we abandon
positivist notions, there is no need to dissociate the historian and
the man of faith or to imagine that there will ever exist a 'scientific' or 'ultimate' history which will leave no room for Christian
faith in the interpretation of history. For history is a matter of
interpretation in the light of personal commitments, accepted
values and existential understanding in a way in which natural
science is not thus a *personal* interpretation of nature. There is a
public and verifiable scientific interpretation of nature, but it does
not answer our deep existential questions; there is no such
public and verifiable interpretation of history, which nevertheless
does convey insight into our existential predicaments, but not
insights which can be verified by scientific means. Faith and
historical interpretation are indissolubly joined together. That is
why there can be a Christian interpretation of history but not a
Christian chemistry. Failure to understand the relation of faith
and history has led recent scholars to offer a 'scientific' account of
the origins of the Christian Church and its faith; so far from being
'scientific', their subjective presuppositions are visible on every
page and determine at every point 'what could not have happened'. The result is a general picture of Christian beginnings at
variance with the evidence of the sources.

Another concern of the existentialist theology is the danger of
false 'objectification'—the turning of existential truths into
tangible occurrences in the historical world: the resurrection of
Christ, it is said, is only a mythological way of bringing out the
eschatological significance of his historical death. We can all agree
that it is wrong to substitute a physical miracle for the inwardness of
the New Testament teaching that the power of Christ's resurrection
must be known personally through faith in him as the living
Lord, and that it is wrong to suppose that a presumption of such
a physical event's having taken place has necessarily anything to
do with faith in the Risen Christ. But the conclusion that should
have been drawn from these insights is that the eighteenth-century
definition of 'miracle', as given, for instance, by Hume, is totally

inadequate to represent what the New Testament means by the mighty act of God in raising Christ from the dead; it should not have been concluded that the resurrection of Christ was not an historical event, or that it is 'something removed from historical scholarship'. Miracles, as defined by Hume and positivism generally, cannot happen (logical 'cannot'), but tautologous definitions of this kind tell us nothing about whether any particular event happened. If it happened, it was not a miracle in Hume's sense. Whether an event happened is determinable only by making a judgment concerning the evidence for it; if a rationally coherent explanation is possible without the judgment that the event occurred, then the historian will say that he sees no reason to think that the event occurred. The weakness of the existentialist theology is that it has given no rationally convincing account of the origin of the Church and its faith on the assumption that the resurrection of Christ was not an historical event. It dissociates the Christian faith from historical testimony to its actual origin and nature, and it attempts to remain 'scientific' while giving existentialist interpretations of the meaning of faith as a substitute for historical explanation. Its explanation of the evidence is unconvincing, because it has not given a satisfying account of how an inward change in the disciples' own self-understanding came to be misinterpreted by those who heard them testify to it as an affirmation that an historical event had taken place, namely, that Christ had risen from the dead. Such a view is by no means self-explanatory, since it contradicts the evidence from which it must necessarily start; that evidence unanimously asserts that it was Christ's resurrection which created the disciples' faith. The problem becomes all the more insoluble in view of the assertion of the Bultmann school that neither Jesus nor his disciples had believed during his earthly life that he was the Messiah or the Son of Man. If there was no prior faith in Jesus' divinity to create the belief in the resurrection, and if there was no historical resurrection to create the faith of the Church, we are left with faith—an undeniable historical reality, Bornkamm's 'last fact' accessible to historians—hanging in the air, to be explained by existentialist analysis rather than historically. Either Christ's resurrection called the Church's faith into being or we must give some more rationally coherent account of how that faith with all its tremendous consequences arose. An eschatological event which is not an event in history is not (as Bornkamm realizes) an event of which historians can take cognizance and it is therefore useless in the interpretation of Christian origins. The Easter event, says Bornkamm, is 'an event *in* this time and in this world, and yet an event which puts an end and a limit to this time and this world. To be sure only faith experiences this (Acts 10.40ff.), for it cannot be observed and demonstrated like any other event in space and time.'[1]

The Unavoidable Decision of Faith

The last chapter of Bornkamm's *Jesus of Nazareth* bears the sincere and moving testimony of a leading contemporary New Testament scholar to faith in Christ's resurrection. The only point of importance—and it is *very* important—on which it is necessary to dissent from his fine exposition is the opinion that the resurrection of Jesus is not an event which can be 'observed and demonstrated like any other event in space and time'. Of course, it cannot be *observed*, since historical judgments are inferences from evidence; the historian cannot observe events in history: he can only infer them. And, of course, it cannot be *demonstrated*, for historical judgments are not capable of proof. The only form of demonstration in history is a demonstration that this judgment of the evidence is more rational than that one. In the physical sciences it is different. For instance, the astronomers Adams in Cambridge and Leverrier in Paris inferred from the evidence of the 'perturbations' of Uranus that there must exist in a particular position an unknown planet which caused them; and in due course there came the 'demonstration' of their hypothesis when Galle in Berlin discovered Neptune on 23 September 1846. In the nature of the case there can be no such demonstrations in history; 'facts' must always remain inferences from evidence, and the historian's judgments of evidence, critically displayed before him, remain judgments. In this sense the resurrection of Christ is either a 'fact' or not a 'fact', and it is to be assessed one way or the other by the historian just like any other event in space and time.

The recognition of this truth will help to correct another false emphasis in positivist thinking about history. This is the notion that before an event can be deemed historical it is necessary to be able to give a detailed account of precisely how it occurred; such

[1] *Jesus of Nazareth*, Eng. trans., 184.

a view arises naturally from the assumption that history is the determination of 'what happened' or 'facts as they occurred'. It seems to be an integral part of the existentialist case against the resurrection as an event of history (*Historie*) that no such account of 'how it happened' can be constructed from the resurrection-stories in the Gospels or from other New Testament sources; the resurrection of Christ may be known to be *geschichtlich* by existential illumination, but it cannot be judged to be *historisch* by the methods of scientific history. We have already agreed that no historical account of the sequence of events on and after Easter Sunday can be built up from the resurrection stories in the Gospels; they do not give us that kind of historical information. But historical evidence of a different kind remains to be explained; and if we are cross-examining it in order to reconstruct 'what happened', then something is preventing us from asking the right questions. One of the right questions would be: how can we explain historically the faith and achievement of the Christian Church, if the resurrection of Christ were not an historical event? A better alternative explanation is the best way of showing that a particular explanation is unsatisfactory. In actual practice historians infer a great number of events of which they can give no satisfactory account of how they happened. The evidence is overwhelmingly strong that Hannibal crossed the Alps with an army, complete with cavalry and elephants, powerful enough to defeat a Roman force of 40,000 men and to go on to a succession of even more spectacular victories after that; the 'fact' is not doubted merely because no historian has been able to reconstruct in detail how this unique and (in the true, non-Humean sense of the word) miraculous feat was accomplished. Such questions will remain matters which can profitably be discussed only by scholars who are expert in dealing with the whole complicated array of evidence. In the matter of the resurrection of Christ a reverent agnosticism about the 'how' is more fitting than strident advocacy of particular theories.[1]

Thirty or forty years ago there was a constant debate between Liberal theologians and the rest as to whether Christ's resurrection

[1] It may be, if the late Professor R. H. Lightfoot is right, that the earliest Evangelist, St Mark, concluded his Gospel at 16.8 because he was deeply aware that the resurrection-manifestations of the Lord were so utterly and mysteriously transcendent as to exceed the power of human words to describe. See R. H. Lightfoot, *The Gospel Message of St Mark*, Oxford, 1950, 80–97.

was 'spiritual' or 'physical'. Here, too, false conceptions of history were responsible for the concentration of attention upon the wrong issues and prevented the right question from being asked. The question of the mode of Christ's resurrection is far too intricate for discussion at the end of this Lecture, involving as it does an immense number of critical minutiae and a variety of interpretative concepts. Perhaps it would be permissible simply to remark that, if we judge that Christ rose from the dead, it is difficult to reconcile this judgment with the theory of a 'spiritual' resurrection; for the latter involves the assumption that, while the disciples were proclaiming that Christ was risen, the body of Jesus lay decomposing in a grave in which it had been buried by a member of the Jewish Sanhedrin. Our purpose has been to show that the question which should have been asked, and which demands an answer, is not the question 'how'; it is not whether Christ's resurrection was 'spiritual' or 'physical', since in the present state of our knowledge we understand so little about 'spirits' and 'bodies'. The right question is whether the resurrection of Jesus was an historical event. And here the historian, even the believing historian, will have to be content with the role of an Adams and a Laverrier; he will point to the 'perturbations' observable in the stream of historical events, and he will make his judgment in the light of a critical examination of the evidence and, if our argument is valid, in the light of his own 'settled convictions' concerning God, man and the world. Apart from faith in the divine revelation through the biblical history, such as will enable us to declare with conviction that Christ is risen indeed, the judgment that the resurrection of Jesus is an historical event is unlikely to be made, since the rational motive for making it will be absent. Historians are not provided by their critical studies with a technique that enables them to escape the decision of faith; and in this matter, as in others, everyman is (in Becker's phrase but not quite in his sense) 'his own historian'.[1]

---

[1] Since this lecture was written the author's attention has been drawn to an essay by Professor H. von Campenhausen of Heidelberg, 'Der Ablauf der Osterereignisse und das leere Grab', in his *Tradition und Leben: Kräfte der Kirchengeschichte*, Tübingen, 1960, 48–113. As an historian, he deprecates the setting aside of historical evidence to make way for psychologizing and existentialist theories; he conducts a careful critical enquiry into the sources, and he concludes that Christ's resurrection and the empty tomb are to be regarded as real events in the light of a strictly historical assessment of the relevant evidence.

7

FAITH AND HISTORY

IN the preceding Lecture we noted that in our present climate of opinion historians, like other people, are predisposed to entertain definite notions concerning what cannot happen. A unique event, to which there is neither parallel in history nor analogy in one's own experience, is normally assumed to be amongst the things that cannot have happened; and in such a case it is natural to conclude that there is no point in looking at the evidence afresh. Any number of witnesses, whether two or two thousand, could not convince people that Christ's resurrection could have happened, if their settled convictions about the nature of man and the world assure them that it could not have happened. It is the startling uniqueness of the resurrection-event which is the stumbling-block; the assumption that only that which can be generalized is capable of becoming knowledge is the basis of the settled conviction that the resurrection could not have happened. It would therefore be profitable to turn our attention to the question of uniqueness in history and ask whether the startling uniqueness of Christ's resurrection constitutes a valid objection to belief in its historicity.

The Unique and the General

The question of the uniqueness of historical events and their relation to general laws is today the subject of much discussion amongst critical philosophers of history; into the intricacies of this philosophical debate it is not necessary for us to enter.[1] There is, of course, a sense in which all historical events are unique; but it is altogether too simple to say that history deals

[1] Reference may again be made to W. Dray, *Laws and Explanation in History*, esp. 44–57, for an introduction to this discussion.

with the particular and unique, while science deals with the general and universal. As we have formerly had occasion to observe, no rational discourse at all is possible without generalization; and historians have their own way of generalizing, being concerned with both the particular and the general. Historical generalizations are, as we have noted, analogical rather than exact like those of natural science. The consequence of this is that conclusions in history cannot be drawn from the general to the particular: for instance, though the historian might classify something now happening in Oceania as a revolution, he could make no predictions from this classification which could not equally well be made by politicians or commonsense observers. A scientist, on the other hand, when he is assured that a complex of events falls into category A, can go on to draw a number of inferences concerning the events B, C and D which are going to follow. Such considerations give rise to a very interesting discussion about the difference between generalization in history and in science; but all that is relevant to our present interest is to note that the process of generalization and inference in history is not nowadays usually considered to be parallel in operation or in result to the process of generalization and inference in the natural sciences. This truth was not so widely recognized thirty or forty years ago as it is now, and it will be recalled that one of the fears of the dialectical theologians, especially Brunner, was that by speaking of Christ's resurrection as historical its significance would be reduced to the status of a mere particular (and therefore problematical) event whose sole function in positivist history was to illustrate a general law. This was so repugnant to the Christian understanding of the significance of Christ's resurrection that it seemed necessary to deny its historical character in order to assert its theological meaning. But today we no longer think in positivist ways, and we are able to make a fresh start.

Let us, then, turn to the question of the uniqueness of Christ's resurrection, which involves 'the scandal of particularity' in its most acute form. Let us ask whether it constitutes a difficulty in the light of a more recent conception of history. When historians speak, for example, of 'the French Revolution', the noun indicates that they refer to a general class ('revolutions'), which is presumed to be recognizable as a type. But by calling it *'the French Revolution'* it is implied that there is a unique and unrepeatable element in the situation which must be understood in its particularity. The particulars could not, of course, have been inferred from the class-concept, but at least the concept 'revolution' guarantees or 'covers' the particular incidents in the sense that it is a familiar characteristic of human observation and experience; revolutions are (for better or worse) something which emphatically cannot be ruled out in advance of the enquiry by any settled convictions concerning the nature of man which would make it impossible to believe that the French Revolution could have occurred. It will at once be apparent that when we speak of Christ's resurrection, the case is quite otherwise. The difficulty now arises that there is no general class of 'resurrections' known to historians. Christians themselves would be the first to assert that the 'resurrections' of (say) Osiris or Lazarus belong to wholly different categories from that of the resurrection of Christ. They would insist that Christ's resurrection is not merely unique in the sense in which all historical events are unique; it is, so to speak, uniquely unique, at least in the sense that there is no covering class-concept of 'resurrections', and in principle there cannot be one. If there were one, the resurrection of Christ would not be what Christians believe it to be. They would have no interest in it merely as providing presumptive evidence of a class of occurrences in nature which had hitherto not been known to exist. Any number of particular resurrections, each of them attested by psychical research, would not provide factual evidence for the truth of the Christian faith. In short, the significance of Christ's resurrection lies precisely in its special uniqueness, that is, in the fact that it does *not* belong to any general class of resurrections.

Here, then, we encounter a real difficulty in any age which has been conditioned by 'the climate of opinion' to look for meaning in the general and universal. 'The historian', says Mr E. H. Carr, 'is not really interested in the unique, but in what is general in the unique.'[1] Even though many historians would wish to qualify the negative part of this statement, it undoubtedly expresses a truth which must not be ignored, namely, that historical explanation involves relating particular events to general or interpretative concepts and thus fitting them into the unbroken tapestry of the historical process. But in the case of Christ's resurrection there appears to be nothing general in the unique, since it does not

[1] *What is History?* 57.

share a common character with other resurrections. It would seem to follow from this that Christ's resurrection cannot be fitted into the causal sequence of historical explanation, since it contains no general element by which it could be grafted into it. It has to be admitted that an absolutely unique event, one which had nothing generally common to other historical events, would be inexplicable because, being isolated from the rest of experience, it could not be integrated into any pattern of rational understanding.[1] To assert that something is inexplicable would negate the very assumption upon which historical thinking is founded, namely, that every *historical* happening is part of an unbroken sequence of historical causation. And here, we should notice, what the historian assumes is only what all of us assume in ordinary everyday life. We sometimes find ourselves saying that a certain happening is totally inexplicable, but we do not really mean it. We know that, if we were wiser, or if we knew all the facts, there must be an explanation somewhere. The activities of scientists and historians combine with the testimony of everyday experience to assure us of the ultimate rationality or explicability of the world; and it is noticeable that those who today have ceased to believe in the omniscience of God are willing to put their faith in computers which shall be able one day to reduce the most obscure complexities of human behaviour to rational explanation. We all know that a lot of things happen which in the present state of our knowledge we cannot explain, but we do not believe that they are in principle inexplicable. This is the root of the objection to miracles, if they are defined as Hume defined them, that is, as causeless and therefore inexplicable happenings. If this is what is meant by miracles, the historian must reject them, since his own activity commits him to the assumption that

[1] Cf. Alfred Cobban, art. 'History and Sociology' in *Historical Studies* III, 1961, 6: 'One answer to Carl Becker is that while facts never speak for themselves, they do "to someone who has an hypothesis to test"; and that if the collection of facts is not guided by an implicit hypothesis, then why collect *these* facts. Historians are fond of stressing the uniqueness of every historical event. Yet it has been truly said that "an absolutely unique event, with no points of significant similarity with other events, would be outside the scope of our understanding". It would be a miracle. History, like all coherent thought, requires general ideas.' (The passages quoted by Cobban are from C. A. Beard and Sidney Hook, 'Problems of Terminology in Historical Writing' in *Theory and Practice in Historical Study: a Report of the Committee on Historiography*, Social Science Research Council Bulletin 54 (1946), 123f. and 133.)

all events must have their place in the one unbroken pattern of historical explanation. We cannot but agree that, if the resurrection of Christ occurred, it must indeed be related to a wider class of historical situations by reference to which it is 'covered'; that is, ceases to be unique in the sense of inexplicable.

But this does not mean that Christ's resurrection could take its place in historical explanation only if a general class of 'resurrections' could first be established. To assume this would prevent us from asking the right question, which is: Is there any sequence of events in history in which the resurrection of Christ fittingly and coherently takes its place, in such a way that a general historical category becomes discernible, with the result that Christ's resurrection ceases to appear as an isolated marvel standing outside the nexus of historical explanation? To put the question in more technical terms: Is it true that Christ's resurrection lacks a 'covering law' or 'covering law model', that is, a known feature of history, into which the event would fit rationally ('naturally') and become intelligible in terms of normal historical explanation?[1] We shall suggest that such a feature is to be found in the sequence of 'disclosure-situations' in the history of Israel, through which Israel's self-understanding in relation to a divine purpose was achieved by means of Israel's commitment to that which was discerned amidst particular historical events.

The Meaning of an Historical Faith

The neglect of the Old Testament has been for a long time a source of weakness in Christian apologetics. In an age of specialism, Old Testament scholars, New Testament scholars, dogmatic theologians, and so on, have tended to concentrate upon their own fields, and it has been nobody's business to interpret the Bible as a whole. Moreover, theologians have a habit of discussing problems like the nature of revelation in history in a special language of their own, which is not understood by those who have not undertaken a sustained study of the theological disciplines. For instance, they have discussed the problem which is now before us in terms of the theological concept of typology, which is indeed illuminating for those who have learned to think in this way: it can clarify the real correspondences in history, not

[1] For a discussion of 'covering law' in this sense see W. Dray, op. cit., 1–21 and *passim*.

merely in fancy, between a 'type' in the past and its fulfilment in subsequent happenings.[1] Here we shall not pursue our question in terms of typology, since the concept is not in general use amongst historians, who do not look for types in history (though they make plentiful use of analogical concepts, e.g. 'revolutions'). The danger of discussing the biblical history in terms of a special language is that the impression is created that it constitutes a special history, a 'sacred history', in which the ordinary conventions of secular history do not apply. It is wrong to give this impression, however, unintentionally, because it obscures the truth that the biblical history is a real history, just as real as the history of the Caesars or the Plantaganets. Too often in the past Israel's history has been treated as something apart from the rest of ancient history, a kind of *Heilsgeschichte* unrelated to the secular history of the nations. Until recently ancient historians did not learn Semitic languages; they regarded Greece and Rome as the fount of civilization, and Israel's history was looked upon as a backwater in the stream of world process. Today the common roots and mutual interpenetration of 'European' and Semitic culture are widely acknowledged and studied, and biblical scholars for their part take it for granted that the whole civilization of the ancient Near East, its philology, archaeology, religious history, literature, and political, economic, social and intellectual evolution, must be taken into account by all who would understand the Old Testament faith. Palestine stood along the central line of development of world history; all the great empires of antiquity had a share in making Israel the particular historical entity which she, in fact, became. Apart from the events of Israel's history, which was real history, part of the history of the world, Israel's faith cannot be understood; it cannot be abstracted from history and treated as a kind of quintessence of religious ideas which remains after the sediment of historical occurrence has been thrown away. When we say that Israel's faith is historical we mean that it is inseparable from the historical events which called it forth. These events were events in the history of the nations, not special religious events, such as might happen in

---

[1] See G. W. H. Lampe, 'The Reasonableness of Typology' in Lampe and K. J. Woollcombe, *Essays on Typology*, London, 1957, 29–31. Cf. also W. Eichrodt, 'Ist die typologische Exegese sachgemässe Exegese?' in Suppl. *Vetus Testamentum* IV, Volume de Congrès, Strasbourg, 1956, 161–80.

some kind of peculiarly sacred history; they were not esoteric happenings, which cannot be investigated by the ordinary methods of the historian; as St Paul remarked concerning the events of a later chapter in the story, these things were not done in a corner (Acts 26.26). Israel shared with many other nations the common history of the Fertile Crescent and thus inevitably inherited the common stock of religious ideas and practices of those nations. Yet Israel came to possess a faith significantly different from the religion of the surrounding peoples, and this constitutes the chief problem in the interpretation of the history of Israel and of her faith. The problem can be stated in the form in which Wellhausen declared it to have no satisfactory solution: Why did Chemosh, the god of Moab, never become the God of righteousness and the Creator of heaven and earth?[1]

The old evolutionary or 'developmental' interpretation of the biblical faith as simply a part of the general religious history of the Fertile Crescent could explain the similarities between Hebrew religion and the religion of the surrounding peoples, but it could give no explanation of the differences, which it therefore tended to overlook. The chief dissimilarity lies in the way in which Israel developed a faith out of her understanding of her own historical existence amidst the world of nations, thus committing herself to a resolute rejection of the unhistorical nature-religions which personified the forces of nature in the religion of the neighbouring peoples. The Bible makes plentiful use of symbolic images and of poetical religious language; it constantly uses such expressions as 'the arm of the Lord', and it speaks of God as acting in historical events, and so on; such language has led many to confuse metaphor with myth and has obscured for them the essential distinction between an historical faith and a mythology. The historical faith of Israel waged an unrelenting struggle against mythology; Israel's religious festivals commemorated the historical deliverances of God's people: they did not solemnize the rebirth of nature, as did the Canaanite festivals; even the earliest strata of the Old Testament have demythologized the notion that the king is god or that the fertility of the crops and cattle is assured by

---

[1] Cf. G. Ernest Wright, *The Old Testament against its Environment*, London and Chicago, 1950, 15. This monograph forms an excellent introduction to the question under discussion in this paragraph.

means of the coronation ritual.[1] From its earliest beginnings the 'theology' of the biblical faith was, in Professor Wright's phrase, 'a theology of recital': 'it is fundamentally an interpretation of history, a confessional recital of historical events as the acts of God, events which lead backward to the beginning of history and forward to its end'.[2] The backbone of the Old Testament faith, like that of the New, is a kerygma, a proclamation of the 'mighty acts' of God for the salvation of his people.[3] Even the harvest thanksgiving in the ancient cultic tradition has already become a credal confession of salvation in history (Deut. 26.5–9); other examples of the recitation of the kerygma will be found in Deut. 6.20–24 and Josh. 24.2–13. The Psalms contain frequent recitations of God's saving acts in Israel's history; as Professor Weiser says, 'a number of them include or allude to the manifestation of the nature of Yahweh in the form of the representation of his saving deeds, that is, the recapitulation of the *Heilsgeschichte* in the form of a cultic drama, following the familiar pattern of the Hexateuch tradition (e.g. Ex. 15.1ff.; Pss. 66.5ff.; 81.6ff.; 89.5ff.; 107.33ff. and often). . . . Such cultic recitals of the tradition of the *Heilsgeschichte* are indicated in the psalms in which the congregation testifies: "We have heard with our ears, O God, our fathers have told us, the work thou didst perform in their days" (Pss. 44.1ff.; 48.8, 13f; 62.11; 75.1; 78.3ff.); here the cult community's duty to pass on and keep alive this tradition is explicitly confirmed (cf. Pss. 81.10; 96.3; 102.21; 105.1f.; 111.4, 6: "He has caused his wonderful works to be remembered; he has caused the power of his works to be made known to his people").'[4]

The earliest principal items of what Weiser calls 'the tradition of the *Heilsgeschichte*' are the Exodus from Egypt, the deliverance at the Red Sea, the journey across the Wilderness and the con-

[1] For an expansion of these assertions see G. Ernest Wright, *God Who Acts*, London and Chicago, 1952, 33–58 and *passim*; Alan Richardson, *Genesis I–XI* (Torch Commentaries), London, 1953, 17–34; *The Bible in the Age of Science*, 136–41.

[2] *God Who Acts*, 57.

[3] The work of Gerhard von Rad is especially important in this connection; see esp. his *Old Testament Theology*, Vol. I, *The Theology of Israel's Historical Traditions*, Eng. trans. by D. M. G. Stalker, Edinburgh, 1962; *Genesis: a Commentary* (Eng. trans. by John Marks, London, 1961, of *Das erste Buch Mose, Genesis* [Alte Testament Deutsch], Göttingen, 1956), 13–18.

[4] Artur Weiser, *The Psalms: a Commentary* (Eng. trans. by Herbert Hartwell, London, 1962, of *Die Psalmen* [Alte Testament Deutsch], 5th ed., 1959), 42f.; cf. also 59 and 68.

quest of Canaan. The Hexateuch (the first six books of our Old
Testament) is compiled from several different 'histories' of these
events (with other traditions), written at various times in Israel's
existence, from the early period of the monarchy to the post-
exilic period. (They are known to scholars by the symbols J, E, D
and P.) Each of these 'histories' was in its day a 'new history',
designed to make clear the relevance of Israel's history in the new
circumstances of the writer's or compiler's own day, though, of
course, each of them incorporates very ancient traditional
material. Excessive concentration upon the literary relationships
of the various strata of the Pentateuch has for a long time tended
to obscure the significance of its several component parts as
reinterpretations of Israel's past in the light of the new challenges
of a later age; furthermore, the positivistic assumption that the
nearer we could get back to the 'bare facts' of uninterpreted
primitive testimony the more adequately we could know 'what
happened', has fostered an unhistorical attitude towards the
inward significance of Israel's faith as itself an interpretation of
history. The labour of the compiler(s), who tried to synthesize the
various historical interpretations of different periods into one
'objective' historical account, has itself obscured the truth that
what we have in the Pentateuch is a series of 'new histories' designed to apply the lessons of Israel's past to the needs of the
present. Once we have grasped that this is an intrinsic character
of historical writing as such, we shall understand better the real
nature of the Old Testament historical accounts as historiography
in the true sense; we shall no longer reject the Old Testament
writers as historians because they know nothing of the Rankean
ideal of scientific history. Today we perceive more clearly that the
significance of historical episodes can be properly understood
only in the light of their final development and that this is why
history has to be written afresh in every age. The Old Testament
historians were interpreters of history who knew this very well,
even if they knew it in a practical and not an academic sense. Thus,
as Professor Knight has reminded us, the P writer understood the
significance of the Tabernacle during the wanderings in the
Wilderness in the light of his fully developed conception of the
Temple in Jerusalem; his theology of the Tabernacle was 'created
by one who already knew the end of the process of theological
growth and development and who could thus see the significance

of the beginning from the end'.[1] All historical interpretation, and therefore all historical writing as such, necessarily involves the seeing of the significance of the beginning from the end. This is the very character of the biblical writings as historical documents; the New Testament itself is a viewing of Israel's story in the light of 'those matters which have been fulfilled among us' (Luke 1.1). This is what is meant in theological language by typology. It is essentially what all history 'in the full sense' unavoidably is. It is not something which makes biblical history different in kind from secular history; for, as we have seen many times, historical judgments of significance can be made only in the light of the end of the process: Bismarck, for instance, can be historically appraised only in the light of 1933 and 1945. The earlier histories are not 'truer' because they stand nearer to the events; in terms of the Pentateuch, J is not necessarily more informative than P. It all depends upon what we are looking for. If we want the factual, archaeological details about the Tabernacle, we do not go to P for them, for P is not an archaeologist and is not concerned with the detailed reconstruction of the past; this is a modern interest, and one which we are able to pursue by reason of the development of modern historical method. If, however, we are concerned about the significance of Israel's religious beginnings, then P will have much to tell us in the light of his knowledge of those developments which were implicit in them. Archaeology is not history, and the biblical writers are historians, not archaeologists.

The Old Testament, then, consists essentially of a series of reappraisals of Israel's history in the light of new experience; this is, of course, not intended to deny that it contains also certain other elements (e.g. the Wisdom Literature). Thus, we have the 'new history' of the Former Prophets and of the Deuteronomic school, and afterwards that of the post-exilic Priestly school. But the most profound of the many reinterpretations of Israel's history which the Old Testament contains is that given to us by the prophets of the Exile, a time of crisis in which all the traditional verities of Israel's faith were called into question by the cruel march of events. A new view of Israel's historical destiny was needed in the light of these events, and it is the unknown prophet of the Return (the so-called Deutero-Isaiah) who supplies

[1] G. A. F. Knight, *A Christian Theology of the Old Testament*, London, 1959, 216.

it in its most profound form. He proclaims the old kerygma of God as the historical deliverer in a relevant contemporary form. He perceives that the disobedient nation could be reborn only by a new divine act of creation-redemption, as at the deliverance at the Red Sea. He declares that he who in the original creation of Israel, his servant-people, had cut Rahab-Egypt in pieces and who smote the dragon of the deep, he who had dried up the sea and made a way for the redeemed to pass over, was he who even now is bringing back his people, the ransomed of Yahweh, with singing to Zion; so that Israel might assuredly know that this same Yahweh, the 'Creator of Israel' (Isa. 43.15), was the God of all the earth (54.5), besides whom there was no other (45.18), and that it was he who had stretched out the heavens and laid the foundations of the earth.[1] Thus, Deutero-Isaiah reinterprets in a new and relevant way the old cultic historical kerygma of Israel. So also the New Testament writers later reinterpret both the old Exodus kerygma and the 'new' kerygma of Deutero-Isaiah in the light of the 'exodus' and deliverance of the New Israel in the historical crisis that culminated in the destruction of Jerusalem in AD 70, in which Jesus-Messiah was the prophet-bearer of deliverance, the Servant of Yahweh, the Messiah.

Disclosure Situations in History

All the characteristic biblical beliefs about God's character and purpose are distillations from Israel's historical experience. That God is righteous, demanding righteousness from men, that he is merciful, delivering those who put their trust in him, and all such credal affirmations, were derived from Israel's historical existence amongst the nations, as interpreted by the prophets. They were not derived from philosophical reasoning; and this is why modern philosophical and linguistic analysis of theological propositions is irrelevant from the standpoint of biblical faith. To attempt to prove God's existence is as foolish as to deny it (cf. Ps. 14.1), since both arise from disobedience, that is, unfaith. God is known in the doing of his will in actual concrete historical situations (cf.

[1] Cf. esp. Isa. 51.9–12, 15f. For a fuller exposition of this theme, see Bernhard W. Anderson, 'Exodus Typology in Second Isaiah' in *Israel's Prophetic Heritage, Essays in honour of James Muilenberg,* ed. B. W. Anderson and W. Harrelson, New York and London, 1962, 177–95. For a New Testament parallel, see Harold Sahlin, 'The New Exodus of Salvation according to St Paul' in *The Root of the Vine,* ed. A. Fridrichsen, London, 1953, 18–95.

Judg. 2.10f.; Jer. 22.16; Matt. 25.34–40; John 7.17). Even the doctrine that God is the Creator of all things is a derivative from Israel's historical experience; it is the logical consequence of the consciousness of having become 'the people whom Yahweh hath made' (cf. Pss. 95.6; 100.3; 149.2). And so all the universe, all men, all nations, the sun and moon and all the heavenly host, could be called upon to confess the name of the one Creator God: 'Let them praise the name of Yahweh, for he commanded and they were created' (Ps. 148.1–5). All the biblical theology is historical theology, that is, the theological interpretation of history.

The distinctive character of Israel's history was that it was built around a series of disclosure situations, which through the activity of prophetic minds became interpretative of Israel's historic destiny and ultimately of the history of all mankind. It is to this distinctive feature that we should look for the beginnings of an answer to the question why it was Yahweh and not Chemosh who was recognized as the God of righteousness and the Creator of heaven and earth. In what we are calling disclosure situations[1] there occurs at certain 'historic' moments the discernment of a meaning which provokes a response to what is discerned, an acknowledgment of an obligation, a commitment to an overriding purpose. The classical example of such a disclosure situation in the Old Testament is that of the Exodus from Egypt and the response to it at the Covenant-making on Sinai, but there are many others (notably the situation of Israel at the time of the Exile and the Return). It is probably beyond the power of historians, using all the resources of modern scientific historical method upon the materials at their disposal, to reconstruct in detail the story of 'what happened' at the coming out of Egypt. Perhaps nothing externally happened in Egypt or at the Red Sea or in the Wilderness which we today would not account for by natural means; perhaps there was no 'miracle' in the Humean

[1] This expression is adopted from the use made of it and similar expressions by Professor I. T. Ramsey in *Religious Language: an Empirical Placing of Theological Phrases*, London, 1957, a most valuable clarification of terminology. We do not here speak of 'revelation', since this is an interpretative concept used by dogmatic theologians and apologists; we speak of 'disclosure situations' in a sense in which any historian would have to acknowledge in them a common feature ('covering law') of certain historical moments which have become for many interpretative clues to other historical situations, especially those in the 'here' and 'now'.

sense. But for Israel, and rightly, what happened was miraculous, a disclosure of the divine purpose and an act of divine redemption in the midst of real, 'secular' history, so that Israel could say, as of all the deliverances in her history, 'This is Yahweh's doing, and it is marvellous in our eyes' (Ps. 118.23). A miracle in the biblical view is not a breaking of the laws of nature (which would be a gross anachronism!) but a personal disclosure of the divine intention in the midst of history, a disclosure, that is to say, to those whose eyes and ears have been opened and who in faith and obedience are willing to make the appropriate response to it. Otherwise it remains a mere 'marvel', however stupendous the occurrence. A miracle is a 'sign' and is therefore a 'disclosure situation', since signs, in order to be signs, require the active presence of a discerning person. It is in this sense that the resurrection of Christ, as an event of history, is a miracle and falls within the general category of disclosure situations, a category which constitutes a recognizable feature of historical explanation.

There is little need to argue the reality of such disclosure situations. We know them in our own experience; there has been some moment, some situation, in our life, probably a time of decision or of crisis, which afterwards we recognize as having been a 'moment of revelation', a 'turning-point', an illumination which has demanded a response; if there has been no commitment, the insight will have faded and its truth grown dim. It has been personal to us; if we have ever tried to explain it to others, we probably found it impossible to communicate its vivid and compelling reality; perhaps others have rejected or derided it. Its character is existential, not public. There are analogies in the historical life of nations, moments of crisis and decision which have become fixed in a people's imagination and have symbolized its ambition, nourished its loyalty and cemented its unity. Often the original situation acquires legendary embellishments, and historians perplexingly find themselves both the guardians of the myths and the destroyers of them. To other nations the cherished interpretation of the situation often appears unconvincing or even repugnant. The Pope blesses the Armada as it sets sail; Queen Elizabeth, after it has met disaster in the storm, strikes a medal: *Deus afflavit et dissipati sunt*. The incident becomes a 'sign' to those who, like John Milton, understand the vocation of 'God's Englishmen' in terms of a high moral purpose and obligation. As time passes, the vision fades, the sense of vocation grows dim; a squalid nationalism takes its place; the 'debunkers' find enjoyment in ridiculing the sublime Miltonic insight, and thoughtful men long for a new vision which will bring a renewed moral commitment in an age of purposeless materialism. In times of prosperity the vision soon fades, as the old Deuteronomist well knew: 'When Yahweh thy God shall bring thee into . . . great and goodly cities . . . and thou shalt eat and be full, then beware lest thou forget Yahweh, who brought thee forth out of the land of Egypt, out of the house of bondage' (Deut. 6.10–12). In times of crisis the vision is renewed, but often it does not last after the crisis has passed; between 1939 and 1945 there were disclosure situations, vivid and efficacious, to bring the nations to a new self-awareness, a new penitence and a renewal of moral purpose: 'when the judgments of God are in the earth, the inhabitants of the world learn righteousness' (Isa. 26.9). But the real tragedy of Western civilization in 1939–1945 is that so many millions could pass through those years of judgment and learn nothing. All this could, in a sense, have been read beforehand in the Old Testament; truly Israel's history *is* our history, the history of mankind.

The disclosure situations attested in the Old Testament are not different in kind from those of other histories. Their distinctive character consists in the depth of their penetration to that ultimate level where the nation, even one's own nation, is stripped of every pretence at self-justification and is brought to the recognition of basic moral issues and of its own costly vocation to serve the righteousness of God in the midst of a concrete historical situation. Though rooted in the particular predicaments of Israel's actual history, these disclosure situations illuminate the truth concerning the predicament of all nations in every age, the real situation of man as man. Israel's history is not unique, except in the sense that every nation's history is unique; other nations have endured similar vicissitudes. What is unique is the faith which arose out of obedience—or rather out of the recognition of a duty of obedience—to the moral truth which had been prophetically discerned in Israel's historical experience. There is no parallel to this discernment of a divine imperative in history amongst the Moabites or any other peoples; throughout the ancient world religion was based upon the mythological interpretation of the cyclical movement of nature, not upon history.

Israel's faith, *per contra*, was from first to last an interpretation of historical experience. This truth has been strongly emphasized by contemporary Old Testament research; as a leading scholar has recently said, 'the special characteristic of biblical revelation is that God binds himself to historical events to make them the vehicle of the manifestation of his purpose'.[1]

'Factors' in History

About a generation ago a major transformation in the method of Old Testament interpretation was taking place among scholars. It corresponded to the change which, as we have noted, was taking place in other fields of historical study. It is instructive to look at the new approach in Old Testament studies in relation to the new historical outlook in its wider aspects. In both cases it might be said that a new emphasis was laid upon historical considerations as over against generalized notions drawn from the anthropological and other sciences. Before that time, in conformity with the widespread historical attitude of their day, biblical scholars had tended to look for the features common to Israelite religion and to the religious pattern of the surrounding peoples; and, of course, they found them in abundance, for they are many. The distinctive element tended to be overlooked, and this was the uniquely historical character of Israel's faith. Instead of taking note of those disclosure situations which gave rise to the differentiating moral quality of Israel's faith, the category of interpretation which was employed was chiefly that of religious experience. By making the 'essence' of the Old Testament consist in the religious experience which it records and evokes, the Liberal theology obscured the intrinsically historical character of Israel's faith. Religious experience tended to become a basically unhistorical conception, in so far as religious experiences were held to be valid for all ages and settings; the time and place of their occurrence were irrelevant to their inner quality and eternal significance. Religious experience thus became a 'factor' in history; its importance in relation to other factors (such as the economic, the political or the climatic) varied in accordance with the importance

---

[1] Edmond Jacob, *Theology of the Old Testament*, Eng. trans. by A. W. Heathcote and P. J. Allcock, London, 1958, 188. In this work the theological content of the Old Testament is expounded in relation to God's activity as Creator of the world and as Lord of history; cf. esp. chap. IV, 'God the Lord of History', 183–232.

assigned to it by the particular historian in his broad philosophical understanding of life as a whole. The Liberal theologians themselves, for the most part, placed a high value upon religious experience, and so it usually became a 'factor of history' of great importance in their interpretation of the Old Testament.

Until a generation or so ago historians were fond of explaining historical development by analysing it into the various factors which they deemed important in it. No one seems to know who invented factors in history, but the notion was given wide currency by the great popularity of Professor A. F. Pollard's *Factors in Modern History* (1907).[1] Discovering hidden factors became a creditable academic achievement; making a corner for oneself in some factor or other was an honourable academic ambition. Hexter suggests that the idea of factors may have been derived from mathematics. Unfortunately the precision of factors in mathematics (there is always a precise number of factors and they exhibit a precise relation to that of which they are factors) stands in complete contrast to the vagueness of factors in history: 'historical factors are models of imprecision; it is never entirely clear what they are factors of, and their number seems to fluctuate at the whim of the historian'.[2] We might think perhaps that 'factors' are more like the elements in old-fashioned alchemy, which were mixed together hopefully in accordance with some esoteric prescription. All that they succeed in doing is to introduce into history a spurious scientific flavour. They are highly subjective, coming into fashion with changes in the climate of opinion or assuming overriding importance according to the commitment of the particular historian or his school. It is worth meditating upon the fact that Livy and Gibbon wrote very successful histories without even knowing that there was such a thing as 'the economic factor'. Nothing could be more arbitrary than the way in which historians have often in recent years dealt with 'the religious factor'; nor could anything better illustrate how a factor which is absent from the historian's personal life is also found to be lacking in his historical interpretation. While imparting a specious

[1] See J. H. Hexter, *Reappraisals in History*, London, 1961, 22–44, 195–201. See also Hexter's chapter on 'The Myth of the Middle Classes in Tudor England' (71–116), in which Pollard's favourite 'factor', the rise of the middle class, is discussed; the discussion suggests profitable reflections upon the mythopoeic faculty of the historian.

[2] Ibid., 196.

scientific air to historical writing, 'factors' all too easily become mythological powers, occult forces which have crept back into 'scientific history' under the prestige of a borrowed name. Thus, amongst certain schools of historians 'the economic factor' becomes a myth, a 'clue to history', an interpretative concept which explains everything. 'The religious factor' has often latterly made only an occasional ghost-like or epiphenomenal appearance in history-writing, having been elbowed from the centre of the stage by its younger and more robust cousins, the political, social and economic factors. But even those Liberal theologians who highly valued religious experience and regarded it as a factor of importance in history failed as thoroughly as did their contemporaries in other fields to perceive that religion as a general factor in human experience, if it is only one element amongst many, has nothing to do with the historical faith of Israel or with any interest that is present amongst the biblical writers themselves.[1] The Bible offers to us a kerygma about history, not a suggestion that we ought to give due weight to the religious factor in the construction of our philosophy of life.

The Revival of Old Testament Theology

The change of attitude amongst Old Testament scholars, which has been so notable a feature of theological thought during the last thiry or more years, has been due not so much to the accumulation of new knowledge (though this, in fact, has been considerable) as to the changed perspective from which they have come to look at their materials. As in other fields, new times have created a demand for a new history. The historical situation through which the scholars were living, especially in Germany and the lands most nearly affected by the rise of Hitlerism, made them look at the Old Testament with new eyes.[2] They saw much

[1] The rediscovery of the historical character of the Bible in recent decades has meant the rejection of the older Liberal interpretation of Israel's history in terms of positivist thought. Thus, for instance, the Dutch Old Testament scholar Th. C. Vriezen speaks of the 'life-and-death struggle between Christian theology and "mere historicism", a theory of interpretation which secularized and humanized Old Testament religion' (*An Outline of Old Testament Theology*, 1949, Eng. trans., 1958, 13. The whole of chap. II, 'The Historical Character of the Old Testament Revelation', is relevant in this connection).

[2] Cf. Norman Porteous, 'Old Testament Theology' in *The Old Testament and Modern Study* (ed. H. H. Rowley), 317: 'It was during the late twenties

that their predecessors had never noticed, because they were not looking for it. A new recognition of the significance of history was born. It is today widely acknowledged that Old Testament theology involves a reliving of Israel's history in such a way that the disclosure situations which gave rise to the prophetic understanding of the divine purpose become for the historian the means of interpreting the historical situation of his own time. In short, Old Testament theology has become nothing more or less than the interpretation of Israel's history, a study of history in the fullest sense of the word. It is generally agreed that Israel's 'religion' cannot be understood from the outside by the 'scientific' methods of the comparative study of religions. 'Let us constantly remind ourselves,' said the late Dr Wheeler Robinson, 'that this religion, like any other, can be understood only from within, or through a sympathy that makes us "resident aliens" (*gērîm*).'[1] The fear that a subjective element of inward understanding will compromise the historian's scientific detachment has been lived down by Old Testament scholars as successfully as by historians in any other field; today it is usual to recognize that, apart from such sympathetic entering into the living faith of Israel, there can be no satisfying interpretation of Israel's history, that is, no adequate theology of the Old Testament.

Professor Porteous has reminded us[2] that as long ago as 1929 Walther Eichrodt had insisted upon the necessity of taking seriously the subjective element in historical interpretation, without which no deep understanding of the Old Testament can be attained.[3] He contended that this did not imply that the biblical scholar possessed or used any special historical methods which were not available to and constantly employed by other historians, since an existential judgment is necessary in the writing of all history in the full sense; there can be no account of Israel's (or of

and especially the thirties of the century that the Church struggle in Germany began to focus attention on the Old Testament and provoke radical thought on its nature and relevance. This grim background to the theological literature of the period should be kept in mind. The discussions which went on during these critical years were by no means purely academic.'

[1] H. Wheeler Robinson, *Inspiration and Revelation in the Old Testament*, Oxford, 1946, 281f.

[2] Op. cit., 322.

[3] 'Hat die alttestamentliche Theologie noch selbständige Bedeutung innerhalb der alttestamentlichen Wissenschaft?' in *Zeitschrift für die alttestamentliche Wissenschaft*, XLVII, 1929, 83–91.

any other) history or religion which is entirely free from preconceptions.[1] It is to be regretted that amongst his contemporaries in
the New Testament field no one understood as Eichrodt did the
real character of historiography, as it was then coming to be perceived, with the result that we have no work on the theology of
the New Testament comparable to Eichrodt's *Theology of the Old
Testament*.[2] At a time when leading New Testament scholars and
dogmatic theologians were still attempting to disengage the
Gospel from real history, out of deference to the canons of positivist historiography, Old Testament theologians were steadily
recovering the biblical understanding of faith as response to an
obligation that had been discerned in history, with most important
consequences for the interpretation of the New Testament as well.
To say this is not to deny that the Old Testament theologians
were stimulated to ask the right questions by the dialectical
theologians, who in action as well as in writing and preaching
were courageously meeting the challenge of the Church struggle
in Germany. It is rather to emphasize the fact that the Old Testament in this stern situation had come alive in a new way; it had
become easier to recognize that Israel's history *is* our history and
to achieve that *Einfühlung*[3]—that feeling of one's way into the
historical situation which confronted the prophets of Israel—by
which in the midst of our contemporary situation we see the truth
which they saw.

Old Testament theology, as, for example, Eichrodt envisages
it, is not different *in kind* from historical research and reinterpretation as understood and undertaken today in other fields. The

---

[1] Porteous (op. cit., 323) thus summarizes part of Eichrodt's contention:
'It is high time that historians should take seriously the fact that there is
inevitably a subjective element in all historical research worthy of the name.
It is an entire mistake when the positivist, for example, tries for the sake of
objectivity to exclude philosophy from the individual sciences. . . . The
historian has to be guided in his work by a principle of selection and by a
goal which gives perspective to his work, but, over and above all that, there
is a principle of 'congeniality'; there must be a certain affinity or relationship
between the historical researcher and the subject of his research, since only so
will the intellectual energy be released which will enable a man to master
his subject. There is, of course, a danger in all this, but unless one is prepared
to run the risk of this danger, the achievement of genuine history will be beyond
one's reach.'

[2] Eng. trans. of Vol. I by J. A. Baker, London, 1961, from the sixth ed.
of *Theologie des Alten Testaments*, Teil I, 1959 (original German ed., 1933).

[3] A term used by O. Procksch, whose *Theologie des Alten Testaments* (2 vols.)
appeared posthumously in 1949–50.

subject-matter is different, of course, and it is undeniable that for many Old Testament scholars the measure of the commitment which their study evokes approaches or attains an absolute quality, a *ne plus ultra* which they cannot even imagine as being transcended. But there is in principle nothing in this process which does not happen to historians in other fields of history; it postulates no special faculty called 'faith' which has no counterpart in 'secular' historiography, no special techniques which are not available to all historians, no supernatural revelation different *in kind* from the illumination which comes to any historian who has recognized his obligation towards his own times through the process of having 'felt his way' into a real situation of the past. If at first sight it seems that to say this involves the denial that biblical faith is a gift of God, it must be replied that such an objection arises from a failure to perceive the teaching of the Bible itself, that faith is nothing other than the acceptance of the divine grace which enables men to be obedient to the disclosure which has been vouchsafed to them in their situation. To confess the biblical faith is to respond to a kerygma, an historical proclamation; it is to make a particular kind of response to the challenge of history. To be an historian in the full sense is (as we have seen) to accept the challenges of history, to be committed to an interpretation of history which is also a participation in history. All historical interpretation involves decision about the present and action in the present; this is true of rationalists (who are invariably reformers) and of Marxists (who would change the world in the act of explaining it) as well as of Jews and Christians. Were it not so, there would never arise the demand for a 'new history'. It is because the Old Testament scholars have in their own field so vigorously responded to this demand of their times that 'Old Testament theology' is perhaps today the most vital and significant of the theological disciplines; it has come to mean the *historical* study of Israel's faith as it arose in a series of disclosure situations which are startlingly relevant to the need for commitment and action in our own time.[1]

[1] The intense activity which has been exhibited in this field during the last thirty years can be appreciated by considering the number of important works which have been published. In addition to the works already cited by G. E. Wright, G. von Rad, A. Weiser, G. A. F. Knight, E. Jacob, Th. C. Vriezen, N. W. Porteous, H. W. Robinson, W. Eichrodt and O. Procksch, we might mention W. Vischer, *Das Christuszeugnis des Alten Testaments*, I,

It would, of course, be wrong to suggest that the revival of Old Testament theology has brought with it unanimity of interpretation amongst scholars. Diversity of view is always a feature of vital historical discussion. Several important issues are now in debate; as Eichrodt remarks, 'we are still in the thick of the argument'.[1] The most significant of these issues from the point of interest of these Lectures is the disagreement between Eichrodt and von Rad concerning the relationship between the Old Testament kerygma and the facts of Israelite history.[2] Von Rad maintains a position in regard to the Old Testament which is similar to that of Bultmann in regard to the New Testament: historical-critical studies do not substantiate the assertion of the kerygmatic tradition that the events took place which were interpreted as the acts of God in Israel's history. What matters is the existential understanding of the individual believer; the relation of such understanding to what actually happened in history is irrelevant. The relation of the Old Testament to the New Testament is thus a matter of existential interpretation, not of real correspondences in historical events. In such a view there is a surrender of the historical basis of Israel's faith and the substitution of an existentialist insight in place of an historical interpretation of real events. The 'existential' meaning of the Old Testament, once it is thus divorced from history, becomes what each individual interpreter cares to make it; the one thing which it cannot be is what the Bible itself unanimously declares that it is, namely, the proclamation of God's sovereignty over history, made manifest through prophetic faith, which discerns his saving acts amidst the crises of Israel's history. By detaching faith from history the existentialist school renders insoluble the problem of how Israel's continuing

---

1934 (Eng. trans., *The Witness of the Old Testament to Christ*, London, 1949) and II, 1942; A. G. Hebert, *The Throne of David*, London, 1941; G. E. Phillips, *The Old Testament in the World Church*, London, 1942; L. Köhler, *Theologie des Alten Testaments*, 1936 (Eng. trans., *Old Testament Theology*, London, 1957); M. Burrows, *An Outline of Biblical Theology*, Philadelphia, Pa., 1946; O. G. Baab, *The Theology of the Old Testament*, 1949; R. C. Dentan, *Preface to Old Testament Theology*, 1950; H. H. Rowley, *The Faith of Israel*, 1956. The list is not exhaustive, and there are, of course, scores of valuable monographs and articles in the learned journals.

[1] *The Theology of the Old Testament*, I, Eng. trans., 118.
[2] The issue is concisely presented in an Excursus to the Eng. trans. of Eichrodt's *The Theology of the Old Testament*, I, 512-20.

faith in Yahweh's saving action in history arose in the first place and was afterwards sustained through many centuries. Eichrodt's position is more in accord with recent historiographical thinking: the deep prophetic interpretation of historical events, which we find in the Old Testament records, is more worthy of the name *history* than any mere chronicle of 'what happened' could ever be. 'In the Old Testament we are not dealing with an anti-historical transformation of the course of history into a fairy tale or poem, but with an interpretation of real events inspired by contact with the mysterious Creatorhood of God who controls history, and from the continual experience of his saving action.'[1]

New Testament Theology

By comparison with the vitality of the discussion of Old Testament theology the study of New Testament theology today seems somewhat anaemic. What is needed is a presentation of New Testament theology as an 'interpretation of real events inspired by contact with the mysterious Creatorhood of the God who controls history, and from the continual experience of his saving action'.[2] There are still many New Testament scholars who question the propriety of writing New Testament theologies, doubtless because they approach the matter from a predominantly literary and non-historical point of view. To them New Testament theology means either an attempt to unify dogmatically the varieties of New Testament thought (which they rightly disapprove) or simply the evolutionist tracing of the development of the Christian religion from its antecedents in the ministry of Jesus to its proliferation in Hellenized second-century Catholicism. They have hardly considered a third possibility. They do not understand the New Testament historically, that is, as a 'new history', a reinterpretation of the existence and faith of Israel in the light of a new historical situation brought about by the coming of Jesus and his Church. They are still dominated by the notion that the earliest records of the sayings and deeds of Jesus must be the soundest source of the history of Jesus and by the correlative notion that all interpretation of 'what happened' must be discounted as history. Since even the earliest records do not give us

[1] Eichrodt, op. cit., 516.
[2] O. Cullmann's *Christology of the New Testament* is a fine example of this kind of presentation.

an uninterpreted account of what happened, the real history of Jesus ('the facts') must in their view remain unknowable.

We hardly need to repeat that such an attitude, though it still survives amongst New Testament scholars, no longer reflects the accepted standpoint of historians generally. Today it is more usually held that history involves a continual process of interpretation and reinterpretation in the light of reflection upon subsequent developments; these developments bring into the foreground elements which were implicit but largely unnoticed in the original situation and whose meaning can be perceived and understood only in the light of them. In all other spheres than that of New Testament study it is generally agreed that history cannot properly be written until after some decades have elapsed; we would not, for example, expect a balanced and satisfying history of the Suez crisis or of the Cuba affair to be achieved for a long time yet. This is not primarily because new facts may come to light, but because the known facts cannot yet be judged in the light of the final outcome of the train of events. What the eye-witnesses and participants report is the raw material of the historian; it is not history itself. In the final resort 'facts' are judgments made not at the time but as a result of reflection upon the long process of causal explanation in which they are seen to cohere. Judgments made today will need to be modified tomorrow, and this process of continuing reassessment constitutes the essence of history. This is why the rewriting of the Bismarck story has been virtually a compulsive preoccupation amongst German historians since 1933 or 1945. It is not true that earlier histories are more 'reliable' than later ones; it is not true that earlier writers, merely because they are earlier, are likely to give us a more 'objective' account of the intention and accomplishment of the historical *dramatis personae*; nor is it true that the success of the modern historian in evaluating earlier histories will depend solely upon his skill in isolating or reconstructing his predecessors' sources, on the assumption that these sources, being earlier, will somehow bring us closer to 'the facts'. Yet all these positivist presuppositions underlie the conclusion of the form-critics that the Gospels are not history but 'only' kerygma, or interpretation, or *Gemeindetheologie*, and so on. A fresh start needs to be made from the basis of the recognition that 'what happened' can be rightly assessed only 'in the perspective of history'.

A single illustration must suffice to show how a more adequately historical approach would raise questions about several of the positions which are today regarded by many New Testament scholars as 'established'. Each generation interprets what has been said and done in the past in the light of its own fixed presuppositions concerning man and the world. The earliest generation of Christians were Jews of limited outlook, with hardly a thought of the world beyond Palestine or of a world-history transcending their own particular crisis of the struggle against the Roman occupying power. It was inevitable that they should interpret the life and intention of Jesus Messiah in terms of this situation and therefore in terms of his near return upon the clouds of heaven; it was natural, too, that the earliest Gentile Christians, an ostracized minority in the cities of their habitation, should at first take over this wishful expectation. It would be entirely unhistorical to suggest that they should have immediately interpreted the events recently fulfilled in terms of a broad geographical and historical outlook which could not have been theirs. But, although it is not difficult to understand how traces of this very old interpretation of the significance of Jesus should have found a place in the Gospel tradition, it would be utterly unhistorical to assume that, because it is the earliest, it gives us an objective representation of the real intention of Jesus himself. It represents merely an early stage in the development of the Church's historical interpretation of the mission of Jesus, a stage which would have to be transcended when in the light of subsequent events a reassessment had become possible. The astonishing expansion of the Christian Church, which had established itself in Rome even before the Apostle of the Gentiles could reach that city, had already created an urgent need for a 'new history', a thorough reappraisal of the meaning of the work and words of Jesus in the light of a new and unanticipated historical situation. Our earliest Gospel, St Mark, gives us just such a reappraisal. The character of any historical reappraisal is that it revives and reinterprets elements in the original situation of which the significance had not formerly been seen, because these elements could be perceived only in the light of historical development. It is thus fatally unhistorical to adopt a fundamentalist attitude towards the earliest interpretation—in this case, that of the original Jewish apocalypticist view—and to say that because it is earliest it is therefore the only truly historical or objective account. The later situation—the existence of the Church in Rome and in many cities within and beyond the Roman world—would have brought out the significance of many formerly neglected elements in the words and deeds of Jesus (for instance, his encounter with a Syrophoenician woman), which could now be understood because there was a context within which their implication had become obvious. The traditions and memories would be searched again to see what guidance could be obtained from 'the mind of the Lord' amidst the perplexities of a new and unexpected historical situation. The intention of Jesus now no longer appeared to have been what it had seemed to the earliest Palestinian Christian congregations. Implicit in what he had done and said, it could now be perceived, was the obligation to 'preach the gospel to all nations' before the End could come (Mark 13.10; Matt. 24.14). Historically it is quite inadmissible to disallow the historicity of the sayings of Jesus concerning the world-mission of the Church on the ground that the earliest historical outlook of the Jewish-Christian community had not understood them; it is, as we have noticed many times, of the essence of historical interpretation that the inner meaning of a particular situation in history should be perceived only when it comes alive in a new situation in which it is existentially relevant and demanding.

The positivist thaw, which has been a marked feature of historiographical thinking during the course of the twentieth century, is slowly bringing about a softening of the presuppositions of the older form-critics, and a new and more historical appreciation of the Gospels is appearing. Today there is a quickening of interest, for example, in the question about the sense in which St Luke is an historian.[1] 'A generation ago, in his inaugural lecture at Cambridge',[2] writes Dr C. K. Barrett, 'Professor Dodd could claim that the Fourth Gospel constituted the most acute and pressing problem in New Testament studies. . . . It would not be far wrong to say that the focus of New Testament studies is now moving to the Lucan writings.'[3] This is doubtless because these writings raise in a pressing way the whole issue of the

[1] See Professor C. K. Barrett's suggestive reflections in his expanded Peake Memorial Lecture, published under the title *Luke the Historian in Recent Study*, London, 1961.

[2] C. H. Dodd, *The Present Task in New Testament Studies*, Cambridge, 1936.

[3] Ibid., 50.

historical character of the New Testament witness. Their author has lived through a critical period of transition in the life of the Church and he has undertaken to supply the new history which is demanded by a new situation. In a fine study of the Lucan books Dr Hans Conzelmann has carefully analysed the many differences of presentation and shifts of emphasis between the original Palestinian tradition of the words and deeds of Jesus and the developed theology of St Luke.[1] In Conzelmann's view the problem which St Luke is wrestling with is that of 'the delay of the Parousia'. According to Luke's sources Jesus and his earliest followers taught that the Parousia was imminent; Luke had therefore to explain the anomaly of an ongoing Church history, which he accomplishes not unsuccessfully by means of his characteristic theology of the Church and the Holy Spirit. This view makes Luke a skilful apologist and a theologian, but hardly an historian. The view is inevitable because of Conzelmann's uncriticized presupposition, namely, that the earliest historical interpretation of Jesus and his work, that of the Palestinian community, must be the basis of all subsequent historical interpretation. But this, as we have seen, is an assumption which would not be made by historians in other spheres. Only after several decades had gone by could the intention and work of Jesus be adequately assessed 'in the perspective of history'. This is precisely what St Luke is doing, and his writings deserve to be called 'history' in the full and proper sense of the word. Not only in respect of the Parousia but also in several other respects—for example, the propriety of the Gentile mission—St Luke perceived truths about the intention of the historical Jesus which were obscured from an earlier generation of interpreters by their own limited historical horizon. Conzelmann regards as important for our understanding of St Luke 'the discrepancies between the ideas in his sources and his own ideas',[2] but his presuppositions unfortunately preclude the possibility that St Luke's 'own ideas' may represent a more satisfactory historical interpretation of the Gospel story than do the 'sources', which are, after all, only earlier and necessarily more limited interpretations of that story. The assumption that modern scholars may freely criticize 'sources', but that St Luke was not in

[1] *The Theology of St Luke*, Eng. trans. of *Die Mitte der Zeit* by Geoffrey Buswell, London and New York, 1960.
[2] Ibid., 95.

a position to do so is quite unjustifiable; after all, he tells us explicitly that he has done so (Luke 1.1–4). The Fourth Evangelist, who gives us a profound historical reinterpretation of the Synoptic tradition, has so successfully concealed his sources that some contemporary scholars, who seem to think that the writing of history consists in copying from 'sources', go to the length of providing them for him and postulate his dependence upon 'south Judaean traditions'.[1] A new approach to the understanding of the New Testament will be achieved when it is generally recognized that 'sources', like 'facts' themselves, are only judgments of evidence, and that earlier sources are inevitably partial and lacking in historical perspective. The later rewriting of the Gospel story (for example, in St John's Gospel) is indeed unlikely to give us many new 'facts', but it may give us a profoundly illuminating representation of the truth of history. In this most important sense the Fourth Gospel is thoroughly historical.

Preoccupation with literary criticism sometimes leads New Testament scholars to suppose that the earliest sources into which the Gospels and Acts can be analysed must present the most objectively historical information accessible to the critic. In the light of our study of history this presupposition is seen to be the reverse of the truth. We need not feel disconcerted, as the old form-critics did, by the discovery that all the Gospel records are written from the point of view of the Easter faith: historians always view events in the perspective of later developments, and the fact that the whole Gospel tradition bears testimony to Christ's resurrection is itself evidence, not that the Gospels are unhistorical, but that the resurrection was an event in history.[2] There is no historical testimony at all to a non-kerygmatic Christ, a rabbi who summoned men to existential decision and did not rise from the dead; and there is no reason to suppose that the Romans would

[1] Cf. Alan Richardson, *The Gospel according to St John* (Torch Commentaries), London, 1959, 25–28.

[2] Cf. Bo Reicke, 'Incarnation and Exaltation: the Historic Jesus and the Kerygmatic Christ' in *Interpretation* (Richmond, Va.), XVI (April 1962), 159: 'After the resurrection of Jesus the apostles and disciples recollected their memories of the crucified One. . . . In doing so they were convinced that the post-resurrection picture of Jesus which had been supplemented by their new Christological insight was more empiric and historic, more adequate, correct and true than the immediate picture had been. They did not intend to transform the original memory-picture into mere fancy when they supplemented it by Christology. On the contrary, they were concerned only with

have found it necessary to execute such a preacher, had he existed. It is true that there were many who met Jesus, who saw nothing kerygmatic about him; *they* might have written about the non-kergymatic Jesus, had they had any interest in doing so. It is for lack of such testimony of unbelievers that the existentialist theologians have imagined that we can have little knowledge of the Jesus of history and that, as Professor Reicke remarks, there has developed on the Continent, as in ancient Corinth, a 'Christ-party' which is not interested in the Jesus of history but only in the kerygma of Christ.[1] The Gospels provide abundant evidence that the Church in the apostolic and sub-apostolic periods did not preach Christ as a faceless eschatological event: it was important that believers should know how the Risen Lord had come to be crucified, how he had lived and what he had taught. It mattered that catechumens should understand how he dealt with people— with fishermen called to discipleship, with blind men and cripples and sorrowing parents, with grasping publicans and religious bigots, with the demon-possessed and with penitents or little children: it mattered because he was the Risen One, who had left an example to be followed by the community of which he was the living Head. The moral appeal of the Jesus of history remains still a strong and converting factor in bringing men to confess him as Lord and Saviour, precisely because he is the Jesus *of history*, not the legendary hero of morality play. But the Jesus *of history* is not the non-kerygmatic object of Schweitzer's 'quest', or even the existentialist non-Messiah of the 'new quest'; he is the Jesus of the developed historical judgment of the Church that is found in the Four Gospels.

The theology of the New Testament, like that of the Old Testament, is essentially an interpretation of history. Even over the relatively short period of less than a century between the earliest 'sources' and the later writings, we can discern a process of the widening and deepening of historical judgment, an increasing objectivity as the perspective of history lengthens and as each

---

correcting what they, according to their sincere conviction, had heretofore not been able to understand in a complete or adequate way.' This did not mean a step into *Gemeindetheologie*, but 'a return to historic reality. They were consciously returning to the reality in which, as apostles and eyewitnesses, they had shared, but which, because of their inertia, they had not adequately experienced and understood.'

[1] Ibid.

new situation brings into focus some hitherto barely understood implication of 'the matters fulfilled among us'. There are thus several 'theologies' within the pages of the New Testament, or, more accurately, there are several stages of the development of that more-or-less unified and accepted 'final' interpretation which is implied by the fixing of a New Testament canon. Taken as a whole, the theology of the New Testament constitutes a new and bold reinterpretation of the theology of the Old Testament in the light of the life, death and resurrection of Christ and of the first going forth of the Conquering Word, as the Church obeyed the intention of her Lord in the preaching of the gospel to all nations.

8

THE WITNESS OF HISTORY

THE growing awareness during the present century of a subjective element in all historical interpretation has raised in an urgent form the question of historical relativism. The problem is not merely an academic one, which can be discussed at leisure by scholars in their inconclusive way while the tides of history ebb and flow. The kingdom of heaven suffers violence, and men of violence take it by force. In our own times we have seen how a revolutionary ideology repudiates history and abolishes ('liquidates') its 'inoffensive professors', those undutiful guardians of the humane tradition who have failed to discharge their responsibility to society. History so easily becomes the lackey of ideologies, whereas in its true nature it is the safest prophylactic against them. The essential prerequisite for successful resistance to ideological pretensions is the presence of a deep, humane historical consciousness, such as only a truly critical and compassionate 'clerisy' of historians could provide.[1] Where this is not forthcoming, history as it is understood in the European tradition perishes. We may discern a 'judgment of history' in the nemesis which has overtaken Marxist thought, which originally developed the notion of ideology in its assault upon the humane tradition and in so doing destroyed both the concept and the practice of history itself.[2] Historical relativism in its extreme forms involves

[1] Cf. Jules Benda, *La trahison des clercs*, Paris, 1927; Eng. trans., *The Great Betrayal*, 1928.
[2] A reviewer in *The Times Literary Supplement* (Sept. 15, 1961, No. 3,107), welcoming the official *History of the Great Patriotic War of the Soviet Union, 1941–45* (*Istoriya Velikoi Otechestvennoi Voiny Sovietskovo Soyuza, 1941–45*, Vol. I, Moscow: Military Publishing House of the Ministry of Defence of the U.S.S.R.), as a sign of better things, has written: 'History as we understand it, especially history dealing with contemporary or recent events, may be said scarcely to have existed in the Soviet Union at all, particularly during the

a denial of the Western belief in the possibility and the value of truth for its own sake and hands over history as a tool of social engineering to an alien totalitarian idea. 'The mutability of the past', we may recollect, was the central tenet of Ingsoc, the official philosophy of the Party in Oceania.[1] At the Ministry of Truth, Winston Smith was employed in helping to create the official version of the past. 'Day by day and almost minute by minute the past was brought up to date . . . All history was a palimpsest, scraped clean and reinscribed exactly as often as was necessary. In no case would it have been possible, once the deed was done, to prove that any falsification had taken place.' The deliberate manipulation of history for ideological ends seems to those nurtured in the European tradition to spell the ultimate degradation of the human person, whose essential nobility consists in his freedom to seek and honour the truth. But is his condition any less miserable, if his enslavement to error derives not from ideological blinkers imposed by human despots but from his own inherent incapacity to perceive the truth of history as it is in itself or to understand history at all except by such forms of subjective interpretation as are possible to him in the transitory 'climate of opinion' of his own age?

Myth and the Interpretation of History

Becker's remark, quoted above,[2] that historians are the wise men of the tribe to whom is entrusted the keeping of the useful myths, contains a truth which needs further elucidation. Even the most dedicated of 'scientific' historians have been revealed as makers and guardians of the useful myths. Some have gone so far as to suggest that the providing of such myths is the sole

---

Stalin epoch. All such history was "arranged" to suit an ideological purpose; the most extreme example of this kind of writing is, of course, the *Short History of the CPSU*, published in 1938 and written by a committee under the direction of Stalin, and later officially attributed to Stalin himself. In this, as we know, the two great geniuses who directed the destinies of Russia since 1917 (and even before) were Lenin and Stalin. Under the Khrushchev régime this book has been substantially, though not very drastically, revised and above all freed of its all-pervading "personality cult" element. But even in this new version there are still numerous facts with which any "objective" historian would quarrel, for instance with nearly everything concerning Trotsky.'

[1] In George Orwell's *Nineteen Eighty-Four*, London, 1949.
[2] 173.

function of the historian,[1] whose activity endows the meaningless flux of events with intelligibility for the time being. Others claim that their interpretation ('myth') of history is scientifically based upon an induction from the empirical evidence,[2] but the reception of their claim by other historians indicates that their conclusions lack the character of verifiability which is usually associated with scientific hypotheses. The general trend of our investigation has suggested that historical interpretations, if they are to command assent, must be established by strictly historical considerations and that they cannot be commended upon scientific and sociological grounds as such. That historians are concerned with myth in the sense of interpretation is doubtless true; but it is important to understand the manner in which historical interpretation ('myth') is a necessary aspect of their work and also the sense in which a prime duty of historians is to be critical of the myths of their age.

In the nineteenth century Friedrich Nietzsche (1844–1900), Burckhardt's colleague at Basle, in revolt both against Hegel's regimented march of the historical process and against the depersonalized historical criticism of the positivists, had asserted the value of myth as the active though unprincipled ally of his daring Life Force.[3] His exaltation of instinct over reason was followed in that depressing line which ran through Houston Stewart Chamberlain[4] to the egregious Dr Alfred Rosenberg's *Myth of the Twentieth Century* (1930), the exposition of the Nazi myth of the superiority of Aryan man. As Professor Pieter Geyl remarks, Nietzsche would no doubt have despised Chamberlain and Rosenberg, but 'these cultivators of the useful myth have nevertheless given the world a terrible object lesson on where history can land us when it is detached from criticism and truth.'[5] The truth is that societies and nations live and shape their policies

---

[1] Notably the German historian Theodor Lessing, who died in 1933, in his *Geschichte als Sinngebung des Sinnlosen* (1919); cf. the position of Karl Popper (*supra*, 114f.).

[2] The outstanding example is Sir Arnold Toynbee in his massive work, *A Study of History* in ten volumes (1934–54); for a critical assessment of it see P. Geyl, *Debates with Historians*, 91–178.

[3] F. Nietzsche, 'Vom Nutzen und Nachtheil der Historie für das Leben' in his *Unzeitgemässe Betrachtungen* (1873–76); this essay is briefly summarized by P. Geyl in his *Use and Abuse of History*, New Haven, 1955, 52–55.

[4] *Grundlagen des neunzehnten Jahrhunderts* (1899).

[5] *Use and Abuse of History*, 55f.

by the myths they believe in, and hence arises the ethical responsibility of the historian. Such myths are ideological interpretations of history and their primary virtue is that they should be useful. Their function is to secure social cohesion, to assure the common man that he belongs to a cause greater than himself, and to create the blissful expectation of well-being hereafter. It is not necessary that the myth should be true, but only that it should be 'useful'. Though ostensibly it interprets the past, its real concern is the future; history is the screen on which the ideal future is projected. Myth is essentially 'practical history'.

It was the French Syndicalist philosopher Georges Sorel 1847–1922) who in his *Réflexions sur la Violence* (1903)[1] gave expression to the conception of myth as a force in history: myths were not descriptions of reality but affirmations of a determination to act. He takes over from Nietzsche and Bergson the idea of the irrational Life Force, which charges on through the course of events, throwing up from time to time the useful myths which serve as the banners which rally the cavalry. His own favourite myth was that of the General Strike, which was the banner of the Anarcho-Syndicalist class war. Sorel's political activity was ineffectual, but Mussolini gave his theorizing a practical application when he utilized the power of the State to propagate and to realize the myth of Fascism, that is, the myth of the greatness of the Italian people, the forerunner of the Nazi myth of the *Herrenvolk*. 'We have created our myth', he declared at Naples in 1922; 'the myth is a faith, it is passion. It is not necessary that it shall be a reality. It *is* a reality by the fact that it is a goad, a hope, a faith, that it is courage. Our myth is the nation, our myth is the greatness of the nation.'[2] As Canon Smyth has said, myths of this kind 'are designed to realize the future they predict by making the group to which they are addressed accept the prediction as a present reality. . . . The myth is a kind of Realized Eschatology.[3] It is scarcely necessary to elaborate further examples of such 'dynamic myths' from our contemporary world—the Marxist 'classless society', 'the American way of life', 'the African per-

[1] Eng. trans. by T. E. Hulme, 1915. On Sorel see John Bowle, *Politics and Opinion in the Nineteenth Century*, 398–413.
[2] George H. Sabine, *A History of Political Theory*, London, 1939, 759, quoted in a perceptive article by Canon Charles Smyth in *Theology*, Vol. LII, No. 352 (October 1949), 369.
[3] Ibid.

sonality', and so on; all around us the myths proliferate and wax strong for good or ill.

It would be a mistake to imagine that myths flourish only in totalitarian countries, where the State propaganda-machine makes them conspicuous and strangles their rivals: every people has its own myth (or public image of itself, as we tend to say now-adays).[1] It grows up unconsciously; no one can say exactly who its originator was; political parties claim to embody it in their policies; journalists articulate it, and historians find it adumbrated in the story which they tell of the people's past. The immense popularity of G. M. Trevelyan's *English Social History* (London ed., 1944) in Britain during the period of post-war reconstruction was doubtless due to its portrayal of the English past as the matrix of the ideals of the Beveridge report (1942) and as the womb of history in which the Welfare State was conceived. To say this is in no way to impugn the value or validity of Trevelyan's inter-pretation of English history. In any case it is the only kind of history in which the layman will be interested, for he cannot see the relevance to his own life and times of the technical history of the specialists. Historians may indeed criticize Trevelyan's con-ception of social history ('history with politics left out'), but at least we are reminded that the layman will get his myth of his historical destiny from some other source, if he does not get it from historians. We shall not doubt the value and utility of a generous and humane portrait of historical development, such as we find in Trevelyan's book, so long as we believe that one historical perspective can be better than another, even though we agree that no perspective is absolute and that in a hundred years' time Trevelyan's history will tell the historians of the period more about the English mood in the 1940s than about the previous ages of English history. If we believe that one historical perspec-tive can be better than another, then at least we are not one kind of historical relativist, the kind which asserts that all perspectives are equally subjective and that there is nothing to choose among them.

[1] Cf. Craig McGregor, art. 'The Uncertain Smile of Australia' in *The Spectator*, No. 6,983 (April 27, 1962), 535: 'Nations live by the myths they believe in, and few people have yet questioned the national myth of mateship and Jack's-as-good-as-his-master. . . . Australians just take it for granted that they are friendly, unsnobbish blokes . . .; because they believe it they usually are.'

If we believe this, however, it will be because of the kind of persons we are, which involves our commitment to a faith, to a point of view, to what Becker called our 'settled convictions as to the nature of man and the world'. It will not be because we have been able to 'read off' the moral and spiritual laws of history as the natural scientist 'reads off' the physical and chemical laws of nature. Interpretations (myths) of history are not (either in Ranke's or in Toynbee's sense) empirically deduced from an objective study of 'the facts', for at every point, even at the point of deciding what are the facts, the personal judgment of the historian is involved.[1] Why do some thoughtful men—we are not now speaking of those who, having no root in themselves, are swayed by demagogues or conditioned by the prevailing 'climate of opinion'—become Marxists and others secular humanists, and so on? The answer can only be that they think as they do because they are what they are, because each man in his separate individuality has become the person he is. This answer may not seem to take us very far, but it brings us to the ultimate mystery of the human person: that in his freedom he may choose to be what he is and to believe what he believes, though he is never wholly free from conditioning factors ('the climate of opinion'), and yet he may be understood historically, at least in principle, by a super-human intelligence such as that of God or, if we prefer it, of the electronic brain of the future. Historical interpretations (myths) are not 'read off' from the records of the past, but are chosen by *persons* in the light of their present experience and their determination to shape the future. To say that all such interpretations are equally subjective is to assert that moral experience is an illusion and that no way of life is better than another; it is to declare that history is a flowing current which we cannot harness or direct, bearing the generations of mankind to a destination over which they have no choice. But the witness of history itself tells against

[1] Cf. Reinhold Niebuhr, *The Nature and Destiny of Man*, London, 1941, I, 151: 'It is impossible to interpret history at all without a principle of interpretation which history as such does not yield. The various principles of interpretation current in modern culture, such as the idea of progress or the Marxist concept of an historical dialectic, are all principles of interpretation introduced by faith. They claim to be conclusions about the nature of history at which men arrive after a 'scientific' analysis of the course of events; but there can be no such analysis of the course of events which does not make use of some presupposition of faith as the principle of analysis or interpretation.'

such views, because our historical experience is political and moral. It may be true that it is not the historian's business to pass moral judgments upon the *dramatis personae* of history; but as the 'guardian of the myths' he must be a moralist or an amoralist, and this involves personal decision. Even if his criterion is strictly that of utility ('the useful myths'), he still must regard historical interpretations as useful *for* something, for some ends which he judges better than others: the utilitarian is inescapably a moralist.

It has often been asserted (by Sorel, for instance) that Christianity is one of the socio-historical myths of the type which we have been considering. Instead of a myth of the *Herrenvolk* or of the classless society, Christianity gives us the myth of the Kingdom of God, according to which man's unhappiness in this world is compensated in the next. It may be true that many frustrated individuals or whole groups of people (for example, in the slave communities) have been attracted to the Gospel in this way. But in so far as it is ever possible to demonstrate an historical statement, it is certain that the Christian faith did not arise as an ideological myth. The latter requires a particular set of social and economic conditions to bring it to birth and to sustain it, as, for instance, the myth of the classless society which arose out of the wretched condition of industrial workers in the nineteenth century, or the myth of the *Herrenvolk* which arose amongst a vigorous people deprived of *Lebensraum* in a capitalist world. By contrast there is a universality about the appeal of the Gospel to man as man—not as proletarian man, or Aryan man, or economic man—which distinguishes it from the social myths, which are by their very aim and character limited and local.[1] But there is also something else which distinguishes the Christian interpretation of history from the myths, and that is that the Christian faith is based upon the actual witness of history in a way in which the social myths are not. The myths use history only as a screen upon which to project their vision of the future. They are fundamentally indifferent to the history which they profess to interpret; their interest in history is not, so to speak, a truly historical interest, a 'passion for the past', a compassion which seeks to understand the real men and women of the past in their actual historical predicament. The ideological myths are fundamentally unhistorical. Their historical 'heroes' are semi-personalized occult forces ('the

[1] See further on this subject Alan Richardson, *Christian Apologetics*, 65–88.

Dialectical Process', the Life Force, Progress, the Nation, the Proletariat, the various 'factors' in history). Such interpretation is not history but mythology.

Now we saw that the differentiating character of biblical faith, when contrasted with the religions of the surrounding peoples, was precisely its kerygmatic aspect, that is to say, its testimony to a disclosure of saving truth in actual historical situations. The characteristic attitude of the Christian believer towards the Bible (whether he be a theologian or a 'plain man') is that he puts himself by every means at his disposal into a disclosure-situation of the biblical history and he finds that this is his own situation, as a man of unclean lips dwelling among a people of unclean lips. This disclosure of the Lord of history, high and lifted up, who yet commissions him in his service in the midst of the tasks and toils of his own historical situation, is vouchsafed in the moment of obedience, of response to that which has been disclosed concerning the purpose of God in the predicament of his own life and times. It is out of real history that the Christian thus finds himself addressed, a history that has come alive for him as his own history, in which he is not a mere spectator but an active participant, challenged to commit himself to moral and personal decision and action. He partakes in the real, continuing historical struggle against the baals, the false deities, the mythological personifications of the forces of nature or of the nation; a struggle which is still today the mark of Christian obedience in the world. The mythological deities, which claim men's belief and worship and service, today have different names—Life-Force, *Volk*, Progress, Dialectical Process, and so on—but they are just as real, or as unreal, as the gods of the nations of the Fertile Crescent some two or three thousand years ago. Just as of old biblical faith was compelled to wage an unrelenting struggle against 'the abominations of the heathen', those hypostatized forces of nature before which men prostrated themselves, so today Christian faith continues the struggle against mythology, against the secular myths which modern men have set up, believing vainly in their power to realize the golden future which they predict. The witness of history shows that they are but idols, powerless to save. Belief in the social myths is a worshipping of the work of men's hands, an idolatry that leads only to disaster or frustration. Christian faith is an historical faith, not a mythology.

Historical Relativism and 'the Climate of Opinion'

Little more than a decade separates the confidence of Lord Acton that, though 'ultimate history' would not be attained in his own generation, objective history was being progressively achieved, and the scepticism of Carl Becker concerning the possibility of objective history at all.[1] There can be little doubt that Acton's standpoint sums up the general optimistic attitude of nineteenth-century historians, but that Becker more nearly represents the viewpoint of historians which has been developing during the course of the twentieth century.[2] A great deal of Becker's contention would now be taken for granted by many, perhaps most, historians.[3] The question is not whether we are to be relativists or not, but how far we are to be relativists.[4] The view to which our argument has led us is that only those who refuse to make or are incapable of making moral decisions in the face of the historical issues of their own day can be in any thorough-going sense historical relativists: their inability to interpret history is the obverse of their incapacity to meet the moral challenge of their own times. Relativism in history is likely to imply a sceptical attitude to ethical questions; if we suppose that there is no

[1] Compare the optimism of Acton's report in 1896 to the Syndics of the Cambridge University Press (*The Cambridge Modern History: its Origin, Authorship and Production*, 1907, 10–12) with the tone of Becker's *Atlantic Monthly* article of 1910 (*supra*, 191–4).

[2] Cf. the midway position of Sir George Clark's introduction to *The New Modern History*, (1957), xxivf., where those scholars are said to be 'impatient' who 'take refuge in scepticism, or at least in the doctrine that, since all historical judgments involve persons and points of view, one is as good as another and there is no "objective" historical truth'.

[3] Commenting upon Orwell's phrase 'the mutability of the past', Charlotte Watkins Smith (*Carl Becker: on History and the Climate of Opinion*, 102f.) says, 'surely something like this is already a central tenet of most present-day historians. . . . Even the most casual reader of the *American Historical Review* . . . realizes that the scientific historian with his definitive picture of what really happened is an extinct breed.' Cf. H. W. V. Temperley, *Research and Modern History*, London, 1930, 18f.

[4] How far Becker himself was a relativist has been endlessly debated; see the works of Charlotte Watkins Smith and Burleigh Taylor Wilkins already cited. See also Maurice Mandelbaum, *The Problem of Historical Knowledge* (New York, 1938), which criticizes historical relativism, and Becker's review of it in *The Philosophical Review*, XLIX (May, 1940). Becker there writes: 'If relativism means . . . that a considerable body of knowledge is not objectively ascertainable, if it means a denial of Mandelbaum's statement that "the *ideal* of objective historical knowledge is possible of at least *partial* attainment"—then I am not a relativist.'

objective right and wrong, but that our moral convictions are only prejudices resulting from our historical and social conditioning, we shall also hold that historical interpretation is a largely subjective procedure.[1] It has been well said that 'if one way of life is no better than another, then no way of life is valuable at all',[2] and to this it may be added that if one historical interpretation is no better than another, then the study of history is of no value at all. The fact that historians (like Becker himself) go on working vigorously, even though they have abandoned the notion of 'objective' history, is sufficient testimony to the truth that the merits of different interpretations of history can be rationally evaluated, that personal viewpoints can be enlarged by mutual discussion and criticism, and that more adequate judgments can be reached through an open-minded willingness to consider that someone else's appraisals may be better than one's own. Those who avow a thoroughgoing relativism, whether in historiography or in morality, probably overlook the very high degree of community of judgment which exists or is attainable through mutual discussion in virtue of the common humanity of the participants, and they ignore the positive value of the clash of differing points of view, which makes historical interpretation fruitful and interesting.[3] The bogey of historical relativism is not very intimidating; we are all relatively relativists nowadays, for no one believes that historical judgments can be 'proved' after the fashion of verification in the natural sciences. And this has made historical study all the more relevant, existential and practical.

Acton regarded history as 'our deliverer . . . from the tyranny of environment and the pressure of the air we breathe'.[4] Becker took an opposite view; for him, as we have seen, the historian was inescapably conditioned by 'the climate of opinion'

---

[1] Cf. Louis Gottschalk, *Understanding History*, New York, 1951, 110f.

[2] Michael Roberts, *The Recovery of the West*, London, 1941, 138.

[3] The monumental dullness of the original *Cambridge Modern History* was doubtless largely due to the deliberate attempt to remove the element of personal judgment and 'the clash of opinion'. Acton instructed the contributors that 'our Waterloo must be one that satisfies French and English, German and Dutch alike' and that no reader should be able to detect 'where the Bishop of Oxford laid down the pen, and whether Fairbairn or Gasquet, Liebermann or Harrison took it up' (*Lectures on Modern History*, 318). Cf. A. J. Toynbee, *A Study of History*, I, 3f.; G. M. Trevelyan, *Clio, a Muse*, 1931, ed., 171.

[4] *Lectures on Modern History*, 33.

of his own day. Again, the right question to ask is not whether we are or are not conditioned by our upbringing and environment, but how far we are conditioned by these things. We shall probably conclude that Acton underestimated and Becker overestimated the influence of 'the climate of opinion'. Acton could confidently appeal to 'the common, even the vulgar, code' of morals, assuming that all men knew what it was; for Becker all scales of value were relative to a particular age and would pass away with it. Becker was impressed by A. N. Whitehead's application of the theory of relativity to philosophical problems, and it was from Whitehead that he took over the seventeenth-century phrase 'climate of opinion', which Whitehead had restored to circulation.[1] We are told that Becker delighted in quoting Whitehead's judgment that 'observational discrimination is not dictated by impartial facts. It selects and discards, and what it retains is arranged in a subjective order of prominence', thus having it on the authority of Whitehead that the scientific objectivity of the Rankeans was so much nonsense.[2]

From this position Becker goes on to elaborate an argument which emphasizes by exaggerating an important aspect of our modern historical-mindedness. 'What is peculiar to the modern mind', he tells us, 'is the disposition and the determination to regard ideas and concepts, the truth of things as well as the things themselves, as changing entities, the character and significance of which at any given time can be fully grasped only by regarding them as points in an endless process of differentiation, of unfolding, of waste and repair.'[3] He contrasts with this mentality the confidence of the former 'unhistorical' ages, when philosophy, theology and deductive reasoning, rather than science and history, were regarded as portals to knowledge. By way of illustration he quotes Aquinas's definition of natural law: it is clear, concise, magisterial, deduced from rational principles valid for all times and all places. Rational creatures (if we may sum-

---

[1] *Heavenly City*, 5; A. N. Whitehead, *Science and the Modern World* (1926). John Bowle (*Politics and Opinion in the Nineteenth Century*, 243) says that the phrase was first coined by Joseph Glanvill (1636–80), Rector of the Abbey Church, Bath, an enthusiast for experimental science and a member of the Royal Society. It was from Glanvill that Matthew Arnold took the legend of the Scholar Gipsy.

[2] Burleigh Taylor Wilkins, *Carl Becker*, 191.

[3] *Heavenly City*, 19.

marize St Thomas's definition) have a share in the Eternal Reason, whereby they have a natural inclination to their proper act and end, 'and this participation of the Eternal in the rational creature is called the natural law'.[1] Because we live in a changed world, Becker tells us, we can no longer think in such terms. We can clumsily translate the words, but we cannot meet the argument on its own ground, because the thought-forms of the thirteenth century are meaningless to us. We can neither assent to them nor dissent from them. If St Thomas were to ask us what natural law is, we could answer him only by telling him the history of the idea. 'Historical-mindedness is so much a preoccupation of modern thought that we can identify a particular thing only by pointing to the various things it successively was before it came to be that particular thing which it will presently cease to be.'[2]

We need spend little time in pointing out the exaggeration of this argument, which leads Becker to the position of 'nearly absolute relativism'. It is not true to say that we cannot think in the thought-forms of St Thomas, for the achievement of the historian of thought is precisely that he is able to think the thought of former generations. Even though we allow Becker to insist that we are interested in the past because we are chiefly interested in the present and the future, it does not follow that we are therefore precluded from thinking past thought and finding in it insights to which our own generation is blind. Perhaps Becker had not met any living Thomists who might have demonstrated to him the possibility of thinking in Thomistic categories in the twentieth century. The great systems of the past—Platonism, Thomism, and so on—do not die because the climate of opinion changes; they dissolve only to refashion themselves in new and living forms, combining with fresh elements in new historical situations to ensure that continuity of development in which all history (including the history of thought) consists. If history as a study is a reliving of the thought and experience of the past, then we should expect to find an intense intellectual excitement as we wrestle with the questions which engaged the whole being of a Plato or an Aquinas. We shall find that their problems are our problems and we shall come to see why men speak of a *philosophia perennis*. An even more striking refutation of Becker's exaggerated

[1] *Summa Theologica*, Part II (First Part), Q. XCI, art. ii.
[2] *Heavenly City*, 19.

denial is to be found in the way in which generations of Christians
—'simple' folk as well as professional theologians—have strug-
gled to think biblically, to allow their whole mind to be re-formed
by the living categories of the biblical history. What Becker is
really telling us (as the scintillating first chapter of his *Heavenly
City* makes clear) is that he personally has been conditioned to
believe that the universe is indifferent to human aspirations and
that God is no longer possible as a term of explanation. And, of
course, we are all keenly aware of those features of the twentieth-
century climate which make relativist notions seem to be necessary categories of thought. But were there not in every age some
people, some prophets, some minority groups, who resisted the
pressure of conditioning influences, there would be no new insights, no reform, no progress. Greek philosophy arose because
certain individuals questioned the assumptions prevalent in the
climate of ancient thought; Hebrew faith arose and was maintained by resistance to the pressure of the climate of opinion of the
whole Fertile Crescent. 'The climate of opinion' is a useful metaphor up to a point, but when it is pressed so far as to suggest
that our thinking is totally conditioned by the assumptions of our
age, it leads to the absurdity of affirming that all our ideas, including this one, are valid only for today and were not true yesterday
and will not be true tomorrow. In short, 'a nearly absolute
relativism' is just as impossible as belief in scientifically objective
history.

Historical Theology

There is, nevertheless, an important truth to which Becker
directs our attention, and we should not allow the exaggerations
of his argument to obscure it. It is true that, as he says, we nowadays identify an idea and express its meaning by recounting its
history. This is one of the consequences of our having become
historically minded. Becker's own example, the idea of natural
law, may be used as an illustration. How would we expect a
lecturer whose theme was the meaning of natural law to deal with
the subject? We would expect him to begin with Plato, or perhaps
even with the pre-Socratics and Pythagoreans, and then to work
his way forward to the Stoics; then he would probably show how
St Ambrose baptized Cicero's thought into the Christian theology
of the Middle Ages. And so he would come to St Thomas and

discuss the development of Thomism down to the present day. After this he would probably turn back to the Reformers' criticism of natural theology and work his way forward to recent statements of the theology of the 'orders' of society; if he were an Anglican, he would doubtless say something about Hooker and the casuistry of the Caroline divines; he would make reference to the rise of ideas about laws of nature in the scientific field from the seventeenth century onwards, and finally he might round off his treatment by discussing rationalism in ethics, mentioning some modern philosophers who have advocated it along with a few of their critics. Then he would stop and say in effect: 'And that is what is meant by natural law.' In short, our habit since the nineteenth century is to identify a conception by giving an account of its history.

And this constitutes 'historical theology'. This is the way we teach theology in universities and seminaries; it is, in fact, one strand, and a very important one, in the wider subject of the history of thought. Its banishment to theological faculties in universities, as to a ghetto of specialists, and its general exclusion from the curricula of other university departments, are responsible for the failure of so many of our Western institutions of higher education to provide any opportunity at all for the fertile study of the humane tradition of Europe in its wholeness and in the richness of its historical content.[1] In recent years 'historical theology' has acquired a bad name in certain quarters, because it has appeared to be one of the duller and least relevant of all the branches of 'technical history', an archaeological exhumation of long-buried skeletons in order that they may be catalogued in dry-as-dust volumes and learned journals. It must be admitted that students of theology have often been expected to learn a number of 'facts' of which the relevance to questions of contemporary faith and life has not been made clear, because they have not been presented historically. That is to say, the student

[1] It should be unnecessary to point out that 'Europe' in this context is neither a geographical nor even an ethnological concept. Europa was originally a Syrian maiden, and in another ancient myth Japhet was a son of Noah—profound expressions (well understood during the Middle Ages) of the truth that the seeds of European civilization are to be found in Asia, a truth which is being rediscovered by modern scholarship. See, e.g., Denys Hay, *Europe: The Emergence of an Idea*, Edinburgh, 1957, and Cyrus H. Gordon, *Before the Bible: the Common Background of Greek and Hebrew Civilizations*, London, 1962.

has not been helped to think himself historically into a vanished world of faith and doubt, of action and conflict, in which the ancient formulations can be seen to be alive with insights into real problems which challenge us to find contemporary answers in the language and thought-forms of today. Students have been expected to know, for example, that according to the Definition of the Council of Chalcedon the one and the same Christ is to be acknowledged in two natures unconfusedly, unchangeably, indivisibly and inseparably, the difference of the natures being in no way removed because of the union, but rather the property of each nature being preserved and concurring into one Person and one Hypostasis. They have been expected to say in their examinations which of the four formidable adverbs was directed against the Apollinarian and Eutychian heresies and which against the Nestorian; and, being anxious to satisfy the examiners, they have done so quite correctly, for these things can be learnt without undue mental strain out of books. When 'historical theology' is reduced to recording a mass of 'facts', that is, the codified and congealed judgments of a number of past scholars, it has been drained of its vitality and interest. The unpardonable crime in the exposition of the history of ideas is dullness, the failure to recognize and communicate the existential challenge of the past to the present. It can be avoided only by those who are vitally concerned with history because they are alive to the urgent questions of their own day. This is why the history of thought is a practical study, not merely an 'academic' one; it is why theology, which in our times has become historical theology, should be studied not in a self-contained private enclosure but in relation to the whole world of present thought and action.[1]

Theology in our times has become historical theology. Because we are nowadays historically minded, we can understand an idea or a doctrine only when we can relate its history; we can identify a concept only by regarding it, not as something static, something which can be defined once for all as in St Thomas's definition of natural law, but as a living, developing entity, to be represented by a series of points in an endless process of differentiation, of unfolding, of waste and repair. Becker is right when he thus

[1] Cf. a suggestive discussion by K. J. Woollcombe in a review-article of J. N. D. Kelly, *Early Christian Doctrines*, Oxford, 1958, in *Theology*, Vol. LXII, No. 469 (July 1959).

describes what is involved in the fact of historical-mindedness. But he is unpersuasive when he imports his own sceptical and relativist point of view into the interpretation of history, in the apparent belief that he has derived his attitude from the study of history itself. He is speaking only for those of his own disposition of mind when he says that the thought-forms of previous centuries are meaningless to us and that therefore there is no point in asking whether the various standpoints of previous ages are true or false. When he says that we cannot meet their arguments on their own grounds, and therefore cannot either assent to them or refute them, he overlooks another possibility, namely that we can be challenged by them to decision and action about the questions of faith and morals that press upon our own times. Becker shares too completely the attitude of the *philosophes* whom he loved and hated with the same breath; the historian's mind was, with Becker, as Voltaire said of Hume, 'superior to his materials'. He could not think in the thought-forms of Aquinas, because the problems which Aquinas was struggling with—as Becker would readily have admitted—were not real problems for him. Historical theology is of compulsive interest to those for whom its problems are real problems, not merely intellectual speculations, but matters of life-and-death significance in their own history. For those who think with Becker that the ideas of former ages must necessarily have lost their value and utility in a changed climate of opinion, historical theology (like every other branch of the history of thought) will be nothing more than a catalogue of dead ideas, irrelevant to our concerns; but for others, who find the history of past faith and thought a source of challenge to understanding and commitment in the present, it will mean a looking at the existential questions of our life from the perspective of the saints and doctors of the Church, and, what is not less important, from the perspective of ordinary everyday believers, 'the holy, common people of God'. The entering into liturgical worship, the prayer of the Church as it has received expression over many centuries of unbroken development, is for millions of Christian people today, intellectual and simple alike, a sufficient refutation of the assertion that in our modern climate of opinion it is impossible to enter into the thoughts and experiences of past generations. Liturgical worship is just such an entering into the deep understanding of the past which Becker's teaching about history declares to be impossible. It involves an escape from our own rarified atmosphere, from the transient and constricting thought-forms of our own day, which Becker held to be the only climate available, into a purer and more universal air in which the essentially human part of us may breathe freely and deeply.

Historical Theology and the Ecumenical Outlook

If historical theology acquired in certain quarters a bad name, that was because its character of a living engagement with the faith and thought of the past had been obscured by the way in which it was taught. Other branches of history have suffered in precisely the same way: history will always seem dull if those who teach it are not alive to the basic human dilemmas which confront the present and the future with the existential challenge of the past. The right remedy for this situation is not to abandon the study of history but to see that it is taught by those who understand something of their own involvement in history. Another objection to historical theology is based upon its apparent acceptance of the relativist outlook; it assumes as the presupposition of its study that all historical thinking (the Chalcedonian Definition, for instance) is of only limited validity and will require restatement when the thought-forms of an age become obsolete. It will not allow us to abstract a frame from the moving film of history (AD 451, for example) and say that this is the once-for-all moment of truth, and that henceforward all further development of thought must be judged in the light of it. The creeds and authoritative definitions of the Church thus cease to be termini and become the channel-buoys of past faith on the flowing tide of history. If this be an objection, its truth must be conceded. The adoption of the historical attitude means that there are no absolutes in history, that no interpretations of history are final. But our modern historical-mindedness does not mean that the ancient signposts, such as the Chalcedonian Definition, have become irrelevant and valueless; on the contrary, they gain a new and more vital significance. They become, when historically understood, the means of the understanding of our own situation, because all the great nodal points of history bear upon the present predicament of man and never lose their relevance to each successive crisis of faith and unbelief, of self-understanding and despair, at the moments of their occurrence which are called 'now'. The ancient formularies of the faith will never be irrelevant if they are *historically* understood; they will never lose their inherent authority, even though their existential meaning will always have to be rediscovered in the response of each new age to the challenge of the past.

Of course, historical theology involves relativism, and this is in no way to be regretted. Relativism in theology is one of the most valuable gifts of the new historical-mindedness to the Church in the twentieth century. Properly understood it could mean that the religious crisis of the eighteenth century, which has extended down to our own times, may at last be resolved. That crisis arose through the discovery that a sacred and infallible history had not after all been disclosed by supernatural revelation; it persisted so long as theologians continued to look beyond history—to religious experience, to transcendental philosophy, to existentialist philosophy, to a supra-historical *Heilsgeschichte*—for a disclosure which had indeed been made in the stuff of ordinary, everyday history. The problem which was raised for theology by the questions of the eighteenth century will be solved for our generation of Christian believers when we understand that the Word became 'flesh', that is, in a contemporary thought-form, history, the history which historians, both believers and unbelievers, handle every day. And this involves on its theoretical side no other assumption than one which is a commonplace of the thinking of historians in the second half of the twentieth century, namely, that the interpretation of history (or, quite simply, history) necessitates the personal involvement of the historian in an act of decision, a judgment of faith. When the twin bogeys of scientific objective history and of 'a nearly absolute relativism' have been laid, the way is open for the Christian understanding of the disclosure of God's purpose in history, a disclosure which in every generation remains to be rediscovered through the opening of the eyes of faith.

Another valuable consequence of the development of the historical attitude in the nineteenth century has been the growth of a new spirit of ecumenical understanding in the twentieth century. The triumph of the historical revolution in the sphere of Christian theology was signalized in this University by the establishment in 1870 of an honour school of Historical Theology and at Cambridge by the decision of the Senate in 1871 to set up the

Theological Tripos. Both within and beyond the ancient universities it became possible for Anglican and Dissenter to study and
teach the Bible and Church History on a common and agreed
basis. For half a century or so this development was doubtless
aided by the prevalence of the Actonian conception of history as a
disinterested search for objective 'facts', which made it seem
possible to ignore 'interpretations' and 'the clash of opinion'. The
delusion was a useful one at first, but where it persisted in the
years between the two World Wars it became a handicap; theologians, often isolated from other currents of thought, were
inhibited by it from a real engagement with the new thinking,
especially the new history, of their times. Moreover, it made
theological study seem dull and irrelevant, a collecting of 'facts'
for their own sake and an avoidance of vital issues which might
give rise to 'the clash of opinion'. By the 1930s such a conception
of theological study, where it survived, had come to seem remote
from the world of mounting ideological tension and of rival
demands for total commitment.

Nevertheless, the change of outlook was bound to come;
newer views of history as an engagement between the present and
the past inevitably began to demonstrate the implications of
historical relativism for the understanding Christian truth. Today
we can look back over this development and see it in perspective.
Theological absolutism—dogmatism in the pejorative sense—had
for centuries been the enemy of truth and of Christian unity. Its
rejection was from the beginning implicit in the rise of modern
historical-mindedness. The very standpoint and method of
historical theology, properly understood, implies that in the light
of history no one interpretation, no one dogmatic system, can
alone be right while all others are wrong. It implies that there is
more of truth to be learnt from those who do not share our perspective than from those who do, and that the limitations of our
own viewpoint may be corrected by our seeking to put ourselves,
like good historians, into the tradition in which others stand, so
that we also may see the truth which they have seen. We now
understand that inter-confessional theological study and teaching
is more than a search for a number of objective 'facts' upon which
all can agree; it is veritably (in George Herbert's expressive
phrase) 'a traffic in knowledge', a mutual enterprise of historical
reappraisal. This is what historical theology is coming to mean

today. The growth of what nowadays we call the ecumenical spirit in the Churches is, in part at least, one of the long-term results of the revolution in historical thinking in the nineteenth century; the true appreciation of tradition (past historical appraisals), and especially of traditions other than our own, is a by-product of historical-mindedness, involving the recognition that there are many perspectives from which the one truth may be seen and that no historical assessments are absolute. The relativism implicit in our new post-Enlightenment historical dimension is something for which we should give thanks; it is a gift of the Holy Spirit of God, who makes men to be of one mind in a house, but, like every divine gift, it will profit us only if it is used aright.

The very act of entering into ecumenical discussion implies that, though we are eager to enlarge our view by trying to widen our angle of vision, we are convinced already that an important aspect of the truth is to be seen from our own standpoint. As the judicious Hooker once remarked, the law of common indulgence allows us to think our own ways at least half a thought the better because they are our own.[1] We would not study the history of ideas at all, nor would we engage in ecumenical discussion, if we did not at bottom believe in a truth which we have seen. Truth is that which demands commitment, for otherwise it ceases to commend itself as true; but commitment to such truth as we see need not deprive us of the humility which acknowledges that there are aspects of truth about which we can learn from others. This is essentially an *historical* attitude.

Christian Dogmatics as Historical Theology

There can be no Christian theology, or thinking about God's relevation in history, which is not itself identified with an historical moment of encounter between the present and the past. Dogmatic systems are as historically conditioned as are philosophical systems, or, for that matter, social and political and economic systems. There can never be a final dogmatics or once-for-all definition of Christian truth. The work of the dogmatic theologian will always be the reassessment of the historical faith in the light of the new situation of his own day. Before the rise of the historical attitude the task of dogmatics was thought to be the formulation of final definitions of revealed truth; today dogmatics is

[1] *Ecclesiastical Polity*, IV, xiv, 1 (ed. Keble, 1845, I, 480).

seen to be the study, both critical and constructive, of the disclosures vouchsafed in the biblical history to those who have found in them a revelation of meaning in their own contemporary history. Dogmatics is the culminating discipline of historical theology. Therefore dogmatics is *not* the philosophy of history, not even the Christian philosophy of history (though it will always involve the *critical* philosophy of history); it is not the interpretation of religious experience, the interrogation of the religious consciousness with a view to assessing its validity or truth; it is not the existentialist analysis of an eschatological apprehension; it is not a special scientific method for comprehending a suprahistorical *Heilsgeschichte*; it is not the systematization of propositional scriptural truths. Dogmatics is the attempt to understand the theology of the Old Testament together with the theology of the New Testament, and this is historical theology because (as we have seen) the theology of the Old and New Testaments can be understood only in the light of our experience of the present, that is, of our *historical* experience (not some peculiarly 'religious' experience), in which what the past has disclosed becomes the challenge to faith and action in the living present.

The object of dogmatics is to make the meaning of the biblical disclosure situations intelligible and challenging in each newly succeeding age. In this sense all dogmatic theology will be relevant to the age in which it is articulated; it will be both conditioning and conditioned. But this does not mean that a dogmatic system is true only for its own day and then ceases to have any value. Such a notion is quite unhistorical. Dogmatic systems change their form and their points of emphasis, but they do not die; they continue to reverberate down succeeding ages, powerfully affecting subsequent development. They become forces in history, past ideas which live and are active in the present; the Christian community may retain them in a largely subconscious way, as a man retains, perhaps unconsciously, the influences which affected him in his formative years and which have helped to make him what he is. The Chalcedonian theology, the mediaeval world view, Thomism, Calvinism, and many other such constellations of past thought, are still active and powerful in the great traditions of Christian faith and practice. That is why dogmatics must always be a reassessment of past historical interpretations; it is why theology cannot be separated from the history of theology, just as philosophy cannot be separated from the history of philosophy. It is only rationalism, with its reforming zeal to abolish the past and to start again *ab initio*, which supposes that the past can be treated as though it had never been. The attitude of the revolutionary is necessarily anti-historical, as Lord Acton noted.[1] This is as true of the philosophical revolutionary as of the political: those who in the nineteen-thirties were hailing 'the revolution in philosophy'[2] were ready to turn their back upon all the history of philosophy before Wittgenstein. That history is studded with revolutionary 'prolegomena to every future metaphysic', but each revolution in its turn takes its place in the lengthening perspective of history and, as it itself becomes an incident in the history of philosophy, is seen to have been just one more palace-revolution. The history of a hundred Christian sects exhibits a familiar parallel pattern; having started with the repudiation of tradition, the sect gradually becomes a church with a strong traditional and formal pattern of its own. The rejection of history is no more possible than the rejection by the individual of his own pre-natal or childhood experiences. Revolutionary rationalism has performed many valuable services in the development of civilization but this does not justify rationalism as a philosophy. In many periods of history it is necessary that dead tradition, an inherited formalism, should be swept away in order that a truly historical encounter with the living past should become possible

---

[1] Cf. *The Internationale:*

> 'No more tradition's chains shall bind us,
> Arise, you slaves, no more in thrall!
> The earth shall rise on new foundations,
> We have been naught, we shall be all.'

[2] Cf. *The Revolution in Philosophy* by Gilbert Ryle and others. Perhaps the clearest sympathetic account of 'the revolution' is to be found in G. J. Warnock, *English Philosophy since 1900* (Home University Library), London, 1958. It is interesting that the author commends 'the revolution' by recapitulating its history, although in true rationalist vein he tells us that 'the history of philosophy, though certainly it is not just history, is not just philosophy either, and hence is for the most part only indirectly or incidentally relevant to the course of philosophy itself' (vii). The problem here implicit is underlined when he tells us at the end of the book that we shall have to await 'the verdict of history' before we can assess the claim of the linguistic philosophers that no *Weltanschauung* is implicit in their work (170f.). In our view there is an important sense in which philosophy *is* the history of philosophy: philosophers, whether consciously or unconsciously, are engaged in the continual reassessment of past thought.

again. The elucidation of the significance of this encounter in the sphere of Christian belief is the substance and task of dogmatic theology.

Dogmatics, like liturgy, arises out of a living involvement with past faith and its expression; it is the attempt to understand present faith in the light of the past and *vice versa*. A dogmatic which merely reaffirms past orthodoxy without engaging the living faith of past ages in the concerns of the present is dead and useless. In this respect dogmatics and liturgy are closely parallel and are involved in each other; both involve the holding together of the living past and the living present in a single moment which transcends time, in the distinctively human way in which men can transcend time. The experience of faith and of worship as *historical* negates the contention that man is entirely conditioned by his own climate of opinion or that his thought is valid only for the age in which he lives. In the act of faith, which is by its very nature historical faith, man transcends his own 'now', which would remain barren and meaningless, if it were not fertilized by the faith of the past. In the act of worship, especially in its liturgical character, the entering into the worship of the Church of all the ages, man likewise transcends his own 'now', which is filled with a richness inconceivable to those who live in an unhistorical present. Faith and worship are not two separate and distinct activities: the historic liturgies contain the historic creeds, the recital of the saving events of history; Christian worship is the response of man in thanksgiving (*eucharistia*) to the disclosure of God's mercy in the history of the world, which is known to Christian faith. Protestant theology (Barth's, for example) is immensely impoverished by its habit of associating dogmatics almost solely with 'the Word of preaching' to the exclusion of liturgical worship.[1] The disclosure of God's past mercies is made a present disclosure not only in preaching but also in the sacraments, in which the worshipper relives the past so that it becomes his own past, which is present to him now. Liturgical worship implies entering into the historical prayer of the Church, which yet paradoxically assures the worshipper of his transcendence over

[1] Cf. Karl Barth, *Church Dogmatics*, Vol. I, Part I, 91: 'The normal and central fact with which dogmatics has to do is, very simply, the Church's Sunday sermon. . . .' But, equally simply, the sermon is not the only Sunday activity of the Church.

the climate of opinion, over time and over death, which for men without faith signifies the victory of time over humanity.[1]

The New Age of Universal History

Within the lifetime of this present generation the expression 'universal history' has acquired a new meaning. Formerly it signified the attempt to write synoptically the history of all the peoples of the world. Orosius was the first to undertake this task; at the instigation of St Augustine he endeavoured to provide the 'new history' required by the nascent Christian civilization then arising amidst the catastrophe of the destruction of the Roman Empire. The framework of the biblical history, into which might be inserted a digest of the classical historians of Greece and Rome, continued to be the pattern of universal history right down to Bossuet's *Discours* (1681) or the celebrated English *Universal History* (1737). Voltaire, as we noted above, attempted in his *Essai sur les moeurs* (1752) to provide the secular 'new history' which his cosmopolitan age required and to widen the scope of history by taking in the Arabs, Persians, Indians and Chinese.[2] The *Essai* has been deemed the first truly universal history.[3] But in the nineteenth century the cosmopolitan outlook gave way to the rising consciousness of nationality, and history in the Rankean era became predominantly the several histories of the value-bearing national states. Moreover, in the nineteenth century, with its vast

[1] An American Anglican, speaking of the ancient words of many of the collects and prayers of the Book of Common Prayer, says: 'Their origin is shrouded in the mists of tradition. They long antedate the "errors" of Rome. . . . Like the dialogue of the Eucharist itself, they have sung themselves into the memories of generation upon generation of worshippers. A mere visitor to a liturgical Church can with difficulty comprehend what they can mean to those whose inmost possession they have become. Such a visitor may be shocked at the manner in which the minister "patters" the liturgy—and this is a grave fault, one may grant, on the minister's part. Yet the visitor might be surprised how little this matters to the liturgically minded parishioners. This is *their* prayer, not the minister's. It is *Common Prayer* . . . The Church as Spirit-moved Body prays. . . . The true nature of liturgical action—a baptism or a eucharist—is, precisely, that of a communal drama, realistic, historical' (Theodore O. Wedel, *The Coming Great Church: Essays on Church Unity*, New York, 1945, 110f.).

[2] Thus remarkably anticipating both the spirit and the recommendations of the Hayter Report (*Report of the Sub-Committee on Oriental, Slavonic, East European and African Studies*, under the chairmanship of Sir William Hayter, to the University Grants Committee; London, H.M.S.O., 1961).

[3] Eduard Fueter, *Geschichte der neueren Historiographie*, 1925, 358.

new accumulations of historical materials, the opening of the archives, the recovery of forgotten languages, and so on, historians were compelled to become specialists; and so we all became accustomed to the idea of history by sections: histories of France, histories of Peru, histories of the Popes, and so on. Universal history was neither a possible nor a desirable enterprise; the pretence that a single mind could compass all history could mislead only the unscholarly. A crusading rationalist like Mr H. G. Wells[1] might write brilliant propaganda-history in the spirit and style of the Enlightenment; Oswald Spengler[2] might dress his pessimistic cyclical philosophy in the garb of history, universalizing the German mood in the hour of defeat; Toynbee might find consolation through an 'empirical' study of the history of all former civilizations in the era of the dissolution of the British Empire; but all such undertakings were essays in the philosophy of history rather than historiography, and academic historians were, for the most part, not impressed. They have gone on cultivating their own gardens, even though they were well aware that a whole world of history lay beyond their garden walls. And from time to time some adventurous nonconformist historian has made a survey of the world beyond the walls.[3]

The debate, for or against the utility of world-history, might have gone on for ever, had not the course of history itself made a decisive intervention. Almost within the lifetime of this generation the history of the world has unified itself in a wholly unprecedented way. The former discussions are today becoming obsolescent. Whereas throughout the past history proceeded to a large extent section by section, because different parts of the globe had relatively separate histories, today the world is rapidly coming to have a unified history. The astonishing development of science and technology in our own times is the agent responsible for the unification of history. When we say 'universal history' from

---

[1] Cf. his *Outline of History* (1920), a remarkable *tour de force*, which exercised a powerful influence over the younger generations between the wars.

[2] *Der Untergang des Abendlandes*, I, 1918; II, 1922; Eng. trans. by C. F. Atkinson, *The Decline of the West*, London, 1926–9.

[3] The most recent of these, and a very stimulating and instructive one, is John Bowle, *A New Outline of World History from the Origins to the Eighteenth Century*, London, 1962. A second volume is promised to bring the story down to today. Much of this latter period is covered by E. Fueter himself in his *Weltgeschichte der letzten Hundert Jahre, 1815–1920*, 1921; Eng. trans. by S. B. Fay, *World History, 1815–1920*, 1923.

henceforward, the expression will have a meaning that it could not have had in any previous generation, because from now onwards the whole world will share a common history. Already a decision taken in New York or Moscow is immediately effective in any part of the world; every nation is at once implicated in what happens in Cuba or the Congo; the philosophical ideas of Gilbert Ryle or A. J. Ayer are discussed in Malaya or Melbourne a month or two after they have been promulgated in Oxford; a statement made in any city of the world may be almost instantly received in any place on the earth's surface; a man in a capsule has this week[1] orbited around the earth three times in less than five hours. As Dr E. H. Carr recently reminded us, the spread of education and technology is bringing millions of people in Asia and Africa into full participation in history for the first time; to which we may add that their *historical* existence (in Carr's sense[2]) will be from the start a participation in world-history. From the twentieth century onwards the histories of different countries will be no more separable from the history of the one world than the history of Oxfordshire or Lancashire is now separable from the history of England. Probably the greatest historical change which has ever overtaken mankind is now occurring all around us; we are entering, for better or for worse, a new age of universal history.

Obviously the new age will set before historians new tasks and new conceptions of their calling; a 'new history' of the world from its beginnings will be required in the light of the new situation. Already certain historians—controversial figures in the academic groves of Clio—are calling for a new history which shall be de-Europeanized (they doubtless also mean de-Americanized, de-Australianized, and so on) and which shall be genuinely universal in outlook. Thus, Professor Barraclough tells us that the new world-history 'means thinking ourselves out of the *milieu* in which we have been reared, breaking through into a new dimension, adopting a global instead of a local (or even a parochial) perspective. For us in Europe, in particular, it means advancing from a view of the past in which Europe is the centre to universal, world-wide standards of judgment.'[3] The Hayter Report seems to

---

[1] May 24, 1962.   [2] Cf. *supra*, 51f.

[3] G. Barraclough, 'Universal History' in *Approaches to History*, ed. H. P. R. Finberg, 100.

adopt a similar attitude. While one may sympathize with the aim, it is still possible to doubt whether the real difficulties have been fully considered—not merely the old difficulty about the possibility of a synoptic grasp of such a vast and complex entity as world-history. The first difficulty is created by the doubt whether 'the historian' is capable of attaining such an impartial, indeed godlike, objectivity as would be required for the pursuit of world-history. Long ago Pierre Bayle insisted that the historian should be not a Frenchman, not a German, and so on, but like Melchizedek, without father and mother; but has anyone, least of all the *philosophes*, succeeded in achieving the ideal? Of course, the rationalist is confident that he can wipe out his past and look upon history 'in that secular spirit from which alone an impartial view can come', but then, he has identified his rationalism with 'the global perspective'. The Hayter Report omits all reference to religion, which is a curious way of beginning the study of (for example) Indian civilization; it starts, that is to say, from a peculiarly European perspective, and one which is a comparatively recent European development at that.

The second difficulty is closely related and brings us into an area where a great deal of fundamental thinking remains to be done. Professor Barraclough says that we must think ourselves out of the *milieu* in which we have been reared, but it is hard to believe that he really means this. Our *milieu* is precisely that of the scientific and historical-mindedness of the European civilization which arose on Christian foundations. Asia and Africa are, in fact, being Europeanized with increasing rapidity; their millions are beginning to participate in 'history'. Such participation involves not only the acceptance of modern science and technology, but also the acquisition of modern historical-mindedness, though the need for this latter quality is less obviously apparent. In the past the Asian civilizations had little sense of history, as Professor Barraclough himself reminds us.[1] It may be that in the

[1] 'The fact remains, however, that this gradual and stumbling approach to world-history . . . has been in all essential ways an achievement of the European peoples, and so far as it has found its way into the Orient, it has been the result of Western influences and largely the result of a Western-educated intelligentsia. Interest in history, belief in the value of history, even the tendency to view events in historical context and historical perspective, which is so natural to us that we are rarely conscious of the extent to which we do it, is a western attitude which has no exact counterpart in China or India. China, indeed, has preserved excellent annals and chronological lists,

nations newly awakened to historical awareness, as in Europe in the nineteenth century, the strong sense of national identity will encourage the view that the nation's historic destiny is the only kind of history that is significant, since it leads to historical activity; already the signs of 'colonialist' exploitation have appeared where the new nations have been strong enough to impose their will on their neighbours. There are, after all, different kinds of Europeanization. Voltairean cosmopolitan rationalism may prove to be as shortsighted in the twentieth century as it was in the eighteenth. It is dangerous to imagine that religious attitudes can be ignored, especially in revolutionary times, and to assume that they will be corroded by what Mr Lippmann long ago called 'the acids of modernity'.[1] The renascent religions of the East and of Africa gain fresh vitality from the nationalist sentiments of new or resurgent peoples, conscious of their entry into history in a new way, eager to abolish the past and finding in their revolutionary zeal that 'bliss was it in that dawn to be alive, and to be young was very heaven'.[2] The myths which may take their place, or, more probably, be intertwined with them, may be borrowed from European sources ('the classless society') or may be native counterparts of familiar European models ('the African personality': 'Aryan man'); what is predictable is that the 'new history' of the emerging nation-states will be designed to show how the golden future portrayed by the myth is already a present reality that has grown out of the nation's past. All this is implied by the statement that the Asian and African millions are 'emerging into history', for the 'history' into which they are emerging is not the academic history of the specialists but the history of a world of ambitions and illusions, of national rivalries and power politics. It is not, of course, European history into which the new peoples are entering, but it is history of the European type. The crisis of Europe in the eighteenth century is now being extended to the whole world; the 'religionless' secular humanism of the Western type is being exported to all the world.

---

which provide at least the bare bones of history; but India before the European invasions has little that, by modern standards, can be called history at all, and both countries have shown very little concern for the preservation of historical records' (ibid., 96).

[1] Walter Lippmann, *A Preface to Morals*, London, 1929.
[2] Wordsworth, *Prelude*, xi, 108.

Governments in every country, however underdeveloped, understand that education for the masses is the condition of a successful
début in 'history', and it is our Western secular education that
they want.[1]

In the light of such considerations as these it is fitting that the
World Council of Churches at its Third Assembly in New Delhi in
1961 should have authorized as its major theme of study during
the coming years before the Fourth Assembly 'the Finality of
Christ in the Age of Universal History'.[2] The Christian Churches
are vitally involved in all the issues raised by the emergence of the
new world-historical consciousness, and particularly in their
educational aspects. After all, it was the missionary labours of the
Churches which began the whole process by first carrying Western
conceptions of education to Asia and Africa, though the fact is
often passed over in an embarrassed silence by 'secular' historians.
Thoughtful Christians today are well aware that it is in the sphere
of the 'secular' that God's will is to be done, and they have no
quarrel with 'secular' education as such. What they are concerned to controvert are the secular myths of history, the bread
which, if people eat, they will hunger again. The unrelenting
struggle against mythology, begun long centuries ago by Israel in
Canaan, will, so far as can be seen, continue yet for centuries to
come. But there is no cause for anxiety or defeatism; the tokens of
victory are already visible to the eyes of faith. There is a universality and finality about the Christian faith which makes it relevant
to the whole human race in every age and place, and which utterly
distinguishes it from all the useful myths. This faith is grounded
upon adequate evidence, historical and contemporary. The six

---

[1] Cf. Mr J. S. Fulton, Vice-Chancellor of the University of Sussex, writing
in *The Times* (London) of August 16, 1961: 'Throughout the world—and
especially in the underdeveloped countries—education is a new universal
religion. Men of every colour, race and creed see in it the key that will open
the doors to self-realization for the individual, to the true independence of
nation or group, to the possibility of co-existence in peace for a divided
human race; and, above all, to influence over the intellectual leaders of the
generations to come. Nothing like this has happened since the foundation
in the Middle Ages of the universities of Western Europe. Today the scale
is far larger, the faith in education perhaps less disinterested; but the power
of the explosive force at work in every continent is as unquestionable as its
effects are beyond prediction.'

[2] See the report of the Committee on the Division of Studies, *The New
Delhi Report: the Third Assembly of the World Council of Churches, 1961*, London,
1962, 164–7, where the methods of the proposed study are outlined.

hundred or so delegates of the Churches who met together at New Delhi in 1961 constituted a more widely representative gathering of the human race than has ever before in the history of the world been brought together under any auspices whatsoever. The kaleidoscopic variety of humanity was represented there. The delegates were divided on most of the social and political questions of our day, but they spoke together frankly and gladly about these matters, because they were united upon one thing: Jesus and the resurrection. What indeed had brought together this representative gathering of all humanity was the very proclamation which had called into being the Church of apostolic days: the resurrection of Jesus Christ from the dead—that and nothing else. There is a universality and an historical reality about Christ and his Church which has no parallel in the history of the world. Already he is confessed by men from the East and from the West, from the North and from the South, the Light of the world and the desire of all nations. And this acknowledged Lord is none other than the historical Jesus, of whom our Gospels tell, born, crucified, risen and ascended, one who is no myth, but part of the history of the world.

An immense vista of tasks to be attempted opens before us as we contemplate the new age of universal history into which we have entered. The crisis of eighteenth-century Europe is now a world crisis. How explosive will be the reaction of the new nations to the Europeanizing process, the new imperialism of eighteenth-century secular idealism to which they are being subjected? Is their apparent ready acceptance of 'the faith in education' merely the necessary appropriation of the tools by which they in their turn can assume the grandeur of empire and the possibility of world domination? Has secularized education the resources within itself to assuage the ferocity of the secular myths of the future age? Can the ecumenical Christian community in every land bring to bear on governments and on popular opinion the realization that rulers are ministers of God, whose duty is to serve and not to overbear, to maintain law and not to manipulate it for their own convenience, to safeguard the freedom of the individual person and the rights of the minority? A hundred such questions concerning the new age of universal history spring to mind, which we cannot even begin to consider here. And so these Lectures must conclude at a point which is only a beginning, with questions which the study of history has raised but has not answered. It is in the nature of history itself to raise questions rather than to supply answers, for history is a never-ending process of reappraisal. History does not deal in conclusions which can be represented as scientifically verifiable results, and each historian who handles the weightier issues must respect the warning, 'According to your faith be it unto you.'

THE DEISTIC CONTROVERSY

IT is obvious that in Locke's thought there were elements which provided more than a foothold for the great deistic attack upon the traditional idea of revelation which was mounted during the first half of the eighteenth century. The deists believed in God as the Intelligent Author of Nature and perhaps even as the Moral Governor of the World, but not as the God who had revealed his love toward mankind. Newton, 'the childlike sage' and 'the sagacious reader of the works of God',[1] told them only of a Great Mechanick in whose clockwork universe mighty planets and falling apples must obey laws which never could be broken and which for their guidance he had made. Newton himself spent more hours of his life searching for revelation in the Scriptures than in searching the heavens with his telescope, but those who received 'the Newtonian philosophy' as an all-sufficient 'natural revelation' felt no need of any supernatural addition to it. Newton's Muse might inspire the intellectual affirmations of Joseph Addison's 'The spacious firmament on high',[2] but not the personal and Christ-centred devotion of his contemporary, Isaac Watts. In an age when deism was intellectually fashionable, and when the orthodox belief of a Locke, a Sherlock or a Butler was itself half-deist, sceptics and downright atheists could shelter behind a façade of deistic respectability. Thus, in 1696, a year after the publication of Locke's *Reasonableness*, there appeared John Toland's *Christianity not Mysterious*, the first step on his journey from deism to pantheism.[3] Locke's disciple and intimate friend, Anthony Collins, passed through deism to the implicit denial of Christianity altogether; ever since his day 'free-thinking' has been generally employed as a synonym for 'atheist'.[4] From Locke's position it was easy to go a step further: if revelation were only an alternative method of establishing

---

[1] William Cowper, *The Task*, Book III, 11, 252f.
[2] *Ode* in *The Spectator*, No. 465, August 23, 1712.
[3] Cf. W. R. Sorley, *History of English Philosophy*, 146–9.
[4] Collins's *Discourse of Free-thinking* appeared in 1713. Amongst his later controversial writings his *Discourses of the Grounds and Reasons of the Christian Religion* (1724) called forth thirty-five replies in two years (Sorley, op. cit., 150).

truths which could be clearly perceived by reason, might not rational men dispense with revelation altogether? Such a position was maintained by the more respectable deists, like Matthew Tindal, a clergyman who retained his fellowship at All Souls College until his death at nearly eighty years of age in 1733. The title of his book, which came to be known as 'the Deist's Bible', was, significantly, *Christianity as Old as the Creation* (1730): primaeval men were not, for the eighteenth-century mind, primitive savages, but noble deists by the light of nature, untrammelled by the priestly corruptions of Catholicism or by Protestant prejudices concerning the Fall of Man and his need of redemption. The subtitle was cleverly culled by Tindal from the writings of the conservative Thomas Sherlock, later Bishop of London: *The Gospel a Republication of the Religion of Nature*; and he contrived to suggest (with some plausibility) that all reasonable English divines thought as he did. For the deists, revelation was either superfluous (as for moderates like Tindal) or perverse (as for extremists like Collins, Toland and poor Thomas Woolston). The Bible compared unfavourably in content, clarity and style with the 'natural revelation' through the light of reason which was found in the *Principia Mathematica* of Sir Isaac Newton.

The orthodox reply to the attack upon revelation was ineffective for the reason that the conservative churchmen understood no better than did the deists the character of the biblical revelation as historical. Their arguments were inept. From the time of Charles Leslie's *Short and Easy Way with the Deists* (1701) the banality of the debate continues to reflect the theological incomprehension of an age which had little understanding of history. Thomas Sherlock (1678–1761), then Bishop of Bangor, replied anonymously to Woolston's argument in his *Discourses* (1727–30) that Christ's resurrection was a shocking fraud unscrupulously perpetrated by the apostles, who had stolen his body. Sherlock's *Tryal of the Witnesses of the Resurrection of Jesus* (1729), though it doubtless has the better of the argument, is markedly irreligious in tone and 'contains no hint of the crucial importance of the event at stake or of the splendour of Christ's person; and the book ends with a touch of comedy in bad taste'.[1]

---

[1] J. S. Lawton, *Miracles and Revelation*, London, 1960, 49. This work contains a useful and compendious account of the controversial literature of this whole period and beyond it.

Daniel Waterland (1683–1740), an influential and much-respected theologian of considerable learning, replied to Tindal's 'Deist's Bible' in his *Scripture Vindicated*; but his arguments in favour of the literalist interpretation of the Old Testament, as Sir Leslie Stephen remarked, are grotesque.[1] Joseph Butler (1692–1752), afterwards Bishop of Durham, buried himself (as Queen Caroline noticed) in his remote rectory at Stanhope in Weardale while he wrote his magisterial reply to Tindal, whom he never actually mentions by name; in 1736 there appeared his famous *Analogy of Religion, Natural and Revealed, to the Constitution and Course of Nature*, the chief apologetic work of the century. Butler is himself half a deist; as a good eighteenth-century thinker, he agrees that 'natural religion is the foundation and principal part of Christianity'.[2] He knows as little as his contemporaries about the significance of an *historical* revelation. For him, as for them, revelation consists in propositions written in a divinely inspired Book. The Book, he admits, is full of ambiguities, difficulties and obscurities, but then, so also is the Book of Nature. There is thus a real analogy between the two Books. The illegibility of the handwriting in both Books, it would appear, creates a presumption in favour of a common authorship. Here below, probability is the guide of life; and if there is even only a 51:49 chance in favour of the biblical revelation, the rational man has no alternative but to order his belief and conduct according to it. Though Butler's reputation as an apologist lasted for more than a hundred years, his enduring place among the immortals was won by his work as a moral philosopher.[3] He was, after all, doing the work of an apologist in a climate of opinion very different from that of our own historically-minded age; his task was to reply as best he could to the philosophical deism of Tindal and his like. We must charitably allow that even the egregious William Warburton (1698–1779), afterwards Bishop of Gloucester, was doing the best that could be done in an age which had no glimmering of that

---

[1] Cf. L. Stephen, *History of English Thought in the 18th Century*, 3rd ed., New York, 1949, I, 258–61.

[2] *The Analogy of Religion*, Butler's Works, Oxford, Clarendon Press, 1874, I, 154.

[3] Butler's chief ethical writings are contained in his *Fifteen Sermons Preached at the Chapel of the Rolls Court* (1726) and in the 'Dissertation on the Nature of Virtue' appended to the *Analogy*. For an estimate of the permanent significance of his contribution to moral philosophy, see C. D. Broad, *Five Types of Ethical Theory*, 53–83.

historical sense which was to dawn even before the eighteenth century had run its course. In his blustering anti-deistic polemic, *The Divine Legation of Moses* (1737–41), he falls back upon the surprising thesis that the Old Testament must be divinely inspired because it contains no reference to a future life. Every rational being knows that belief in the hereafter, with its rewards and punishments, is essential to morality. Other nations could practise the virtues of civil government because by the light of nature they knew all about the divine sanctions of the after-life. But the Jews, because they possessed the divine legation (law-giving) of Moses, could dispense with the intimations of natural religion and yet remain moral. Today such arguments seem to us jejune beyond belief, and we wonder how learned divines could ever have seriously put them forward. Historical problems to which a properly instructed Sunday-school child could today suggest the answers lay entirely beyond the grasp of the wisest theologians of the Age of Reason.[1]

[1] There is, of course, a parallel in the earlier development of natural science, when Galileo and his fellows were struggling to solve problems which seem to us elementary. Cf. H. Butterfield, *Origins of Modern Science*, 2: 'Things which we find it easy to instil into boys at school, because we see that they start off on the right foot—things which strike us as the ordinary natural way of looking at the universe, the obvious way of regarding falling bodies, for example—defeated the greatest intellects for centuries, defeated Leonardo da Vinci and at the marginal point even Galileo, when their minds were wrestling on the very frontiers of human thought with these very problems.'

APPENDED NOTE II
CLASSICAL HISTORY, ANCIENT AND MODERN

THE revival of classical learning during the fifteenth and sixteenth centuries coincided with the rise of a new civic and national consciousness in Europe, especially in Italy. The new times demanded a new history, and the humanist scholars found conveniently to hand the ancient classical histories upon which to model their own. Their importance in the development of historiography lies in the stimulus which they gave to interest in 'profane' history, dormant for so many centuries, and in their setting before themselves the standards of the classical writers of history. So awed were they by the wisdom of the ancients that it never occurred to them to criticize the classical historians or to imagine that it might be possible to advance beyond them.[1] It was not until after the new science of Galileo and his fellows had overthrown the scientific cosmology of the ancient world that literary men dared to imagine that modern achievements in literature, drama and history might equal or even surpass the masterpieces of the ancients.[2] A long time was to elapse before men became accustomed to the idea that the modern age was not a period of decline and fall from the excellence of the classical intellect, and it was the gradual recognition of the superiority of modern science which eventually effected the change of view. In

[1] Professor Butterfield (*Man on his Past*, 2n.) quotes A. Momigliano: 'To the best of my knowledge, the idea that one could write a history of Rome which should replace Livy and Tacitus was not yet born in the early seventeenth century' ('Ancient History and the Antiquarian' in *Contributo alla Storia degli Studi Classici*, Rome, 1955, 75). Until the end of the eighteenth century history in the English universities primarily meant commenting upon the works of the ancient historians.

[2] This bold idea was debated at the end of the seventeenth century; cf. Sir William Temple's 'Four Essays upon Ancient and Modern Learning' in his posthumous *Miscellanea* (1705) and the early work of Dean Swift (who had once been Temple's secretary), *The Battle of the Books* (1704), a satire in which the ancient books fought against the modern ones in St James's Library. More important, however, is Fontenelle's *Digression sur les anciens et les modernes* (1688), which foreshadows the idea of progress; his argument that all past achievements will be left behind through the sheer accumulation of scientific knowledge anticipates the theories of Buckle in the nineteenth century.

our own century the process of overvaluing the modern at the expense of our European classical heritage has been accelerated alarmingly; fifty years ago the traditional humanist disciplines were still regarded as the norm of education, at least for the *élite*; today they are struggling for survival.[1] The very word 'humanism' is virtually obsolete in its original sense and is now widely used, prefixed by the word 'scientific', to denote confidence in modern a-theistic man's ability to make himself at home in the universe.[2]

The historiography of the renaissance humanists is not to be thought of as 'modern' in anything like the sense in which we speak of nineteenth-century historiography as 'modern'. It is modern, however, in the sense which *they* gave to the word and which was usual until, in the nineteenth century, the notion of a threefold division of history into ancient, mediaeval and modern began to replace it. Obviously the men of what we call the Renaissance could not have thought of 'modern history' as beginning in 1485 or 1494 or 1500. For them, and for centuries after them, modern history began where ancient history stopped, that is, with the barbarian invasions.[3] They had to look back across the centuries to the age before the fall of Rome in order to find models for their own new history, and these models they used with skill. They read the classical authors with an appreciation which their predecessors had hardly shown since at least the time of Bede; they rekindled the 'humane' conviction that 'there is no learning so proper for the direction of the life of man as Historie'.[4]

[1] Cf. R. R. Bolgar, *The Classical Heritage and its Beneficiaries*, Cambridge, 1954, esp. the Introduction and the concluding chapter.

[2] The word 'humanist' properly meant 'classical', especially 'Latinist' (cf. the professorships of Humanity in the Scottish Universities and elsewhere), before it became more widely applied to the study of the 'Humanities'; in this sense it is entirely legitimate to speak of a humanist renaissance in the fifteenth and sixteenth centuries. Cf. Bolgar, op. cit., chap. VII.

[3] This was the period intended when the Regius chairs of Modern History were established in Oxford and Cambridge by George I in 1724. Professor Butterfield points out that it was the philologists who fixed the use of the term 'mediaeval' by using it to denote the kind of Latin met with after the fall of Rome (ibid., 45 f.). Cf. also Marc Bloch (*The Historian's Craft*, 178–81), who recalls the opening sentence of Voltaire's *Essai sur les moeurs*: 'You wish ultimately to overcome the disgust you feel at Modern history since the decline of the Roman Empire. . . .' (in the ed. of the *Essai* edited by J. Marchand, Editions Sociales (Les Classiques du Peuple), Paris, 1962, 25.)

[4] Sir Henry Savile in the preface to his translation of Tacitus (1591), quoted by Herbert Davis in his illuminating essay entitled 'The Augustan Conception of History' in *Reason and the Imagination*, ed. J. A. Mazzeo, 217.

If their work was imitative rather than pioneering, moralist rather than scientific, practical rather than critical, it at least achieved the important result of restoring the standards which the best classical historians had attained. If the stream did not rise higher than its source, it refreshed what had become the arid wastes of profane history and reinvested it with the sense of its genuinely human interest and dignity. The new historians recovered a neglected portion of the humane inheritance of Europe.

Niccolo Machiavelli (1469–1527) is often said to have in-augurated 'modern' political thinking with his controversial study *The Prince* (1513); he had considerable experience of responsibility for the political affairs of his native Florence, largely because his principal, the Chancellor, was himself a distinguished humanist scholar who devoted much of his time to his studies. He was thus well qualified by humanist standards to undertake the writing of his *History of Florence* (1525), one of the earliest of the modern humanist historical works. He had made a special study of Livy, whom the humanists regarded as their model *par excellence*, and his work resembles that of his master both in its strong sense of narrative and in its uncritical use of sources. His younger con-temporary, Franscesco Guicciardini (1483–1540), the leading historian of the humanist renaissance in Italy, after having en-gaged in public affairs in the papal service, spent the last six years of his life writing his *History of Italy*. It covered the period from the French invasion of Italy in 1494 to the date of its author's retirement from public life in 1534, and is thus a history of his own times. It illustrates how much had been learned from the example of the classical historians; it is shrewd, realistic and conscientiously accurate, and it reflects the ideal of Tacitus that history should be written without recrimination or partisanship.[1]

Davis shows how the humanist attitude to history persisted into the eigh-teenth century; he refers to the influential *De Ratione et Methodo legendi Historias Dissertatio* of Degory Whear (1623), the first Camden Reader in Ancient History at Oxford. The study of history was, in the humanist view, 'of the utmost importance for all those who might be in any way concerned with public affairs'.

[1] Tacitus, *Annals*, i, 1: 'My purpose is to relate a few facts . . . without either bitterness or partiality (*sine ira et studio*), being far removed from any motives (*causas*) for such things.' (In Latin usage 'annals' (*annales*) was the word employed when the events narrated were known to a writer only indirectly, while 'history' (*historiae*) often referred to the events of the writer's own day.)

The humanist renaissance was not, however, confined to Italy, for in those days European scholarship and culture were international in character and books and ideas travelled quickly. Sir Thomas More's *History of King Richard III* appeared in 1513 (and his *Utopia* in 1516), before Machiavelli's and Guicciardini's histories. These histories of particular times and places, imitating classical precedents, began the process of narrowing down the conception of history to something like its nineteenth-century proportions, but the general connotation of history still covered a vast area of 'enquiry', as it had done for Herodotus. Sir Walter Raleigh had adventured across the empty seas into the New World, but his *History of the World* (1614), immensely popular in the seventeenth century, is based on Old Testament chronology and stops with the fall of Macedonia; it is larded with personal reminiscence and crowded with edifying digressions on theology, mythology, politics, military strategy, and so on, as indeed ancient historical writing often was.[1] Even so, at the end of the century Sir Isaac Newton, who with his telescope had adventured into remote worlds across the empty skies, was still labouring to corroborate the ancient biblical-classical chronological scheme by means of his scientific researches. The humanist historians were not 'modern' in our sense of the word, but they made a first move in the direction of our post-eighteenth-century historical view when they took their stand on the achievements of classical historiography.[2]

Classical history was essentially practical. Polybius had laid it down that a necessary qualification for the historian was that he should have engaged in political life.[3] Livy is the outstanding exception, having had no direct practice in the conduct of public affairs, but his intense patriotism and moral concern remove him

---

[1] Cp. the seven books entitled *Origines*, the first historical work in the Latin language, written by M. Porcius Cato, who having turned author in his old age, 'perpetuated the conflicts of his career in Forum and Senate. . . . A peculiar conglomerate—local antiquities and Hellenic erudition, the annals of the Roman wars, and not a little autobiography' (Ronald Syme, *Tacitus*, Oxford, 1958, II, 566).

[2] Cf. Sir E. L. Woodward (*British Historians*, 16f.), speaking of More and Raleigh: 'These men were not "modern"; they were the grandsons and great-grandsons of mediaeval men. Neverless, for better or worse, our own "modern" ideas, and secular outlook, our scientific culture reach back to the years in which Greek and Latin authors were read in a new way, and scholars and artists recovered a lost continuity with the ancient world.'

[3] Polyb., xii, 25e.

entirely from that class of historian which today we might call 'purely academic'. It is highly significant that the work which perhaps most clearly formulates the ideals of classical historiography is Cicero's *De Oratore* (55 BC), which deals with the qualifications of those who aspire to address the Senate, the law-courts or the public in a useful and persuasive manner. The connection between history and rhetoric, the art of persuasion, had long been taken for granted. History, especially the great and edifying history of Greece and Rome, was the proper education for men of affairs, a view which was still unchallenged in Jowett's Balliol; it is no accident that at the Renaissance humanist history was studied and written by men who were active participants in public life. History was inseparable from the lessons of history; it was in itself a curriculum of training, inculcating morals, instilling patriotism, reproving vice and folly, teaching the art of political success. For the humanists as for the classical mind, history was an art, not a science, and it is absurd to condemn classical history (as Mommsen's generation of 'scientific historians' anachronistically did) for not being something of which there was as yet no conception in existence.[1] History before the nineteenth century was not an enquiry which could be 'scientifically' detached from religion, ethics, patriotism and practical action; because it was vitally important to the life of man and of society, it must be presented with all the persuasive arts of rhetoric and literary elegance. Then it might become what Cicero in a famous sentence declared it to be: '*testis temporum, lux veritatis, vita memoriae, magistra vitae*'.[2]

The ancient historians were indeed conscious of their obligation to record the truth, to avoid partisanship and to reject the legendary.[3] But their chief concern was with 'what edifies' rather than with 'what happened'. It is therefore hardly surprising that contemporary scholars should find that one of the principal points of difference between classical historians and post-Rankean historians lies in their different attitudes to their sources. Some ancient writers, such as Polybius and Tacitus,[4] are more careful

---

[1] Cf. A. H. McDonald, 'The Roman Historians' in Maurice Platnauer, *Fifty Years of Classical Scholarship*, Oxford, 1954, 384f.

[2] *De Oratore*, ii, 36.

[3] Cf. Cicero, ibid., ii, 36, 62, etc.

[4] For Tacitus's use of his sources see R. Syme, op. cit., I, 178–216; 378–407.

than others, but on the whole they are content to take from
earlier authors what suits their convenience without undertaking
any critical assessments and with little attempt to verify their
accuracy.[1] Failure to search out and evaluate the original documentary evidence constitutes the main indictment of Livy, the
model historian of the renaissance humanists, as of Roman
historiography generally.[2] The history of the classical authors is
furthermore distorted by their didactic intentions. Poetry, too,
had a didactic function, but because it was not bound by facts as
history was, its effect was more superficial, a temporary affecting
of the emotions.[3] Historians were therefore responsible for
inculcating the profitability of virtue and the unhappy consequences of vice. Tacitus is quite explicit: 'My purpose is not
to relate everything at length, but only such things as were conspicuous for excellence or notorious for infamy. This I regard as
the highest function of history, to let no worthy action be un-
commemorated, and to hold out the reprobation of posterity as a
terror to evil deeds and words.'[4] When such is the conscious aim
of the historian, the mythopoeic function of historiography is
virtually avowed: Polybius and Livy become propagandists of the
myth of Roman Greatness.[5] And this, of course, is just what
makes them interesting to us and explains why we still read them.
If today we want to know the 'facts' about Roman history, we do
not go to Livy but to some recent historian or to the second half-
dozen volumes of the *Cambridge Ancient History*, completed in
1939. In what he was trying to do (not in what *we* think he ought
to have tried to do) Livy succeeds admirably; the historical myth

[1] P. G. Walsh (*Livy, his Historical Aims and Methods*, Cambridge, 1961,
109) quotes the younger Pliny: 'If my subject is an ancient period already
discussed by others, my material will be ready at hand' (Ep. v, 8).

[2] See P. G. Walsh, ibid., 110.

[3] Cf. Aristotle, *Poetics*, 9.2f. See *supra*, 57.

[4] *Annals*, iii, 65.

[5] Cf. P. G. Walsh, op. cit., 109: 'Livy's moral and patriotic preoccupations
lead him to depict a series of leaders as the embodiment of the Stoic virtues
of prudence, justice, courage and moderation, and of the other virtues which
the Roman tradition extolled. In these characterizations Livy has allowed his
pursuit of edifying examples to take preference over a truthful account, not
merely by distortion of emphasis, but even by the suppression of unpalatable
facts. Contrariwise, he has sought out the signal examples of vice in all its
forms in order to demonstrate its destructive effect on the individual and the
community. It is this conception of history, dominated by idealized heroes
and denigrated villains, which is ultimately responsible for the most serious
defect in Livy's work. He falsifies history not by error but by design.'

by which a cultured Stoic lived in the days of Caesar Augustus comes alive for us in the pages of the *Ab Urbe Condita* and the spirit and ideals of Roman greatness are rekindled by the spell of its romantic patriotism. The paradox of every great historical work is that it comes to be valued for what it tells us about its author's own age rather than about the past of which he was writing. When we understand what Livy did for the renaissance humanists we are better able to appreciate his essential quality.

By contemporary standards the classical historians failed completely in their understanding of the nature of historical explanation. They knew of only two causal factors in history: the actions of individual men (especially 'great men') and the inscrutable operation of Chance, Tyche or Fortuna. They never suspected the existence of the 'economic factor' or of 'social factors', much less of 'ideological factors', in history. History is either what men decide and dare and do,[1] or else it is what they suffer at the hands of capricious Fate. Their use of the latter notion in whatever form—Chance, Necessity, Fate, Luck—would correspond to the behaviour of a contemporary historian who, when baffled in his search for rational explanation, was content to attribute an occurrence to 'imponderable factors' in history, but the difference between them and him is that they really believed in an irrational factor which governed the course of things, or perhaps in a mysterious balancing agent which always restored the equilibrium of things at the appointed time. Varying conceptions of this irrational factor in history were current amongst the classical historians; Tacitus claims to suspend judgment about 'whether it is Fate and unchangeable Necessity or Chance which governs the revolutions of human affairs'; he remarks that there were conflicting views even amongst 'the wisest of the ancients'.[2] The Stoic Livy identifies Fortuna with the World-Intelligence which governs all things; for the Epicureans, the fatal arbiter is Nature, the random movement of the atoms. Even the allegedly rationalist Thucydides believes that history

[1] Cf. P. G. Walsh, ibid., 34: 'The central feature of ancient historical writing . . . is the prominence attached to the individual—his thoughts, his emotions, his words, his acts, his character; these are the stuff of history, the motivators of events. So Thucydides, in his analysis of the Peloponnesian War, and Polybius, in his discussion of the origins of the Hannibalic War, both assume that the causes lay in human decisions, thoughts and emotions.'

[2] *Annals*, vi, 22.

fatalistically repeats itself, and the matter-of-fact Polybius is content to attribute the rise and fall of empires to the workings of Fate.[1] In fact, classical historiography was through and through religious, though the religion which informed it was neither the official religion of the State deities nor the popular evangelical nonconformity of the mystery religions, but rather the religion of the 'higher paganism', which conceived of deity as 'ultimate reality'. This inscrutable deity manifested itself in history as Necessity or Luck; it was an open question whether it was intelligent (Stoicism) or blind (Epicureanism); the important thing was for men to be on the right side of Fortune. Happy was the historian whose story led to the conviction that Fortune would continue to smile upon his own people. The classical historians were the keepers of the useful myths.

Such was the conception of the nature and task of historiography which the renaissance humanists inherited from the classical world. Of course, there were adjustments to be made, especially in regard to the concept of Fate. It was not difficult to replace this notion by the Christian idea of Providence and thus to make possible in the future a more adequate conception of the character of historical explanation as a search for rationality. There was indeed the ever-present danger that pagan notions would creep back into historiography, but on the whole the pitfalls were avoided. It was fashionable amongst rationalist thinkers fifty years ago to exult that a healthy 'secular' attitude towards history, reviving the 'scientific' spirit of classical historiography, was achieved by the renaissance humanists, who freed 'science' from the stranglehold of 'theology'.[2] But the outlook and ideals of post-eighteenth-century rationalism were not those of the classical historiographers, whose primary concern was with the historical myths, the practical religious cement of society. Like most thoughtful men of the Graeco-Roman world, they sat loose

[1] Cf. Lecture II, *supra*, pp. 60f.; also W. Warde Fowler, 'Polybius' Conception of Tyche', *Classical Review*, 17 (1903), 445ff.

[2] The achievement was usually linked with that of Copernicus, who was supposed to have 'dethroned' man from his 'privileged position' at the centre of the universe (cf. J. B. Bury, *The Idea of Progress*, 335). It is true that medieval cosmology, following Greek science, located man's terrestrial habitat only a layer or two away from the centre of the physical universe; but the latter was at the farthest point of distance from the divine realm and was usually identified with hell. Man stood precariously near the bottom of the Ladder of Being; he was not 'enthroned' and held no 'privileged position'.

to the conventional religious orthodoxies of their times; in the characteristically religious-superstitious manner of their age, they believed not so much in God or the gods as in 'ultimate being', of which the historical appellation was Tyche or Fortuna. Cultus, the conventional religious observances, might be considered socially beneficial; its useful 'stories' and symbolic ceremonies induced healthy and patriotic attitudes; even so might an enlightened Empiricist regard expressions of Christian belief and worship today.[1] Amongst the renaissance humanists there were several scholarly sceptics, some of them in high places in the ecclesiastical hierarchy, whose attitude towards conventional orthodoxy and forms of worship was of the same order. But they hardly represented the outlook of the humanist movement as a whole, least of all in England. It is true that the later years of the humanist period in England (the Age of Reason) were not notable for religious fervour, and that a Bolingbroke might strenuously assert the humanist conception of the moral utility of history while surpassing in bitterness many of the deistic attacks upon the Church and upon orthodox beliefs. But the mildly theological tone of the humanist outlook in the Augustan age is caught more exactly by Pope in the *Essay on Man*, with its lingering belief that all things, even the most repulsive, have their appointed place in the Great Chain of Being and are necessary for the perfection of the whole:

> All Nature is but art unknown to thee,
> All Chance, direction which thou canst not see,
> All Discord, harmony not understood;
> All partial evil, universal good;
> And, spite of pride, in erring reason's spite,
> One truth is clear, Whatever is, is right.[2]

Humanist history was a means of inculcating theological truths as well as moral sentiments. The doctrine of Providence had replaced the idea of Chance or Necessity. The opening lines of the *Essay* sum up the Augustan humanists' conception of history and are all the more intriguing because they are addressed to Bolingbroke himself ('Awake, my St John! . . .'), who had cast himself

---

[1] Cf. R. B. Braithwaite, *An Empiricist's View of the Nature of Religious Belief*, Cambridge, 1955.
[2] Epistle i, 284ff.

for the role of the humanist statesman-historian, and who wrote so much about history but never actually managed to write any history. He is exhorted to

> Expatiate free o'er all this scene of man,
> A mighty maze! but not without a plan. . . .
> Eye Nature's walks, shoot Folly as it flies,
> And catch the Manners living as they rise;
> Laugh where we must, be candid where we can,
> But vindicate the ways of God to Man.

APPENDED NOTE III

THE PHILOSOPHY OF HISTORY

THE philosophy of history is a nineteenth-century phenomenon, if we mean by the phrase the attempt to explain
the historical process as a whole. St Augustine (as we
noticed in Lecture II) based his interpretation of history not upon
philosophical reasoning but upon scriptural revelation, and his
view is therefore better described as a theology of history. In the
twentieth century, although there have been notable attempts to
construct a philosophy of history (e.g. Spengler, Toynbee), many
philosophers have decided that philosophy (metaphysics) is not
an independent source of knowledge and cannot answer questions
like that of the meaning of history as a whole. Consequently the
philosophy of history in the nineteenth-century sense has gone
out of fashion.

But there is another sense in which the expression 'philosophy
of history' is used today, namely, the *critical* philosophy of history,
that is, the philosophical criticism of the kind of thinking which
we call historical, the methods used by historians, the nature of
historical 'facts', and so on.[1] Historical knowledge confronts
philosophers with many difficult problems. For example, the past
by definition has ceased to be; if, then, it does not exist, are
historians talking about nothing, non-being? Some philosophers
have concluded that all historical facts are present facts (idealism:
Croce, Collingwood), but the theory sounds unconvincing to
historians who are keenly aware that they are talking about *past*
facts and yet are not talking about non-existence. In what sense,
then, does the past exist?[2] The more abstruse of these critical

[1] The best introduction to the subject in both the above senses is to be
found in W. H. Walsh, *An Introduction to the Philosophy of History*, London,
1951. See also Raymond Aron, *Introduction to the Philosophy of History: an
Essay on the Limits of Historical Objectivity,* Eng. trans. by G. J. Irwin, London,
1961; original French ed., 1938; revised, 1948.

[2] Students of the Bible come across this problem in a most interesting
form in the Hebrew conception of 'remembering', that is, making past events
present again, so that the past becomes 'the living past' and enters dynamic-
ally into the here and now. Cf. J. Pedersen, *Israel*, I–II, Eng. trans., London,
1926, 245–59; III–IV, Eng. trans., London, 1940, 410ff.; A. G. Hebert, art.
'Memory' in Alan Richardson, ed., *A Theological Word Book of the Bible*, 142f.

philosophical problems fall outside the range of interest of these Lectures, but others are very important for our discussion (e.g. the nature of historical 'facts', considered in Lecture VI).

In the latter part of the eighteenth century the quickening of interest in history and the steady accumulation of historical knowledge were forcing thoughtful men to reconsider the Cartesian scepticism concerning the possibility of historical knowledge. Already before the century closed Immanuel Kant (1724–1804) had attempted to answer the question, 'How is historical knowledge possible?' But his solution of this problem was less influential than his answer to the parallel question about how scientific knowledge is possible. It will be recalled that Hume's philosophical criticism of the idea of causation had raised the problem about scientific knowledge; but from the confident manner in which Hume undertook to write 'impartial' history he would seem to have had few doubts about the possibility of historical knowledge. Indeed, the problem of historical knowledge did not engage the attention of philosophers in any very serious way until towards the end of the nineteenth century (Dilthey, Bradley). Kant did not succeed in focusing attention upon the critical problem of historical knowledge in a manner comparable to that in which his answer to the question about scientific knowledge had directed attention to the epistemological problems raised by the progress of the natural sciences. This is doubtless because throughout the nineteenth century, despite the unparalleled enlargement of historical knowledge, the prestige of the natural sciences tended to dominate the thinking of philosophers. Up to the time of Dilthey and Bradley it was widely assumed that historical knowledge was only a variety (and perhaps an inferior variety) of scientific knowledge in general (positivism); and the distinctive character of historical knowledge was hardly perceived (except in the line of thought stemming from Burke and Coleridge) until the twentieth century, which has witnessed a decline of positivist influence.

Kant himself was concerned with the moral issue raised by the problem of history, a concern less likely to be felt in an age in which history was usually held to be strictly scientific. For Kant, as for the men of the Enlightenment generally, history was nothing if it was not moral. Thus, he found himself compelled to ask whether speculative philosophy can demonstrate on *a priori* grounds that, despite its chaotic and disquieting features, the history of mankind is nevertheless a rational progress towards a goal which commends itself to the moral reason. His answer provides a philosophical rationalization of the incipient idea of progress of the late eighteenth century. He argues that it is a requirement of the moral reason that the course of history as a whole should issue ultimately in the fulfilment of those moral possibilities inherent in human nature which the life-span of particular individuals or societies cannot realize. Modestly aware of his own ignorance of general history, he leaves it to working historians to provide empirical corroboration for his speculative conclusion. When we pass from Kant to J. G. Herder (1744–1803), who had once been Kant's pupil, we move from the rationalistic atmosphere of the Enlightenment to the warmer climate of the Romantic Movement, with its trust in feeling and intuition. But the result is much the same: man's historical destiny is disclosed by the moral potentialities of human nature.[1]

In Herder, however, a significant change in European thought is becoming manifest. The Great Chain of Being has begun to move; the Ladder has become an escalator which goes only upwards. The idea of progress, of history as evolution towards a goal, which dominated nineteenth-century thought, has begun to fascinate the European intelligence. Instead of the Ladder, standing itself fixed and motionless between earth and heaven, there is the upward ascent of the creation on the moving staircase. Even the Middle Ages have ceased to be a stagnant society; they are joyfully discovered to be themselves a pageant of the upward progress of humanity. The whole of the past is re-animated; it possesses an interest and a value which it did not have for the men of the Enlightenment. The new quality of historical-mindedness was coming to birth; and, though the shadow of eighteenth-century rationalism would extend across the nineteenth century, obscuring the existential significance of the new historical approach for a long time to come, a movement of thought was taking place which was not less significant for the future of the world than the scientific revolution of the seventeenth century had been. Herder is of immense importance in the development of the new attitude towards and enthusiasm for history which charac-

[1] For the speculative views of Kant and Herder see W. H. Walsh, op. cit., 119–36.

terized the nineteenth century and which underlay its truly astonishing activity in historical research and historical writing. This intense historical activity testifies to the genuine but inarticulate conviction of the century of Ranke, bemused as it was by the grey and oppressive phantom of 'scientific history', that the secret of human existence and destiny is somehow locked away not in the inexorable rhythms of atoms in motion but in the self-understanding of man in his history.[1]

The most impressive attempt of speculative philosophy to explain *a priori* the course of development which history *must* follow was made by G. W. F. Hegel (1770–1831), who became the dominant philosophical mind in Germany after he succeeded Fichte in the chair of philosophy at Berlin in 1818.[2] Since for Hegel the real is the rational, all historical process must conform to the laws of logic. The rational pattern of history does not have to be discovered by historians following empirical methods; it is demonstrated by metaphysics, or, in Hegel's language, logic. The working historian is concerned with particular facts, which (as Lessing had said) can never demonstrate the necessary truths of reason; the philosopher is not concerned with particular facts but with those necessary laws of logic which govern the course of historical development. The movement of thought, and therefore of history, is dialectical, that is, it proceeds like an argument from a thesis to an antithesis and then to a resolution of the conflict between them in a new synthesis. The goal of history, the final synthesis, is the emergence of the consciousness of freedom on the part of Reality or Spirit and the progressive realization of freedom in historical societies and institutions. The historian will supply empirical confirmation of the logician's *a priori* dialectical scheme,

[1] Cf. Karl Barth, *From Rousseau to Ritschl*, on Herder, esp. 209–13: Herder's passionate feeling for humanity, made in the Creator's image, drove him to the discovery of man in history—in such unlikely places as Hebrew poetry, German folk-song, the despised Middle Ages, the Reformation; in fact, 'it was just those aspects of history which had made it particularly suspect, and even an object of hatred, to the Enlightenment . . . that Herder emphasized with love and care, counselling his contemporaries to esteem and respect them as the very ones which were absolutely essential to the concept of history' (209). 'In what concerns history Herder shouted what Lessing had whispered. History, for him, is nothing else but living experience . . .' (211).

[2] Hegel's lectures on *The Philosophy of History* were put together by his admirers and published after his death from cholera at the height of his fame; Eng. trans. by J. Sibree, 1857.

so far as his evidence goes; Hegel himself goes beyond logic in applying his dialectical notion to the actual process of world-history. In the beginning there was despotism of the oriental type, when only one man (the despot) was free; then by way of anti-thesis came the Graeco-Roman extension of freedom to all citizens (but not to slaves); finally there comes the synthesis, the fulfilment by the Germanic nations of the Christian ideal of the infinite value and freedom of every individual, the historical self-realization of the Absolute Idea. Thus, the culmination of world-process is to be found in the perfection of the political develop-ment of the Prussian State round about 1830. The movement of historical development is from East to West (though it is not clear how this can be deduced by logic); doubtless Hegel never contemplated the possibility that the process would continue its westward course and cross the Atlantic. The provincial and ideological character of Hegel's logic soon became apparent, though in its day it served the purpose of bolstering the myth of Prussian greatness. Hegel himself held that his philosophy had made articulate the spiritual content of the Christian religion, which by its naïve and childish dogmas had in the past com-municated truth pictorially to minds hitherto incapable of under-standing the philosophy of the Spirit.

Strange though it may now seem to us, Hegel's influence was considerable. In theology the Tübingen School applied his dialectic to the history of the early Church,[1] but after Ritschl's break with the Tübingen theology in 1857, the movement of thought associated with his name rejected speculative philosophy as a method of theological understanding. Like Kierkegaard, who ridiculed Hegelianism, it anticipated the critical attitude of twentieth-century English philosophers towards metaphysics as such. But in England a remarkable renaissance of Hegelian ideal-ism occurred in the later nineteenth and earlier twentieth centuries under the leadership of T. H. Green, Edward Caird, Bernard Bosanquet, F. H. Bradley and others; these thinkers created the 'stable background' of the dominant idealistic philosophy in which William Temple's generation grew up.[2] In Germany itself,

[1] See p. 121, *supra*.
[2] Cf. W. Temple, art. in *Theology*, Nov. 1939; also the preface to his *Christus Veritas*, London, 1924, and the essay by Dorothy M. Emmet in F. A. Iremonger, *William Temple, Archbishop of Canterbury, his Life and Letters*, London, 1948, 521ff.; Temple was a pupil of Edward Caird at Balliol.

however, Hegel's disciples after his death had split into factions and it soon became obvious that a logic capable of so great a variety of forms could hardly possess *a priori* validity. Hegel's philosophy, curiously enough, exerted its most enduring posthumous influence under the patronage of revolutionary political messianism, which found that the logic of history could be diverted to quite un-Hegelian ends. The youthful Karl Marx (1818–83) had imbibed the fashionable Hegelian teaching on entering the University of Berlin five years after Hegel's death. He combined the materialism of the Encyclopaedists with Hegel's notion of the dialectical movement of history, thereby 'standing Hegel on his head' and endowing atoms with logical necessity ('dialectical materialism'). The course of history could be predicted by means of the scientific principles of Marxist philosophy:[1] the material (or economic) forces of history were the basic realities, and they moved with a pre-determined logical inevitability towards the Hegelian goal of freedom, now interpreted by Marx in terms of the classless society. The Marxist myth of history remains a powerful force in the world today, 'an extremely dangerous intellectual anachronism',[2] a means of changing history rather than of explaining it. In the nineteenth century other 'scientific' theories of history were put forward, claiming to be based upon laws as verifiable as those of contemporary physics (Comte, Buckle), but Marxism was the only one which contrived to get itself backed by a revolution that placed behind it an immense weight of economic and military power; it owed its success to the religious fervour generated by its myth of the messianic proletariat destined to fulfil the purpose of history.[3]

[1] That the theory can still be taken seriously by intellectuals in the West is illustrated by V. Gordon Childe, *History*, London, 1947. A very full bibliography of Marxist thought will be found in J. Witt-Hansen, *Historical Materialism, Exposition and Critique,* Book I, 'The Method', Copenhagen, 1960. In relation to our theme we might mention S. Hook, *From Hegel to Marx*, London, 1936; probably the best short introduction to Marx is Isaiah Berlin, *Karl Marx, his Life and Environment*, Oxford, 2nd ed., 1948 (with short bibliography); for the political aspect see the two chapters on Marx and Engels in John Bowle, *Politics and Opinion in the Nineteenth Century*, 298–347.
[2] John Bowle, op. cit., 347.
[3] Cf. Reinhold Niebuhr, *Faith and History*, 210f.: 'Marxism is a secularized version of messianism without the knowledge of the (Hebrew) prophets that the judgment of God falls with particular severity upon the chosen people. . . . Its non-prophetic messianism endows a particular social force in history with unqualified sanctity and its post-Christian utopianism prompts

The philosophy of history in both its nineteenth-century modes, the speculative and the positivist (or 'scientific'), are discredited today. In the twentieth century there has arisen the existentialist philosophy, with its own conception of the significance of history. The fountain-head of this philosophy, Martin Heidegger, remains inaccessibly remote from most English-speaking students,[1] and such understanding of it as they possess is chiefly derived *via* Bultmann and his interpreters. We have endeavoured to distinguish between *existentialist* (philosophical theory) and *existential* (the personal understanding of one's self as a being in history),[2] and we have noted that the latter word is useful (though not indispensable) in speaking about historical study as a challenging personal encounter with the past, a characteristic of historical activity which is recognized by many historians today. It remains for us to point out that in these Lectures we have been concerned with history, not with the philosophy of history (although, of course, the *critical* philosophy of history touches our enquiry at almost every point). History means the interpretation of evidence from the past in the light of experience in the present, and this interpretation is the proper task of the historian. The doing of it does not turn him into a philosopher; philosophers may criticize the formal methods and concepts of the historian, but they do not themselves construct interpretations or perform the historian's task for him: this is implied when it is said that philosophy is not an independent source of knowledge. The historian in his turn will, if he is wise, listen carefully to what the critical philosophers have to say. (In practice, of course, the historian and the critical philosopher of history are often the same man, but this does not affect the distinction here made between the historian and the philosopher.) The historian, *qua* historian, even the historian of ideas, is not the philosopher; we no longer accept the view that the historian ascertains the 'facts' and then the

---

the illusion of a kingdom of perfect righteousness (i.e. a classless society and an anarchistic brotherhood) in history. . . . Its materialism is, on the whole, a justified reaction to pietistic religions which do not understand the social character of life. . . . Its ostensible atheism is less significant than its idolatry. It worships a god who is the unqualified ally of one group in human society against all others.'

[1] Despite the prodigious efforts of his translators to unscrew the inscrutable; see his *Being and Time*, Eng. trans. by John Macquarrie and Edward Robinson, London, 1962, esp. 424–55.

[2] *Supra*, 149f.

philosopher 'interprets' them. The historian *is* the interpreter, because the 'facts' themselves are his interpretations.

A very important corollary follows concerning the nature of the enquiry into the history of ideas which has been pursued in these Lectures. That enquiry has been *historical* in character, since it has been concerned with the interpretation of history. The point is an important one, because there is much confusion today concerning the nature of theology. Many philosophers nowadays are accustomed to class theological statements with metaphysical ones, bringing them into the same condemnation. This is a mistake, a confusion of categories, so far as *Christian* theology is concerned. If our approach has been correct, theological statements are historical, not metaphysical, in character. Such statements as 'God is love' or 'the world was created by God'[1] are historical in that they are brief summaries of a long and well-considered process of reflection upon historical 'facts', which are themselves interpretations of historical evidence. Christian dogmatics, is, in essence, the Christian interpretation of history. The verification of theological statements involves us in the interpretation of history, which is the task of the historian *qua* historian; verification is not the task of the philosopher *qua* philosopher, because the relevant evidence is historical. Verification, again, is not to be sought in the natural sciences (though, of course, the historian will have to take into account all available knowledge, including scientific knowledge, when he comes to make his interpretation). In the last resort, as in all historical interpretation, the interpreter's own personal experience of involvement in history will be the deciding factor in his judging, because all historical judgment is unavoidably personal and existential. There is no escape from personal decision by the fiction of an objective or 'scientific' history, which can determine the existential questions of historical interpretation in the kind of 'public' manner which is expected of the natural sciences. The sciences tell us much about the stage on which the drama of history is enacted; they can even help us to set the stage in such a way that the play may be better acted and better seen; but the meaning of the drama is perceived not by attending to the stage mechanism, but by involvement in the tragedy enacted under the lights focused by the historian's skill.

[1] Cf. *supra*, 223f.

BIBLIOGRAPHY

A SELECTION of the more important, especially the more recent, books and articles bearing upon the subjects touched upon in these Lectures. Other works are mentioned in the footnotes to the Lectures.

Abbreviations used in this Bibliography:

AHR	= *American Historical Review, A Quarterly*, The Macmillan Co., New York
CUP	= Cambridge University Press
ET	= English translation
ExT	= *Expository Times*, Edinburgh
Interpretation	= *Interpretation, a Journal of Bible and Theology*, Richmond, Virginia
JR	= *Journal of Religion*, Divinity School, the University of Chicago
JTS	= *Journal of Theological Studies*, OUP (Clarendon Press)
Mind	= *Mind, a Quarterly Review of Psychology and Philosophy*, Edinburgh
NS	= New Series
OUP	= Oxford University Press
PQ	= *Philosophical Quarterly*, University of St Andrews
SBT	= Studies in Biblical Theology, Student Christian Movement Press, London, and Allenson, Naperville, Illinois
SJT	= *Scottish Journal of Theology*, Edinburgh
ThEH	= *Theologische Existenz Heute*, Munich
Theology	= *Theology: a Monthly Review*, SPCK, London
ZThK	= *Zeitschrift für Theologie und Kirche*, Tübingen

ACTON, J. E. E. D., first Baron, 'The Study of History' (Inaugural Lecture, 1895) in *Lectures on Modern History*, ed. with introduction by J. N. Figgis and R. V. Laurence, London, 1907.
— *Historical Essays and Studies*, London, 1908.
ADAMS, H. P., *The Life and Writings of Giambattista Vico*, London, 1935.
ALTANER, BERTHOLD, *Patrology*, ET, Edinburgh, 1960; esp. chap. VI, 'Hagiographers, Historians and Chroniclers of Christian Antiquity'.
ALTHAUS, PAUL, *The So-Called Kerygma and the Historical Jesus*, ET by David Cairns, Edinburgh, 1959.
ANDERSON, HUGH, 'Existential Hermeneutics' in *Interpretation*, XVI, No. 2 (April 1962).
ANGUS-BUTTERWORTH, L. M., *Ten Master Historians*, Aberdeen Univ. Press, 1961.
ARENDT, HANNAH, *Between Past and Future: Six Exercises in Political Thought*, London, 1961.
ARON, RAYMOND, *Introduction to the Philosophy of History: an Essay on the Limits of Historical Objectivity*, ET by G. J. Irwin, London, 1961; original French ed., 1938; revised, 1948.
ASHLEY-MONTAGU, M. F., ed., *Toynbee and History: Critical Essays and Reviews* (by some thirty well-known historians; includes Toynbee's statement, 'What I am Trying to Do'), Boston, Mass., 1956.
ASUBEL, HERMAN, *Historians and their Craft*, New York: Columbia, 1950.
AUBYN, GILES ST, *A Victorian Eminence: the Life and Works of Henry Thomas Buckle*, London, 1958.

BAGBY, PHILIP, *Culture and History: Prolegomena to the Comparative Study of Civilizations*, London, 1958.
BAILLIE, DONALD M., *God was in Christ: an Essay on Incarnation and Atonement*, London, 1948.
BAILLIE, JOHN, *Our Knowledge of God*, OUP, 1939.
— *The Belief in Progress*, OUP, 1950.
— *Natural Science and the Spiritual Life*, OUP, 1951.
— *The Idea of Revelation in Recent Thought*, OUP, 1956.
BAKER, HERSCHEL, *The Wars of Truth*, Cambridge, Mass., 1952.
BALTHASAR, HANS URS VON, *Karl Barth: Darstellung und Deutung seiner Theologie*, Cologne, 1951.
BARNES, HARRY ELMER, *History of Historical Writing*, Oklahoma Univ. Press, 1937.
BARR, JAMES, *Biblical Words for Time*, SBT, London, 1962.
— *The Semantics of Biblical Language*, OUP, 1961.

BARRACLOUGH, GEOFFREY, *The Historian in a Changing World*, OUP, 1955.
— 'Universal History' in H. P. R. Finberg, q.v.
— 'Europe and the Wider World in the Nineteenth and Twentieth Centuries' in A. O. Sarkissian, q.v.

BARRATT, C. KINGSLEY, *Luke the Historian in Recent Study*, London, 1961.

BARTH, KARL, *Church Dogmatics*, ed. by G. W. Bromiley and T. F. Torrance (ET of *Die Kirchliche Dogmatik*, 1932–), Edinburgh:
Vol. I, Part 1, 1936; later Parts, 1955–62.
Vol. I (two Parts), The Doctrine of the Word of God.
Vol. II (two Parts), The Doctrine of God.
Vol. III (four Parts), The Doctrine of Creation.
Vol. IV (three Parts: Part 3 is in two halves), The Doctrine of Reconciliation.
— *Der Römerbrief* (1919); cf. esp. preface to 2nd ed., 1923, for critique of 'Historismus'; Neue bearb., Munich, 1933; ET by Sir Edwyn Hoskyns, *The Epistle to the Romans*, OUP, 1932.
— *From Rousseau to Ritschl*, ET by Brian Cozens of eleven chapters of *Die Protestantische Theologie im 19 Jahrhundert* (Zürich, 1952), London, 1959.
— *God, Grace and Gospel*, ET by J. S. McNab (*SJT* Occasional Papers, 8), Edinburgh, 1959.

BARTSCH, HANS WERNER, *Das historische Problem des Lebens Jesu*, *ThEH*, Neue Folge 78, Munich, 1960.
— ed. *Kerygma und Mythos*, five vols., various contributors, Hamburg, 1951–5; partial ET by R. H. Fuller, *Kerygma and Myth*, I, 1953, II, 1962 (London).

BEARD, CHARLES A., 'Written History as an Act of Faith' in *AHR*, XXXIX, 1934, 219–31.
— and HOOK, SIDNEY, 'Problems of Terminology in Historical Writing' in *Theory and Practice in Historical Study: a Report of the Committee on Historiography*, Social Science Research Council Bulletin 54 (1946).

BECKER, CARL L., 'Detachment and the Writing of History' in *The Atlantic Monthly*, CVI, Oct. 1910.
— *The Heavenly City of the Eighteenth-century Philosophers*, Yale Univ. Press, New Haven, 1932.
— *Everyman His own Historian: Essays on History and Politics*, New York, 1935.
— 'What are Historical Facts?' in *Western Political Quarterly*, VIII, 1955, 327–40; also in P. L. Snyder, q.v.

BELLER, E. A., and LEE, M. DU P., Jr., *Selections from Bayle's Dictionary*, Princeton Univ. Press, 1952.

BELLOT, H. HALE, *American History and American Historians: a Review of Recent Contributions to the Interpretation of the History of the United States*, Univ. of London, Athlone Press, 1962.

BENSON, LEE, *Turner and Beard: American Historical Writing Reconsidered*, Glencoe, Ill., 1960.

BERDYAEV, NICHOLAS, *The Meaning of History*, London, 1936.

BERGIN, T. G., and FISCH, M. H., *The New Science of Giambattista Vico*, ET, Cornell Univ. Press, Ithaca, N.Y., 1948.

BERLIN, SIR ISAIAH, *Historical Inevitability*, Auguste Comte Trust Memorial Lecture, 1, London, 1954.
— *The Hedgehog and the Fox: an Essay on Tolstoy's View of History*, London, 1954.

BLACK, J. B., *The Art of History*, London, 1926.

BLOCH, MARC, *The Historian's Craft*, ET by Peter Putnam of *Apologie pour l'histoire, ou métier d'historien* (Paris, 1949), Manchester Univ. Press, 1954.

BOBER, M. M., *Karl Marx's Interpretation of History* (1927), CUP, 1950.

BODENSTEIN, WALTER, *Neige des Historismus: Ernst Troeltschs Entwicklungsgang*, Gütersloh, 1959.

BOLGAR, R. R., *The Classical Heritage and its Beneficiaries*, CUP, 1954.

BOMAN, THORLEIF, *Hebrew Thought Compared with Greek*, ET by Jules L. Moreau, London, 1960.

BOND, H. L., *The Literary Art of Edward Gibbon*, OUP, 1960.

BORNKAMM, GÜNTHER, *Jesus of Nazareth*, ET of *Jesus von Nazareth* (Stuttgart, 1956) by Irene and Fraser McLusky with James M. Robinson, London, 1960.

BOWLE, JOHN, *Politics and Opinion in the Nineteenth Century: an Historical Introduction*, London, 1954.
— *A New Outline of World History from the Origins to the Eighteenth Century*, London, 1962.

BRADLEY, F. H., 'The Presuppositions of Critical History' in *Collected Essays*, I, OUP, 1935.

BRONOWSKI, J., and MAZLISH, BRUCE, *The Western Intellectual Tradition from Leonardo to Hegel*, London, 1960.

BROWN, ROBERT, *Explanation in Social Science*, London, 1962.

BRUMFITT, J. H., *Voltaire: Historian*, OUP, 1958.

BRUNNER, EMIL, *The Mediator*, ET by Olive Wyon, London, 1934.
— *The Divine-Human Encounter*, ET by Amandus W. Loos of *Wahrheit als Begegnung*, London, 1944.
— *Revelation and Reason*, ET by Olive Wyon, Philadelphia, Pa., and London, 1946.

BUCHDAHL, GERD, *The Image of Newton and Locke in the Age of Reason*, London and New York, 1961.

BULTMANN, RUDOLF, 'The New Testament and Mythology' (ET of *Offenbarung und Heilsgeschehen*, 1941), in *Kerygma and Myth*, I (see under Bartsch).

— *Jesus*, Berlin, 1926; ET by Louise Pettibone Smith and Erminie Huntress Lantero, *Jesus and the Word* (1936), Fontana ed., 1962.

— *Glauben und Verstehen*, I, Tübingen, 1933.

— *Glauben und Verstehen*, II, Tübingen, 1952; ET by J. C. G. Greig, *Essays Philosophical and Theological*, London, 1955 (esp. 'The Problem of Hermeneutics').

— *Theology of the New Testament*, ET by K. Grobel, 2 vols., New York and London, 1952, 1955.

— *The History of the Synoptic Tradition*, ET by John Marsh, Oxford, 1963, from 3rd German ed. (1957).

— *Primitive Christianity in its Contemporary Setting*, ET by R. H. Fuller, London, 1956.

— *History and Eschatology* (Gifford Lectures, 1955), Edinburgh, 1957.

— *Das Verhältnis der urchristlichen Christusbotschaft zum historischen Jesus*, Sitzungsberichte der Heidelberger Akademie der Wissenschaften, Heidelberg, 1960.

— 'Is Exegesis without Presuppositions Possible?' in *Existence and Faith: Shorter Writings of R. Bultmann*, ET by Schubert M. Ogden, q.v.

BUTTERFIELD, HERBERT, *The Whig Interpretation of History*, London, 1931.

— *The Englishman and his History*, CUP, 1945.

— *Lord Acton* (Historical Association Series), London, 1948.

— *Christianity and History*, London, 1949.

— *The Origins of Modern Science, 1300–1800*, London, 1949.

— *Christianity in European History*, London, 1951.

— *History and Human Relations*, London, 1951.

— *Man on his Past: the Study of the History of Historical Scholarship*, CUP, 1955.

— *George III and the Historians*, London, 1957.

BURCKHARDT, JACOB, *Reflections on History*, ET by M. D. H., London, 1943.

— *Judgments on History and Historians*, ET by H. Zohn, London, 1958.

— *Weltgeschichtliche Betrachtungen*, Bern, 1947.

— *Letters*, see under Dru.

BURY, J. B., 'The Science of History' (Inaugural Lecture, 1903) and 'Cleopatra's Nose' (1916) in *Selected Essays*, ed. by H. W. V. Temperley, CUP, 1930.

— *The Ancient Greek Historians*, London, 1909; new ed., New York, 1958.
— *The Idea of Progress: an Inquiry into its Origins and Growth*, London, 1928.
— *A History of Freedom of Thought*, London, 1932.

CAIRNS, DAVID, *A Gospel without Myth? Bultmann's Challenge to the Preacher*, London, 1960.
CAM, HELEN, *Historical Novels* (Historical Association Series), London, 1961.
CAMPENHAUSEN, HANS FREIHERR VON, 'Der Ablauf der Osterereignisse und das leere Grab' in *Tradition und Leben: Kräfte der Kirchengeschichte: Aufsätze und Vorträge*, Tübingen, 1960.
CAPONIGRI, A. R., *Time and Idea: the Theory of History in Giambattista Vico*, London, 1953.
CARPENTER, J. ESTLIN, *The Bible in the Nineteenth Century*, London, 1903.
CARR, E. H., *What is History?* (Trevelyan Lectures, 1961), London, 1961.
CASSIRER, ERNST, *An Essay on Man: an Introduction to a Philosophy of Human Culture*, Yale Univ. Press, New Haven, 1954.
— *The Philosophy of the Enlightenment*, ET by F. C. A. Koelln and J. P. Pettegrove, Princeton Univ. Press, 1951.
— *The Logic of the Humanities*, ET by C. S. Howe, Yale Univ. Press, New Haven, 1961.
CHADWICK, HENRY, *Lessing's Theological Writings*, selections in translation with an introductory essay, London, 1956.
CHEYNE, T. K., *Founders of Old Testament Criticism*, London, 1933.
CHILDE, V. GORDON, *Man Makes Himself*, London, 1936.
— *What Happened in History*, London (Penguin), 1942, new ed., 1960.
— *History*, London, 1947.
CHILDS, BREVARD S., *Myth and Reality in the Old Testament*, SBT, London, 1961.
CLAGGETT, MARSHALL, *The Science of Mechanics in the Middle Ages*, Univ. of Wisconsin Press, Madison, 1959.
CLARK, SIR G. N., *The Seventeenth Century*, OUP, 1929; 2nd ed., 1947.
— *Science and Social Welfare in the Age of Newton*, OUP, 1937.
— *Historical Scholarship and Historical Thought* (Inaugural Lecture), CUP, 1944.
— 'History and the Modern Historian', General Introduction to *The New Cambridge Modern History*, I, CUP, 1957.
CLARKE, M. L., *George Grote*, London, 1962.

COHEN, J. M., *Montaigne's Essays*, translated with introduction, London (Penguin), 1958.

COBBAN, ALFRED B. C., *Edmund Burke and the Revolt against the Eighteenth Century*, London, 1929; with new preface, 1960.

— *In Search of Humanity: The Role of the Enlightenment in Modern History*, London, 1960.

— 'History and Sociology' in *Historical Studies*, III, ed. James Hogan, London and Cork, 1961.

COCHRANE, C. N., *Christianity and Classical Culture: a Study of Thought and Action from Augustus to Augustine*, OUP, 1940.

COLLINGWOOD, R. G., *The Idea of History*, OUP, 1946.

— 'The Theory of Historical Cycles', *Antiquity*, I, 1927: (i) 'Osward Spengler', 311–25: (ii) 'Cycles and Progress', 435–46.

CONZELMANN, HANS, *The Theology of St Luke*, ET of *Die Mitte der Zeit* (1954) by Geoffrey Buswell, London and New York, 1960.

— art. 'Jesus Christus' in *Religion in Geschichte und Gegenwart*, 3rd ed., III, Tübingen, 1959.

— 'Jesus von Nazareth und der Glaube an den Auferstandenen' in Ristow and Matthiae, qv.

— 'Rudolf Bultmann' in *Studium Generale*, 1961.

— ,EBELING, G., and FUCHS, E., *Die Frage nach dem historischen Jesus*', *ZThK*, Beiheft, 1959.

CRAGG, G. R., *The Church and the Age of Reason, 1648–1789*, Pelican History of the Church, London, 1960.

CREIGHTON, MANDEL, 'The Teaching of Ecclesiastical History' (Inaugural Lecture, 1885) in *Historical Essays and Addresses*, 2nd imp., London, 1904.

CROCE, BENEDETTO, *Theory and History of Historiography*, ET by D. Ainslie, London, 1921.

— *History as the Story of Liberty*, ET by S. Sprigge, London, 1941.

CROMBIE, A. C., *Augustine to Galileo: the History of Science, AD 400–1650*, London, 1952.

CRUMP, C. G., *History and Historical Research*, London, 1928.

CULLMAN, OSCAR, *Christ and Time*, ET by Floyd V. Filson, London, 1951.

— *Christology of the New Testament*, ET by S. C. Guthrie and C. A. M. Hall, London, 1959.

— 'Unzeitgemässe Bemerkungen zum "historischen Jesus" der Bultmann-Schule' in Ristow and Matthiae, q.v.

DANCE, E. H., *History the Betrayer: a Study in Bias*, London, 1960.

DANIÉLOU, JEAN, *Reflections on the Inner Meaning of History*, ET by Nigel Abercrombie, London and Chicago, 1958.

D'ARCY, M. C., *The Sense of History: Secular and Sacred*, London, 1959.

DAVIS, HERBERT, 'The Augustan Conception of History' in J. A. Mazzeo, q.v.

DAWSON, CHRISTOPHER H., *The Making of Europe*, London, 1946.
— *Religion and the Rise of Western Culture*, London, 1950.
— *The Dynamics of World History*, ed. by J. J. Mulloy, London, 1957.
— *The Historic Reality of Christian Culture: a Way to the Renewal of Human Life*, London, 1960.

DEHIO, LUDWIG, 'Germany and the Epoch of World Wars' in Hans Kohn, q.v.
— 'Ranke und der deutsche Imperialismus' in *Historische Zeitschrift*, CLXX, 1950, 307–28.

D'ELIA, PASQUALE M., *Galileo in China*, Cambridge, Mass., 1960.

DIEM, HERMANN, *Dogmatics*, ET by Harold Knight, Edinburgh, 1959.
— *Kierkegaard's Dialectic of Existence*, ET by Harold Knight, Edinburgh, 1959.
— *Grundfragen der biblischen Hermeneutik*, Munich, 1950.

DILTHEY, WILHELM. See under Hodges; Rickman.

DINKLER, ERICH, 'Existentialist Interpretation of the New Testament' in *JR*, XXXII, 1952, 87–96.

DOCKHORN, KLAUS, *Der deutsche Historismus in England*, Göttingen, 1949.

DODD, C. H., *History and the Gospel*, London, 1938.
— *The Interpretation of the Fourth Gospel*, CUP, 1953 (esp. Appendix: 'Some Considerations upon the Historical Aspect of the Fourth Gospel').

DORN, WALTER L., 'The Heavenly City and Historical Writing on the Enlightenment' in R. O. Rockwood, q.v.

DOUGLAS, DAVID C., *English Scholars*, London, 1939.

DOVRING, FOLKE, *History as a Social Science: an Essay on the Nature and Purpose of Historical Studies*, The Hague, 1960.

DRAKE, STILLMAN, *Galileo's Dialogue concerning the Two Chief World Systems—Ptolemaic and Copernican*, Univ. of California Press, Los Angeles, 1953.

DRAY, WILLIAM, *Laws and Explanation in History*, OUP, 1957.

DRU, ALEXANDER, *The Letters of Jacob Burckhardt*, selected and translated, London, 1955.

EBELING, GERHARD, *The Nature of Faith*, ET by R. Gregor Smith, London, 1961.

— *Die Geschichtlichkeit der Kirche und ihrer Verkündigung als theologisches Problem,* Tübingen, 1954.

— *Word and Faith,* ET by J. W. Leitch, London, 1963 (essays on the historical Jesus and Christology, the Word of God and Hermeneutics, the significance of the critical historical method for theology, etc.).

See also under Conzelmann.

EICHRODT, WALTHER, *Theology of the Old Testament,* Vol. I, ET by J. A. Baker from 6th ed. (1959) of *Theologie des Alten Testaments,* Teil I, 1933.

ESTLIN CARPENTER, J. See under Carpenter.

FINBERG, H. P. R., ed., *Approaches to History: a Symposium,* London, 1962.

FINLEY, M. I., *The Greek Historians,* New York, 1959.

FIRTH, SIR CHARLES, *Essays, Historical and Literary,* OUP, 1938.

— *Modern Languages at Oxford, 1724–1929,* OUP, 1929, esp. chap. I, 'George the First's Experiment'.

FITCH, ROBERT E., 'Reinhold Niebuhr's Philosophy of History' in *Reinhold Niebuhr: his Religious, Social and Political Thought,* ed. C. W. Kegley and R. W. Bretall, New York, 1956.

FLEW, A. G. N., *Hume's Philosophy of Belief,* London, 1961 (esp. chaps. VIII and IX).

FLINT, ROBERT, *History of the Philosophy of History,* Edinburgh, 1893.

FOAKES JACKSON, F. J., *A History of Church History: Studies of some Historians of the Christian Church,* Cambridge, 1939.

FORBES, DUNCAN, *The Liberal Anglican Idea of History,* CUP, 1952.

FOSTER, M. B., *Mystery and Philosophy,* London, 1957.

— 'The Christian Doctrine of Creation and the Rise of Modern Natural Science', *Mind,* XLIII (1934), 446–68.

— 'Christian Theology and Modern Science of Nature', *Mind* XLIV (1935), 439–66 and XLV (1936), 1–27.

FOX, LEVI, ed., *English Scholarship in the Sixteenth and Seventeenth Centuries* (Dugdale Society Conference Papers), OUP, 1956.

FREEMAN, E. A., *Methods of Historical Study,* London, 1886.

FRIEDMAN, MAURICE S., *Martin Buber: the Life of Dialogue,* Chicago and London, 1955 (esp. chap. XXIV).

FUCHS, ERNST, 'Die Frage nach dem historischen Jesus' in *ZThK,* LIII, 1956, 210–29.

— 'Glaube und Geschichte' in *ZThK,* LIV, 1957, 117–56.

— *Hermeneutik,* 2 Auflage mit Erganzungsheft, Bad Cannstatt, 1958.

— 'Zum hermeneutischen Problem in der Theologie' in *Gesammelte Aufsätze,* I, Tübingen, 1959.

— 'Zur Frage nach dem historischen Jesus' in *Gesammelte Aufsätze*, II, Tübingen, 1960.   (ET in preparation.)
See also under Conzelmann.

FUETER, EDUARD, *Geschichte der neueren Historiographie* (1911), Munich and Berlin, 1932; *Histoire de l'historiographie moderne*, traduit par E. Jeanmaire, Paris, 1914.

FULLER, REGINALD, H., *The Mission and Achievement of Jesus: an Examination of the Presuppositions of New Testament Theology*, SBT, London, 1954.

FUSSNER, F. SMITH, *The Historical Revolution: English Historical Writing and Thought, 1580–1640*, London, 1962.

FÜTER, EDUARD. See under Fueter.

GARDINER, PATRICK, *The Nature of Historical Explanation*, London, 1952.

GAY, PETER, 'Carl Becker's Heavenly City' in R. O. Rockwood, q.v.

GEORGE, H. B., *Historical Evidence*, OUP, 1909.

GEYL, PIETER, *Debates with Historians*, The Hague, 1955.
— *The Use and Abuse of History*, Yale Univ. Press, New Haven, 1955.

GILMORE, MYRON P., *The World of Humanism, 1453–1517*, paperback ed., New York, 1962.

GODSEY, JOHN D., *The Theology of Dietrich Bonhoeffer*, London, 1960.

GOGARTEN, FRIEDRICH, *Demythologizing and History*, ET by N. Horton Smith of *Entmythologisierung und Kirche* (1953), London, 1955.

GOLLWITZER, HELMUT, 'Der Glaube an Jesus Christus und der sogenannte historische Jesus' in Ristow and Matthiae, q.v.; ET by A. G. Hebert in *Theology*, LXV, No. 501 (March 1962).

GOOCH, G. P., *History and Historians in the Nineteenth Century*, London, 1913.

GOODFIELD, JUNE. See under Toulmin.

GOTTSCHALK, LOUIS, *Understanding History*, New York, 1951.

GRANT, A. J., *English Historians*, London, 1906.

GRESHAKE, GISBERT, *Historie wird Geschichte: Bedeutung und Sinn der Unterscheidung in der Theologie Rudolf Bultmanns* (Beiträge zur ökumenischen Spiritualität und Theologie, Herausgeber: Thomas Sartory), Essen, 1963.

GRIFFITH, G. T., 'The Greek Historians' in M. Platnauer, q.v.
— art. 'Historiography' (Greek and Roman) in *Chambers's Encyclopaedia* (ed. 1950), Vol. VII.

GUERLAC, HENRY, 'Newton's Changing Reputation' in R. O. Rockwood, q.v.

HALÉVY, D., *Histoire d'une historie*, Paris, 1939.

HALL, A. RUPERT, *From Galileo to Newton, 1630–1720*, London, 1963.

— 'The History of Science' in H. P. R. Finberg, q.v.

HALL, BASIL, 'Reformation without Tarrying for Theology', *JTS*, NS, XI, Part I, April 1960. (A comment on *The New Cambridge Modern History*, Vol. II, *The Reformation, 1520–1559*, ed. G. R. Elton.)

HALLER, WILLIAM, *The Rise of Puritanism*, New York, 1938.

HALPHEN, LOUIS, *Introduction à l'histoire*, Paris, 1946.

HARNACK, ADOLF VON, *What is Christianity?*, ET of *Das Wesen des Christentums* (1900), paper-back ed., New York and London, 1958.

HART, H. ST. J., ed., *Coleridge's Confessions of an Inquiring Spirit*, London, 1956.

HAUSRATH, A., *David Friedrich Strauss und die Theologie seiner Zeit*, Heidelberg, 1876.

HAY, DENYS, *Europe: the Emergence of an Idea*, Edinburgh, 1957.

HAZARD, PAUL, *The European Mind, 1980–1715*, ET by J. Lewis May (of *La crise de la conscience Européenne, 1680–1715*, 3 tomes, Paris, 1935) London, 1953.

— *European Thought in the Eighteenth Century: from Montesquieu to Locke*, ET by J. Lewis May (of *La pensée Européene au XVIIIéme Siécle*, Paris, 1946), London, 1954.

HEIDEGGER, MARTIN, *Being and Time*, ET by John Macquarrie and Edward Robinson, London, 1962, from 7th ed. of *Sein and Zeit* (1927).

HEITSCH, E., 'Die Aporie des historischen Jesus als Problem theologischer Hermeneutik' in *ZThK*, LIII, 1956, 192–210.

HENDERSON, IAN, *Myth in the New Testament*, SBT, London, 1952.

HEXTER, J. H., *Reappraisals in History*, London, 1961.

HOCKETT, HOMER CAREY, *The Critical Method in Historical Research and Writing*, New York, 1955.

HODGES, H. A., *Wilhelm Dilthey: an Introduction*, London, 1944 (contains selected passages in translation).

— *The Philosophy of Wilhelm Dilthey*, London, 1952.

HOFER, WALTHER, 'Towards a Revision of the German Concept of History' in Hans Kohn, q.v.

HOOK, SIDNEY, *From Hegel to Marx: Studies in the Intellectual Development of Karl Marx*, London, 1936; paper-back ed., Ann Arbor, Michigan, 1962.

— *Marx and the Marxists: the Ambiguous Legacy*, Princeton Univ. Press, 1955.

— ed., *Religious Experience and Truth: a Symposium*, Edinburgh, 1962. (A discussion by several well-known American philosophers and theologians of an original paper by Paul Tillich on 'The Religious Symbol' printed in an appendix.)

HOSKYNS, SIR EDWYN C., *The Fourth Gospel*, ed. by F. N. Davey, London, 1940; 2nd ed. 1947, esp. pp. 58–85, 'The Historical Tension of the Fourth Gospel'.

— and DAVEY, F. NOEL, *The Riddle of the New Testament*, London, 1931.

HUIZINGA, JOHAN, *Men and Ideas* (Essays), ET by J. S. Holmes and H. van Marle, London, 1960.

INGE, W. R., 'The Idea of Progress' in *Outspoken Essays*, II, London, 1922.

JACKSON, J. F. J. See Foakes Jackson.

JACOB, EDMOND, *Theology of the Old Testament*, ET by A. W. Heathcote and P. J. Allcock, London, 1958.

JAMES, D. G., *The Life of Reason: Hobbes, Locke, Bolingbroke*, London, 1949.

JASPERS, KARL, *The Origin and Goal of History*, London, 1953; ET of *Vom Ursprung und Ziel der Geschichte*, 1949.

JEREMIAS, JOACHIM, 'The Present Position in the Controversy concerning the Problem of the Historical Jesus' in *ExT*, LXIX, No. 11, August 1958.

JONES, GERAINT V., *Christology and Myth in the New Testament*, London, 1956.

JONES, R. F., 'The Humanistic Defence of Learning in the Mid-Seventeenth Century' in J. A. Mazzeo, q.v.

KÄHLER, MARTIN, *Der sogenannte historische Jesus und der geschichtliche biblische Christus*, Leipzig, 1892 and 1896; reprinted 1956.

KAMLAH, WILHELM, *Christentum und Geschichtlichkeit: Untersuchungen zur Entstehung des Christentums und zu Augustins 'Bürgschaft Gottes'*, 2 Auflage, Stuttgart, 1951.

KÄSEMANN, ERNST, 'Das Problem des historischen Jesus' in *ZThK*, LI, 1954, 125–53.

KENDRICK, T. D., *British Antiquity*, London, 1950.

KIERKEGAARD, S., *Philosophical Fragments*, ET by David F. Swenson, OUP and New York, 1936.

— *Concluding Unscientific Postscript to the Philosophical Fragments*, ET by David F. Swenson, Princeton Univ. Press, 1941.

KILBURN, K. *Lucian*, Loeb Classical Library, ET, London, 1960; contains Lucian's essay, 'How to Write History.'

KLIBANSKY, R., and PATON, H. J., eds, *Philosophy and History: Essays presented to Ernst Cassirer*, OUP, 1936.

KNIGHT, G. A. F., *A Christian Theology of the Old Testament*, London, 1959.

KNOWLES, DAVID, *The Historian and Character*, CUP, 1955.

— *The Evolution of Mediaeval Thought*, London, 1962.

KNOX, JOHN, *Criticism and Faith*, London, 1953.

KOHN, HANS, ed., *German History: Some New German Views*, London, 1954.

KRAELING, EMIL, *The Old Testament since the Reformation*, New York, 1955.

KRAUS, H. J., *Geschichte der historisch-kritischen Erforschung des Alten Testaments von der Reformation bis zur Gegenwart*, 1956.

KRAUS, MICHAEL, *The Writing of American History*, Univ. of Oklahoma Press, 1953.

KRONER, RICHARD, 'The Historical Roots of Niebuhr's Thought' in *Reinhold Niebuhr: his Religious, Social and Political Thought*, ed. C. W. Kegley and R. W. Bretall, New York, 1956.

KÜMMEL, W. G., *Promise and Fulfilment*, ET by Dorothea M. Barton, SBT, London, 1957.

— *Kirchenbegriff und Geschichtsbewusstsein in der Urgemeinde und bei Jesus*, Symbolae Biblicae Upsalienses, I, 1943.

— *Das Neue Testament: Geschichte der Erforschung seiner Probleme*, Verlag Karl Alber, 1958.

LAMPE, G. W. H., and WOOLLCOMBE, K. J., *Essays on Typology*, SBT, London, 1957.

LAMPRECHT, KARL, *What is History? Five Lectures on the Modern Science of History*, ET by E. A. Andrews, London and New York, 1905.

LAWTON, J. S., *Miracles and Revelation*, London and New York, 1959.

LEAVIS, F. R., ed., *Mill on Bentham and Coleridge*, London, 1950.

LECKY, W. E. H., *History of the Rise and Influence of the Spirit of Rationalism in Europe*, 2 vols., London, 1865; one-vol. ed., 1910.

LEFF, GORDON, *Mediaeval Thought from St Augustine to Ockham*, Penguin: London, 1958.

LEIPOLD, HEINRICH, *Offenbarung und Geschichte als Problem des Verstehens: eine Untersuchung zur Theologie Martin Kählers*, Gütersloh, 1962.

LESSING, THEODOR, *Geschichte als Sinngebung des Sinnlosen*, Berlin, 1919.

LEVIN, DAVID, *History as Romantic Art*, Stanford Univ. Press and OUP, 1960. (Studies of Bancroft, Prescott, Motley and Parkman.)

LEVY-BRUHL, L., 'The Cartesian Spirit and History' in Klibansky and Paton, q.v.

LICHTENBERGER, F., *History of German Theology in the Nineteenth Century*, ET, Edinburgh, 1899.

LIEB, FRITZ, 'Geschichte und Heilsgeschichte in der Theologie Rudolf Bultmanns' in *Evangelische Theologie* (Munich), XV, 1955.
— 'Die Geschichte Jesu Christi in Kerygma und Historie: ein Beitrag zum Gespräch mit R. Bultmann' in *Antwort: Festschrift für Karl Barth*, Zollikon-Zürich, 1956.

LIEBESCHÜTZ, HANS, *Ranke* (Historical Association Series), 1954.

LIGHTFOOT, R. H., *History and Interpretation in the Gospels*, Bampton Lectures for 1934, OUP, 1935.

LILLEY, A. L., *Religion and Revelation*, London, 1932.

LOVEJOY, ARTHUR O., *The Great Chain of Being: a Study of the History of an Idea*, Harvard Univ. Press, Cambridge, Mass., 1936.
— *Essays in the History of Ideas*, New York, 1955, esp. 'The Historiography of Ideas', 'Herder and the Enlightenment Philosophy of History'.

LOW, DAVID MORRICE, *Edward Gibbon, 1737–1794*, London, 1937.

LÖWITH, Karl, *Meaning in History: the Theological Implications of the Philosophy of History*, Chicago Univ. Press, 1949.

LUCAS, JOHN R., 'On Not Worshipping Facts' in *PQ*, Vol. 8, April, 1958, 144–56.

MCDONALD, A. H., 'The Roman Historians' in M. Platnauer, q.v.

MCINTYRE, JOHN, *The Christian Doctrine of History*, Edinburgh, 1957.
— 'Christ and History' in *The Reformed Theological Review* (Melbourne, Vic.), VIII, No. 3, August, 1949.

MCLACHLAN, H., *Sir Isaac Newton: Theological Manuscripts*, selected and edited with an introduction, Univ. of Liverpool Press, 1950.

MACMURRAY, John, *The Clue to History*, London, 1955.

MACQUARRIE, JOHN, *An Existentialist Theology: a Comparison of Heidegger and Bultmann*, London, 1955.
— *The Scope of Demythologizing: Bultmann and his Critics*, London, 1960.
— *Twentieth-century Religious Thought: the Frontiers of Philosophy and Theology, 1900–1960*, London, 1963.

MALEVEZ, L., *The Christian Message and Myth: the Theology of Rudolf Bultmann*, London, 1958.

MANDELBAUM, MAURICE, *The Problem of Historical Knowledge*, New York, 1938.

MANSON, T. W., 'The Life of Jesus: Some Tendencies in Present-day Research' in *The Background of the New Testament and its Eschatology*, ed. W. D. Davies and D. Daube, CUP, 1956.

MANUEL, FRANK E., *The Eighteenth Century Confronts the Gods*, Harvard Univ. Press, Cambridge, Mass., 1959.

MARCHAND, JACQUELINE, *Voltaire: Essai sur les moeurs et l'esprit des nations*, with introduction and notes, Editions Sociales, Paris, 1962.

MARLÉ, RENÉ, *Bultmann et l'interprétation du Nouveau Testament*, Paris: Aubier, 1956.

MARSH, JOHN, *The Fulness of Time*, London, 1952.

MARTIN, ALFRED VON, 'Historians and History' in Hans Kohn, q.v.

MARXSEN, W., *Der Evangelist Markus*, Göttingen, 1956.

MATHEW, DAVID, *Acton: the Formative Years*, London, 1946.

MAZLISH, B. See under Bronowski.

MAZZEO, J. A., ed., *Reason and the Imagination: Studies in the History of Ideas, 1600–1800*, New York and London, 1962.

MEINECKE, FRIEDRICH, *Die Entstehung des Historismus*, Munich and Berlin, 1936 and 1959.

— 'Ranke and Burckhardt' in Hans Kohn, q.v.

— *Schaffender Spiegel*, Studien zur deutschen Geschichtsschreibung und Geschichtsauffassung, Stuttgart, 1948.

— *Zur Theorie und Philosophie der Geschichte*. Stuttgart, 1959.

MILBURN, R. L. P., *Early Christian Interpretations of History*, Bampton Lectures for 1952, London, 1954.

MISES, LUDWIG VON, *Theory and History*, Yale Univ. Press, New Haven, 1957; London, 1958.

MOELLENDORFF. See under Wilamovitz-Moellendorff.

MONTAGU, M. F. A. See under Ashley-Montagu.

MOSSNER, E. C., *The Life of David Hume*, London, 1954.

MOWAT, R. B., *The Age of Reason: the Continent of Europe in the Eighteenth Century*, London, 1934.

MUNZ, PETER, *Problems of Religious Knowledge*, London, 1959.

— 'Historical Understanding' in *PQ*, Vol. 3, No. 12, July 1953.

NAMIER, SIR LEWIS B., 'History' in *Avenues of History*, London, 1952.

NIEBUHR, H. RICHARD, *The Meaning of Revelation*, New York, 1941.

NIEBUHR, REINHOLD, *Beyond Tragedy: Essays on the Christian Interpretation of History*, New York, 1937.

— *The Nature and Destiny of Man: a Christian Interpretation*, Gifford Lectures, 2 vols., New York, 1941 and 1943; one-vol. ed., 1949.

— *The Irony of American History*, New York, 1952.
— *The Self and the Dramas of History*, New York, 1955.
NIEBUHR, RICHARD R., *Resurrection and Historical Reason: a Study of Theological Method*, New York, 1957.
NIETZSCHE, FRIEDRICH, 'Vom Nutzen und Nachtheil der Historie für das Leben' in *Unzeitgemässe Betrachtungen* (1873–76); published separately, the Sammlung Birkhäuser, Basel, n.d., *circa* 1950.
NINEHAM, D. E., 'Eye-Witness Testimony and the Gospel Tradition' in *JTS*, NS, in three sections; I, Vol. IX, Part I, April 1958, 13–25; II, Vol. IX, Part II, Oct. 1958, 243–52; III, Vol. XI, Part II, Oct. 1960, 253–64.
NORDAU, MAX, *The Interpretation of History*, ET by M. A. Hamilton, London, 1910.
NORTH, C. R., *The Old Testament Interpretation of History*, London, 1946.

OAKESHOTT, MICHAEL, *Experience and its Modes*, CUP, 1933.
— 'The Activity of Being an Historian' in *Historical Studies*, I, ed. T. Desmond Williams, London and Cork, 1958.
— *Rationalism in Politics and Other Essays*, London, 1962 (also includes 'The Activity of Being an Historian').
OGDEN, SCHUBERT M., *Existence and Faith: Shorter Writings of Rudolf Bultmann*, translated with introduction, New York, 1960; London, 1961.
— *Christ without Myth*, London, 1962.
OMAN, SIR CHARLES, *On the Writing of History*, London, 1939
OTT, HEINRICH, *Geschichte und Heilsgeschichte in der Theologie Rudolf Bultmanns*, Tübingen, 1955.
— *Denken und Sein: der Weg Martin Heideggers und der Weg der Theologie*, Zollikon-Zürich, 1959.
— *Die Frage nach dem historischen Jesus und die Ontologie der Geschichte*, Zollikon-Zürich, 1960.
OWEN, H. P., *Revelation and Existence: a Study in the Theology of Rudolf Bultmann*, Univ. of Wales Press, Cardiff, 1957.

PANNENBERG, WOLFHART, 'Heilsgeschehen und Geschichte' in *Kerygma und Dogma*, V, 1959.
— and others, *Offenbarung als Geschichte* (*Kerygma und Dogma* Beihefte), Göttingen, 1961.
PARES, RICHARD, *The Historian's Business and Other Essays*, OUP, 1961.
PARKIN, CHARLES, *The Moral Basis of Burke's Political Thought*, CUP, 1956.

PATTISON, MARK, *Essays*, ed. H. Nettleship, 2 vols., OUP, 1889.
— *Isaac Casaubon, 1559–1614*, London, 1875 and 1892.
PEARDON, T. P., *The Transition in English Historical Writing, 1760–1830*, Columbia Univ. Press, New York, 1933.
PERRY, MICHAEL C., *The Easter Enigma: an Essay on the Resurrection with special reference to the Data of Psychical Research*, with an introduction by Austin Farrer, London, 1959.
PFLEIDERER, OTTO, *Development of German Theology since Kant*, New York, 1890.
PIPER, OTTO, *God in History*, New York, 1939.
PLATNAUER, MAURICE, ed., *Fifty Years of Classical Scholarship*, OUP, 1954.
POLANYI, MICHAEL, *Personal Knowledge: Towards a Post-Critical Philosophy*, London and Chicago, 1958.
POMEAU, RENÉ, *La religion de Voltaire*, Nizet, 1956.
POPKIN, RICHARD H., *The History of Scepticism from Erasmus to Descartes* (Wijsgerige Teksten en Studies), Assen, Van Gorcum, 1960.
POPPER, KARL R., *The Open Society and its Enemies*, 2 vols., London, 1945; 4th ed., 1962.
— *The Poverty of Historicism*, London, 1957.
PORTEOUS, NORMAN W., 'Old Testament Theology' in H. H. Rowley, q.v.
POWICKE, SIR F. M., *Modern Historians and the Study of History: Essays and Papers*, London, 1955.
PRESTIGE, G. L., *God in Patristic Thought*, London, 1936.
— *Fathers and Heretics*, Bampton Lectures for 1940, London, 1940.

RAD, GERHARD VON, *Old Testament Theology*, I, 'The Theology of Israel's Historical Traditions', ET by D. M. G. Stalker, Edinburgh, 1962.
RAMSEY, IAN T., *Religious Language: an Empirical Placing of Theological Phrases*, London, 1957.
— ed., *Locke's Reasonableness of Christianity*, London, 1958.
RANTZAU, JOHANN ALBRECHT VON, 'The Glorification of the State in German Historical Writing' in Hans Kohn, q.v.
RAWLINSON, A. E. J., *The New Testament Doctrine of Christ*, Bampton Lectures for 1926, London, 1926.
— *Christ in the Gospels*, OUP, 1944.
REICKE, BO, 'Incarnation and Exaltation: the Historic Jesus and the Kerygmatic Christ' in *Interpretation*, XVI, No. 2, April 1962.
RENIER, G. J., *History, its Purpose and Method*, London, 1950.

RICHARDSON, ALAN, *Miracle Stories of the Gospels,* London, 1941.
— *Christian Apologetics,* London, 1947.
— *Introduction to the Theology of the New Testament,* London, 1958.
— *The Bible in the Age of Science,* London, 1961.
RICKMAN, H. P., *Meaning in History: W. Dilthey's Thoughts on History and Society,* London, 1961.
RISTOW, HELMUT, and MATTHIAE, KARL, eds., *Der historische Jesus und der kerygmatische Christus,* Berlin, 1960; contains essays by forty-eight New Testament scholars.
RITTER, GETHARD, 'The German Professors in the Third Reich' in *The Review of Politics,* VIII, No. 2, 1946, 242–54.
— 'Die Fälschung des deutschen Geschichtsbildes im Hitlerreich' in *Deutsche Rundschau,* LXX, No. 4, 1947, 11–20.
ROBERTS, T. A., *History and Christian Apologetic,* London, 1960.
ROBINSON, H. WHEELER, *Redemption and Revelation in the Actuality of History,* London, 1942.
— *Inspiration and Revelation in the Old Testament,* OUP, 1946.
ROBINSON, JAMES M., *A New Quest of the Historical Jesus,* SBT, London, 1959.
ROCKWOOD, RAYMOND O., ed., *Carl Becker's Heavenly City Revisited,* a Symposium, Cornell Univ. Press, Ithaca, N.Y., 1958.
ROWLEY, H. H., ed., *The Old Testament and Modern Study: a Generation of Discovery and Research,* OUP, 1951.
ROWSE, A. L., *The Use of History,* London, 1946.
RUST, E. C., *The Christian Understanding of History,* London, 1946.

SABINE, GEORGE H., *A History of Political Theory,* London, 1939.
SANDERS, E. K., *Jacques Bénigne Bossuet,* London, 1921.
SANDYS, SIR JOHN EDWIN, *A History of Classical Scholarship,* 3 vols., CUP, 1906–8.
SANTILLANA, G. DE, *The Crime of Galileo,* London, 1958.
— Introduction to Galileo's *Dialogue on the Great World Systems* (the Salusbury Translation), Chicago, 1953.
SARKISSIAN, A. O., ed., *Studies in Diplomatic History and Historiography in Honour of G. P. Gooch,* London, 1961.
SCHWARTZ, EDOUARD, *Griechische Geschichtsschreiber* (Kommission für spätantiker Religionsgeschichte bei der Deutschen Akademie der Wissenschaften zu Berlin), Leipzig, 1957.
SCHWEITZER, ALBERT, *The Quest of the Historical Jesus: a Critical Study of its Progress,* ET, London, 1910, of *Von Reimarus zu Wrede,* Tübingen, 1906.
SÉE, HENRI, *Science et philosophie de l'histoire,* 2nd ed. revised, Paris, 1933.

SELIGMAN, EDWIN R. A., *The Economic Interpretation of History*, Columbia Univ. Press, New York: Columbia Paperbacks, 1962.

SHOTWELL, JAMES T., *An Introduction to the History of History*, Columbia Univ. Press, New York, 1922.

SIMPSON, C. A., 'An Inquiry into the Biblical Theology of History' in *JTS*, NS, XII, Part I, April 1961.

SMITH, CHARLOTTE WATKINS, *Carl Becker: on History and the Climate of Opinion*, Cornell Univ. Press, Ithaca, N.Y., 1956.

SMITH, R. GREGOR, J. G. *Hamann, 1730–1788: a Study in Christian Existence*, with selections from his writings, London, 1960 (esp. pp. 88–102).

SMYTH, CHARLES, 'Christianity and the Secular Myths' in *Theology*, LII, No. 352, Oct. 1949, 368–74.

SNYDER, P. L., ed., *Detachment and the Writing of History*, Cornell Univ. Press, Ithaca, N.Y., 1958; OUP, 1959.

SORLEY, W. R., *A History of English Philosophy*, CUP, 1920.

SOCIAL SCIENCE RESEARCH COUNCIL (230, Park Av., New York, 17), A Report of the Committee on Historiography: *The Social Sciences in Historical Study*, Bulletin 64, 1954.
See also under Beard.

SPENGLER, OSWALD, *The Decline of the West*, London, 1926–9; ET by C. F. Atkinson of *Der Untergang des Abendlandes*, I, 1918; II, 1922.

SPINK, J. S., *French Free-Thought from Gassendi to Voltaire*, London, 1960.

SPRIGGE, C. J. S., *Benedetto Croce: Man and Thinker*, CUP, 1952.

ST AUBYN. See Aubyn.

STARK, W., *Montesquieu: Pioneer of the Sociology of Knowledge*, London, 1960.

STEPHEN, SIR LESLIE, *History of English Thought in the Eighteenth Century*, 1876; 3rd ed., New York, 1949.

STERN, FRITZ, *The Varieties of History: from Voltaire to the Present* (selected passages), New York and London, 1957.

STROMBERG, R. N., *Religious Liberalism in Eighteenth-century England*, OUP, 1954.

STROUT, CUSHING, *The Pragmatic Revolt in American History: Carl Becker and Charles Beard*, Yale Univ. Press, New Haven, 1958.

SWABEY, MARIE COLLINS, *The Judgment of History*, New York, 1954.

SYKES, NORMAN, *Man as Churchman*, CUP, 1960.

SYME, SIR RONALD, *Tacitus*, 2 vols., OUP, 1958.

TALMON, J. L., *The Origins of Totalitarian Democracy*, London, 1953.

TAVARD, G. H., *Paul Tillich and the Christian Message*, London, 1962.

TAYLOR, A. E., *David Hume and the Miraculous*, CUP, 1927.

— *The Faith of a Moralist*, 2 vols., London, 1930 (esp. Vol. II, chap. IV, 150–96).

TEGGART, FREDERICK J., *Theory and Processes of History*, Univ. of California Press, Los Angeles, 1960.

TEMPERLEY, HAROLD W. V., *Research and Modern History*, London, 1930.

— 'The Historical Ideas of J. B. Bury' in J. B. Bury, *Selected Essays*, q.v.

THOMPSON, A. HAMILTON, *Gibbon* (Historical Association Series), London, 1941.

THOMPSON, JAMES WESTFALL (with the collaboration of Bernard J. Holm), *A History of Historical Writing*, 2 vols., I, From Earliest Times to the End of the Seventeenth Century; II, The Eighteenth and Nineteenth Centuries, New York, 1942.

TILLICH, PAUL, *The Interpretation of History*, New York, 1936.

— *Systematic Theology*, I, London, 1953; II, London, 1957.

TILLYARD, E. M. W., *The Elizabethan World Picture*, London, 1943.

TOULMIN, S. E., and GOODFIELD, J., *The Fabric of the Heavens*, London, 1961.

TOYNBEE, SIR ARNOLD J., *A Study of History*, 10 vols., OUP, 1934–54; cf. esp. the section 'The Quest for a Meaning behind the Facts of History' (Vol. X, 126–44).

— *A Study of History*: abridgement by D. C. Somervell, 2 vols., London, 1946, 1957.

— *An Historian's Approach to Religion*, London, 1956. See also under Ashley-Montagu.

TROELTSCH, ERNST, art. 'Historiography' in *Hastings's Encyclopaedia of Religion and Ethics*, VI, 716ff., Edinburgh, 1913.

— *Der Historismus und seine Probleme*. Buch 1: *Das logische Problem der Geschichtsphilosophie*; Neudruck der Ausgabe 1922, Aalen, 1961. (Gesammelte Schriften, 3.)

TULLOCH, JOHN, *Rational Theology and Christian Philosophy in England in the Seventeenth Century*, 2 vols., Edinburgh, 1872.

ULLMANN, RICHARD K., *Between God and History: The Human situation exemplified in Quaker thought and practice*, London and New York, 1959.

VOGT, JOSEPH, *Geschichte des Altertums und Universalgeschichte*, Stuttgart, 1957.

— *Wege zum historischen Universum: von Ranke bis Toynbee*, Stuttgart, 1961.

VRIEZEN, TH. C., *An Outline of Old Testament Theology*, ET, London, 1949.

WALSH, P. G., *Livy: his Historical Aims and Methods*, Cambridge, 1961.

WALSH, W. H., *An Introduction to the Philosophy of History*, London, 1951.
— 'The Limits of Scientific History' in *Historical Studies*, III, ed. James Hogan, London and Cork, 1961.

WEBB, CLEMENT C. J., *Studies in the History of Natural Theology*, OUP, 1915.
— *The Historical Element in Religion*, OUP, 1935.

WEBER, ALFRED, *Farewell to European History, or The Conquest of Nihilism*, ET by R. F. C. Hall, London, 1947.

WEBSTER, SIR CHARLES, *Art and Practice of Diplomacy*, London, 1961.

WEDGWOOD, C. V., *Truth and Opinion*, London, 1960.

WELLS, H. G., *Outline of History*, 1920.

WESTON, JOHN C., Jr., 'Edmund Burke's View of History' in *The Review of Politics*, Univ. of Notre Dame Press, Indiana, XXIII, No. 2, April 1961, 203–29.

WHITEHEAD, A. N., *Science and the Modern World*, London, 1926.

WIDGERY, ALBAN G., *Interpretations of History: Confucius to Toynbee*, London, 1961.

WILAMOVITZ-MOELLENDORFF, ULRICH VON, *Greek Historical Writing, and Apollo*, ET by Gilbert Murray, OUP, 1908.

WILKINS, BURLEIGH TAYLOR, *Carl Becker: a Biographical Study in American Intellectual History*, Cambridge, Mass., 1961.

WILLEY, BASIL, *The Seventeenth Century Background*, London, 1934.
— *The Eighteenth Century Background: Studies on the Idea of Nature in the Thought of the Period*, London, 1940.
— *Nineteenth Century Studies: Coleridge to Matthew Arnold*, London, 1949.
— *More Nineteenth Century Studies: a Group of Honest Doubters*, London, 1956.

WILLIAMS, C. H., *The Modern Historian*, London, 1938.

WITT-HANSEN, J., *Historical Materialism, the Method, the Theories*: Book I, The Method, Copenhagen, 1960.

WOODWARD, SIR E. L., *British Historians*, London, 1943.

WOOLLCOMBE, K. J. See Lampe.

WRIGHT, G. ERNEST, *The Old Testament against its Environment*, SBT, London, 1950.
— *God Who Acts: Biblical Theology as Recital*, SBT, London, 1962.

YOUNG, G. M., *Gibbon*, London, 1932.

ZAHRNT, HEINZ, *The Historical Jesus*, London, 1963, ET by J. S. Bowden of *Es begann mit Jesus von Nazareth*, Stuttgart, 1960.

ZEEDEN, ERNST WALTER, 'Der Historiker als Kritiker und Prophet: die Kritik des 19 Jahrhunderts im Urteil Jacob Burckhardts' in *Die Welt als Geschichte*, XI, 1951, No. 3, 154–73.

INDEX OF NAMES

Acton, Lord J. E. E. D., 33, 35n., 65n., 105n., 106, 114, 160, 166, 172f., 176, 250–2
Adams, J. C., 210, 212
Addison, Joseph, 273
Aeschylus, 158
Alaric the Goth, 55
Albertus Magnus, 70n.
Alembert, J. le R.d', 18, 90, 93
Alexander the Great, 62
Alfred, King, 24n.
Allen, Don Cameron, 9f.
Althaus, Paul, 130
Anderson, Bernhard W., 223n.
Anderson, Hugh, 148n.
Anne, Queen, 98n.
Annet, Peter, 45
Aquinas, 21, 27, 70n., 74f., 252f.
Aristotle, 21, 57, 66, 71, 73–77, 97, 158
Arnold, Matthew, 252n.
Arnold, Thomas, 169–72
Aron, Raymond, 287n.
Arthur, King, 30
Ashton, J. F., 189n.
Astruc, Jean, 118
Athanasius, St, 23, 67
Aubyn, Giles St, 113n.
Augustine, St, 23n., 55–64, 66n., 67, 188, 265, 287
Augustus, Caesar, 41, 283
Aulard, Adolphe, 49n.
Ayer, A. J., 267

Baab, O. G., 233n.
Bacon, Francis 31, 42, 47
Baillie, D. M., 61n., 128n.
Baillie, John, 28n., 120n.
Baker, Herschel, 31n.
Baker, Sir Richard, 32
Bampton, John, 13–15, 17, 47
Barker, Sir Ernest, 166n.
Barnes, Harry Elmer, 204n.

Baronius, Caesare, 33f.
Barr, James, 57n.
Barraclough, G., 43n., 175, 267f.
Barrett, C. Kingsley, 237
Barth, Karl, 120n., 122n., 126, 131f., 134–8, 140, 149n., 172, 207, 264, 290n.
Bartsch, H.-W., 137n., 140n., 147n.
Bayle, Pierre, 25f., 43n., 85, 88, 96, 268
Beard, C. A., 117n., 191n., 205, 216n.
Becker, Carl, 17, 28n., 50, 53, 63, 93n., 100n., 103n., 173–5, 177, 191–3, 194n., 195, 201–5, 212, 216n., 243, 247, 250–4, 256–8
Bede, the Venerable, 65, 278
Bellarmine, Cardinal, 70n.
Beller, E. A., 88n.
Benda, Jules, 242n.
Bentham, Jeremy, 168
Bentley, Richard, 19, 25, 42f.
Bergin, T. G., 96n.
Bergson, H., 245
Berkeley, Bishop George, 47
Berlin, Sir Isaiah, 107n., 160n., 292n.
Bernard, St, 67
Beveridge, Lord, 246
Beyschlag, W., 123n.
Bismarck, Otto von, 175–8, 180, 222, 235
Black, J. B., 97n., 98n., 100n.
Bloch, Marc, 39, 170n., 189n., 278n.
Bochart, Samuel, 87
Bodley, Sir Thomas, 37
Bolgar, R. R., 278n.
Bolingbroke, Viscount (Henry St John), 22n., 26, 35, 38, 46n., 86f., 92, 98n., 285n.
Bolland, John, 40

Bolton, Edmund, 30n.
Boman, Thorleif, 59n., 68n.
Bonaventura, St, 70n.
Bonhoeffer, D., 81n.
Bornkamm, Günther, 121, 124, 132, 146, 148, 190, 196, 198n., 209f.
Bosanquet, B., 291
Bossuet, J. B., 24f., 80, 85, 91, 97f., 138, 171
Boswell, James, 84n.
Bousset, W., 128, 139, 265
Bowle, John, 111n., 245n., 252, 266n., 292n.
Boyle, Sir Robert, 19, 30n., 42, 76n., 165
Bradley, F. H., 189n., 192, 194n., 288, 291
Brady, Robert, 86
Braithwaite, R. B., 285n.
Broad, C. D., 45n., 275n.
Bronowski, J., 48n.
Brumfitt, J. H., 25n., 43n., 91n., 96, 97n.
Buchdahl, Gerd, 19n.
Buckle, H. T., 105f., 113f., 116, 169, 179, 277n., 292
Buffon, G. L. L., 97n.
Bull, George, 34
Bunyan, John, 25n.
Burckhardt, Jakob, 77n., 156, 172, 178–83, 244
Burghley, Lord, 37
Burke, Edmund, 22n., 105, 150, 166–9, 171, 174, 184, 288
Burnet, Gilbert, 39f.
Burrows, Millar, 233n.
Bury, J. B., 56n., 63f., 105, 108f., 284n.
Butler, Joseph, 21, 27, 45f., 49, 273, 275
Butterfield, Herbert, 18n., 33n., 43n., 73, 77n., 78n., 79n., 90n., 107n., 119n., 159, 162n., 166, 173n., 276n., 277n., 278n.

Caird, Edward, 41n., 111n., 291
Cajetan, Thomas, 70n.

Calmet, Antoine, 24
Camden, William, 37
Campenhausen, H. von, 212n.
Caponigri, A. R., 96n.
Carlyle, Thomas, 97f.
Carpenter, J. Estlin, 119n., 122n.
Carr, E. H., 51–53, 98n., 104n., 110n., 117n., 138, 160n., 174n., 215, 267
Carr, H. Wildon, 164n.
Casaubon, Isaac, 34
Cassirer, Ernst, 43n., 88n., 116n., 117
Catherine de' Medici, 159
Cato, M. Porcius, 280n.
Celeste, Sister Maria, 76n.
Chadwick, H., 28n., 95n., 120n.
Chamberlain, H. S., 244
Chambers, E. K., 168
Charlemagne, 38
Chastellux, F.-J., 93n.
Cherbury, Lord Herbert of, 27
Chesterfield, Earl of, 38, 87
Childe, V. Gordon, 292n.
Cicero, 61, 281
Claggett, Marshall, 77n.
Clarendon, Earl of (Edward Hyde), 40f.
Clark, Sir G. N., 19, 31n., 40, 41n., 78n., 95n., 106n., 250n.
Clarke, Samuel, 22
Cleopatra, 98n.
Cobban, Alfred B. C., 41n., 51, 53, 90, 92, 117n., 168n., 216
Cochrane, C. N., 61
Cohen, J. M., 83n.
Coleridge, S. T., 105n., 150, 168f., 171, 288
Collingwood, R. G., 57, 162–6, 184, 189, 191f., 287n.
Collins, Anthony, 25, 273f.
Commynes, 105
Comte, Auguste, 109–12, 292
Condillac, E. B. de, 51
Condorcet, Marquis de, 55, 94
Conzelmann, Hans, 238
Copernicus, 19, 42f., 77, 284n.
Cortés, Hernando, 158

Cotton, Sir Robert, 37
Coverley, Sir Walter de, 32
Cowper, William, 273n.
Cragg, G. R., 47n.
Creighton, Mandel, 117n., 160n.
Croce, Benedetto, 160–6, 179n.,
    184, 191f., 287n.
Cullmann, Oscar, 134n., 234n.

d'Alembert, see Alembert
Darwin, Sir Charles, 32n., 97
Daube, D., 147n.
Davies, Godfrey, 35n.
Davies, Sir John, 80
Davies, W. D., 147n.
Davis, Herbert, 35n., 278n.
Dawson, Christopher, 55
Dehio, Ludwig, 175n.
Dentan, R.C., 233n.
Descartes, René, 19, 22, 26, 42,
    47, 76n., 82–85, 96
De Wette, W. M. L., 119
d'Holbach, see under Holbach
Diderot, Denis, 18, 22n., 51, 90,
    93, 94n.
Diem, Hermann, 126n., 147n.
Dilthey, Wilhelm, 117, 162f., 166,
    288
Dionysius the Areopagite, 70n.
Dionysius of Halicarnassus, 87n.
Dodd, C. H., 196n., 237
Douglas, David C., 37n., 84n.
Drake, Stillman, 76n.
Dray, William, 117n., 162n.,
    213n., 217n.
Drews, Arthur, 207
Droysen, J. G., 177
Dru, Alexander, 178, 179n., 180n.
Dryden, John, 73n., 91n.
Duchesne, Louis, 33n.
Dugdale, Sir William, 38

Ebeling, Gerhard, 198f.
Eichhorn, J. G., 119
Eichrodt, Walther, 218n., 230f.,
    232n., 233f.
Eliot, George, 121n.
Elizabeth I, Queen, 36, 225

Emmet, Dorothy M., 291n.
Empedocles, 71
Engels, F., 292n.
Erasmus, 179
Erigena, John Scotus, 70n.
Estlin Carpenter, J., 119n., 122n.
Eusebius of Caesarea, 23n., 64

Fairbairn, A. M., 128n.
Farrar, A. S., 47n.
Farrer, F. W., 123n.
Feigl, H., 115n.
Finberg, H. P. R., 20n., 35n.,
    43n., 116n.
Finley, M. I., 54, 57n.
Fisch, M. H., 96n.
Flacius, Matthias, 33
Flew, A. G. N., 188n., 189n.
Flint, R., 24n., 89n.
Foakes Jackson, F. J., 11n.
Fontenelle, B. le B. de, 90, 113,
    277n.
Forbes, Duncan, 105n., 169–71
Foster, M. B., 76n.
Fowler, W. Warde, 284n.
Fraenkel, P., 132n.
Freud, S., 48
Fridrichsen, A., 223n.
Fuchs, Ernst, 146, 148n., 150n.
Fueter, Éduard, 166, 265n., 266n.
Fulton, J. S., 270n.
Fussner, F. Smith, 36n., 37n., 43n.

Galileo, 19, 43n., 76f., 108, 276n.,
    277
Galle, J. G., 210
Gardiner, Patrick, 117n., 142n.,
    161n.
Gardiner, S. R., 101n.
Gasquet, Cardinal F. A., 251n.
Gatterer, J. C., 119
George I, King, 278n.
Geyl, Pieter, 106f., 167n., 177, 244
Gibbon, Edward, 40, 44, 92f., 99,
    103, 164, 167, 187, 228
Gibson, Edmund, 36n.
Ginsberg, Morris, 112n.
Glanvill, Joseph, 252n.

Godsey, John D., 82n.
Goethe, J. W. von, 178, 182
Gollwitzer, Helmut, 147n.
Gooch, G. P., 49n., 56n., 105, 169, 171n.
Goodfield, June, 69n.
Goodspeed, D. J., 117n.
Gordon, Cyrus H., 255
Gottschalk, L., 251n.
Grant, A. J., 31n.
Green, T. H., 291
Griffith, G. T., 54n.
Grote, George, 105, 111n., 112, 114, 169, 174n.
Guerlac, Henry, 22n.
Guicciardini, Franscesco, 279f.
Gunkel, H., 128

Halévy, Daniel, 167n.
Hall, A. R., 20n.
Hall, Basil, 106n.
Hallam, H., 105, 169
Haller, W., 31n.
Hammond, Henry, 34
Hampshire, Stuart, 161n.
Hannibal, 211
Hare, J. C., 169
Harley, Robert, first Earl of Oxford, 37f., 86
Harnack, Adolf von, 122, 128, 140, 144
Harrelson, W., 223n.
Hart, H. St J., 168n.
Hay, Denys, 64n., 255n.
Hayter, Sir William, 265n., 267f.
Hazard, Paul, 49, 53f., 95n., 96, 118n., 120n.
Hearne, Thomas, 38, 86
Hebert, A. G., 147, 233n., 287n.
Hegel, G. W. F., 55, 121, 244, 290-2
Heidegger, Martin, 144n., 149, 293
Heitmüller, W., 128
Helvétius, C. A., 51
Hempel, C. G., 115n.
Henderson, Ian, 144n.
Herbert, George, 260
Herder, J. G., 55, 289, 290n.

Herodotus, 54, 59, 280
Herring, Archbishop, 99
Herrmann, W., 122
Hexter, J. H., 228n.
Hickes, George, 38, 86
Hitler, A., 51, 176
Hobbes, Thomas, 20n., 22, 26, 48n., 82, 85f., 96
Hobsbawm, E. J., 186n.
Hodges, H. A., 56n., 162n.
Hofer, Walther, 175n., 183n.
Holbach, P. H. D. von, 22n., 51
Holbein, 179
Holtzmann, H. J., 123n.
Hook, Sidney, 117n., 216n., 292n.
Hooker, Richard, 261
Hort, F. J. A., 25, 172
Hoskyns, Sir Edwyn, 126n.
Huet, Bishop Pierre Daniel, 39
Hulme, T. E., 129, 245n.
Hume, David, 17, 26, 43f., 47, 91, 99-103, 118, 157, 185, 187-9, 195f., 208f., 216, 288

Iago, 74
Iremonger, F. A., 291n.

Jackson, F. J. Foakes, 11n.
Jacob, Edmond, 227, 232n.
James, D. G., 86n.
Jay, E. G., 75n.
Jeremias, Joachim, 147n.
Johnson, A. R., 128n.
Johnson, Samuel, 84
Jones, R. F., 36n.
Josephus, 23
Jowett, Benjamin, 281
Justin Martyr, 59n.

Kähler, Martin, 130n.
Kant, Immanuel, 191, 288f.
Käsemann, Ernst, 146
Keim, Th., 123n.
Kelly, J. N. D., 256n.
Kepler, J., 19, 71, 76n.
Kierkegaard, S., 125-7, 291
Kingsley, Charles, 98
Klibansky, R., 85n.

Knight, G. A. F., 221f., 232n.
Knowles, David, 160n.
Knowling, R. J., 122n.
Knox, John, 189n.
Knox, R. A., 94
Köhler, L., 233n.
Kohn, Hans, 175n., 178
Kümmel, W. G., 142n., 147

La Mothe le Vayer, 89
Lampe, G. W. H., 218n.
Lamprecht, Karl, 116
Law, William, 46, 48
Lawton, J. S., 45n., 274n.
Leavis, F. R., 93n.
Lee, M. du P., 88n.
Leibnitz, G. W., 47
Lenin, V. I., 243n.
Leonardo da Vinci, 276n.
Leslie, Charles, 274
Lessing, G. E., 28, 55, 95, 118–21, 125f., 148, 290ff.
Lessing, Theodor, 244n.
Leverrier, U. J. J., 210, 212
Levy-Bruhl, L., 84
Lewes, G. H., 111n.
Liebeschutz, Hans, 177n.
Lightfoot, John, 24f., 42
Lightfoot, Bishop J. B., 25, 172
Lightfoot, R. H., 211n.
Lilley, A. L., 78n.
Lipsius, Justus, 24, 39
Livy, Titus, 24n., 35, 62, 64, 228, 277n., 279f., 282f.
Locke, John, 19–21, 27, 47, 51, 86, 273
Lods, A., 118n.
Louis XIV, 18, 98, 114, 179
Lovejoy, Arthur O., 9f., 11, 70n., 167n., 169n.
Lowes, J. L., 73n.
Löwith, Karl, 24n., 59n., 94, 179n.
Lucas, J. R., 155n.
Lucretius, 161n.
Lundsteen, A. C., 118
Luther, Martin, 27, 173, 177, 202f.
Lyell, Sir Charles, 97

Mabillon, Jean, 32, 35, 39, 41f., 83, 105, 109
Macaulay, Lord T. B., 105f., 169
McDonald, A. H., 281n.
McGregor, Craig, 246n.
Machiavelli, 279f.
McIntyre, John, 130f.
Macmurray, John, 115n.
Macquarrie, John, 144n., 293n.
Madox, Thomas, 38
Malebranche, N., 84f.
Malevez, L., 144n.
Mandelbaum, M., 250n.
Manson, T. W., 147n.
Marlborough, Duchess of, 98n.
Marlowe, Christopher, 72
Marsham, Sir John, 87
Martin, Alfred von, 179n.
Martineau, Harriet, 111n.
Marx, Karl, 48, 55, 108, 112, 292
Mascall, E. L., 67n., 76n.
Matthiae, Karl, 147n.
Mazlish, B., 48n.
Mazzeo, J. A., 31n.
Meinecke, Friedrich, 175n., 176, 177n., 181f.
Michaelis, J. D., 118
Michelet, Jules, 77n., 91n., 112, 114, 167n.
Middleton, Conyers, 43f.
Milburn, R. L. P., 24n.
Mill, James, 105, 106n., 169
Mill, J. S., 93n., 104n., 110n., 168
Milton, John, 31, 80, 225
Moellendorff, U. von Wilamo-vitz-, 54, 57n.
Momigliano, A., 277n.
Mommsen, Theodor, 174n., 281
Monmouth, Geoffrey de, 30
Montaigne, Michel de, 83
Montesquieu, C. L. de S., 51, 89f., 95, 97, 98n., 99, 103
Montfaucon, Bernard de, 39
More, Sir Thomas, 280
Moses, 24f., 85
Mossner, E. C., 99n., 101n.
Muirhead, J. H., 168n.
Muratori, L. A., 40, 92

Murray, Gilbert, 54n.
Mussolini, B., 245

Newman, J. H., 45n.
Newton, Sir Isaac, 19, 20–24, 27,
  32, 42, 51, 73n., 76n., 80, 112f.,
  175, 273f., 280
Newton, John, 67n.
Nicolson, Harold, 186n.
Nicolson, William, 36n.
Niebuhr, B. G., 169, 171
Niebuhr, Reinhold, 59n., 127n.,
  247, 292n.
Nietzsche, Friedrich, 179n., 244
Nineham, D. E., 189n., 196n.

Oakeshott, Michael, 47, 117n.,
  160n., 161n.
Ogden, Schubert M., 139n., 141n.,
  145
Origen, 60
Orosius, 23n., 64, 265
Orwell, George, 243n.
Ott, Heinrich, 137n., 144n.
Owen, H. P., 144n.

Parker, Archbishop Matthew, 36f.
Parkin, Charles, 168n.
Pascal, Blaise, 19, 76n., 98n.
Paton, H. J., 85n.
Pattison, Mark, 21, 28, 34f., 112–
  14, 121
Paulus, H. E. G., 120
Pearson, Bishop John, 34
Pedersen, J., 287n.
Pericles, 41, 174
Petavius, D. (Petau), 70n., 87
Pfleiderer, O., 122n.
Phillips, Godfrey E., 233n.
Platnauer, M., 281n.
Plato, 60, 69, 73f., 158, 253
Pliny, the Younger, 282n.
Plotinus, 73
Polanyi, Michael, 159n.
Pollard, A. F., 156, 228
Polybius, 54, 60–62, 102, 280–2,
  283n., 284
Pope, Alexander, 27n., 35, 285
Popper, Karl, 104n., 114–16, 244n.

Porteous, Norman W., 229n., 230,
  231n., 232n.
Powicke, F. M., 29n., 32n.
Prestige, G. L., 67
Procksch, O., 231n., 232n.
Protagoras, 158
Pseudo-Dionysius, 70f., 74
Ptolemy of Alexandria, 69, 73,
  158
Pyrrho, 88n.

Rad, Gerhard von, 220, 232n., 233
Raleigh, Sir Walter, 25n., 280
Ramsey, Ian T., 21n., 225n.
Rancé, Amand de, 39
Ranke, Leopold von, 30, 63n.,
  92f., 100, 104, 107n., 108–10,
  119, 172–8, 180–2, 184, 247,
  290
Rantzau, J. A. von, 181n.
Raven, C. E., 76n.
Ray, John, 76n.
Raymond of Sebonde, 75
Reicke, Bo, 239n., 240
Reimarus, H. S., 25, 118f.
Reitzenstein, R., 128
Renan, E., 123
Richardson, Alan, 82n., 109n.,
  121n., 132n., 134n., 142n.,
  174n., 220n., 239n., 248n.
Rickman, H. P., 162n.
Riley, Athelstan, 70n.
Ristow, Helmut, 147n.
Ritschl, Albrecht, 122, 172, 291
Roberts, Michael, 251n.
Robinson, Edward, 293n.
Robinson, James M., 139n.,
  140n., 145, 147n., 149n., 150–3
Robinson, H. Wheeler, 230, 232n.
Rockwood, Raymond O., 22n.,
  191n.
Rosenberg, Alfred, 178, 244
Ross, W. D., 57n.
Rousseau, J.-J., 28n., 49, 51, 93n.,
  167f.
Rowley, H. H., 128n., 229n.,
  233n.
Ryle, Gilbert, 10n., 263n., 267

Sabine, G. H., 245n.
Sahlin, Harold, 223n.
Saint-Real, Abbé de, 89n.
Sanders, E. K., 85n.
Sandys, Sir J. E., 39n.
Santillana, G. de, 76n.
Sarrailh, Jean, 51n.
Savile, Sir Henry, 278n.
Scaliger, J. J., 24, 39, 42, 87
Schirach, Baldur von, 178
Schleiermacher, F. D. E., 121, 126, 169n.
Schlözer, J. G., 119
Schnabel, Franz, 175n.
Schweitzer, Albert, 118, 124, 129, 139
Scott, Sir Walter, 105
Secker, Archbishop Thomas, 46
Seeley, Sir John, 123n.
Seifert, F., 116n.
Sellars, W., 115n.
Semler, J. S., 119
Shakespeare, W., 72n., 73n.
Sherley-Price, Leo, 65n.
Sherlock, Bishop Thomas, 196, 273f.
Sidney, Sir Philip, 38n.
Simon, Richard, 85
Sira, Ben, 38
Smalley, Beryl, 65n.
Smith, Adam, 17
Smith, Charlotte Watkins, 191n., 201n., 202n., 250n.
Smith, Lacey Baldwin, 186n.
Smyth, Charles, 245
Socrates, 54, 60, 72
Sorel, Georges, 245, 248
Sorley, W. R., 43n., 273n.
Soustelle, Jacques, 159n.
Spelman, Sir Henry, 37
Spencer, Herbert, 111
Spengler, Oswald, 266, 287
Spinoza, 47, 85
Sprigge, C. J. S., 164
St Aubyn, Giles, 113n.
Stalin, J., 51, 243n.
Stanley, A. P., 169
Stark, W., 90n., 99n.

Stephen, Leslie, 44n., 275
Stillingfleet, Bishop Edward, 34
Stirling, J. H., 41n.
Stone, Archbishop, 99
Stow, John, 37
Stranks, C. J., 46n.
Strauss, D. F., 188n., 121, 126, 180
Stromberg, R. N., 45n., 46n.
Stubbs, Bishop William, 116n., 251n.
Suetonius, 24n.
Swenson, David F., 125n., 126n.
Swift, Dean, 35, 277n.
Sybel, H. von, 177
Syme, Sir Ronald, 280n.
Sykes, Norman, 39n.

Tacitus, 102, 277n., 279, 281-3
Taine, Hippolyte, 49, 91n., 116, 142, 190n.
Talmon, J. L., 50f., 95n.
Tavard, G. H., 131n.
Taylor, A. J. P., 56n.
Temperley, H. W. V., 250n.
Temple, Archbishop William, 291
Temple, Sir William, 35, 277n.
Terence, 157n.
Thirlwall, Bishop Connop, 169f.
Thomas, St, see Aquinas
Thucydides, 54, 57, 59f., 86, 283
Tillich, Paul, 127-32
Tillotson, Archbishop John, 21, 87
Tillyard, E. M. W., 10, 65n., 71, 72n., 80
Tindal, Matthew, 25n., 27, 45, 274f.
Tomassin, Père, 89
Toland, John, 45, 273f.
Toulmin, Stephen, 69n.
Tout, T. F., 116n.
Toynbee, Sir A. J., 244n., 247, 251n.
Treitschke, Heinrich von, 177, 178n.
Trevelyan, Sir G. M., 109n., 246, 251n.

Trevor-Roper, H. R., 51n., 101n.
Trotsky, Leo, 243
Tyrrell, George, 124
Tyrrell, James, 86

Ussher, Archbishop James, 24, 42, 80, 87

Valla, Lorenzo, 33n.
Vico, Giambattista, 95f., 103, 171
Vogel, Heinrich, 81n.
Vischer, Wilhelm, 232n.
Voltaire, 18, 24, 41, 51, 56, 91–98, 101, 103, 120, 179, 265, 278n.
Voysey, C., 118n.
Vriezen, Th. C., 229n., 232n.

Walsh, P. G., 282n , 283n.
Walsh, W. H., 107n., 109n., 117n., 287n., 289n.
Wanley, Humfrey, 38, 86f.
Warburton, William, 21, 100, 275
Warnock, G. J., 263n.
Waterland, Daniel, 275
Watts, Isaac, 67n., 273
Webb, C. C. J., 75n.
Webster, Sir Charles, 164
Wedel, T. O., 265n.
Weiser, Artur, 220, 232n.

Weiss, Bernhard, 123n.
Weiss, Johannes, 124
Wellhausen, J., 219
Wells, H. G., 175n., 266
Wesley, John, 45n., 46, 48
Westcott, Bishop B. F., 25, 172
Weston, John C., Jr., 168n.
Wette, W. M. L. De, 119
Whear, Degory, 279n.
Whiston, William, 22f.
Whitehead, A. N., 76n., 252
Wilamovitz-Moellendorff, see Moellendorff
Wilkins, Burleigh Taylor, 191n., 201n., 204n., 205n., 250n., 252n.
Willey, Basil, 10, 74n., 111n.
Witt-Hansen, J., 292n.
Woodward, Sir E. L., 36, 38n., 280n.
Woollcombe, K. J., 218n., 256n.
Woolston, Thomas, 25, 45, 274
Wootton, Lady Barbara, 109n., 112n.
Wright, G. Ernest, 219n., 220, 232n.

Xanthippe, 60
Xenophon, 54

Zahrnt, Heinz, 81

INDEX OF SUBJECTS

(Only the more important references are given)

Abstraction in modern thought, 81f.

Accident in history, 60f., 76, 98, 283

Age of Reason, 17n., 41–45, 273–6

Almagest, 73

'Ancient' and 'modern', 273, 277n., 278

'Anglican' School, The, 166–72

Antiquarianism, 170

Antiquaries, The, 35–38

Aristotelian-Ptolemaic system, 69–71

Aristotelian natural theology, 73–77

Art, History of, 179

Astrology, 73

Aufklärung, 41n.

Aztecs, 158f.

Battle of the Books, 277n.

Biblical criticism, 25, 41–44, 85, 118–22, 169f.

Cartesian attitude to history, 84–88

Causal explanation in history, 97–99, 152, 185–90, 195f., 209f., 213–17

Chain of Being, 69f., 289

Chalcedonian Formula, 151, 256

Chance, 60f., 76, 98, 283

China, 91f.

Civilization, History of, 92, 96, 179–81

Civitas Dei and *civitas terrena*, 61–64

Classical historiography, 54–62, 280–4

— naturalism, 59

— rationalism, 57

Cleopatra's Nose, 98n.

'Climate of Opinion', 201f., 205, 252

Compassion, 159, 181

Copernican revolution, 77

'Copernican revolutions' in historiography, 43n.

Covering law, 217

Critical philosophy of history, 192, 287, 293

Criticism, biblical; see Biblical

Culture and history, 179–81

Cyclical view of history, 55–61, 283f.

Deism, 21, 45, 273–6

Demythologizing of nature-myths, 56f., 219f.

— of the New Testament, 81, 143f.

Dialectic of history, 121, 290f.

Dialectical materialism, 292

Disclosure situations in history, 223–7

Dogmatics, The nature of, 261–4

Ecclesiastical history, 33–35

Education, New religion of, 270

Empathy, 162

Empiricism, 47, 101, 285

Encyclopaedia, The French, 18, 88

Enlightenment, the word, 41n.

Enlightenment, The, 41–45, 51, 90–99

— historiography, 90–103

Epicureanism, 283f.

Erudites, The, 29–41

Europe, European, 64, 255n., 267–9

Europeanization, 267–71

Evolution, Theory of, 97
Existentiale, existentielle, existentialism, 149f., 293
Existentialist hermeneutics, 147–53
Explanation in history, 57, 61, 97–99, 196f.
Experience, religious, 227–9
—, historical, 223–7, 262

Facts, 154–6, 190–4
Factors in history, 227–9
Faith, 132–5, 205, 208, 248f.
Fate, 57, 98, 210, 283
'Finger of God' as historical explanation, 25, 99, 138
Fortuna, Fortune, 60f., 283f.
French Revolution, 49f., 165f., 186, 214f.

Geisteswissenschaften, 162f.
Geschichte and *Historie; Geschichtlichkeit,* 150, 155
Generalization in history, 110, 117, 186, 214–17
Göttingen historians, The, 119
'Great Men', 97f., 160n.
Greek and Hebrew thought, 11f., 56–59
Greek historiography, 54–60, 280f.

Harmony, 73f.
Hayter Report, 265n., 267f.
Hegelianism, 290–2
Heilsgeschichte, 133–9, 220
Historein, 11n.
Historical experience; see Experience.
— explanation; see Causal; Explanation
— faith, 217–23.
— interpretation; see Interpretation
— myths; see Myth
— revolution, 12; see Revolutions in history
— theology, 254–64

Historical-mindedness, 12, 32, 58, 78n., 268
Historicism, the word, 104n., 115, 131n.; see also Positivism
Historie, 155n.
Historismus, 181
History, the word, 11, 59
— as scientific; see under Scientific History; Positivism
— as source of existential knowledge, 12, 57f., 148–51, 170n., 232
History of Religions School, 128f., 139f., 143, 207
Horse-shoe Nail theory, 98
Humane, humanity, 156–62, 179, 183, 278
Humanities, The, 156, 278n.
Humanism, Scientific, 110n., 278
Humanist, the word, 278n.
Humanist history, 29–32, 277–80
Humanity, Religion of, 110n.

Idealism, 163, 191f., 287, 291
Ideas, The History of, 9–11, 53
Ideological myths, 248f.
Ideology, 107f., 174, 183
Impartiality in history, 99–102, 191–4, 200–5
Individual, Value of the, 50, 62
Inevitability, Historical, 61, 107n.
Intellectual history, 9, 53
Interpretation in history, 190–4, 208f., 293f.; see also Myth
Intuition, 162
Involvement, 162–83

Jesuit Missions, 24
Jesus of History, The, 123f., 133, 135, 140f., 240
Judgment in history, 57, 61f., 64, 159–62
Judgments of evidence, 192

Kerygma theology, 139–47

Laws of history, 102, 110–14, 186, 189

Liberal theology, 122–4, 131, 134, 138

'Life of Jesus Movement', 123f.

Liturgical worship, 257f., 264, 265n.

Lucan writings, 237f.

Luck, 61, 283f.

Marxism, 55, 108, 112, 232, 242, 247f., 292

Maurists, 39

Mediaeval piety, 66f.

— view of history, 64–66

— world-view, 68–75

Miracles, 28, 44, 187–90, 208f., 224f.

'Modern' history, 278–80

Moral indignation, 160

— judgments in history, 159–62

Morals in history, 83f., 87, 93f., 281f., 285

Music of the spheres, 73f.

Myth as historical interpretation, 52, 208–12, 247f.

Mythology, 56f., 143f., 219f., 249

Myths of history, 52, 57, 61f., 107–9, 173–8, 182f., 243–9, 270, 284

Nation, nationalism, 176–8, 181, 269

Natural law, 252–5

Natural theology, 68–75

Naturalistic view of history, 56f., 59; see Positivism

Nature, nature myths, 56–58, 75, 78

— as source of revelation, 27, 78f., 273f.

Necessity, 283f.

Nemesis, 59

'New history', 29, 165–8, 175, 221f.

New Quest of the Historical Jesus, 145–7

New Testament Theology, 234–41

Newtonian Philosophy, The, 18–20

Nineteenth-century historical developments, 12, 103–18

'Objectification', 152, 208

Objectivity in historiography, 138, 183, 250–4

Old Testament Theology, 229–34

Paradox, 126f.

Personal factors in judgment of evidence, 200–5

Personification of nature, 56f.

Philosophe history, 90–99

Philosophia perennis, 253

Philosophy of history, The, 55, 57, 262, 287–94

Positivism, positivist views of history, 57, 109–18, 128, 143, 153f., 181

Practical history, 164f., 170n., 256, 280

Presuppositions in history, 142f., 192n., 200–5

Probability in history, 28, 83–85, 114, 129–32

Profane, the word, 25n.

— history, 25–28, 88f.

Progress, 55f., 63, 289

Providence, 61, 285

Prussian myth, The, 176–8

Ptolemaic system, 69–71

Quest of the Historical Jesus, 123f., 129f., 133–5, 145–7

Rationalism, 47–49, 101–3, 105f., 263

Rationalist myth, The, 77, 106–9, 284

Rationalistic theology, 27, 78

Recital, Theology of, 220

Reformation, Reformers, 33, 78

Regius Chairs of History, 278n.

Relativism, Historical, 242f., 250–4

Religion, religionless, 81n., 268f.

Religionsgeschichtliche Schule, 128f., 139f., 143, 207

Renaissance, The, 77n.
Resurrection (of Christ), 144f., 190, 195–217, 225, 239f.
Revelation, 12, 25–27, 65, 131, 135, 223–7, 232, 273–6
Revolution, as a general concept, 186
— in historiography, 12, 43n.
— in philosophy, 263
— The Scientific, 12, 19f., 79n.
Revolutions, 117n.; see also French Revolution
Rheteric, 55, 281
Ritschlianism, 122–4
Romantic History, 166f., 289
Romanticism, 167, 169n., 289f.

Sacred History, 23–25, 88f., 133–9
Scientific history, 56–59, 102f., 109–16, 173, 182f.; see also Positivism
— humanism, 110n., 278
— Revolution, see Revolution
Sociology, social sciences, 111–17, 162f.

Soviet historiography, 242n.
State, The, 50, 62, 64, 176, 291
Stoicism, 283f.
Subjectivity, 126, 192–4, 200–5

Technical history, 107
Thomism, 252f.
Timaeus, 73
Tübingen School, 121, 291
Tyche, 60f., 76, 284
Typology, 217f., 222

Ultimate history, 106, 114, 173
— reality, 81, 285
Unhistorical attitudes, 58, 78, 84–88, 95–97, 103f., 166–8
Uniqueness of historical events, 213–17
Universal history, 24f., 64, 265–72
Uranus, 210, 212
'Useful myths', 173, 243–6, 270

Wie es eigentlich gewesen, 104, 173